Blasted Literature

Edinburgh Critical Studies in Victorian Culture

Series Editor: Julian Wolfreys

Volumes available in the series:

In Lady Audley's Shadow: Mary Elizabeth Braddon and Victorian Literary Genres
Saverio Tomaiuolo
978 0 7486 4115 4   Hbk

Blasted Literature: Victorian Political Fiction and the Shock of Modernism
Deaglán Ó Donghaile
978 0 7486 4067 6   Hbk

William Morris and the Idea of Community: Romance, History and Propaganda, 1880–1914
Anna Vaninskaya
978 0 7486 4149 9   Hbk

Blasted Literature

Victorian Political Fiction and the Shock of Modernism

Deaglán Ó Donghaile

Edinburgh University Press

© Deaglán Ó Donghaile, 2011

Edinburgh University Press Ltd
22 George Square, Edinburgh

www.euppublishing.com

Typeset in 10.5/13 pt Sabon
by Servis Filmsetting Ltd, Stockport, Cheshire, and
printed and bound in Great Britain by
CPI Antony Rowe, Chippenham and Eastbourne

A CIP record for this book is available from the British Library

ISBN 978 0 7486 4067 6 (hardback)

The right of Deaglán Ó Donghaile
to be identified as author of this work
has been asserted in accordance with
the Copyright, Designs and Patents Act 1988.

Contents

Series Editor's Preface

'Victorian' is a term at once indicative of a strongly determined concept and, simultaneously, an often notoriously vague notion, emptied of all meaningful content by the many journalistic misconceptions that persist about the inhabitants and cultures of the British Isles and Victoria's Empire in the nineteenth century. As such, it has become a by-word for the assumption of various, often contradictory habits of thought, belief, behaviour and perceptions. Victorian studies and studies in nineteenth-century literature and culture have, from their institutional inception, questioned narrowness of presumption, pushed at the limits of the nominal definition, and sought to question the very grounds on which the unreflective perception of the so-called Victorian has been built; and so they continue to do. Victorian and nineteenth-century studies of literature and culture maintain a breadth and diversity of interest, of focus and inquiry, in an interrogative and intellectually open-minded and challenging manner, which are equal to the exploration and inquisitiveness of their subjects. Many of the questions asked by scholars and researchers of the innumerable productions of nineteenth-century society actively put into suspension the clichés and stereotypes of 'Victorianism', whether the approach has been sustained by historical, scientific, philosophical, empirical, ideological or theoretical concerns; indeed, it would be incorrect to assume that each of these approaches to the idea of the Victorian has been, or has remained, in the main exclusive, sealed off from the interests and engagements of other approaches. A vital interdisciplinarity has been pursued and embraced, for the most part, even as there has been contest and debate amongst Victorianists, pursued with as much fervour as the affirmative exploration between different disciplines and differing epistemologies put to work in the service of reading the nineteenth century.

Edinburgh Critical Studies in Victorian Culture aims to take up both the debates and the inventive approaches and departures from convention that studies in the nineteenth century have witnessed for the last half century at least. Aiming to maintain a 'Victorian' (in the most positive sense of that motif) spirit of inquiry, the series' purpose is to continue and augment the cross-fertilisation of interdisciplinary approaches, and to offer, in addition, a number of timely and untimely revisions of Victorian literature, culture, history and identity. At the same time, the series will ask questions concerning what has been missed or improperly received, misread, or not read at all, in order to present a multi-faceted and heterogeneous kaleidoscope of representations. Drawing on the most provocative, thoughtful and original research, the series will seek to prod at the notion of the 'Victorian', and in so doing, principally through theoretically and epistemologically sophisticated close readings of the historicity of literature and culture in the nineteenth century, to offer the reader provocative insights into a world that is at once overly familiar, and irreducibly different, other and strange. Working from original sources, primary documents and recent interdisciplinary theoretical models, Edinburgh Critical Studies in Victorian Culture seeks not simply to push at the boundaries of research in the nineteenth century, but also to inaugurate the persistent erasure and provisional, strategic redrawing of those borders.

Julian Wolfreys

Acknowledgements

While writing this monograph, I benefited from the encouragement and advice offered by a number of friends, colleagues and mentors. It began as a PhD thesis at Trinity College, Dublin, under the supervision of Nicholas Daly, now of University College, Dublin, who continues to help my work. His advice and critical insight (not to mention a fair amount of his time) have been invested in this project for some years, and I will always be grateful for his guidance. Whilst at Trinity, I also gained much from the wisdom and practical support offered on countless occasions by Darryl Jones, Kate Hebblethwaite and Stephen Matterson. Terence Brown gave a helping hand at the very beginning of my research, and his kindness will always be remembered.

When my research entered its postdoctoral phase at the Department of English at the National University of Ireland, Maynooth, it benefited enormously from the institutional support, scholarly expertise and friendship offered by a number of colleagues. First among these is Joseph Cleary, who carefully mentored its transition from thesis to book. I have learned much from his theoretical skill, critical rigour and profound insight into literary and cultural history, and am honoured that my work became associated with him. Margaret Kelleher also gave generously of her time to read my work in preparation, and her support and advice continue to be keenly appreciated. Others at NUI Maynooth helped this project along the road to completion with some fine conversation and insightful advice. Conor McCarthy helped me to hone my thinking on *The Secret Agent*, while Emer Nolan, Stephen O'Neill, Colin Graham and Moynagh Sullivan helped me, in different ways, to focus my theoretical perspectives. As Head of Department, Chris Morash facilitated my research at every request and his unstinting support and frequently given counsel are deeply appreciated.

My work has benefited enormously from the advice and support offered by David Glover, and I will always be grateful for his generosity

and critical insight. Stephen Arata also read drafts of my work on literature and anarchism, and his advice helped me to formulate a far more
focused argument on this subject. Linda Dryden has read my work
with a brilliantly critical eye and, since our first meeting at RLS 2004 in
Edinburgh, has always been on hand to offer support and encouragement. I have also benefited greatly from the help and kindness given so
freely by Laurence Davies. Nicholas Allen of NUI Galway has also been
a fine friend and supporter of my research.

My heartfelt thanks go to Cáthal McGlinchey and Elaine Treanor,
who housed my work for longer than they had ever anticipated, and a
very special and sincere debt of gratitude goes their way. Some of our
long discussions of the relationship between literature and history have
made their way into this book. Willie McLaughlin of Derry guided me
toward the path of scholarship some time ago, and I have the great
fortune to enjoy his insight as a teacher and humanist of the highest
order. Other friends and colleagues who have helped me to shape my
thinking include Mark Quigley, University of Oregon, whose interest in
Irish literature gave me much to work with recently, while David Lloyd
of USC also gave generously of his time and insight into the politics of
literary culture.

Most recently, the final draft of this monograph found a welcoming
and enormously supportive home at Liverpool Hope University, where I
have gained much from the practical and intellectual support offered by
my colleagues at the Department of English. Steve Brie, Elaine Hartnell-
Mottram, Zoe Kinsley, Will Rossiter, Bill Blazek, Caroline Bennet, Jan
Jobling, Linda McLaughlin, Manel Herat and Salman Al-Azami have all
had some hand in the final formulation of my arguments. Special thanks
are due to Cindy Hamilton who, as Head of Department, ensured that
this vital phase of my writing enjoyed all of the institutional support that
it needed. As Dean of Arts and Humanities, Terry Phillips also took a
deep interest in my research and offered much in the way of practical
support. Michael Holmes, who eased the transition from Maynooth to
Merseyside, has also been an invaluable friend. As well as helping me
to find my feet in a new scholarly community, all of my colleagues at
Liverpool Hope University afforded me the vital time that was required
to put the finishing touches to my work.

This work has benefited enormously from the help and guidance
offered by Edinburgh University Press. The press's Head of Publishing,
Jackie Jones has shown great patience and understanding, and I have
had the great fortune to work closely with Julian Wolfreys who, as
Series Editor, paid attention to the overall contours of this monograph
as well as to its finest details. I would also like to thank my anonymous

readers at the press, whose criticism and advice gave greater focus and direction to my writing.

And finally, my deepest thanks go to family. My earliest memories are of reading books alongside my mother and father, Martina and Michael Donnelly, and their guidance and example has informed my work on this monograph in so many ways. My brother, Ruairí Ó Donghaile, and his partner, Catherine Kelly, encouraged this work from the very beginning, as did my sisters Úna, Caoimhe and Niamh, who have had to endure living with my papers and books for years. My beloved nephew and nieces, Oisín, Aoibhínn and Clódagh, can now grow up safely in the knowledge that they won't have to spend years tripping over the notes and books that I scattered over their parents' homes. Mary Sweeney has always been there for my family when I was elsewhere doing research, and Eamonn Sweeney has heard so much about it that I hope he will not be put off reading the end product.

Although theirs are the last names mentioned here, my greatest debt is to my partner, Helen Sweeney, and to our little daughter, Niamh. Their love and support have sustained my work in countless ways. During the long absences necessitated by research trips, conferences and teaching, they gave up so much and, in doing so, they gave more to this project than I can ever begin to express. This book is for them, and for my parents.

Funding

My postdoctoral work was funded by an IRCHSS Government of Ireland Postdoctoral Research Fellowship, which was awarded from 2007–2009 and held at the National University of Ireland, Maynooth. This vital funding was supplemented by further material support and funding from the Department of English and from the Office of Research, where my requests for support were always met by Professors Chris Morash and John G. Hughes, respectively. In 2009 the Royal Irish Academy supported my research at Cornell University and the New York Public Library with the award of a generous mobility grant. During its later stages, my writing also benefited from the award of a UCLA William Andrews Clark Memorial Library Fellowship, and my deepest thanks are extended to the Regents of the University of California and, in particular, to Peter H. Reill, Director of the UCLA Center for Seventeenth- and Eighteenth-Century Studies.

Special thanks are due to the staff of the following libraries: the Library of Trinity College, Dublin, particularly the Department of

Early Printed Books, the National Library of Ireland, Dublin, the NUI Maynooth Library, and the Liverpool Hope University Library, the William Andrews Clark Memorial Library at UCLA, the Rare Books and Manuscripts Collections at the Carl A. Kroch Library, Cornell University, the New York Public Library, the British Library (and especially the staff at the Newspaper Library at Colindale), the Bancroft Library, UC Berkeley, and the National Library of Scotland, Edinburgh.

Introduction: Shock, Politics, Literature

In 1894 *Strand Magazine* sent a correspondent into the carefully guarded Crime Museum of New Scotland Yard. The journalist was despatched to report on a new exhibit containing every 'dangerous species' of bomb, or 'dynamite relic' that had been found intact during the Fenian campaign of the 1880s. The contents of the Black Museum, as it was also known, were, like the exhibits in British Museum's *Secretum*, never intended for public inspection as they were considered by the authorities to be far too hazardous for popular consumption. Instead, these volatile specimens were put on display for the sole and very serious purpose of instructing the Metropolitan Police in the latest developments in subversive activity. Here, budding detectives, and the occasional if very strictly vetted visitor, became acquainted with what the *Strand* termed the 'almost historic' materials amassed by Her Majesty's Chief Inspector of Explosives, Sir Vivian Majendie, CB, HM. However the curious public, on the other hand, could only learn about these explosive and 'too precious' artefacts from a safe distance in the pages of the popular journal as part of a course of necessary lessons on the important but little understood topic of political violence. The exhibits in the Black Museum, it promised, would never become a public attraction, even though readers were assured that the experience of viewing them was 'the finest and most complete nerve-tester in the world!' Their purpose within this special museum was to educate officers in the most recent developments in the lethal technology of the 'infernal machine', or improvised bomb. They included devices capable of causing 'deferred' explosions and a particularly fiendish type of bomb that was disguised as a baby's bottle. Other examples of terrorist hardware included explosive cigars and top hats, explosives concealed inside lumps of coal, devices hidden in seemingly harmless barrels of cement and oilcans, and even an early version of the letter bomb addressed and posted to the Chief Secretary of Ireland at the House of Commons. Inside every one of these unassuming objects, reported the *Strand*, lay mechanisms possessing 'deadly wrecking powers' that were capable of shattering 'anything between our nerves and our residences' (pp. 127, 119). Foremost of all was Majendie's most treasured if least ingenious acquisition: the simple but 'essentially man-killing' machine known as the 'Daly bomb'; the grenade was named after a Limerick republican who was captured on his way to the Houses of Parliament armed with three of these devices, which he planned to throw at MPs from the Strangers' Gallery.[1]

These closely guarded and most secret of exhibits were, as the *Strand* made clear, very special artefacts because they were not relics from antiquity but the 'actual weapons' that had just been invented and put to deadly use on English soil by the Fenians, Irish revolutionaries who had set out to destroy the British Empire from within by bombing political and symbolic targets across a number of cities. Unlike the ancient objects held in the British Museum, such as the contents of its popular and rapidly expanding Department of Egyptian and Assyrian Antiquities, these far more contemporary, if absolutely forbidden, 'mementoes' had a more thrilling immediacy. Carefully displayed so as to allow detectives to inspect the 'various movements' of their internal workings, like the delicate and elaborate 'clockwork pattern' of the time bomb (pp. 119, 127), these strange but deadly curiosities had to be contained and kept out of the public view. This was because when they were taken apart they revealed the secret knowledge of bomb technology, information that, should it enter popular consciousness, could cause further disruption and political chaos. In a similar way, the late nineteenth-century dynamite novel was used by imperialist writers to mystify the British public about the political motivations that inspired men like John Daly to plant bombs in England, a strategy that involved presenting Fenianism as apolitical. And like the bombs themselves, which served as violent statements of Irish anti-imperialism, other novels written by Irish separatists were designed to shock British readers into recognising their desire for independence.

As the models and designs of the most recent Fenian bombing campaign, Majendie's devices were, for those important enough to get by the museum's strict vetting policies, all the more thrilling to behold because they were valuable material evidence of these 'almost historic' deeds.[2] I begin with this unusual example of late Victorian museum culture because it neatly describes the inherent modernity of terrorism. The very language with which the bombs are described – they are constantly referred to by the *Strand* and in other journalism, fiction and polemical writing of the period as 'infernal machines' – suggests that the late Victorian public was conscious of the technological and politically symbolic novelty of the 'portable volcano'[3] that was the home-made bomb. The term 'infernal machine' also describes an entity that was both deadly and inorganic since the bomb's capacity to frighten lay in its potential to bring the normally inert substance of high explosives into lethal being and to shatter not just physical matter but also the very nervous system of its political target. In other words, the explosion of Fenian bombs did not just damage buildings, bridges or even people: they were in themselves shocking messages that forced the British public to acknowledge the radical conceptual force of modern Irish republicanism and its anti-imperial goals. According to their own logic, Fenians like Daly were bombing more than infrastructure or the high-ranking individuals whom they associated with imperial power: by planting bombs at the metropolitan heart of the British Empire they aimed to attack its symbolic mechanisms and undermine its ideology of a United Kingdom.

Now safely defused and laid out in the Black Museum, their insides exposed, the bombs were, according to the *Strand*, devilish contraptions invented for the sole purpose of destroying human life. But their formidable, if now forgotten presence in late nineteenth- and early twentieth-century literary culture reveals how terrorism served as much more than a violent political strategy. Certainly, it frightened the public, but many late Victorian readers found having their 'nerves', or political-conceptual faculties, shattered a very thrilling experience, as proven by their eager consumption of popular narratives of revolutionary violence, and especially of those that showcased the kind of destructive workmanship featured in the *Strand*. Fenian bombs entertained as much as they terrified and appealed to sensation-hungry readers of penny dreadfuls and popular magazines. This examination of the phenomenon of terrorism as it appears in popular literature, radical journalism and modernism maps the connections between these bombs and the literature that they inspired. The explosions that shook Britain during the 1880s added a shocking *frisson* to Irish nationalism and, as spectacularly destructive statements of Irish anti-imperialism, provided the press with suitably shocking headlines. In this way the political violence of the late Victorian *fin de siècle* resembles the more recent attacks of 2001, which the novelist Martin Amis defined as 'political communication by other means'.[4] The explosion of dynamite bombs on the streets of British cities like London, Glasgow and Liverpool was made even more 'audible' by newspaper reports in a process that was, in turn, repeated by popular novelists who appropriated the news and recycled it as popular fiction. From the penny evening papers to more authoritative publications like *The Times*, the newspaper industry communicated facts about terrorist outrages, aiding the media-conscious *dynamitards* by publicising their efforts. Indeed, the condescending, dismissive and imperial tone of *The Times* was interpreted as provocation by the Fenian dynamiters, who countered its imperial authority with their own kind of 'plain speaking'[5] when they bombed its offices in 1883.

With advances made in the development of high explosives in the 1860s, terrorism became a signally modern insurrectional strategy. Far more powerful, portable and stable than the cumbersome gunpowder with which the Fenians razed Clerkenwell in 1867, Alfred Nobel's dynamite, which was patented in the same year, transformed insurgency. On becoming commercially available for industrial purposes, dynamite made revolutionary violence a far more spectacular affair, allowing Irish bombers to attack targets chosen from the imperial spectrum of 'Social, Political and Commercial London'.[6] Designed to shatter imperial prestige, capture the popular imagination and, ultimately, shock the British public into conceding to their demands, these bombs combined sensory shock with political impact.

Planted at politically sensitive spaces like Nelson's Pillar, the Tower of London, Scotland Yard and, most spectacularly, the Houses of Parliament at Westminster, Fenian bombs were, to borrow from Paul Virilio, expressions of a consciously modern 'image strategy'.[7] Westminster, as described by Coulson Kernahan in his Edwardian shilling shocker, *The Red Peril*, was at once the 'brain' and 'central . . . electric battery of the British Empire'. In bombing it, the Fenians were attacking what he imagined to be both the power source and nervous system of the imperial establishment. For Kernahan parliament was not only a dynamo but also the rational and intelligent centre of the imperial grid. The Fenians' goal was to short-circuit this system and bring it to its knees. By highlighting its vulnerability, they hoped to damage its symbolic prestige as the place where loyal British subjects could 'stand solid and four square to the world'.[8] As the centre of the world's most powerful empire and its 'most jealously guarded institution',[9] as Edgar Wallace described it, Westminster was, to the Fenians, an irresistible target.[10]

Terrorism, Shock and Political Degeneration

Whence, then, the connection between bombs and books? Max Nordau diagnosed this juncture in the opening pages of his famously pessimistic analysis of European culture, *Degeneration*, published in 1895. This bleak description of political, moral and social decline identified anarchists, artists and authors as members of a single, diseased 'anthropological family'. Degenerates, he warned, were not only criminals, prostitutes and lunatics, but also those 'who satisfy their unhealthy impulses with the knife of the assassin or the bomb of the dynamiter', as well as those who did the same 'with pen and pencil'.[11] Nordau's model of modernity as a literary and cultural crisis amplified by the interplay of aesthetics and revolutionary ideology presents the bond between art and political chaos as the key to understanding the rot in European culture. Thanks to the abandonment of traditional social and even sensory controls, he complained, the popular imagination was running riot at the *fin de siècle*. Nordau's warning that a 'frenzied' modernity complete with its 'chaos of phenomena' was threatening the delicate 'impressionability of the nerves and brain' reveals how the political and nervous balance of Europe were regarded as linked phenomena by conservative intellectuals.[12] The beliefs of anarchists and other revolutionaries were symptomatic of the wider breakdown of rational thought that threatened to overstimulate the popular European imagination. Already subjected to the shocks of everyday experience, it was only a small step for the modern subject whose consciousness had been worn down by less conspicuous sources of degeneracy (such as popular books, modern painting, religious worship) to erupt in a murderous outbreak of anarchic revolt.

Anarchist doctrine, particularly its abandonment of the established moral laws, had, for Nordau, direct literary analogues in the new cultural tendencies of decadence, symbolism and aestheticism, all of which were infusing art and literature with ever greater levels of insanity. Nordau believed that writing had especially political implications and warned that the range of available literature, with its limitless flow of information, both political and aesthetic, threatened to reduce the modern subject to the intellectual level of an incoherent 'imbecile': 'If attention fails,' he warned, 'the world appears to the beholder like a uniform stream of enigmatic states which emerge and disappear without any connection'.[13] Nordau remarked how the difference between attentive and inattentive man was the same as the contrast between 'the reproduction of the scenes of nature by a good painter and a photographic plate'. By suggesting that, as a more organic form, painting suppresses aspects of phenomena while simultaneously bringing others into prominence, so that it 'at once permits a distinct external incident, or a definitive internal emotion of the painter to be recognised', he tried to politicise aesthetics. In contrast to the discriminatory power of the painter, the perfectly reproduced image found in a photograph represents a scene and all of its details 'indiscriminately, so that it is without meaning, until the beholder brings into play his attention, which the sensitive plate could not do'.[14] Warning that the new, 'super-sensuous world'[15] had accomplished perfect levels of impressionability and, therefore, had abandoned its capacity for discrimination, Nordau predicted the end of all psychic balance because the photograph, with its flawless reproduction of phenomena, was an apt reflection of the super-sensitivity of the degenerate mind.

For Nordau, the cure for degeneration would be preventive. Rather than identifying individual degenerates (an impossible task, given the epidemic scale of the problem), levels of popular sensitivity, he suggested, could be controlled. In this regard, aestheticism appeared as a particularly threatening subversion of the politics of representation. Whereas the information contained in a photograph can be interpreted by its 'beholder', aestheticism, like its political analogue, anarchism, overwhelms consciousness and short-circuits this discriminatory power, transforming the modern subject into a passive receiver of unadulterated emotion. Drawing on the conservative French novelist Paul Bourget's model of society as an 'organism' fuelled by the 'subordinate energy' of its cells and vulnerable to the 'decadence' of anarchy, Nordau employed the metaphor of the bomb to discuss the mental condition of the anarchist and aesthete: 'If the normal actions of the brain-cells may be compared to quiet combustion, the action of morbidly-irritable groups of cells may be said to resemble an explosion'. Employing an ironic blend of Paterian language and symbolism, Nordau identified the unpredictably explosive mental condition of the degenerate as the psychological state wherein 'stimulus . . . flames forth in consciousness . . . a train of presentations, conceptions, and reasonings, which suffuse the mind as with the glare of conflagration, outshining all other ideas'.[16] By interiorising external data without mediating it, aestheticism, like anarchism, undermined the necessary management of information and emotion, eroding the sense of balance and authority inscribed in the discriminating consciousness which, quite literally, it threatens to blow up. Thus, for Nordau, the popular 'aesthetic thrill' posed a clear political threat. A consequence of the 'fatigue and exhaustion . . . of contemporary civilization' with its 'vastly increased number of sense impressions and organic reactions,' it threatened bourgeois subjectivity itself, where 'perceptions, judgements and motor impulses' were now being violently forced.[17]

Throughout *Degeneration*, Nordau describes how this state of social 'vertigo'[18] has both literary and political manifestations. By including authors, artists and anarchists in his roll call of the degenerate, Nordau tried to implicate the 'mad-house literature' and 'fugitive periodicals' of the literary world with the threat of revolution, thereby revealing the connection between the forces bringing about the collapse of mental and political states.[19] Appealing to the 'hysteric reader' hooked on sensory rushes and aesthetic thrills, modern literature represented the *acme* of degeneration: aestheticism was for Nordau 'the literature of diabolism', and its 'violent' pleasures were the 'aberrations' and 'perversions' that would ruin the mind of a healthy man.[20] By lumping all of these European literary movements together, Nordau grandly claimed that avant-garde writers were 'ego-maniacs' and 'anarchists, i.e., enemies of all institutions'. The political consequence of their literary endeavours would be the spread of chaos and 'the ruin of the community'[21] (Nordau also called Henrik Ibsen an anarchist and compared Walt Whitman to the French terrorist, Ravachol).[22] Calling for a cultural task force or 'critical police' to halt this epidemic, defend the established order and restore normality,[23] Nordau made the connection between modern literature and revolution a key element of his popular psychological theories.

Yet, the promise of unbridled cultural and political chaos appealed to writers, ranging from the authors of 'low-brow' potboilers to more esoterically inclined modernists like Joseph Conrad, Ezra Pound and Wyndham Lewis. The looming disaster that Nordau prophesised appealed to Coulson Kernahan, whose dynamite novels exploited the thrills of 'impending, if averted catastrophe'. For Kernahan's readers, partial to the 'consciousness that a dislodged pebble, a spoken word, may bring down an avalanche which shall sweep thousands of petty mortals at one stroke ... into the waste pit of the universe', political and social breakdown was a glamorous subject investing 'the humdrum human life of today with the august dignity and glamour of doom'. Conrad was also drawn to this model of fear, wherein '(a)ll other sensations and emotions' are swept away by the conceptual and psychic force of 'a wave of sheer terror'.[24] As such, the literature of terrorism underlines Michael Denning's suggestion that distinguishing between elite and popular culture is a problematic affair as it offers us a particularly clear example of how the penny dreadful can be read as an analogue to the more literary novels, stories and manifestos of modernism.[25]

The rise of mass culture towards the end of the nineteenth century in Britain saw a corresponding increase in literacy that fuelled demand for both news and popular fiction. The Education Act of 1870 created a lower middle-class reading public (whose advance across Europe was the real target of Nordau's reactionary cultural analysis) and transformed reading practices by creating demand for cheap, mass-produced and quickly digestible literature.[26] The dual popular texts of the daily newspaper and the cheap novel were particularly suited to the literary needs of this new reading public; their form and content overlapped as information from newspaper reports appeared on the pages of rapidly written shilling shockers like Robert Louis Stevenson's *The Dynamiter*, which offered a slightly displaced form of political discourse. As Patrick Joyce has shown, nineteenth-century urban culture was closely connected to the economic sphere of consumption, in its aesthetic as well as its material manifestations, which meant that long before postmodernism 'the city had to be presented in aesthetic forms', particularly in literary ones. Joyce draws attention to the representative literature of the city, including directories, guides, travel writing, journalism and, of course, fiction.[27] The dynamite novel, with its themes of urban terror and political meltdown, is an important subcategory in its own right; this best-selling genre exploited the theme of modern political violence not just as political matter, but as a form of literary capital as well. Whether made in a throwaway manner in sensation novels such as Marie Corelli's 1895 shocker, *The Sorrows of Satan*, which opens by condemning the 'moral cancer' of poverty for leaving men 'inclined to the use of dynamite',[28] or making a more central appearance in Conrad's 1907 novel, *The Secret Agent*, the theme of terrorism saturated the late Victorian and Edwardian literary consciousness.

In order to examine the engagement between literature and terrorism, I have drawn on a variety of popular novels and stories, journalism and modernist texts. These fictions, political periodicals and avant-garde journals reveal the centrality of terrorism to the literary imagination during the period dating, roughly, from 1880 until 1915, when a range of writers exploited the connection between aesthetics and the shocks of political violence. Nordau's intensely conservative belief that new, 'malevolent' prerogatives in writing would undermine the essentially organic and genuine qualities of art is a reflection of contemporary anxiety over the transformations that occurred in literary production during this moment. His disgust at the entertainment provided the mass-produced texts that delivered so many political frights, moral shocks and aesthetic thrills reveal his distaste for the systematic experiences of modernity. Conrad's fiction provides particularly clear evidence of the longevity of this phenomenon and reveals how the shocks of political violence held a special appeal for the modernist imagination. His most famous tale of anarchy, *The Secret Agent*, emerged after a lengthy enough engagement with these popular political themes and was not published as a novel until after he had worked through the theme of anarchism with his short stories of 1906, 'An Anarchist' and 'The Informer' (the novel emerged at this time out of an earlier, much shorter draft entitled *Verloc*, which was serialised in the journal *Ridgeways:*

A Militant Weekly for God and Country). These shorter tales link the modernism of the novel to the more popular mode employed by writers like Stevenson and Richard Henry Savage. As Frederic Jameson suggests, Conrad is a pivotal presence in this moment of literary and cultural transformation. Locked somewhere between the popular tradition of the romance and the avant-garde of modernism, the style and content of his fiction belongs equally to both of these concurrent literary tendencies. For Jameson, these processes are most evident in Conrad's far-flung imperial romances, *Lord Jim* and *Nostromo*, but they are also clearly present in the domestic fictions that are infused with the political content of the popular dynamite novel.[29] Like many of Conrad's shorter works, 'An Anarchist' and 'The Informer' do not carry the high modernist freight of *The Secret Agent* but their themes of political trauma and personal tragedy connect them to the popular, thrilling style of the political romance of the 1880s and 1890s. Conrad's exploration of these themes, culminating with the fatal Greenwich Park explosion around which *The Secret Agent* hinges, connects his earlier tales of anarchy to the aesthetic radicalism of avant-garde modernism, bridging the gap between the shilling shocker and the deliberately provocative 'shock modernism' of Vorticism. With its combative polemical style, reliance on manifestos and use of explosive imagery, Vorticism had revolutionary political and aesthetic intentions that drew on this earlier literature of political trauma.

This monograph builds upon themes explored by Barbara Arnett Melchiori in her 1985 study, *Terrorism in the Late Victorian Novel*, which analyses nineteenth-century political fiction as the expression of middle-class anxiety over domestic and foreign radicalism. By focusing on the political qualities of the plots of various dynamite novels, Melchiori has argued that these tales satisfied popular demand for 'dynamite sensation'. With their emphases on the shadowy, threatening presence of the usually foreign conspirator, such narratives portrayed revolutionary violence as the result of the personal and psychological tics of subversive maniacs rather than as evidence of the political and cultural crises at the heart of the British Empire.[30] In doing so, Melchiori stresses the limits of the conservative Victorian social and literary conscience, which was troubled by certain figurative tropes of the fictional terrorist, such as his anonymity. As Melchiori has shown, the terrorist was an irritant to the political sensitivities of the British middle class. But while she has brought attention to the problems that are inherent in the dynamite novel's support for the 'unquestioned' norms of imperialism and for a conservative political and social world view (the Tory and anti-liberal ideology of many of these fictions usually manifests itself in the containment of dynamite plots or the prevention of explosions), Melchiori has overlooked their exploitation of the conceptual and political shocks that were embodied in the revolutionary demands of Fenians and anarchists, nor has she linked these earlier tales to the production of literary modernism. More recently, Alex Houen has suggested that the dynamite novel was an exercise in the containment of Irish or anarchist threats, which it achieved through the absorption of terror 'into the quotidian'. As an attempt to normalise revolutionary violence through the very process of narration, the genre ultimately failed in the endeavour to depict political violence as a purely textual phenomenon. Instead, according to Houen, this process had the reverse effect, underlining instead the ways in which sensation literature can actually magnify the terror-effect by protracting its impact upon the imagination of the reader. In his study of terrorism's place within the American literary consciousness, Jeffory A. Clymer also draws attention to the connection between literary and political shock, claiming that in the American popular consciousness 'writing about dynamite and throwing dynamite are two versions of the same action'.[31]

This book contends that popular fiction (both British and Irish) and modernism are linked together by their treatment and outright exploitation of the explosive shocks of late nineteenth-century terrorism. Not only were these shocks visceral but, in the case of Fenian and anarchist bomb attacks, they were also a deeply conceptual affair because violence in these cases was linked to the Fenian demand for the destruction of the British Empire or to the anarchist's desire to see the overthrow of the state. No previous study has shown how these conceptual and political phenomena are related to one another, or how the act of dynamiting became translated into modernism's militant blasts against the inert weight of the literary establishment. The symbolic political destructiveness of the Fenian and anarchist bomb had a literary analogue in modernism's desire to blow up the norms of literary tradition and reconstitute writing as a revolutionary and intensely personal form of expression (in this way modernist shock reacts against its origins in the popular mass reading of the 1880s and 1890s). The points of contact between these modes of political and literary disruption have so far gone unexplored: Melchiori deals almost exclusively with popular late nineteenth-century texts, and Houen, largely, with modernism; neither has fully addressed the linkages between the ways in which these literary tendencies dealt with the aesthetically productive subject of terrorism.[32] Likewise, Clymer's study of terrorism's impact upon the American consciousness does not address the presence of Fenianism and anarchism in British literary culture, nor does it assess their impact upon the modernist imagination. This book adds to our understanding of terrorism's purpose as a cultural as well as a political phenomenon by exploring its twofold literary status at the close of the nineteenth century and at the beginning of the twentieth.

The Political *Flâneur*

Just as terrorism lies at the heart of the imagination of urban chaos, so too does its corresponding characteristic – invisibility. The imperceptibility of the stateless anarchist is underlined by his or her trans-national character. Like the Fenians of the 1880s, anarchists subverted the modern state, along with the power of its policing systems and agents. While the fictional detective has garnered much critical attention, that of his double, the mysterious and charismatic terrorist (a related character is the criminal mastermind, who, in manifestations such as Arthur Conan Doyle's super-villain, James Moriarty, has a subliminally political quality), has gone relatively unnoticed. The Irish dynamiters who arrived in Britain from the United States under the direction of the mysterious 'Number One' were the first actual representatives of this type. By the 1890s the European anarchists who sought sanctuary in Britain from persecution in their own countries filled the imaginative void left by the Irish bombers. By causing indiscriminate explosions such as the 1893 attack on the Liceo Theatre in Barcelona, which killed twenty, and by carrying out what appeared to be random assassinations with pistols and even daggers, these relatively invisible terrorists not only confused police forces but also undermined popular notions of national identity at a moment when champions of the visible such as Francis Galton and Alphonse Bertillon claimed that the observation of an individual's 'peculiarities' and 'patterns' of identity was the key to solving crimes. For Galton, identifying the guilty was a simple, even predictable, matter of following 'symmetry, correlation, and the nature of genera',[33] a method practised time and time again by the infallible Sherlock Holmes. But terrorists defied this linear approach because they were political subversives, not private criminals motivated by a desire to acquire wealth; as Havelock Ellis warned his readers in 1890, the 'political criminal . . . does not easily admit of scientific discussion'.[34]

The period in which this literature was produced was characterised by new understandings of urban space, new practices in journalism and new kinds of literary writing. Patrick Joyce has stressed that, as places of 'free circulation', its streets had a theatrical quality that allowed modern subjects, as independent agents, to participate in the urban 'spectacle'. Yet, precisely because it facilitated such freedom, the imperial metropolis contained an inherent potential for conflict and disruption,[35] a fact that was not lost on the *Illustrated London News*. After Westminster was struck twice by Irish bombers on 26 January 1885, the 'well-remembered' day that became known as 'Dynamite Saturday', the paper blamed the liberal values of British democracy for tolerating terrorism: 'Anyone is at liberty to enter Westminster', it complained, and 'the dastardly scoundrels who ignited blocks of dynamite in these places' had hidden among the innocent crowds of 'men, ladies, and children, who came to see the interior'. Robert Louis Stevenson was equally horrified by a third, simultaneous attack that wrecked the armoury at the Tower of London on the same afternoon, terrifying 'the poor little sight-seers'.[36] Westminster was a political spectacle in its own right where ticket-holding visitors could pass policemen at the Norman Porch and enter the House of Commons Chamber to view the very centre of Britain's imperial power. One bomb shattered the Speaker's Bar and another went off in St Stephen's Crypt ,while, according to the *Illustrated London News*, the third bomb was smuggled into the Tower inside 'a man's hat' or, even worse, 'in a woman's dress'.[37] Just as the fugitive in Edgar Allan Poe's short story 'The Man of the Crowd' resists the surveillant gaze, or 'calm but inquisitive interest' of his pursuer, and evades detection by dissolving into an urban 'mob',[38] the terrorist appeared able to move at will in and out of late Victorian Britain's most significant political sites thanks to the uncontrollable nature of metropolitan crowds. It was feared that the bombers who disguised themselves as tourists and planted these 'infernal machines' were no more conspicuous than the next man or woman waiting in line to view the cultural and political sights of London. Making use of urban crowds, both as camouflage and as target audience, whose attention he or she sought, the Femian bomber wanted, above all, to capture the imagination of the late Victorian public. In doing so, the Irish revolutionary became another curiosity among a wider panorama of urban mysteries. As well as ensuring a place for his or her handiwork in the cabinet of explosive curiosities at the Crime Museum of Scotland Yard, this also guaranteed a place in the public consciousness for the dynamiter as one of the most enigmatic figures of the era.

A uniquely marginal urban type, the terrorist must be added to the pantheon of metropolitan characters presented by Judith R. Walkowitz in her critique of the social and cultural milieu of the late-Victorian metropolis, *City of Dreadful Delight: Narratives of Sexual Danger in Late-Victorian London*. Reading anxieties of class and gender as projections of a fragmenting modernity, Walkowitz posits the imperial capital as an increasingly contested, public and therefore democratic landscape, wherein the privileged position of the *flâneur* unravelled owing to competition from new figures like the gambler and the prostitute. While these characters posed particularly personal dangers by threatening to undermine selfhood via the transmission of sexually transmitted disease or enslavement to gambling, the terrorist played on more objective and rational fears. Unlike these interiorised threats, political violence posed the subject with the random public peril of the bomb attack. The unpredictable likelihood of being blown up by a Fenian device did not require personal involvement with fixed or visible sources of danger like the brothel and gambling den: one had only to be in the wrong place at the wrong time to be destroyed by hidden explosives. The terrorist should be numbered among 'new urban travellers' identified by Walkowitz because both the Fenian dynamiter and the stateless anarchist helped to construct the now familiar aura of the late Victorian metropolis as a locus of thrill, terror and nervous excitement.[39] For example, in Robert Louis Stevenson's bestseller of 1885, *The Dynamiter*, the Irish revolutionary becomes a clearly politicised version of the unreadable figures of the *flâneur* and *flâneuse* (both men and women practise political violence in the novel) and the threatening qualities of the 'mysterious' conspirators of Richard Henry Savage's 1894 novel *The Anarchist: A Story of To-Day* are heightened by excessive mobility and their characteristically metropolitan identities.[40]

Michael Denning has described popular fiction, particularly the spy thriller, as ideologically driven 'cover stories' that reveal and narrate the political values not just of their authors, but also of the cultures in which they are produced. As Denning has shown, the narrative structures of these tales are built around contemporary fears, to the extent that nineteenth-century British imperial culture was reflexively defined by the fiction with which society was entertained. These narratives were ideologically motivated because they made sense to individual readers of the grander, collective system of which they were part: 'these narratives are not only *of* the culture but are *about* the culture'.[41] But while Denning has stressed their function and significance as barometers of British imperial and class anxiety, he has not addressed how they treat the crucial theme of resistance to empire: the novel of espionage may narrate the adventures of defenders of the realm and their foes from rival states, but they do not reveal to us the inner machinations of the political separatist out to destroy the British Empire or his enemies engaged against him in counter-insurgency. Denning exclusively examines tales of espionage in which imperial crises are secretly acted upon and threats contained by spies operating within the parameters of the

'Great Game' of national intelligence: in contrast to these narratives of the discrete rivalry between states, there is no imaginative restriction in the fiction of terrorism. The novels with which this book opens are far less circumspect in their treatment of Irish and anarchist threats to the British Empire. The authors and readers of these political shockers had no patience for the subtleties of intrigue and instead preferred to luridly describe or read about catastrophic attacks upon symbolic sites of imperial and financial power like the Palace of Westminster and the City of London. Written from both the pro- and anti-imperial positions, these tales are as figuratively loaded as Denning's cover stories but as political and cultural narratives their very forms encoded the opposed ideologies on behalf of which they were written. Therefore the pro-empire novels of Robert Louis Stevenson and Coulson Kernahan take the form of quest narratives in which Fenians are hunted across London, while the nationalist novelists Tom Greer and Donald MacKay employ science fiction as a means of discussing the unlimited political possibilities of Irish independence.

Rather than reading 'high' and 'popular' literature as two entirely distinct modes of aesthetic expression, as Tzvetvan Todorov has done in his seminal essay, 'The Typology of Detective Fiction',[42] I have mapped the political connections that bind the shilling shocker more closely to modernism than has hitherto been recognised. In doing so, I have drawn on Nicholas Daly's model of the romance as a form of 'popular modernism'. Like Denning, Daly insists that the popular romances that displaced the realist novel as the literary mainstay of late nineteenth- and early twentieth-century Britain offered middlebrow readers with a self-reflexive 'narrative theory' of cultural change. Although Daly focuses on the late Victorian gothic romance, his account of the contamination that occurred between the not-so-distinct 'high' and 'low' literary cultures of this moment is of particular relevance to the political fiction, journalism and modernism with which I engage. For Daly, the very term 'popular', when applied to the literature of the late Victorian and Edwardian periods, is problematic because it contains within itself an oxymoronic ambivalence. During this moment popular culture was less distinguishable from modernism, or 'less easily broken down in terms of its class address' than subsequently became the case. Changes in the marketing of fiction and in very appearance of the book itself were accompanied by a transformation in what Daly terms the 'modality' of literature. For example, the relatively sudden displacement of the realist, three-decker volume as the principle medium of novel-length fiction by the mass-produced shilling shockers by the 1890s represented not just a revolution in production, but also a profound shift in literary tastes. As Daly has shown, the cultural uncertainties of the late nineteenth and early twentieth centuries were manifested in popular fiction and modernism, both of which turned their narrative gaze inward toward the processes that produced them, and went about examining the unstable cultural, class and imperial terrain upon which they stood. The late Victorian, Edwardian and modernist fictions that showcased terrorism were also evidence of the slippage between early modernism and mass culture. While the two expressions of modernism with which I deal – Conrad's anarchist fictions and the anarchic literary individualism of Vorticism – are very different kinds of modernism (Lewis positioned *Blast* within a much higher literary and aesthetic sphere than, say, Conrad's short stories, 'An Anarchist' and 'The Informer'), they nevertheless share a stylistic debt to the political potboilers and radical journalism of the 1880s and 1890s. With the publication of *The Secret Agent* in 1907, a novel that was followed with the shocking opening sequence of *Under Western Eyes* in 1910, the political thrills of these earlier texts became recycled as perfectly modernist literary *materiel* (the productiveness of the engagement between 'popular' and 'modernist' writing is most evident in the exchange between Fenian scare fiction of the 1880s and *The Secret Agent*).[43] As Daly suggests, the exchange between the seemingly polarised practices and texts of both tendencies can be read as a culturally profitable phenomenon, rather than as a fatal collision that generated two distinct or oppositional literary forms.[44]

Explosive Reads

Chapters 1 and 2 of this monograph examine, in turn, how urban adventures, detective fiction and thrillers, as well as several of Joseph Conrad's tales, translated the shocks of Fenianism and anarchism into popular and then modernist literary capital. In doing so, these narratives of political chaos exploited together what Daly has described as the late Victorian and Edwardian 'community of the nervous'.[45] While literary representations of Fenianism and anarchism are considered separately here, the overlapping and deliberate confusion of Irish and hard-left ideology in some of these works suggests that realism and historical accuracy were, for many authors, secondary to the flashy exploitation of political violence.

Both types of dynamite novel processed political news as political fiction. Writers of these genres raided other models of popular literature for inspiration, producing a number of variations ranging from politicised detective stories and quest adventures to narratives of mass death and tales of reversed invasion, and even creating the sub-genre of political science fiction. Satisfying the demand for contemporary and up-to-date thrills, the adaptable popular genre of the dynamite novel was also ideologically determined as its authors sought to pander to the political beliefs of their readers: while some authors Like R. L. Stevenson criticised Fenianism as immoral, others like Tom Greer defended it as the inevitable result of imperial misrule in Ireland. Dynamite fiction also reveals the extent to which the Irish-American 'dynamite press' – consisting of organs like *The Irish World*, *The Irish People*, *The United Irishman* and *Ireland's Liberation* – influenced the late Victorian imagination. Publicising the chaos and destruction caused by Fenian attacks, these journals also exploited 'the terror of the public' by performing within the nineteenth-century forerunner of the super-mediated 'society of the spectacle'.[46] Henry James, on the other hand, regarded political violence as a suitable vehicle for the inspection of the relationship between cultural history, literary form and the need to preserve the exisiting political dispensation.

The dynamiters understood their dependence on media coverage, as did their sponsors who appreciated how the report of an explosion was most effectively conveyed in newspaper print (one American subscriber to *The United Irishman* submitted '$2 for my yearly subscription for the "United Irishman", and $1 for dynamite' which he considered 'the most consistent remedy for old tyrant England').[47] Clearly, the US-based Irish separatist press engaged in important publicity work for bombers at large in England, underlining Clymer's suggestion that nineteenth-century terrorism was a form of 'dramatic public violence' that occurred within an expanded media environment. Fenianism, like the American anarchism that Clymer describes, operated within a capitalist and, in the case of Britain, imperial culture that was saturated by a print media that was itself aided by rapidly developing communication technologies like the telegraph and photography. All of these factors greatly increased the potential of revolutionary violence to generate publicity for radical political causes: as Clymer has shown, publicity was so important to modern terrorism that revolutionary politics and modern journalism matured together in this period.[48]

For the anarchists, this was also an age characterised by relentless capitalist cruelty and violence. For Élisée Réclus, the only possible answer to the crushing poverty and inequality bearing down upon the poor of Europe was the revolutionary violence or 'external shocks' that would 'change the form of society'.[49] According to the Russian revolutionary and novelist Sergei Kravchinski, or 'Stepniak', the anarchist was an inevitable by-product of the instability of late nineteenth-century

Europe. Writing from exile in London, Stepniak explained that because it left the proletariat entirely destitute of any political rights, the very concept of government and its repressive structures systematised terror. Poverty, he warned, was the offshoot of the ruthless organisation of capital but so too was violent resistance to the capitalist state: 'The one', he warned, 'is the material substratum of the other'.[50] Mikhail Bakunin also blamed the 'filthy . . . hierarchical world of middle-class civilization' which, 'with its smooth Western façade', for concealing 'the most awful debauchery of thought, feeling attitude and actions'. For Bakunin, the dehumanisation of the poor and autocratic tyranny were not uniquely Russian phenomena but existed in every capitalist state where 'aimless emptiness' was the only freedom to be had.[51] For anarchists, then, the terrorist was a response to the suffering inflicted by capitalism. He or she was, in Stepniak's words, a distinct 'type of modern humanity . . . reproduced in hundreds of forms throughout the world',[52] and from this perspective, government was the source and 'creation of terrorism'. For the anarchists, resistance to capitalism was more than physical force: in their eyes it crystallised 'an idea, a tendency, and a system'.[53] From this perspective, revolutionary violence amounted to the expression of individual agency. The anarchists who shocked governments by virtue of their rejection of all political norms found a suitable weapon in dynamite, which they regarded as 'the accredited symbol of anarchy' and the stuff of a new era in politics.[54]

As one journalist complained, dynamiting was 'not an ordinary crime' but 'a new one':

> Assassination of individual rulers, or ministers, we have had from old, but the modern dynamiter, the wholesale indiscriminate assassin, in comparison with whom the Thug was an embodiment of sweetness and light – this monstrosity, until it sprang into existence, was a creature that the ordinary mind was incapable of even imagining.[55]

Political violence has its own place in the history of aesthetics. Written in 1757, Edmund Burke's *A Philosophical Enquiry into the Origins of Our Ideas of the Sublime and Beautiful* describes how fear 'robs the mind of all its powers of acting and reasoning'. Burke defined terror as the paralysis of emotion and consciousness, a near-physical condition that 'operates in a manner that resembles actual pain'. Yet he also recognised that the short-circuiting of these capacities could induce pleasure, 'for terror', he wrote, 'is a passion which always produces delight'.[56] Three decades later, Burke returned to this theme in his *Reflections on the Revolution in France*, in which he complained that with the overthrow of the *ancien régime*, conspiracy and murder had become the stuff of social change.

Presenting the revolution as a gory political spectacle that threatened to displace the proper but 'bloodless' methods of reform, Burke acknowledged the magnificence of its 'stage effect' and its potential to 'rouze' its torpid but potentially murderous popular audience.[57] His analysis of the shocking, sensory impact of revolutionary terror updated and politicised his earlier writing on the sublime, in which he had already pointed to the theatrical nature of state power as displayed in the torture and execution of Robert Francis Damiens, who had attempted to assassinate Louis XV.[58] But the French Revolution, with its spectacularly levelling policies, threatened to turn the European establishment on its head; once the extent of the threat posed by the republican mob was fully realised, the spectacular implications of terror began to recoil backward on the conservative imagination.[59] By focusing on the trauma caused by violent political change from below, Burke portrayed revolution as a purely shocking phenomenon lacking in political content. He was not the only writer to play on contemporary fears of sans-culottism as political fear fuelled late eighteenth-century English and Irish gothic fiction, sensational genres that displaced very faintly the subject of Jacobin violence. For example, the 'shocking event' with which Matthew Lewis's 1796 novel, *The Monk*, closes, sanitises these fears by presenting them as apolitical horror and the vengeful crowd that beats the Prioress to death is a clear stand-in for the republican mob. Mary Shelley also exploited political distress in *Frankenstein*, in which the dæmon's political consciousness of the 'strange system' of property leads it to attack barriers of 'rank, descent, and noble blood'. Likewise, the Irish legacy of colonial occupation and dispossession informs the ultimately political shocks of Charles Maturin's supernatural tale of 1820, *Melmoth the Wanderer*.[60]

Burke's influential interpretation of the French Revolution held long into the following century. Thomas Carlyle described the overthrow of Louis XVI as the 'Crowning Phenomenon of our Modern Time' but his interpretation of the French Revolution was fundamentally an anxious exploration of Chartism and the Swing Riots gripping southern and eastern England during the 1830s. Carlyle's alarmism haunted the fearful mid nineteenth-century British middle class, in whom he instilled panic over domestic manifestations of Jacobinism. Although the 'chimera' of British radicalism was contained by the late 1840s,[61] the spectre of revolutionary politics returned in anti-imperial guise with the outbreak of the Fenian rebellion of 1867, which included bombings, arms raids and prison escapes, all carried out on English soil and later, in 1881, monarchies across Europe were reminded of their vulnerability when the Tsar, Alexander II, was blown up by Nihilists in St Petersburg.

As Clymer suggests, the unstable conceptual meaning of the word 'terrorism' lies in its confused historical origins, which he traces to the dishonest practices and ideological evasiveness of modern industrial capitalism.[62] The word is notoriously pejorative, and I will not enter the definitional debates that surround it, other than to draw attention to its historical usage. It was, after all, employed in this period by revolutionaries like Patrick Ford to describe their own activities. The editor of *The Irish World and American Industrial Liberator*, Ford praised Fenian dynamiters for carrying out 'savage, unrelenting, unremitting warfare against England – *in England*' and encouraged them to continue until its cities were left 'scourged by day and terrorized by night'. Clearly, this bombing campaign was intended to inspire widespread fear by leaving the British public in a sublime, drawn out 'agony of suspense'. Ford had no problem describing the Fenians as terrorists because, unable to defeat the British through conventional military means, they used the mediated violence of the 'explosive demonstration'. This tactic had a twofold purpose: to frighten the British public and to underline the politically jarring demand of Irish independence.[63] While writers like Ford regarded terrorism and its offshoot of printed propaganda as the natural extension and modernisation of anti-imperial politics, anarchist sympathisers like Havelock Ellis were careful to portray political offenders as the innocent victims of a despotic state. As someone who was not guilty of committing anti-social offences, the revolutionary, Ellis insisted, could not be described as criminal since the application of the word 'crime' to the expression of alternative national feelings or radical political opinions was in itself an abuse of language that guaranteed the illegitimate power of abusive governments.[64]

The Fenians who arrived in England in the 1880s to conduct a campaign that would be 'sublime in volume and terrible in intensity'[65] were conscious of the cultural impact of political violence. Launched with a fatal explosion at Salford Barracks in January 1881 and lasting until 1885,[66] their campaign fits the conceptual definition according to which we understand modern terrorism: the targeting of symbolic buildings, persons and places associated with the political power of an enemy government by non-state actors in order to force the passage of political concessions. The following decade saw Britain's political order and, according to some writers, the nation's very identity, threatened by anarchism (although in England anarchist 'outrages' were more imagined than real). But with Fenianism and anarchism the *septembriseur* of the revolutionary Massacres was replaced in the popular imagination by the more modern figure of the lone, bomb-wielding terrorist. Of course, such tactics were not new in the 1880s – Friedrich Engels criticised the Communards who burned swathes of Paris for their 'desire to appear shocking'[67] – but what distinguished this new revolutionary strategy was its use of cutting-edge bomb technology.

Like Edmund Burke, the writers of the 1880s were faced with a new, performative and spectacularly violent form of political protest. But what distinguishes their perspective from Burke's is their lack of patience. For Burke, shock lingered in the imagination, but the explosive scares of Fenianism and anarchism registered more suddenly, even instantaneously, within the Victorian consciousness. Given the material history of the explosives that they contained, these bombs can be thought of as delivering the masses with industrially produced violence. As such, they owed their momentary quality to the fact that people did not contemplate them for very long. Unlike the drawn-out French revolutionary Terror of 1793, the explosions of the 1880s and 1890s were aimed at a public conditioned to absorb political shock far more systematically than Burke's contemporaries had ever been by the culture industries of the latter part of the nineteenth century. As a public of modern consumers, it was far less inclined to contemplate the gradual impact of violence upon 'the natural frame and constitution'[68] of the human mind than Burke's contemporary readers because, in the late Victorian consciousness, terror was not a qualified or measured experience but an immediate one. Burke's theory explains the workings of the sublime upon an eighteenth-century imagination but, by the 1880s, images of – and texts about – catastrophe were being mass produced and consumed in a much more rapid manner. Whether conveyed by the popular press or in the pages of sensation novels and penny dreadfuls, these words and images were served to readers who demanded racier thrills than had their predecessors of the previous century. The rise of industry, democracy and mass literacy meant that, by the time that the first Fenian bomb exploded in Salford Barracks, political violence registered on an entirely different psychic and cultural level than it had in Burke's time.

Terror still produced delight but in an altogether different way because, put simply, the late Victorian public had a shorter, less contemplative attention span. The bombers who vied for its attention provided political violence that was ready-made for their mediated age, when economies, industries and technologies of image production were modernising and reorganising social reality.[69] Because they inhabited an age characterised by its rapidity, disjunction and defamiliarisation, Fenians and anarchists were conscious of the need for suddenness and unexpectedness in their attacks (the attacks on Westminster and the Tower of London were carried out without warning) and in their propaganda, to the extent that stories in O'Donovan Rossa's *The United Irishman* and Helen and Olivia Rossetti's anarchist journal, *The Torch*, were published in order to terrify. Occurring within an age of media saturation and pronounced subjective dislocation, and having been adapted to suit it, the practice of dynamiting represented a new departure in the history of political violence as it did not allow for a great deal of contemplation. Its lack of predictability – the very fact that it could not be anticipated – is what distinguishes this modern terrorism from earlier models of revolutionary violence. For Burke, terror had a psychic as well as a physical effect but the 'unprecedented sensory complexity and intensity' of the late nineteenth century, with its new media and technologies of communication, such as the penny evening paper, the telegraph and the cinema, meant that new competitors seeking the public's attention would have to go to considerable lengths to get it. As Wolfgang Schivelbusch has pointed out, nineteenth-century industrial modernity was saturated with themes of trauma and popular images of potential disaster,[70] and the explosion became a competing medium in the atmosphere of sensory overload that was the late nineteenth-century city.[71] Fenian bomb attacks against 'conspicuous public edifices',[72] aimed as they were against symbolic cultural, historical and political targets, reveals how dynamiting was a distinctly modern form of political protest aimed at capturing the popular imagination, transforming the appearance of revolution from what it had been during the 1790s. Planting bombs was a more chaotic practice than the refined terrors of that earlier moment appear to us. This book considers how modern political fear fits into the chapter in literary history that opens with the dynamite novel of the 1880s and closes in 1915 with the final publication of *Blast*.

Notes

1. This was John Daly, who was sentenced to life imprisonment in 1884 and served twelve years. After his release he was elected Mayor of Limerick in 1899. According to *The Times*, Daly was intent on 'the wholesale murder of the most eminent men in the country'. See 'The Dynamite Party, Past and Present', *The Times*, Saturday, 24 April 1886, p. 8.
2. 'Crimes and Criminals. No. 1. – Dynamite and Dynamiters', *The Strand Magazine*, Vol. VII, Jan–June 1894, pp. 119–32, p. 119.
3. Richard Henry Savage, *The Anarchist: A Story of To-Day* (Leipzig: Bernhard Tauchnitz, 1894), 2 vols, Vol. 1, p. 86. Subsequent quotations are from this edition.
4. The responses of writers to September 11th differ from those of their nineteenth-century counterparts, as novels like Ian McEwan's *Saturday*, John Updike's *Terrorist*, Claire Messud's *The Emperor's Children* and Don De Lillo's *Falling Man* can hardly be considered as penny dreadfuls. In contrast to the more literary response provoked by the Al Qaeda attacks against

the United States, Fenianism was associated with more 'lowbrow' writing from the outset. See Martin Amis, 'The Second Plane', *The Second Plane* (London: Jonathan Cape, 2008), p. 3.

5. *United Irishman*, untitled cutting, dated 1882, Chief Secretary's Office, Dublin, B 171, National Archive, Dublin.
6. 'England's Fright', *The Irish World and American Industrial Liberator*, 26 January 1884, p. 5.
7. Paul Virilio, *Ground Zero*, trans. Chris Turner (London: Verso, 2002); originally published as *Ce qui arrive* (Paris: Éditions Galilée, 2002), p. 42.
8. John Coulson Kernahan, *The Red Peril* (London: Hurst & Brackett, 1908), p. 323.
9. Edgar Wallace, *The Four Just Men* (Oxford: Oxford University Press, 1995), p. 20.
10. 'It is in that English Parliament', wrote the dynamite propagandist, Jeremiah O'Donovan Rossa, that 'the chains for Ireland are forged'. See Diarmuid (Jeremiah) O'Donovan Rossa, *Rossa's Recollections, 1838–1898* (Shannon: Irish University Press, 1972; originally published New York, 1898), p. 145.
11. Max Nordau, *Degeneration* (London: Heinemann, 1895), p. vii.
12. Nordau, *Degeneration*, Book I, p. 42; Book II, p. 145; Book II, p. 283.
13. Nordau, *Degeneration*, Book II, p. 73; Book I, pp. 145–6.
14. Nordau, *Degeneration*, Book I, pp. 145–6.
15. Nordau, *Degeneration*, Book I, p. 5.
16. Nordau, *Degeneration*, Book II, pp. 62, 301.
17. Nordau, *Degeneration*, Book I, p. 42.
18. Ibid.
19. Nordau, *Degeneration*, Book II, pp. 102–3.
20. Nordau, *Degeneration*, Book II, p. 135; Book II, p. 297; Book II, p. 283.
21. Nordau, *Degeneration*, Book I, p. 144.
22. Nordau, *Degeneration*, Book I, pp. 231, 357.
23. Nordau, *Degeneration*, Book I, p. 535.
24. See Coulson Kernahan, *The Red Peril*, p. 48. See Joseph Conrad, 'The Informer', from *The Lagoon and Other Stories* (Oxford and New York: Oxford University Press, 1997), p. 105.
25. See Michael Denning, *Cover Stories: Narrative and Ideology in the British Spy Thriller* (London: Routledge & Kegan Paul, 1987), p. 3.
26. See John Carey, *The Intellectuals and the Masses: Pride and Prejudice Among the Literary Intelligentsia, 1880–1939* (London: Faber and Faber, 1992), pp. 155–6.
27. Patrick Joyce, *The Rule of Freedom: Liberalism and the Modern City* (London: Verso, 2003), p. 189. See especially chap. 5, 'The Republic of the Streets'.
28. Marie Corelli, *The Sorrows of Satan* (Oxford: Oxford University Press, 1998), p. 3.
29. Nordau, Book II, p. 320. See Frederic Jameson, *The Political Unconscious: Narrative Theory as a Socially Symbolic Act* (London: Routledge, 1996), especially chap. 4, 'Romance and Reification: Plot Construction and Ideological Closure in Joseph Conrad'.

30. See Barbara Arnett Melchiori, *Terrorism in the Late Victorian Novel* (London: Croom Helm, 1985), pp. 2–5, p. 37.

31. Jeffory A. Clymer, *America's Culture of Terrorism* (Chapel Hill and London: The University of North Carolina Press, 2003), p. 1.

32. Houen interprets *The Secret Agent* as a discussion of the social and political implications of contemporary thermodynamic theory, or as a novel in which an 'entropic' anarchism is positioned against capitalism (with Conrad's discussion of heat, particularly solar heat, running on 'borrowed capital' suggesting the fragility of the political and social establishment). Thus, Conrad's reflection on physical force occurs via a metaphorical discussion of physics and *The Secret Agent* is read as a novel about politics as the dispensation of pure energy, and terrorism as the unleashing of 'pure force'. See Alex Houen, *Terrorism and Modern Literature: From Joseph Conrad to Ciaran Carson* (Oxford: Oxford University Press, 2002), pp. 29–30, 41–2, 57.

33. See Francis Galton, *Finger Prints* (London: Macmillan & Co., 1892), p. 1.

34. Havelock Ellis, *The Criminal* (London: Walter Scott, 1890), p. 2. Emma Goldman, who read Ellis and found models for her own anarchist thought in his work, described the European anarchist 'Attentäter' as a 'sensitive human being' and the revolutionary as a 'modern Christ'. See Emma Goldman, 'The Psychology of Political Violence', *Anarchism and Other Essays* (New York: Dover Publications, 1969), pp. 79–108. Quotations from pp. 82, 93. See also Goldman, *Living My Life* (New York: Dover Publications, 1970), 2 vols, Vol. 2, p. 889.

35. See Joyce, *The Rule of Freedom*, pp. 148, 149, 189.

36. See 'Crimes and Criminals,' *The Strand Magazine*, p. 129. See Niall Whelehan, 'Skirmishing, *The Irish World*, and Empire, 1876–86', *Éire-Ireland: An Interdisciplinary Journal of Irish Studies*, 42.1 & 2, Spring/Summer 2007, pp. 180–200, p. 196. See 'Dynamite Explosions: The Tower and the Palace of Westminster', *The Illustrated London News*, 31 January 1885, p. 123. See Robert Louis Stevenson, 'Confessions of a Unionist: An Unpublished "Talk on Things Current"' (Cambridge, MA: privately printed, 1921), pp. 11–12, 14–16.

37. *The Illustrated London News*, 31 January 1885, p. 127.

38. Edgar Allan Poe, 'The Man of the Crowd', *Tales of Mystery and Imagination* (London: Dent, 2000), pp. 108, 112.

39. See Judith R. Walkowitz, *City of Dreadful Delight: Narratives of Sexual Danger in Late-Victorian London* (London: Virago, 1992), pp. 17–18. Deborah L. Parsons has added to Walkowitz's list of enigmatic urban types by drawing attention to the 'Woman in the Crowd', or *flâneuse*. See Deborah L. Parsons, *Streetwalking the Metropolis: Women, Gender and Modernity* (Oxford: Oxford University Press, 2000).

40. In Savage's novel the forever shifting 'werewolf of anarchism' is embodied in the figure of the Jewish intellectual and political villain, Professor Carl Stein, who infiltrates the American capitalist elite by posing as a harmless academic and private tutor. See Savage, *The Anarchist*, Vol. 1, p. 5; Vol. 2, p. 237. As Walter Benjamin pointed out in *Charles Baudelaire: A Lyric Poet in the Era of High Capitalism*, the *flâneur* is, essentially, a cipher, or 'unknown man' of the city. See Walter Benjamin, *Charles Baudelaire: A*

Lyric Poet in the Era of High Capitalism, trans. Harry Zohn (London: Verso, 1997), p. 48.

41. Denning, *Cover Stories,* p. 24.
42. See Tzvetan Todorov, 'The Typology of Detective Fiction', *The Poetics of Prose,* translated from the *La Poétique de la Prose* by Richard Howard (Oxford: Basil Blackwell, 1977), pp. 42–52.
43. This genealogy is charted in my essay 'Conrad, The Stevensons and the Imagination of Urban Chaos', in Stephen Arata, Laurence Davies and Linda Dryden (eds), *Conrad and Stevenson: Writers of Land and Sea* (Lubbock: Texas Tech University Press, 2009).
44. Daly's critique of this cultural phenomenon and its critical history is found in the Introduction to his *Modernism, Romance and the Fin de Siècle: Popular Fiction and British Culture, 1880–1914* (Cambridge: Cambridge University Press, 1999). See especially pp. 4–12. Quotations are from p. 9.
45. See Nicholas Daly, *Literature, Technology, and Modernity, 1860–2000* (Cambridge: Cambridge University Press, 2004), especially chap. 2, 'Sensation Fiction and the Modernization of the Senses'. This quotation is from p. 36.
46. See 'The Dynamite War: A Well-Planned Engagement, and Brilliant Achievements of the Irish Forces', *The Irish World and American Industrial Liberator,* 14 June 1884, p. 3. The dynamiters disrupted a late Victorian capitalist and imperial 'society of the spectacle' that predates Guy Debord's model of 'integrated', commodity-fuelled twentieth-century modernity. Marshall Berman has shown that capitalist modernity and its 'modernisms' have roots that can be traced to the late eighteenth century, while Ben Singer has shown how capitalist modernity was already providing a unified field of perception and experience at the end of the nineteenth. While his often nebulous analysis theorises, too easily, in my view, a distinctly separate modernity and postmodernity, Debord nonetheless usefully describes processes of 'spectacular modernization' that were underway in Europe and North America during the second half of the nineteenth century. Capital, and its concomitant commodity culture, in which the complicated, unpredictable events of history are fused into a series of simplified media events by means of a network of 'spectacular' systems, were advanced enough in the period with which I deal to suggest that Debord's theory of a networked postmodernity ought to be read alongside histories of a grander, more comprehensive modernity. See Guy Debord, *The Society of the Spectacle,* trans. Donald Nicholson-Smith (New York: Zone Books, 1999; originally published as from *La société du spectacle* (Buchet-Castel, 1967). See Marshall Berman, *All That is Solid Melts Into Air: The Experience of Modernity* (Harmondsworth: Penguin, 1982, reprinted 1988). See Ben Singer, *Melodrama and Modernity: Early Sensational Cinema and Its Contexts* (New York: Columbia University Press, 2001). See also David Harvey, *The Condition of Postmodernity: An Enquiry into the Origins of Social Change* (Cambridge, MA and Oxford: Blackwell, 1990).
47. Quoted in K. R. M. Short, *The Dynamite War: Irish-American Bombers in Late-Victorian Britain* (Dublin: Gill and Macmillan, 1979), p. 104.
48. While Clymer concentrates on the impact of political violence on American literature, his argument that 'heavy press coverage . . . contributed to the

spread of terrorism as a modern style of political confrontation' (p. 8) is relevant to my own discussion of the relationship between Fenians, anarchists, British and Irish literature and the media. See Clymer, *America's Culture of Terrorism*, pp. 7–9.

49. See Élisée Réclus, 'An Anarchist on Anarchy', *Contemporary Review*, vol. xlv (January-June, 1884), May 1884, p. 638; and *Evolution and Revolution* (London: International Publishing, 1886, 3rd edn), p. 3.

50. Sergius Stepniak (Sergei Kravchinski), 'Terrorism in Russia and Terrorism in Europe', *The Contemporary Review*, Vol. xlv, March 1884, pp. 325–41, p. 336.

51. Mikhail Bakunin, letter to Sergei Nečaev, 2 June 1870 (translated from the Russian by Olive Stevens), *Selected Writings* (London: Jonathan Cape, 1973), p. 186.

52. Sergius Stepniak, *The Career of a Nihilist* (London: Walter Scott, 1901), Preface to the Second Edition, x.

53. Stepniak, 'Terrorism in Russia and Terrorism in Europe', pp. 325, 330.

54. See Stepniak, ibid. p. 325.

55. 'Detectives and Their Work', *All the Year Round*, 25 April 1885, quoted in Melchiori, *Terrorism in the Late Victorian Novel*, p. 29.

56. See Edmund Burke, *A Philosophical Enquiry into the Origins of Our Ideas of the Sublime and Beautiful* (Oxford: Oxford University Press, 1998). Quotations from pp. 53, 42.

57. See Burke, *Reflections on the Revolution in France* (London: Penguin, 1986, first published, 1790). Quotation from pp. 93, 156.

58. Burke, *A Philosophical Enquiry*, p. 36. Damiens's is also the example with which Michel Foucault opened his foundational critique of state power, *Discipline and Punish*.

59. Anthony Kubiak suggests that because it is a mimetically constructed phenomenon, political violence is an inherently theatrical construction in which coercion is 'acted out'. See Anthony Kubiak, *Stages of Terror: Terrorism, Ideology, and Coercion as Theatre History* (Bloomington and Indianapolis: Indiana University Press, 1991), p. 12.

60. See Matthew Lewis, *The Monk* (Oxford: Oxford University Press, 1998), pp. 355–6. See Ann Radcliffe, *The Mysteries of Udolpho* (Oxford: Oxford University Press, 1998), pp. 240, 241. See Mary Shelley, *Frankenstein*, collected in *Making Humans* (Boston and New York: Houghton Mifflin Company, 2003), pp. 108, 97. See Charles Maturin, *Melmoth the Wanderer* (Oxford: Oxford University Press, 1989).

61. See Thomas Carlyle, *The French Revolution: A History* (New York: Modern Library, 2002), pp. 16, 179, and *Chartism* (Boston: Charles C. Little and James Brown, 1840), pp. 3–4. See Eric Hobsbawm and George Rudé, *Captain Swing* (London: Phoenix, 2001). See Eric Hobsbawm, *The Age of Capital*, 1848–1875 (London: Abacus, 2001), especially chap. 6, 'The Forces of Democracy'.

62. See Clymer, *America's Culture of Terrorism*, p. 5.

63. See 'A Merciless War Must be waged against the Pirate Empire', *The Irish World and American Industrial Liberator*, 26 January 1884, p. 3, 'A Grand Hunt All Round England for Dynamite', *The Irish World and American Industrial Liberator*, 29 March 1884, p. 1, and 'Set a Thief to Catch a

Thief', *The Irish World and American Industrial Liberator*, 12 January 1884, p. 4.

64. See Ellis, *The Criminal*, p. 2.
65. 'An Emergency Fund', *The Irish World and American Industrial Liberator*, 5 January 1884, p. 4.
66. While K. R. M. Short insists that the campaign resumed again briefly in 1887 with the 'Jubilee Plot', a plan to blow up Westminster Cathedral during Victoria's jubilee celebrations, Christy Campbell has proven that this was a fiction dreamt up by the Secret Service in an attempt to undermine Irish nationalism. See Christy Campbell, *Fenian Fire: The British Government Plot to Assassinate Queen Victoria* (London: HarperCollins, 2002).
67. Friedrich Engels, 'The Programme of the Blanquist Commune Refugees' (1874) in Eugene Schulkind (ed.), *The Paris Commune of 1871: The View from the Left* (London: Jonathan Cape, 1972), pp. 237–8. Quotation is from p. 238.
68. Burke, *A Philosophical Enquiry*, p. 41.
69. For the best discussion of optical culture in this period, see Jonathan Crary's *Techniques of the Observer: On Vision and Modernity in the Nineteenth Century* (London and Cambridge, MA: MIT Press, 1990). See also his *Suspensions of Perception: Attention, Spectacle, and Modern Culture* (Cambridge, MA: MIT Press, 1999).
70. See Wolfgang Schivelbusch, *The Railway Journey: The Industrialization of Time and Space in the 19th Century,* trans. Carl Hanser Verlag from *Geschicte der Eisenbahnreise* (Berkeley and Los Angeles: University of California Press, 1986; Munich, 1977), p. 130.
71. See Singer, *Melodrama and Modernity*, pp. 2, 8.
72. *The Illustrated London News*, 31 January 1885.

Chapter 1

Robert Louis Stevenson, Henry James and the City of Encounters

The bombs planted in British cities by Irish Fenians during the 1880s had a literary impact as well as a political one. The popular genre of the 'dynamite novel' marked the beginning of the influence of Irish political violence on literature, a phenomenon that continued into the 1890s. The influence of Fenianism can also be found in later literary modernism, as we will see in Chapters 3 and 4. The shock waves generated by these bombs were also felt in some of the more highbrow novels of the 1880s, with discussions of revolutionary politics also appearing in classics such as Henry James's *The Princess Casamassima* and George Moore's *A Drama in Muslin*. These ultimately uneventful but consciously stylish works differ from the more lurid adventures offered by Robert Louis Stevenson in his 1885 potboiler, *The Dynamiter*, which James praised for combining 'high-flown' extravagance with what he regarded as its unusually 'steep' political content.[1] However, in his own dynamite novel James refused to indulge the popular taste for frantic plots laced with excitement, danger and explosions, and instead used anarchism as a vehicle for an extended discussion of the need for culture, as opposed to chaos, in late Victorian Britain. Unlike popular political novels, which served the literary needs of the mass market by affording readers exciting brushes with Irish and anarchist terrorism, James presented his readers with the aesthetic, rather than anarchic, dilemmas that were raised by late Victorian revolutionaries. The genre of the dynamite novel offered tales ranging from the popular shock-fests of the penny dreadful market (for many hack writers like Coulson Kernahan, and even for respected ones like Stevenson, this proved a commercially lucrative sub-genre of late Victorian detective and adventure fiction),[2] to the more consciously literary efforts of James and Moore. What differentiates both modes of writing about terrorism is that, while political shockers like Stevenson's *The Dynamiter* are full of action, novels like James's metropolitan tale, *The Princess Cassamassima*, and Moore's Irish melodrama, *A Drama in Muslin*, provide little in the way of thrills, opting instead to use revolutionary politics as a platform for discussing of the grander cultural crises of the day. Stevenson's and James's novels reflect the popular pre-occupation with political violence and, while both texts function within their own, distinct literary registers, they express a shared preoccupation with terrorism's function as a symptom of urban modernity. These novels treat the revolutionary as a political by-product of the inherent chaos of London, while their shared, specifically metropolitan bent suggests that despite their generic and stylistic differences, Stevenson and James were equally taken by the role of Fenian and anarchist activity within part of the wider cycle of the late Victorian urban imaginary. For James, the story of his tragic protagonist, Hyacinth Robinson, 'sprang up', almost spontaneously, 'out of the London pavement' (p. 35) because, as he explained to readers in his highly stylised Preface, he could not find, in the British capital, 'a street, a corner, an hour . . . that was not an advantage' (p. 37). Stevenson's political romance is underlined by London's status as 'the city of encounters', or 'the Bagdad of the West', where anything might happen to or be witnessed by unsupposing *flâneurs* like James (p. 1). Along with this shared concern with the relationship between political violence and late Victorian urban modernity, Stevenson's urban political thriller and James's melodrama are also concerned with the relationship between political violence and culture. In the case of *The Princess Casamassima*, this is presented by James as a dialectical exchange between the stabilising (and historical) forces of taste, which must be protected from the anarchists, whom he depicts as the opponents of culture. Stevenson, on the other hand, while accepting that culture is a contested phenomenon, presents the clash between Fenianism and his trio of heroic amateur investigators in a more desperate light.

The Dynamiter

Appearing in 1885, less than a year before the publication of *The Strange Case of Dr Jekyll and Mr Hyde* (which Stevenson considered 'dam [*sic*] dreadful'),[3] *The Dynamiter* is a uniquely 'lowbrow' piece, even for the author of violent horror stories like *The Strange Case of Dr Jekyll and Mr Hyde* and 'The Body Snatcher'. A sequel to his 1882 collection, *New Arabian Nights*, the tale's arbitrary plot shifts variously from Utah, to London and Cuba. Co-written with his American wife, Fanny Van De Grift Stevenson, the precise authorship of the entire piece is unclear although it is likely that Stevenson composed the Irish-related material while the tale of Mormon terror, 'Story of the Destroying Angel', was at least influenced by Fanny.[4] *The Dynamiter* functions on two levels by, firstly, depoliticising Irish separatism and presenting it as a purely criminal and insane endeavour. It also offers a cultural commentary on the strangeness of metropolitan experience, which, it suggests to the reader, effects the modern subject through an ongoing process of 'profound abstraction' (p. 9).[5] Opening with a dedication to a pair of policemen who were injured while removing one of the Westminster bombs, it even blames the Irish parliamentary leader, Charles Stewart Parnell, for promoting terrorism. But despite Stevenson's claims to moral superiority, his novel ruthlessly exploits popular fascination with Irish political violence. Written or possibly dictated by Stevenson when he was under considerable financial pressure,[6] its manipulation of the panicky *zeitgeist* of the mid-1880s was so successful that it underwent no less than three print runs within twelve weeks of its first publication.[7] Stevenson's anti-Irish sentiment is inarguable: privately, he called for the application of lynch law and the use of Gatling guns to silence nationalist dissent.[8] His views on Irish separatism provide *The Dynamiter* with a contemporary appeal with which the novel's theme of the metropolitan uncanny is underlined. As a result the novel fulfilled a similar cultural role to the fragmented but nonetheless 'ideologically charged' images of contemporary events communicated by the conservative press.[9]

The tale centres on the efforts of three bored gallants, Edward Challoner, Paul Somerset and Harry Desborough, to thwart a Fenian bombing campaign and win a reward offered for the capture of a mysterious Irish dynamiter. As well as expressing imperialist ideology the novel also reveals how the modern urban subject becomes defamiliarised, or 'lost in terrors' (p. 10) as a result of the terrorism that occurs within the city, which Stevenson describes as a 'labyrinth' (p. 8). London's chaotic metropolitan character renders it an unreadable 'hieroglyph' (p. 59), the result of its status as the centre of empire and of having absorbed much belonging originally to the cultures that Britain has colonised. Stevenson's amateur sleuths find themselves being forced into confronting the city's political underground, which functions as a fragment of, or one of many coordinates within, what Julian Wolfreys has termed the 'ever-changing cartographic conceit' of the metropolis.[10] Here, they enter a transgressive world of nightwalkers, tramps and lodging houses, where 'the continual stream of passers-by . . . the sealed fronts of houses . . . the posters that covered the hoardings, and . . . every lineament and throb of the great city', contain 'the elements of adventure . . . streaming by . . . as thick as drops of water in the Thames' (p. 59). However, what they encounter is the erosion of identity as, by uncovering and becoming implicated in the Fenian conspiracy, they become as amorphous as the fluid and indistinct urban elements that Stevenson describes as composing the metropolis. Identity is never secure and often untrustworthy within this environment, and the friends take part in a series of quest adventures of the type usually associated in contemporary popular fiction with distant colonial exploits. In Stevenson's fantasy of imperial recoil the alien culture of the colonised, so central to the appeal of the genre of the far-flung imperial romance, is transplanted directly onto the already orientalised streets of the metropolis.[11] Henry James, who was struck by the originality of the 'very happy idea' of 'placing a series of adventures which are pure adventures in the setting of contemporary English life, and relating them in the placidly ingenuous tone of Scheheradze', believed that Stevenson's combination of exoticism and contemporary politics in *The Dynamiter* guaranteed its success.[12] Stevenson's imperial logic exploits domestic fear and fascination with the colonised Other, placing the Irish bomber in the same popular imaginative territory as more exotic villains from further afield, such as Arthur Conan Doyle's murderous pigmy, Tonga, or H. Rider Haggard's African empress, Ayesha.[13] The 'noise of battle' (p. 7) that emanates from 'that great bazaar of dangerous and smiling chances, the pavement of the city' (p. 67) echoes the violence of contemporary imperial wars taking place in Egypt and the Sudan during 1881–6, where the British were bloodily suppressing nationalist revolts led by Urabi Pasha and El Mahdi while Stevenson was composing his tale; for contemporary readers of *The Dynamiter*, the report of a Fenian bomb was an uncomfortable reminder of the possible reversal of the until-now one-sided dialectic of imperial violence.[14]

Like other popular urban narratives, such as George W. M. Reynold's *The Mysteries of London* (1846–8) and the bleak sociological analysis presented in George R. Sims's *How the Poor Live* and *Horrible London* (1883), *The Dynamiter* operates between the discursive-literary poles of policing and entertainment that have been described by Mark Seltzer.[15] This is stated explicitly by Stevenson in his dedication to the policemen who were injured removing a bomb from the crypt at the Palace of Westminster in January 1885, where he criticised the British public for treating Fenian activity 'like the schoolboy with the penny tale, applauding what was specious' (p. viii). Charles Stewart Parnell, the real target of Stevenson's ire, is blamed for the explosion, and for the Fenian campaign as a whole, for refusing to condemn it, while 'the police, so little recognized, so meagrely rewarded, have at length found their commemoration in an historical act' (pp. vii–viii). Late Victorian political romances featured a variety of sleuths, ranging from idealistic imperialists to more mercenary types and adventurists, but what unites them is their contradiction of the normative epistemological thrust of the detective tale, embodied so famously in the rational practices and empirical theories of detectives such as Arthur Conan Doyle's Sherlock Holmes and Edgar Allan Poe's Auguste Dupin. Thus, in *The Dynamiter*, amateur Fenian-hunters like Edward Challoner experience counter-terrorism as a process of deepening mystification and confusion. Rejecting the standard movement of the classic detection narrative – the journey towards enlightenment via exposure of the criminal's method and motivation – Stevenson's protagonist finally reaches the conclusion that he is dealing with an unfathomable phenomenon – the 'great and confused war of politics' (pp. vii) that is Irish nationalism. Unlike the material clues that inform the rational judgement of other fictional detectives (for example, Doyle's vividly rendered imperial commodities), the information that Challoner uncovers while hunting for Fenian bombers serves only to disengage his mind from the source of these political troubles.

The adventure begins when Stevenson's heroes read an advertisement in the *Standard* offering a reward of £200 to anyone capable of proving the identity and whereabouts of a man seen behaving suspiciously in the Green Park. They must accept the challenge, Somerset insists, because they are entitled to do so:

> 'Do you then propose, dear boy, that we should turn detectives?' inquired Challoner.
> 'Do I propose it? No, sir,' cried Somerset. 'It is reason, destiny, the plain face of the world, that commands and imposes it. Here all our merits tell; our manners, habit of the world, powers of conversation, vast stores of unconnected knowledge, all that we are and have builds up the character of the complete detective. It is, in short, the only profession for a gentleman.' (p. 4)

This self-reflexive elaboration on the political subtext of the detective genre is articulated through Somerset's belief in bourgeois entitlement. Citing middle-class identity as forming the moral and therefore professional basis of detection, Somerset suggests that the skills of this profession are based on inherent qualities such as superior manners, habit, unusually keen conversational skill (by which he means discursive authority and power) and information. According to this logic, it is thanks to, and therefore on behalf and in defence of, his class position that the 'gentleman' sleuth acts. Yet Stevenson undermines this construction by emphasising the disconnectedness of the bourgeoisie's 'vast stores' of knowledge because Somerset and his friends are unaware of how these privileges might relate to the 'web' (p. 7) of imperial structures that surrounds them. *The Dynamiter* hinges upon the refusal of otherness by the Victorian imperial consciousness and exploits this phenomenon by using it to emphasise the inherent strangeness of the British metropolis. This is registered in the obvious orientalism of the novel's opening, which Stevenson couples with the political indecipherability of Fenian activity.

Although they lack the specialised knowledge of the detective who fights 'ordinary' crime, such omniscience would be of no use to Stevenson's heroes as they are dealing with an unreadable form of deviance, which he describes in the dedication as the 'ugly devil' of Irish 'political crime' (p. vii). In this tale the modern bourgeois subject, represented by the amateur sleuth, experiences a process of defamiliarisation during his pursuit of the bomber:

> A great and troubled curiosity, and a certain chill of fear, possessed his spirit. The conduct of the man with the chin-beard, the terms of the letter, and the explosion of the early morning, fitted together like parts in some obscure and mischevious imbroglio. Evil was certainly afoot; evil secrecy, terror, and falsehood were the conditions and the passions of the people among whom he had begun to move, like a blind puppet . . . (p. 55)

In contrast to popular champions of rational empiricism like Holmes and Dupin, Challoner finds himself locked in a spiral of mystery and unfulfilled curiosity that erodes his own sense of agency and transforms him into a mere puppet of the dynamiters. This spiral of deepening confusion (he feels lost in the metropolitan 'labyrinth') underlines the dynamite novel's purpose as a literary intervention in the sphere of politics because in the case of Stevenson's contribution to the genre, the construction of terrorism as the exploitation of pure, irrational fear obscures any notion that dynamiting might be a politically motivated activity. Pro-empire dynamite novels shored up imperialism by denying Fenianism's political motivations, with villains bombing the metropolis, according to a contemporary reviewer, 'as much for the love of the thing as from hatred of tyrants'.[16] As Ronald R. Thomas has shown, the nineteenth-century detective is a distinctly literary type who, on discovering the truth of a given case, is empowered with the authority to narrate the stories of those involved in his investigations.[17] *The Dynamiter*, in contrast, avoids treating its readers to an explanation as Stevenson declines to conclude with the exposure of the miscreant, opting, instead, for his destruction and refusing to narrate his political story. Instead of describing the villain's rationale, the novel closes with the de-explanation of his actions, effectively containing the political and cultural threat posed by the Irish bomber, whose presence in London adds to the mysteriousness of the city. In doing so, Stevenson presents the Fenian as a demonic political actor motivated by wanton, even satanic wickedness. As suggested by the operational nom de plume of

'Zero' that is adopted by the dynamiter, the marauding bomber is not so much a presence as an anti-presence, the nihilistic other to heroes like Challoner who protect the Empire from a threat that is never fully described. Their valorous purpose is 'to deracinate occult and powerful evil' from the metropolis (p. 6), not to engage with the Irish question that was so central to British imperial politics during the 1880s. By constructing terrorism as an obscure phenomenon and promoting detection as a 'profession of intrigue' (p. 7) rather than enlightenment, Stevenson attempts to exorcise the imperial metropolis of its political other, the Irish bomber, by denying the political significance of Irish separatism.[18]

The adventure introduces the Irish conflict directly into the British capital when Challoner stumbles across a premature explosion that wrecks a tenement lodging-house:

> he was startled by a dull and jarring detonation from within. This was followed by a monstrous hissing and simmering as from a kettle of the bigness of St Paul's; and at the same time from every chink of door and window spurted an ill-smelling vapour ... Within the lodging-house feet pounded on the stairs; the door flew back emitting clouds of smoke; and two men and an elegantly dressed young lady tumbled forth into the street and fled without a word. The hissing had already ceased, the smoke was melting in the air, the whole event had come and gone as if in a dream, and still Challoner was rooted to the spot. (p. 9)

In the atmosphere of 'appalling silence' that follows the explosion, Challoner, guiltily aware of the 'staring' windows of the surrounding tenements (p. 10), escapes the site of the explosion, but his subsequent complicity in Fenian activity is much more difficult to shirk off. The guilt he experiences at the scene of the explosion suggests that the feelings of urban alienation described by a host of Victorian novelists, sociologists and journalists are intensified by the unexpected shocks of political violence, and that the 'battle' that constitutes metropolitan existence necessitates struggling against such isolation. Sharon Marcus has explained the inherently political dimension of nineteenth-century urban space, wherein buildings were 'both social products and conduits for social production'.[19] Their function as sites of such processes is underlined by Stevenson's exploding tenement which, with its concealed bomb factory, is a doubly insecure space containing Irish subversives along with its usual, transient population. The social and political diversity of this under-class of slum-dwellers contradicts the bourgeois and imperial ideals of domestic space that was, as Marcus points out, ideologically constructed in the capitalist imagination as a firmly sealed and happily sterile environment.[20]

Failing to realise that a bomb has exploded inside the building,[21] the naive hero quickly becomes implicated in the dynamiters' plot as a young woman who has escaped the blast asks him to deliver a letter along with 700 pounds to her contact in Glasgow, named M'Guire (her male colleagues have abandoned her). Driven by sexual desire, which he conceals under a guise of gentlemanly chivalry, Challoner agrees, since 'the cultured tone of her voice, her choice of language, and the elegant decorum of her movements cried out aloud against a harsh construction', not to mention her 'flashing' at him a glimpse of her ankle (pp. 13–14). Arriving by train in Glasgow, Challoner finds the address to which he has been sent in a slum where, 'as in the streets of London, he was impressed by the sense of city deserts' (p. 50). Here, he gives the note and the money to the Fenian, M'Guire, before realising that he has been duped by the bombers into carrying out the errand. Narrowly escaping a police raid, Challoner is taken by one of the Fenians to a basement where he is given a disguise of a 'degrading ulster' and badly fitting hat that transforms him from a bourgeois into a rough-looking tramp. Dejected, he returns to London after spending the night walking the streets of Glasgow and although he has the outward half of a first-class ticket, he decides to travel in a third-class compartment, his appearance preventing him, 'for decency', from mixing with 'his equals'. His bourgeois and imperial identity has been eroded as Challoner, wandering the 'obscurer' streets of the Scottish city, has become part of the furniture of the modern urban labyrinth. His anxiety is not just the result of his shame but the product of his awareness that, by aiding the dynamiters, he has transgressed class boundaries. This, rather than treason, is the crime that 'cut him to the heart' (p. 58), as he has, if only briefly, abandoned his bourgeois self and entered the twilit world of political conspiracy (all of the action, up until this point, occurs either at dawn or at dusk) and assumed the identity of the vagrant terrorist.

Stevenson's preoccupation with the subversion of London's interior spaces, along with the class and imperial demarcations that they represent, continues in the next adventure. 'The Superfluous Mansion' introduces terrorism to suburbia by bringing Paul Somerset into contact with the dynamiters in a wealthy park. A mysterious elderly lady (who is really Miss Fonblanque in disguise) brings Somerset to her 'stately and severe' home (p. 62) which turns out to be the mansion in which Prince Florizel, the protagonist of 'The Suicide Club' in *New Arabian Nights*, survives an assassination attempt. She claims to be searching for her estranged daughter who left her to work for 'oppressed nationalities – Ireland, Poland, and the like' (p. 73) (liberalism irritated the unionist Stevenson, who criticised Gladstone for pandering to 'the insidious influence of all the favourite catchphrases of the period', including 'oppressed nationality').[22] Promising to look after the property while she retires to a continental spa, Somerset sublets to the suspiciously anonymous Mr. Jones whose visitors include an American who panics on dropping a suitcase: 'What, he (Somerset) asked himself, had been the contents of the black portmanteau? Stolen goods? the carcass of one murdered? or – and at the thought he sat upright in bed – an infernal machine?' (pp. 100–1). On searching Jones's room, which has 'the exact appearance of a lodging-house bedroom', he finds a 'diabolical' arsenal of dismantled pistols and clocks, various chemicals and an assortment of disguises. Transformed into a bomb factory by a man who is not at all what he seems, the suburban 'palace of delight' has become part of the chaotic reality of the metropolis: 'Here were the locks of dismounted pistols; clocks and clockwork in every stage of demolition, some still busily ticking, some reduced to their dainty elements; a great company of carboys, jars, and bottles; a carpenter's bench and a laboratory table' (p. 103). This scene, with its themes of urban terror, shifting identities and scientific apparatus anticipates the horror of *The Strange Case of Dr Jekyll and Mr Hyde*, where fear has a more psychological than political impact.

Jones confesses that he is Zero, the leader of the Fenian cell (his anti-identity being a pun on Jeremiah O'Donovan Rossa's operational nom de plume, 'Number One'), and explains his reliance upon anonymity to Somerset:

> 'If you love romance (as artists do), few lives are more romantic than that of the obscure individual now addressing you. Obscure yet famous. Mine is an anonymous, infernal glory. By infamous means, I work towards my bright purpose. I found the liberty and peace of a poor country desperately abused; the future smiles upon that land; yet, in the meantime, I lead the existence of a hunted brute, work towards appalling ends, and practice hell's dexterities.' (p. 106)

Zero's bombing campaign is a consciously modern affair. It occurs in an age of advertising and mass consumption in which colour, language and design inspire the 'poetry' of his dynamite outrages, and he goes on to explain the popular aesthetic and symbolic qualities of the 'star of dynamite', the high explosive that has 'risen for the oppressed' (pp. 106–7) and democratised warfare through its availability, simple utility and suitability to an age of media:

> What with the loss of plant and the almost insuperable scientific difficulties of the task, our friends in France are almost ready to desert the chosen medium. They propose, instead, to break up the drainage system of cities and sweep off

whole populations with the devastating typhoid pestilence: a tempting and scientific project: a process, indiscriminate indeed, but of idyllical simplicity. I recognize its elegance; but, sir, I have something of the poet in my nature; something, possibly, of the tribune. And for my small part, I shall remain devoted to that more emphatic, more striking, and (if you please) more popular method of the explosive bomb.' (pp. 107–8)

Dynamite is not just a high explosive: it is the 'chosen medium' of the conspirator who uses it to convey a message and, in trying to depoliticise the motivations of Irish bombers, Stevenson suggests that their method is a wickedly artistic one. Unlike other weapons like the bacteriological culture chosen by H. G. Wells' anarchist in his short story of 1892, 'The Stolen Bacillus', dynamite is the ultimate symbolic weapon because it has popular appeal. As well as discussing the political shocks of late Victorian terrorism, Stevenson is also making a statement about popular literary form as the aesthetic value of dynamite lies, according to Zero, in its simplicity. By reducing revolutionary politics to the striking image of the explosion it seems the perfect source of thrills for the writers and readers of popular fiction who, like the Irish bomber, are devoted lovers of romance. This Fenian and self-confessed 'believer' in dynamite (p. 108) also links bombing to the explosive poetics of his subversive propaganda, suggesting that the dynamite campaign serves as its own message, or as its own reality, distinct from the value judgements of the world at large: 'Whatever may strike fear, whatever may confound or paralyse the activities of the guilty nation, barrow or child, imperial Parliament or excursion steamer, is welcome to my simple plans' (p. 108). His appreciation of dynamite's power to shock, and of the destructive power of his bombs, is a playfully politicised version of the artistic consciousness outlined by Walter Pater in his 1873 collection of essays on aesthetics, *The Renaissance*. Describing all art, including 'music, poetry, artistic and accomplished forms of human life', as 'receptacles of so many powers or forces', he represents the aesthetic consciousness as a receiver of intense experiences, or 'impressions' locked into a state of supreme sensitivity to the 'powers or forces producing pleasurable sensations'. This theory of art-as-force is echoed in Zero's insistence on the beauty, or 'bright purpose', of his cause as its purely destructive medium carries its ultimate meaning. Stevenson ridicules the notion that the critical temperament is deeply affected by both the power and the presence of the beautiful but, by equating Pater's theory with the romantic appeal of revolutionary politics, he also suggests that terrorism has a uniquely aesthetic purchase and that the pure energy of Zero's explosions can be compared to the 'heat of . . . genius', as celebrated in the Paterian imagination.[23] Pater's own designs for aestheticism, which he envisioned as the 'outbreak' of a 'spirit of rebellion against the moral and religious ideas' that dominate any given epoch,[24] add a subtle political edge to his discussion of art. Clearly, in this scene in *The Dynamiter*, bombing is read as the expression of uncontrolled political aestheticism or avant-gardism. The artistic quality of a 'striking act of dynamite' suggests that terrorism is distinctively different from other forms of political violence; Stevenson's reflection on this aspect of his intensely mediated age, in which high explosives are another medium for political expression, explains why blowing things up is a particularly modern practice: when Zero asks Somerset, 'what could be more pictorial, what more effective, than the explosion of a hansom cab as it sped rapidly along the streets of London?' (p. 116), he underlines the powerful impression left on the popular imagination by setting off bombs. As the sketches and photographs accompanying reports on Fenian attacks in the popular *Illustrated London News* reveal, these 'striking' acts of terror had a particularly visual quality that appealed to late Victorian news consumers.

Zero repeats this point on the roof of the mansion, where he shows Somerset the urban 'plain of battle':

> 'Here,' cried Zero, 'you behold this field of city, rich, crowded, laughing with the spoil of continents; but soon, how soon, to be laid low! Some day, some night, from this coign of vantage, you shall perhaps be startled by the detonation of the judgment gun – not sharp and empty like the crack of cannon, but deep-mouthed and unctuously solemn. Instantly thereafter, you shall behold the flames break forth. Ay,' he cried, stretching forth his hand, 'ay, that will be a day of retribution. Then shall the pallid constable flee side by side with the detected thief. Blaze!' he cried, 'blaze, derided city! Fall, flatulent monarchy, fall like Dagon!' (p. 123)

Zero intends to leave his targets enchanted by the sublime, shocking and destructive power of his 'incommunicable terrors' (p. 12) and their levelling power. Reminiscent of the gothic clifftop *finales* or revelations that characterise Matthew Lewis's *The Monk* (1796) and Charles Maturin's *Melmoth the Wanderer* (1820), Zero's revenge fantasy also suggests his demonic, Miltonian qualities. But whereas these earlier political fantasies end with their protagonists poised over fathomless gulfs, what distinguishes Zero from gothic villains is his intention to create a void out of the crowded imperial city. A practitioner of 'hell's dexterities', his satanic flamboyance is mirrored by one of J. D. Maginn's fictional bombers, General Thaddeus T. O'Hara, who, in *Fitzgerald the Fenian*, similarly declaims with 'theatrical language and gesture', yelling 'I am a Fenian, and I have imbued my hands in British gore' (p. 207). Dynamiting likewise appears as 'devil's work' in Robert Thynne's 1901 potboiler, *John Townley: A Tale for the Times*, a practically unreadable novel that does not mince its political message with the warning that 'Irish separatism would be the commencement of Irish anarchy'.[25]

The Dynamiter concludes with Zero's auto-destruction in a scene that explains the manner in which the terrorist and the terrorised are both enchanted by the destructive spectacle of the explosion. Zero's campaign comes to an end when he is killed grabbing a newspaper on a crowded railway platform. Desperate to read a report about one of his explosions, he is blown to pieces when the bomb that he is carrying detonates prematurely:

> the train for Liverpool was just about to start, another had but recently arrived; and the double tide made movement difficult. As the pair reached the neighbourhood of the bookstall, however, they came into an open space; and here the attention of the plotter was attracted by a *Standard* broadside bearing the words: 'Second Edition: Explosion in Golden Square.' His eye lighted; groping in his pocket for the necessary coin, he sprang forward – his bag knocked sharply on the corner of the stall – and instantly, with a formidable report, the dynamite exploded. When the smoke cleared away the stall was seen much shattered, and the stall keeper running forth in terror from the ruins; but of the Irish patriot or the Gladstone bag no adequate remains were to be found. (p. 182)

Zero's end is loosely modelled on the death of William Mackey Lomasney, a dynamiter and veteran of the American Civil War who was killed in a premature explosion along with two colleagues during an attempt on London Bridge. With his death, noted *The Times*, Irish terrorism had become 'of merely historical interest', adding, with relish: 'there is something reassuring in the demonstration that the criminals who act – whatever may be the case with those who merely plot – do not work with impunity ... and that two, literally hoist with their own petard, lie dead at the bottom of the Thames'.[26] *The Dynamiter* concludes on a similarly self-satisfied note but its final explosion, occurring on a train platform by a newspaper stand and among a crowd of onlookers, is loaded with self-reflexive and symbolic meaning. Addicted to media coverage of his work, Zero is vaporised while reaching for a newspaper report on his latest attack, and is ironically undone by the media impact of his bombing campaign. His death occurs within the circulation of modernity and its media, with his final explosion – itself marked by the 'report' of the blast – marking terrorism's assimilation within the *schema* of urban modernity, so that instead of disrupting the modern imperial metropolis he becomes part of its very matter: exploding upon the platform and amid the moving crowd, his atomised remains are fused with the disintegrated texts of daily papers, detective novels and other popular reads sold at the news stand.[27] While the reputation of the ratiocinative protagonists of such popular narratives, like Arthur Conan Doyle's iconic detective, Sherlock Holmes, depends on their ability to solve mysteries by making something out of nothing, *The Dynamiter* ends not with the satisfying resolution of detection and the exposure of a villain but with Stevenson's literal reduction of the Irish revolutionary to nothing. Having already renamed and re-identified the real-life Number One as Zero, his entire being – consisting of his physical body *and* his separatist political beliefs – is annihilated by the mediating processes of the press and the bomb. According to the cultural and political logic of the tale, which closes with the late Victorian *leitmotif* of the self-destructing, ineffectual bomber, it might not be possible to ignore the terrorist events that so fascinated contemporary readers but, according to Stevenson, their conceptual and political power could be limited or contained by means of narration. With *The Dynamiter*, Stevenson attempted to desublimate terrorism by suggesting that its political shocks could be absorbed by a resilient modern imperial culture. Dynamiting was itself a consciously modern revolutionary tactic but with this reassuring closure Stevenson suggested that its terrors had become part of the wider cycle of urban modernity and that it could be halted by the very processes that it was designed to disrupt.

Terrorism and the Problem with Culture: *The Princess Casamassima*

Henry James also suggested that culture could protect capitalist society from political meltdown in his 1886 novel, *The Princess Casamassima*, in which he explored the threat posed by the other great radical threat to British society – anarchism. James constructed the novel around the idea that the political chaos occurring in London could be deflected from society by the protective membrane of culture surrounding all that is superior. According to James, culture itself is maintained by the 'finely aware' protectors of society, whose role as its culturally conscious vanguard is to relay their authoritative experiences with the 'maximum of sense' (p. 35),[28] and thereby counter the destructive efforts of revolutionaries whose aesthetic consciousness is inferior to the highly focused sensibilities of the elite. But whereas Stevenson engaged directly with the Irish question, James was careful not to name the Fenians as his 'startled game' (p. 33) in *The Princess Casamassima* and instead associated the threat of political and cultural collapse with the European anarchist movement. As a result, anarchism is portrayed in the novel as an expression of cultural envy by the 'have-nots' of late Victorian society, while it is simultaneously presented as the result of an acute process of urban degeneration. James's bottom line on anarchism – a position that fuses both literary and political conservatism – is that it threatens culture and cannot cope with its complexity, and functions, in the end, as an 'aggressive, vindictive, destructive social faith' (p. 44), offering the notion that the best action to take is none at all.[29] As Mark Seltzer has pointed out, James's views on culture, including his technical stress on the art of writing fiction, are a reflection of his inherently conservative political consciousness. Pointing to James's own attempts to obscure the relationship between his literary and political views in *The Princess Casamassima*, Seltzer suggests that he disguises his realist 'aesthetic of power' as an exchange between a supposedly neutral cultural sphere and the author's own, apparently disinterested, political position.[30] However, while Seltzer offers a Foucauldian reading of the novel as a discourse on surveillance and its 'specular' networks of observation, I am more interested in its engagement with the city as an aesthetically productive site of political chaos.[31] Like Stevenson, who regarded dynamiting as a product of 'the burned atmosphere of cities' (p. 9), James also treated the London streets as a fascinating, if pathological territory where anything might happen. James also portrayed terrorism as a fascinating by-product of the 'atmospheric mixture' that constituted the metropolis (p. 443) but insisted on treating his subject in a more mundane manner than the author of *The Dynamiter*, whom he admired for presenting readers with tales loaded with 'dangers and thrills'. James praised Stevenson's adventures, including *The Dynamiter*, for showcasing his faith in heroism and 'personal gallantry', and for doing so 'with extreme psychological truth', admiring his subject matter as much as his style. He recognised in Stevenson an urban writer who described city 'streets . . . so full of history and poetry . . . of associations springing from strong passions and strange characters',[32] but was also careful to qualify his enthusiasm for these tales, particularly *The Dynamiter*, which he found both extravagant and specious, and lacking the psychological thrust of *The Strange Case of Dr Jekyll and Mr Hyde*.[33] However, despite the obvious aesthetic differences between Stevenson's dashed off political thriller and James's much more introspective work, *The Princess Casamassima* shares common political ground with *The Dynamiter*. Collin Meissner has read the novel as an essay on the shortcomings of 1880s aestheticism and its 'stereotypic' responses to questions of sensory reception and experience,[34] but the novel consistently pits art and culture against the destructiveness of revolutionary ideology. Just as Stevenson denies the political motivations that underlined Fenian activity, James also attempts to hollow out the political core of his subject matter, anarchism, which he recasts as a vehicle for the narrow-minded cultural jealousy of a cabal of embittered malcontents. While anarchism never comes anywhere near to threatening the political establishment in the novel, the most shocking characteristic of James's revolutionaries remains their desire to undermine the cultural pillars that support late Victorian society.[35]

The novel's political discussion draws on a particularly urban aesthetic, with anarchism emerging out of the 'vast vague murmur' (p. 33), or background noise, of the late Victorian metropolis. James's realism renders the city in a very different light to Stevenson's more colourful metropolis as it focuses on the indistinct condition of Britain's spectacular, if monotone capital. London is again orientalised but in a less colourful manner and the 'great grey Babylon' (p. 34) serves as an appropriate setting for a political novel within which intrigues are played out as the workings of an indeterminate and 'shady' political underground, wherein misguided idealists like Hyacinth Robinson become trapped in the hopeless miasma of 'revolutionary politics of a hole-and-corner sort'. Agency is not an option for James's half-hearted plotter, who prefers the pleasures of consumption to the difficulties that have to be endured by the revolutionist and discovers that, by walking through the portal of culture, as he does at the Princess's countryside retreat at Medley Hall, he can experience the 'warmer glow of things'. Upon experiencing for himself the settled, or 'appeased and civilized state' of bourgeois normality (p. 44), Hyacinth gradually attains an intensely refined condition of political transcendence and discovers that class warfare is both unnecessary and irrelevant for the aesthetically conscious. As Taylor Stoehr has pointed out, the novel offered a more literary perspective on political chaos than any contemporary fiction did, but in a manner that does not reflect much of the reality of the revolutionary activity of its day.[36] For James, the precariousness of modern culture lies in the strangely bifurcated nature of modern society, where pleasure is made possible by unseen horrors, such as poverty and inequality, that are fostered by capitalism. Woven together by what Hyacinth describes as a network of 'invisible, impalpable wires' (p. 330), the parallel worlds of the late Victorian bourgeoisie and the urban poor are proximate but also markedly distinct enough to exist as separate realities offering distinct types of experience to their inhabitants. The novel's ideological position supports their necessary separation, as the world of culture depends on the suffering that it generates in the realm that constitutes its political and cultural other – the disruptive reality described by James as the 'sinister anarchic underworld, heaving in its pain, its power and its hate'. As Thomas Peyser suggests, these worlds meet around the spectacle of consumption, where the display of commodities forms 'the still centre' of 'an entire phase of culture',[37] and Hyacinth's work as a bookbinder can be regarded as a site of this convergence. The world of the poor and of the revolutionaries functions as an alternative realm of overwhelmingly negative experience lacking in 'sharp particulars'. Their undefined world is conditioned by the constant movement of 'loose appearances, vague motions and sounds and symptoms'. James suggests that bourgeois culture and its attendant 'stuff' constitutes a far more definite aura than this ever-shifting environment of 'just perceptible presences and general looming possibilities' and, as a result, *The Princess Casamassima* hinges on his paradoxical consciousness of the appeal of urban mystery and irrationality. London is imagined in the novel not in the solid terms of the capitalist world that it so determinedly defends, but as an unstable reality that must, as James argues in his preface, be subjected to a focused literary examination: 'To haunt the great city and by this habit to penetrate it, imaginatively, in as many places as possible – *that* was to be informed, *that* was to pull wires, *that* was to open doors, *that* positively was to groan at times under the weight of one's accumulations' (p. 48). For James this paradox is embodied in the figure of the novelist who, as a 'painter of the human mixture', must become immersed in metropolis and its 'abyss of ambiguities' in order to produce a realistic literary representation of the 'exposed and tangled state' of the political condition of late nineteenth-century urban modernity (p. 37).

Hyacinth's difficulty and, ultimately, his tragedy, lie in the ambiguity of the position that he occupies as an individual who attempts to reconcile revolutionary ideology with an appreciation of culture. As Margaret Scanlan argues, this problem was related to form quite deliberately by James, whose unavoidably loose and consciously heterogenous fiction 'suggests that the novel as high art is in an improbable object, aiming at truth and beauty but unable to disguise its low connections'.[38] Standing between the defined sphere of the bourgeoisie and its art products, which James regarded as being intimately linked to capital, and the uncertain alternatives being offered by the anarchists, Hyacinth's 'much-mixed', extremely conflicted and ultimately tragic state of consciousness is the result, as James claimed, of his own appreciation of the material conditions of the metropolis: 'my gathered impressions and stirred perceptions, the deposit in my working imagination of all my visual and all my constructive sense of London . . . my fresh experience of London – the London of the habitual observer, the preoccupied painter, the pedestrian prowler' (p. 47). Like Stevenson's *flâneur* heroes, the realist author is, for James, both an urban detective and chronicler of experience whose perspective allows him to negotiate the city and its political underground with sensitivity to the necessary, if flimsy, barrier that has been erected, and must also be maintained by the novelist, between culture and the chaos of revolution. According to James's politicisation of aesthetics, conflict must occur between those who experience only 'degrees of feeling – the muffled, the faint, the just sufficient, the barely intelligent', and the aesthetically focused elite, who, appreciating 'the acute, the intense, the complete', possess 'the power to be finely aware and richly responsible'. With their finely tuned sensory equipment, these materially able receivers of culture are the figures who, for James, offer the best subject matter to the writer of fiction because they function not just as observers but as active 'participators' in their lot (p. 35).

James insisted that *The Princess Casamassima* was an essentially urban tale that grew out of his 'habit and . . . interest of walking the streets', a practice that, he claimed, was undertaken for the purpose of literary 'acquisition'. Exposure to what he termed 'assault' by a multiplicity of impressions, he claimed, generated the novel, which was the result of his 'attentive exploration' and 'mystic solicitation' of the streets of London, where images, impressions and interpretations were forced upon him. As a result of these unpredictable phenomena, the metropolis, he advises the reader, is a political 'garden bristling with an immense illustrative flora' where '(p)ossible stories, presentable figures, rise from the thick jungle as the observer moves'. However, while Robert Louis Stevenson, as James himself put it, offered his readers an exciting 'gospel . . . of adventure' in his *New Arabian Nights* (p. 128), he sought instead to use political violence as a vehicle for a discussion of the necessary separation of culture from democracy. This is why Hyacinth's native environment, his 'natural and immediate London', is repeatedly characterised as a zone of uncertainty. 'Truly,' as James stressed, 'there are [in] London mysteries (dense categories of dark arcana) for every spectator'. But, while the boundary between bourgeois society and these shadier areas of experience must be maintained, it is only by transgressing this line on the level of the street that the artist can produce an accurate representation of the metropolis, because 'it's in a degree an exclusion and a state of weakness to be without experience of the meaner conditions, the lower manners and types, the general sordid struggle, the weight of the burden of labour, the ignorance, the misery and the vice' (p. 35). While, historically, Fenianism was one of these mysterious 'arcana', James preferred to obscure its influence by portraying his villains as anarchists and, in doing so, avoided engaging with the opposed ideologies and cultural politics of empire and Irish separatism. Simultaneously, this allowed him to focus with a clearer perspective, undisturbed by the imperial question, on London's status as a more politically contained and controllable site. By ignoring the Fenian reality and replacing it with his anarchist fantasy, James avoided addressing culture as a phenomenon that was laced with colonial associations and instead constructed his tale around a more limited version of the metropolitan experience. As a result the boundary that he drew between the classes is more firmly maintained and far less fluid than it is in Stevenson's tale of tenement explosions and suburban bomb factories.

As with Stevenson's construction of political violence as an inexplicable and even occult phenomenon, James describes the novel's literary capital – 'the value I wished most to render and the effect I wished most to produce' – as owing much to its obscurity. Its unreadable effects are, James insists, the quite indeterminate feelings produced by the mysteriousness of revolutionary politics which, he maintained, was an aesthetically productive affair. This explains how the novel developed out of 'our not knowing, of society's not knowing, but only guessing and suspecting and trying to ignore, what 'goes on' irreconcilably, subversively, beneath the vast smug surface' (p. 48). Irish nationalism, even in its militant form of Fenianism, with its demands for political independence, was an ideology that, when examined closely, had little of the 'subterraneous politics and occult affiliations' offered by anarchism (p. 48) which, with its demand for the abolition of *any* form of government, was a radically other doctrine.[39] Like *The Dynamiter*, *The Princess Casamassima* is also a tale of city experiences, but while the metropolis is a source of romance for Stevenson, James explored the aesthetic and cultural threats posed by his more abstract construction of revolutionary change, which allowed him to present the possibility of any radical social transformation as an inherently negative, fundamentally anti-cultural and distinctly urban phenomenon. With this accomplished, the novel serves as a discourse about the engagement between revolutionary politics, culture and capital by pointing to the threat posed to bourgeois pleasure by the possibility of any degree of political renovation in British society.

James's views on revolution are expressed through the regretful reflections of the burned-out and fatalistic revolutionary veteran and musician, Anastasius Vetch:

> The idea of great changes . . . took its place among the dreams of his youth; for what was any possible change in the relations of men and women but a new combination of the same elements? If the elements could be made different the thing would be worth thinking of; but it was not only impossible to introduce any new ones – no means had yet been discovered for getting rid of the old. The figures on the chessboard were still the passions and jealousies and superstitions and stupidities of man, and their position with regard to

each other, at any given moment, could be of interest only to the grim, invisible fates who played the game – who sat, through the ages, bow-backed over the table. (p. 367)

Human nature, like culture, is essential and unchanging and, in Vetch's fatalistic opinion, the 'elements' that compose human consciousness, rather than wider political or social structures, require transformation. The structural situation that James imagines is, of course, one of entrapment, whereby agency is dissolved by the controlling and unseen fates whose role it is to constantly frustrate humanity. In his preface to the novel, James underlined this view by declaring that the agents of his drama were appealing only in proportion to the degree to which they could 'feel their respective situations' and appreciate their own limitations, which is precisely the dilemma that the reader is presented with in the figure of Hyacinth Robinson. The illegitimate son of a working-class French mother, Florentine Vivier, and, he suspects, an 'extremely immoral' peer (p. 58), whom she murders for abandoning her, Hyacinth is torn between his Gallic heritage on one side of his divided political self and his possibly aristocratic English origins on the other. James consistently links Hyacinth's attraction to revolutionary politics to his French ancestry, while terrorism, which is held to be another one of the impressions generated by the 'carboniferous London damp', is, although clearly and consistently associated with the metropolis, no less portrayed as an inherently foreign phenomenon. Emerging from the city's hybridisation of 'blurred and suffused' images (p. 106), anarchist political violence is one of many ill-defined urban spectacles, such as 'halos and dim radiations, trickles and evaporations' that characterise the fluid underside of the metropolis (p. 106). Any hope of restitution and normality exists outside this rather uncertain zone which, and within the more grounded and exclusive sphere of culture, appears all the more real to James because it is so heavily dependent on capital.

Hyacinth's problem is that he, like the city of which he is a product, lacks a suitably defined identity: 'he wished to go through life in his own character', James insists, but the bookbinder is checked by 'the reflection that this was exactly what, apparently, he was destined not to do'. Realising that he is most likely the illegitimate son of a rakish lord and a French seamstress, Hyacinth is excluded from the character forming imperatives that underline the bourgeois drive for self-definition: 'His own character? He was to cover that up as carefully as possible; he was to go through life in a mask, in a borrowed mantle; he was to be, every day and every hour, an actor' (p. 109).[40] His work in the suitably 'exquisite' art of bookbinding provides him with some access to culture, but the path that it provides is a fragile one because, until he is given the opportunity to travel across Europe on his adoptive guardian, Pinny's, quite modest bequest, he remains 'buried in a squalid corner of London, under a million of idiots' (p. 112). Yet, slight as its aesthetic purchase might seem, thanks to its dual function as labour and art, bookbinding is the activity that allows Hyacinth to maintain a deeply personalised investment in the world of culture. His work in Crookenden's Soho bindery involves him in the materialisation of literary art, and although his mentor there, Eustache Poupin, is himself a former communard, this work, along with his literary interests, differentiates Hyacinth from the rest of his comrades in the anarchist movement.[41] Poupin, the cultured socialist who draws Hyacinth into the orbit of revolutionary politics, is his 'protector', 'godfather' and a rare if particularly French combination of the qualities of 'a cold conspirator and an exquisite artist'. It is his work that makes possible Vetch's presentation to the fifteen-year-old Hyacinth of a copy of Bacon's essays, a purchase that has lasting consequences for him not only in terms of its literary freight but also because it brings the pair together:

> No man knew better the difference between the common and the rare, or was more capable of appreciating a book which opened well – of which the margin was not hideously chopped and of which the lettering on the back was sharp. It was only such a book that he could bring himself to offer even to a poor little devil whom a fifth-rate dressmaker . . . had rescued from the work-house. So when it became a question of fitting the great Elizabethan with a new coat – a coat of full morocco, discretely, delicately gilt – he went with his little cloth-bound volume, a Pickering, straight to Mr Crookenden, whom every one that knew anything about the matter knew to be a prince of binders . . . The work had been accomplished with a perfection of skill which made him ask who he was to thank for it (he had been told that one man should do the whole of it), and in this manner he made the acquaintance of the most brilliant craftsman in the establishment, the incorruptible, the imaginative, the unerring Eustache Poupin. (p. 115)

The key theme of *The Princess Casamassima*, the distinction between 'the common and the rare', is staged across the novel, but especially so in the very constitution of the delicate volume presented to the bindery by Vetch. The binder is at first drawn to Popuin by his 'love of the art', and the Parisian's books are treated by James not as commodities but as art objects. They are exquisite artefacts of capitalist culture and, as exemplified by the Bacon volume, objects that can also transmit capitalist ideology. James uses this concept of literature-as-object to stage within the novel, for the first time, the paradoxical position of the revolutionary who enjoys art. Unlike Vetch, who is 'a mere scoffer at effete things', the reflective and humanitarian Poupin is, we are told, a 'constructive' revolutionary whose skills and sensibilities make him 'the type of intelligent foreigner whose conversation completes our culture'. On seeing his collection of bindings ('the most precious trophies of his skill'), Hyacinth is introduced to the world of culture both in its material and more 'esoteric' manifestations (p. 116), and is immersed in the processes whereby the materiality of literature is either preserved or restored through binding: 'on the spot', we are told in language that anticipates his later recruitment into the cabalistic anarchist movement, he is 'initiated' into its 'fascinating mystery' (p. 117). In becoming enchanted by these works, he detaches himself from the indistinct phenomena that characterise the metropolis and, as he does so, shifts further away from the poverty that, as an anarchist, he initially sought to cure.

The enigma of art, or what Benjamin later described as its 'aura', even when subjected to industrial-style modes of production, as happens in Crookenden's bindery,[42] comes into direct competition with Hyacinth's loyalty to the political and, frankly, occult fraternity of the anarchists. It becomes clear from this point that the situation at stake in novel is the situation of culture, which James makes very obvious through Hyacinth's ambition to acquire knowledge, when he observes that: 'Reading was his happiness, and the absence of any direct contact with a library his principal source of discontent' (p. 119). Hyacinth's bohemian political consciousness is put to the test by his exposure to culture (as are his Gallic, and therefore inherently radical, qualities) because, even if he is genetically predisposed towards anarchism, and is mistakenly accepted by the radicals as 'one of the pure' because of his partially French origins, he struggles with their ideology and with its conflict with culture as a consequence of his finer British aristocratic 'qualities' (p. 127). His binding is superior, appearing 'delicate' and charming', providing him with an 'education of the taste' that allows him to develop his 'perception of beauty' and 'hatred of ugliness' (p. 156). The refinement of this sensibility turns him away from vulgar working-class pastimes like drinking, and from the base scene of the city's gin palaces:

> For this unfortunate but remarkably organized youth, every displeasure or gratification of the visual sense coloured his whole mind, and though he lived in Pentonville and worked in Soho, though he was poor and obscure and cramped and full of unattainable desires, it may be said of him that what was most important in life for him was simply his impressions. They came from everything he touched, they kept him thrilling and throbbing during a considerable part of his waking consciousness, and they constituted, as yet, the principal events and stages of his career. Fortunately, they were sometimes very delightful. Everything in the field of observation suggested this

or that; everything struck him, penetrated, stirred; he had, in a word, more impressions than he knew what to do with – felt sometimes as if they would consume or asphyxiate him. (pp. 157–8)

Hyacinth is hypersensitive to the impressions that he receives and the sensations that he experiences; while Zero claims that his own production of shocking images of political violence qualifies him as an artist of the popular sort, it is impossible, James suggests, for an individual whose consciousness is truly aesthetic to take part in any kind of revolutionary activity. As Mike Fischer has argued, Hyacinth is rendered an ultimately conservative figure because he is not so much torn between politics and art as he is unable to recognise his own complicity in the forces of industrial capitalism. An 'unwitting' but no less involved collaborator in 'the reproduction of the conditions of production' that he sets out to destroy,[43] Hyacinth is both a creator and receiver of impressions whose labour is less consciously mediated – and therefore of a much less modern and more lasting quality – than Zero's violently political work. As a 'real artist', vibrating and alive with inspirational surroundings, Hyacinth, despite this duplicity, still finds himself adrift in the metropolis, where:

the great, roaring, indifferent world of London seemed to him a huge organization for mocking at his poverty, at his inanition, and then its vulgarest ornaments, the windows of third-rate jewellers, the young man in a white tie and crush-hat who dandled by, on his way to a dinner-party, in a hansom that nearly ran one over – these familiar phenomena became symbolic, insolent, defiant, took upon themselves to make him smart with the sense that he was out of it. (p. 164)

Hyacinth prevents himself from fully participating in the capital's mainstream culture because he is aware of the necessity of artistic detachment which, as James would like the reader to believe, is at odds with political commitment and, despite the novel's attempted denials, reveals the problematic nature of the foundations upon which bourgeois existence rests and depends. Poverty and alienation are the real measures of the immediate culture that he distrusts and, as he will also realise, of the grander, more enduring pleasures that he will experience outside London:

he couldn't (with any respect for his own consistency) work, underground, for the enthronement of the democracy, and continue to enjoy, in however platonic a matter, a spectacle which rested on a hideous social inequality. He must either suffer with the people, as he had suffered before, or he must apologise to others, as he sometimes came so near to doing himself, for the rich. (p. 165)

At this stage, Hyacinth is convinced that the rich and the poor are on course for an inevitable 'death-grapple' that will have implications for culture (p. 165) and it is the inescapable tension between his responsibility as a creative artist and his role as a revolutionary 'exterminator' (p. 173) that finally undermines his ability to function as a committed socialist. The 'little bookbinder who had so much more of the gentleman about him than one would expect' (p. 184) is, ultimately, unable to resist, never mind destroy, capitalism, nor bring himself to assassinate any individual associated with it. He is even transformed into an aesthetic object by the Princess, who regards all art as decadent and corrupt because it is simply 'a synthesis made in the interests of pleasure' (p. 246). Yet, despite her claims to be 'modern and democratic and heretical *à outrance*' (p. 251) she regards the urban poor as no more than material for her own rather voyeuristic study. Viewing the possibility of social redistribution as a process of cultural negation, James defends the class system throughout the novel by orienting its political narrative around Hyacinth's refusal to write off its 'finer' (p. 454) qualities. Hyacinth, as a result, is torn between the Princess, who views British society as being in such an advanced state of decline that it is re-enacting the 'decadence' of a 'gouty, apoplectic, depraved, gorged' and doomed Roman Empire, and his own appreciation of culture. Like James, he opts to wallow in its splendour and the reader experiences a decisive shift in his ideological position when, on inspecting the library at the Princess's rural retreat at Medley Hall, he fantasises about being locked up in the room for months. Surrounded by books, the scope of his limited 'cockney vision' expands as he imagines that this aristocratic repository of culture will provide him with true fulfillment (p. 302). Exposed to Victorian commodity culture in all of its glory at the Hall, which is located in 'the real country' and not somewhere along 'the mere ravelled fringe of London', Hyacinth finds its 'strangely pure' location representative of a more complex world formed of 'larger spaces and a more complicated scene' (p. 299). In contrast to his densely labyrinthine native environment in London, rural and aristocratic England necessitates deeper thinking and a more considered perspective on Hyacinth's part:

> There was something in the way the gray walls rose from the green lawn that brought tears to his eyes; the spectacle of long duration unassociated with some sordid infamy or poverty was new to him; he had lived with people among whom old age meant, for the most part, a grudged and degraded survival. In the majestic preservation of Medley there was a kind of serenity of success, an accumulation of dignity and honour.

Despite the fact that the (presumably) aristocratic owners have had to lease their property to anarchists, the house retains an aura of authenticity because it is grounded in history, and because its very existence represents an alternative reality to the kind of daily struggles experienced in the capital. Guilty as it may seem (and James does not dispute this), it is the success of the winning side that facilitates aesthetic and cultural development through the preservation of sites like Medley, where fine things are to be found, enjoyed and protected. Hyacinth's exposure to culture (and, for James, culture could only mean high culture) in the opulent library housed in the stately home highlights the interdependency of culture and capital:

> A fire of logs crackled in a great chimney, and there were alcoves with deep window-seats, and arm-chairs such as he had never seen, luxurious, leather-covered, with an adjustment for holding one's volume; and a vast writing-table, before one of the windows, furnished with a perfect magazine of papers and pens, inkstands and blotters, seals, stamps, candlesticks, reels of twine, paper-weights, book-knives. Hyacinth had never imagined so many aids to correspondence, and before he turned away he had written a note to Millicent, in a hand even more beautiful than usual – his penmanship was very minute, but at the same time wonderfully free and fair – largely for the pleasure of seeing 'Medley Hall' stamped in crimson, heraldic-looking characters at the top of his paper.

This scene, set in 'the country' and at a safe distance from the chaos of London, describes an environment that is removed from the artificial urban surfaces upon which, according to James, political conspiracies are hatched. Here, culture is, quite literally, mediated by aristocratic privilege and locked away from the political pressures of London. Sealed off from these concerns within the library at Medley, Hyacinth begins to realise a clearer view of society and of his own role in history, and begins to appreciate its grander meanings. This occurs as James stages the real drama of the novel as the dilemma that confronts a revolutionary who must trade in his radical beliefs for a chance to share in the 'perfect' world of literary and aesthetic production. The library, as Hyacinth experiences it, contains the necessary materials for literary output but there is also something recent, rather *nouveau* and even corrupt about the supposed permanence of things at Medley Hall, where a host of commodities provide the necessary support required by even simple literary activity like writing letters. This is emblematised for Hyacinth in the heraldic label printed on the paper on which he writes, and for the reader in the subtle but significant diminishment of his experience of guilt over the state of things. Here, James interrogates the difficulties faced by the young bookbinder as a conflict over the value of material culture but, already, we find Hyacinth preferring complicity in the bourgeois system (for, what else does the collection of writing aids represent other than the workings of a system?) to opposing it. As a producer of the most culturally oriented of commodities, books, Hyacinth is unable to deflect their power, but these are not just commodities with straight-forwardly utilitarian value, as books, pens, paper and stamps, along with their associated paraphernalia (blotters, book-knives, and even twine and paper-weights) facilitate the mediation of culture. This luxurious stuff is beyond rational value and is of special worth in Hyacinth's imagination because they are key to his own work, and his value of it – not to mention of himself, as a cultural producer.

The transformation from revolutionary to conservative comes even closer when Hyacinth discovers masterful examples of his own trade on display in the library, where, as Madame Garndoni tells him, the volumes are covered by 'the dust of centuries':

> In the course of an hour he had ravaged the collection, taken down almost every book, wishing he could keep it a week, and put it back quickly, as his eye caught the next, which appeared even more desirable. He discovered many rare bindings, and gathered several ideas from an inspection of them – ideas which he felt himself perfectly capable of reproducing. Altogether, his vision of true happiness, at that moment, was that, for a month or two, he should be locked into the library at Medley. He forgot the outer world, and the morning waned – the beautiful vernal Sunday – while he lingered there.

Both as a reader and expert restorer of books, Hyacinth finds his radical political beliefs coming into conflict with his sense of the unique cultural value of literature and of the book-as-commodity. According to James's logic, which Hyacinth ultimately accepts as the cost of his radical beliefs, these products and the system that produces and archives them, making them available for reading and for the inspection of their material condition and workmanship, must be protected from the dangers of short-sighted revolutionaries. In comparison to well defined locations like Medley Hall and, later, post-Haussmann Paris, London appears 'vague and blurred, inarticulate and dim' (p. 382), providing the vulgar and 'indifferent' environment where, in the absence of such conspicuous display, anarchism develops in the city's deep cultural void (p. 330). Accepting the necessity of class, Hyacinth rejects socialism in exchange for a share in what he perceives to be the timeless struggle of culture, which is rather obviously symbolised by James in the 'wonderful', gilded and weather-beaten clock tower at Medley Hall (p. 299).

However the transition is a complicated process and, traumatised by the disconnection of radical politics from 'wider fields of knowledge' and their 'higher sensations' (p. 396), all of which have been made possible by the accumulation of capital, Hyacinth chooses to take his own life rather than announce his conversion to the side of reaction to the anarchists. While James relies on the popular literary convention of the oath-bound secret society led by an authoritarian master-anarchist, whose orders none of his subordinates will dare refuse, Hyacinth commits suicide not because he feels hopelessly entrapped by the terrorists but because of the irreconcilability of the Jamesian model of 'civilisation' with the revolutionary underground. The charismatic German anarchist, Hoffendahl, who is also known to his subordinates as 'the Master', functions as a super-aesthete whose status, as well as suggesting manipulation, also points to his role as a counter-cultural figure. Despite its barbarism, then, anarchism also has an aesthetic quality:

> Hyacinth's little job was a very small part of what Hoffendahl had come to England for; he had in his hands innumerable other threads. Hyacinth knew nothing of these and didn't much want to know, except that it was marvelous, the way Hoffendahl kept them apart. He had exactly the same mastery of them that a great musician – that the Princess herself – had of the keyboard of the piano; he treated all things, persons, institutions, ideas, as so many notes in his great symphonic revolt. The day would come when Hyacinth, far down in the treble, would feel himself touched by the little finger of the composer, would become audible (with a small, sharp crack) for a second.

However the 'exquisite' experience of drinking in the much stronger 'wine of . . . civilization' at Medley Hall (p. 325) overwhelms Hyacinth and persuades him to abandon his political project, and the second half of the novel charts his growing interest in culture, which develops at the cost of his radical political convictions, and his gradual abandonment of the revolutionaries' 'sacred cause' (p. 396). Terrorism, for James, underlines the necessity of culture and of its separation from the alternative and chaotically aesthetic world of the anarchists.

Hyacinth outlines his belief in the gulf between culture and revolutionary politics in his letter to the Princess from the 'enchanted' city of Venice, where he is transformed by his experience of its overwhelmingly 'ineffable impressions' (p. 394). On his eye-opening tour of Europe, he addresses what James viewed as the absolute separation that distinguished the material production of art from the dangers of socialism. Here, Hyacinth recognises and accepts this distinction, announcing that the 'clearest result of extending one's horizon' is the acceptance of 'the sense, increasing as we go, that want and toil and suffering are the constant lot of the immense majority of the human race'. Despite encountering these moral, practical and economic problems in every country that he has visited, he admits that they do not disturb his faith in art because, thanks to the efforts of those who have suffered throughout the course of history, he has witnessed 'the great achievements of which man has been capable . . . the splendid accumulations of the happier few'. Although these have been accomplished by privileged artists whose work was accomplished on the backs of the 'miserable many', such productions remain, in his view, 'inestimably precious and beautiful'. These works exist in a condition that is beyond valuation and greater than the anarchists' short-sighted plans for the immediate or even long-term political 'rectification' of modern society:

> I feel myself capable of fighting for them. You can't call me a traitor, for you know the obligation that I recognize. The monuments and treasures of art, the great palaces and properties, the conquests of learning and taste, the general fabric of civilization as we know it, based, if you will, upon all the despotisms, the cruelties, the exclusions, the monopolies and the rapacities of the past, but thanks to which, all the same, the world is less impracticable and life more tolerable. (p. 396)

Hyacinth comes to realise that Hoffendahl, who would 'cut up the ceilings of the Veronese into strips, so that every one might have a little piece', and his fellow-revolutionaries cannot appreciate the value of such treasures. The anarchists regard these triumphs as cheap, rendering revolution 'something in which I can't somehow believe as I do in things with which the aspirations and the tears of generations have been mixed' (p. 396). Medley Hall, with its collection of beautifully produced books and its 'timeless' clock tower (with which James rams home the point that historical role of culture, after all, bears a structural relationship to society), serves as a local, British version of what Hyacinth encounters on the streets of continental cities and in their museums, conditioning him for his later declaration that 'I don't want every one to have a little piece of anything'. Along with his 'great horror of that kind of invidious jealousy which is at the bottom of he idea of a redistribution', Hyacinth, speaking now for James, finally comes to understand that the politics of socialism and its 'odious stain' (p. 397) offers nothing but a programme of cultural degeneration. Rejecting any form of radical political belief as worthless and deciding that high culture alone is worth fighting for, he is 'purified' by his experience of it to the extent that he considers abandoning bookbinding in order to write because the material production of commodities, even handcrafted ones, 'charming as the process might be', is, like the realities of suffering and inequality that make art possible, 'less fundamental' and less obvious to the development of an elegant society (p. 403). Although Hyacinth remains a worker until his very end, James offers a glimpse of the kind of individual that he might have been, had he allowed his 'wretched little bookbinder' (p. 112) to assume and fulfill the expectations inherent in the other half of his genetic make-up – that of his 'delicate and high-bred' father, some of whose aristocratic manner he inherited when, as a child, he appeared to Pinny to resemble a 'little nobleman' (p. 63).

Inspired by his time at Medley, then in the museums and boulevards of Paris (the pleasure experienced by Hyacinth on these 'magnificent creations of the arch-fiend of December', Louis Napoleon, is particularly guilt-ridden (p. 405)) and on the streets of Venice, Hyacinth's transformation from terrorist to cultured reactionary is coloured by the contrast between these exciting places and the bland and 'dirty drapery' of his work as a binder (p. 404), which takes place within the 'not very fresh' atmosphere of London (p. 556). Unlike Stevenson, who invests London with colour by orientalising the city, James presents a squalid metropolis where, despite his acknowledgement of its usefulness and appeal as a source of documentary material, culture rests uneasily alongside reality. London, as he insists in the novel's preface, is uniquely inspiring for the writer of modern realism, but this, he insists, is not the same thing as the centuries'-long inheritance that Hyacinth discovers in Europe. Venice, therefore, has not transformed Hyacinth's views so much as it has affirmed them, along with James's belief in heredity in cultural as well as political matters. The revolutionary position, which is outlined in Vetch's attacks against bourgeois philistinism, are presented by James as diatribes against the cultural finery that can only be sustained and maintained, in his view, by capital. Unlike its structures, which are presented as organic phenomena, revolutionary ideology spreads from an 'ulcer of envy' (p. 405) and the anarchist, like any other kind of revolutionary, is driven by misguided and defective passion. The unsoundness of their political views is expressed by the Princess, who announces that '"I don't care about the artists"' (p. 411) and declares that she has no time for '"objects I don't care for"' because, when '"thousands and tens of thousands haven't bread to put in their mouths, I can dispense with tapestry and old china"' (p. 412). James's position is clear: books, tapestries and china do matter, and it is impossible, as the anarchists believe, for the world to become 'beautiful enough when it becomes good enough' (p. 413). The closest that any of them comes to revealing an aesthetic sensibility occurs when the Princess tells Hyacinth that of all the environments she has experienced, she likes 'humble' London best (p. 416). This aspect of the 'huge, luxurious, wanton, wasteful city' city (p. 464) functions both as seedy art and degraded space, where values are 'cockneyfied' and uniqueness dissolves until 'lost among the London millions' (p. 420). She recognises that the city might restore Hyacinth to his original, revolutionary condition because its wretchedness excites his political consciousness but, as James insists, the capital, while fascinating, is, in the end, a 'black gulf' (p. 478) containing an uncontrollable 'sea of barbarism' (p. 477). Hyacinth's auto-destruction is, for James, an act of recovery that serves to protect culture, which, even if it is a product of the 'congested rich' (p. 481), is worth preserving along with the social inequalities that make it possible.

This contradiction becomes so unendurable for Hyacinth that he decides to commit suicide rather than live with the separation of culture and politics. The problem with revolutionaries, according to James, is that they lack any significant cultural 'feeling' (p. 396). Their failure to appreciate finer and superior sensations explains why there is no assassination at the end of *The Princess Casamassima*, which abandons an outwardly violent conclusion in favour of the more contained logic of Hyacinth's suicide. For James, culture is a private affair, at odds with the material and unjust processes of the 'outer world' and the flighty Princess (following on from her earlier enthusiasm for religion and belief in the supernatural, anarchism is her latest fad) understands Hyacinth's troubled condition as that of being denied access to the kind of culture that she, as an aristocratic revolutionary, freely enjoys: "'Fancy the strange, the bitter fate: to be constituted as you are constituted, to feel the capacity that you must feel, and yet to look at the good things of life only through the glass of the pastry-cook's window!'" (p. 337). As the Princess admits, her comrades are modern 'barbarians' who regard such culture and consumption as decadent and requiring destruction. Her only desire is to attack privileged English society which, for James, includes all that is cultural, and to 'blow it up' (pp. 312–13).

With the publication of *The Dynamiter* in 1885 and *The Princess Casamassima* in 1886, readers were presented, via the polar tendencies and literary practices of Robert Louis Stevenson and Henry James, with the subject of political violence. Both novels explore the particularly metropolitan conditions that produce and sustain terrorism, and in different ways they address its cultural impact upon the late Victorian imagination. Stevenson, as we have seen, exploited the thrills of Fenianism while, at the same time, making sure to limit the imaginative possibility that Irish nationalism could ever undermine or subvert imperial rule. James, in contrast, opted to occlude the immediate political problem of Irish separatism from his fiction by devising a tale in which revolutionary political reform equalled the ransacking of centuries' of achievement. There could be no compromise between the two positions for the 'Master', whose 'finer' literary sensibility screened out the possibility of chaos, while Stevenson, whom he admired, insisted upon it. Yet both novels, in very different ways, extracted literary capital from the political crises that emerged in Britain during the mid-1880s.

Notes

1. Henry James, 'Robert Louis Stevenson', originally published in *Century Magazine*, July 1883, reprinted in Leon Edel (ed.), *The House of Fiction: Essays on the Novel by Henry James* (London: Rupert Hart-Davis, 1957), pp. 114–38, p. 133.
2. Barbara Arnett Melchiori discusses the range and variety of the different types of dynamite novels that were popular during the 1880s and 1890s. As Melchiori has discovered, many of these dealt with Fenian plots, anarchist terrorism and even non-political crime masquerading as revolutionary violence. See Barbara Arnett Melchiori, *Terrorism in the Late Victorian Novel* (London: Croom Helm, 1985).
3. Letter to Sidney Colvin, late September or early October 1885, *The Letters of Robert Louis Stevenson*, Vol. 5, July 1884–August 1887 (New Haven and London: Yale University Press, 1995), p. 128.
4. Frank McLynn argues that Stevenson had little, if any, hand in the writing of *The Dynamiter* and offers the unlikely theory that Fanny, out to cash in on her husband's literary reputation, wrote most of the tale. See Frank McLynn, *Robert Louis Stevenson: A Biography* (London: Hutchinson, 1993).
5. Robert Louis and Fanny Vandegrift Stevenson, *The Dynamiter*, originally published 1885 (reprinted Thrupp: Alan Sutton Publishing, 1997). Subsequent citations are provided in the text.
6. Stevenson told W. E. Henly that the adventure was composed 'with the bailiff at my heels'. See Stevenson to W. E. Henly, 6 November 1884, *Letters*, p. 21.
7. McLynn, *Robert Louis Stevenson*, p. 114.
8. Stevenson, letter to Edward L. Burlingame, 6 January 1888, *Letters*, p. 100. In a letter to the *Pall Mall Gazette*, Grant Allen criticised Stevenson's portrayal of the Fenians, whom he regarded as sincere if misguided Irish patriots. Attacking *The Dynamiter* for its conservative tone and 'moral feeling', Allen defended the bombers as 'brave and resolute' individuals who had been goaded by British injustice into using 'desperate means of righting their ill-used country'. Stevenson's unapologetic reply was aired in the essay 'Confessions of a Unionist'. Although his riposte to Allen's criticism was intended to appear in *Scribner's Magazine*, it went unpublished until 1921, thanks to its calls for the application of lynch law and the deployment of Gatling guns in Ireland. See Grant Allen, letter to the *Pall Mall Gazette*, 5 August 1887, reprinted in Stevenson, *Letters*, Vol. 5, footnote, p. 439. See Stevenson, 'Confessions of a Unionist: An Unpublished "Talk on Things Current"' (Cambridge, MA: privately printed, 1921), p. 9. Allen's own foray into the territory of the dynamite novel was *For Maimie's Sake: A Tale of Love and Dynamite* (1886), a bizarre domestic melodrama featuring a subplot in which Russian Nihilists invent silent explosives. See Grant Allen, *For Maimie's Sake: A Tale of Love and Dynamite* (New York: International Book Company, n.d.).
9. See L. Perry Curtis, *Jack the Ripper and the London Press* (New Haven and London: Yale University Press, 2001), p. 9.

10. Julian Wolfreys, *Writing London, Vol. 3: Inventions of the City* (Houndsmills: Palgrave Macmillan, 2007), p. 7
11. Other examples of this inversion of the popular imperial narrative include Richard Marsh's *The Beetle* (1897), Bram Stoker's *Dracula* (1897), and Arthur Conan Doyle's 'The Sign of the Four' (1890), 'The Adventure of the Speckled Band' (1892), and 'Lot No. 249' (1892).
12. Henry James, 'Robert Louis Stevenson', p. 133.
13. See H. Rider Haggard's 1886 adventure, *She*, in which Ayesha, like Bram Stoker's Count Dracula, intends to relocate some day to Britain (London: Penguin, 2001).
14. See Whelehan, ibid.
15. Mark Seltzer, *Henry James and the Art of Power* (Ithaca and London: Cornell University Press, 1984), p. 31.
16. 'Recent Novels', *The Times*, Wednesday, 9 June 1897, p. 11.
17. See Ronald R. Thomas, 'Revaluating Identity in the 1890s: The Rise of the New Imperialism and the Eyes of the New Detective', in *Transforming Genres: New Approaches to British Fiction of the 1890s* (Basingstoke: Macmillan, 1994), pp. 193–214, p. 194. See also Ronald R. Thomas, *Detective Fiction and the Rise of Forensic Science* (Cambridge: Cambridge University Press, 1999).
18. In assuming such positional superiority over the Fenian dynamiter, the novel also indulges in a politics of representation that assigns otherness to the Irish in much the same way that imperialist culture objectifies the more 'exotic' colonial subjects of the orient. For contemporary readers the connection between the Irish threat against the empire and farther-flung adventures was an obvious one: *The Dynamiter* was the sequel to Stevenson's 1882 collection, *New Arabian Nights*, and was originally published under the title *More New Arabian Nights*. See Edward Said, *Orientalism* (London: Penguin, 1995).
19. See Sharon Marcus, *Apartment Stories: City and Home in Nineteenth-Century Paris and London* (Berkeley: University of California Press, 1999), pp. 6, 7, 9.
20. Richard Whiteing's jubilee plot novel, *No. 5 John Street*, also features a tenement bomb factory. Based in a lodging house that is 'impartial to its uses within the law' and that resembles 'a sort of railway junction' catering to the dispossessed, anarchist conspirators use the property as a printing house, explosives laboratory and lecture hall. See Richard Whiteing, *No. 5 John Street* (London: Grant Richards, 1899). Quotations from pp. 83, 101.
21. The encounter occurs as he wanders through the slums of the capital, his *flâneur*-ship underlining Walter Benjamin's notion that 'it takes a heroic constitution to live modernism'. For Benjamin, such idle wandering and observation inevitably gave rise to amateur detection. See Walter Benjamin, *Charles Baudelaire: A Lyric Poet in the Era of High Capitalism*, trans. Harry Zohn (London: Verso, 1997), pp. 74, 69.
22. Stevenson, 'Confessions of a Unionist', p. 20.
23. Walter Pater, *The Renaissance: Studies in Art and Poetry* (Oxford: Oxford University Press, 1998), Preface, pp. xxix–xxxi.
24. Pater, *The Renaissance*, p. 16.
25. Zero's outburst echoes the young Stevenson's terrorisation by his fanatical

protestant nursemaid, Alison 'Cummy' Cunningham, who told him morbid Calvinist stories (his collection of poems, *A Child's Garden of Verses*, is famously dedicated to her, 'My second mother, my first wife, / The angel of my infant life'). Her influence is also discernible in his uncanny 1881 story, 'Thrawn Janet', in which a young rustic woman is possessed by 'the de'il', the 'singular' and malevolent 'Black Man' of Scottish folk superstition, and must then be redeemed by a righteous minister. The evil Mr Hyde, who carries 'Satan's signature' on his countenance, also shares the dynamiter's devilish intentions. See Robert Thynne, *John Townley: A Tale for the Times* (London: Henry T. Drane, 1901), pp. 56, 63. See McLynn, *Robert Louis Stevenson*, p. 13. See Robert Louis Stevenson, 'To Allison Cunningham', *A Child's Garden of Verses* (Hertfordshire: Wordsworth, 2000), p. 5; 'Thrawn Janet', in *The Body Snatcher and Other Stories* (London: Phoenix, 1999), pp. 26, 30; and 'The Strange Case of Dr Jekyll and Mr Hyde', in *Dr Jekyll and Mr Hyde and Other Stories* (London: Penguin, 1979), p. 40.

26. 'The Dynamite Party, Past and Present', *The Times*, 24 April 1886, p. 8.
27. Tom Gunning describes the cultural importance of the metropolitan railway station which served as much as a site for the circulation of popular texts as it did for the movement of people: it was 'not only an emblem of the modern city and its energy and immediacy, but also the place where detective stories are sold *en masse*'. See Tom Gunning, 'Lynx-Eyed Detectives and Shadow Bandits: Visuality and Eclipse in French Detective Stories and Films Before WWI', *Yale French Studies*, No. 18, *Crime Frictions* (2005), pp. 74–88.
28. Henry James, *The Princess Casamassima* (Macmillan & Co, 1886; reprinted London: Penguin, 1987). Citations are hereafter given in the text.
29. As Joyce L. Jenkins argues, the novel's political position is far more problematic than the rapturous praise offered in Lionel Trilling's seminal essay, 'Henry James', would suggest. For Jenkins, the real tragedy of the novel is not Hyacinth's suicide but its lawed morality that 'leaves its practitioners doing nothing at all.' See Joyce L. Jenkins, 'Art Against Equality', *Philosophy and Literature* 22.1 (1998), pp. 108–18, p. 108.
30. Seltzer, *Henry James*, p. 14.
31. Building on Seltzer's reading of the novel, David Stivers has argued for a more epistemic interpretation by suggesting that James's representation of an anarchist conspiracy 'unconfined by nationality, ethnicity, language, gender, or class', functions as an 'imagined synthesis' that gathers momentum beneath the ruptured surfaces of late Victorian bourgeois normality. As Stivers maintains, it is the political underground and not the state that exercises a more pressing influence on the novel, providing the tale with its most central and consistent image of surveillance: 'It sees all and is everywhere – a perfection of spectatorship and action, theory and practice. Neither suffering the objectifying gaze nor conscribed by another's text, it is the only unifying element of the novel'. See David Stivers, 'Narrative Mediation in *The Princess Casamassima*', *The Henry James Review* 28 (2007), pp. 159–73. Quotation from p. 171.
32. Henry James, 'Robert Louis Stevenson', pp. 120–1, 124.
33. Henry James, 'Robert Louis Stevenson', p. 133. However, James disapproved of 'the business of the powders, which seems to me too explicit and

explanatory'. In offering a scientific and material explanation for Jekyll's murderous rampages, Stevenson, James felt, directed the story away from the realm of the psychological. Likewise, *The Princess Casamassima* directs the reader away from the explosive politics of anarchism towards a depoliticised discussion of the motivation (and inevitable demotivation) of the revolutionary. See 'Robert Louis Stevenson', p. 136.

34. See Collin Meissner, '*The Princess Casamassima*: "a dirty intellectual fog"', *The Henry James Review* 19.1 (1998), pp. 53–71.

35. As Paul Hollywood has argued, anarchism also had greater appeal for writers than Fenianism owing to its suitability for the political and aesthetic debates of the late Victorian and modernist periods, as anarchist rhetoric concentrated on 'the point where the future is created: always on the next moment, where a dialectic of creation and destruction operates and does away with the present to create the new'; see Paul Hollywood, *The Voice of Dynamite: Anarchism, Popular Fiction and the Late Political Novels of Joseph Conrad*, PhD thesis, University of Kent at Canterbury, 1994, p. 12.

36. As Stoehr has argued, James's 'conception of the anarchist peril was more refined, if no less inaccurate, than that of the popular imagination'. Lionel Trilling has attempted, unconvincingly, to praise the novel for its historical accuracy and its superior 'moral realism' but, when read from an informed anarchist perspective, such as that offered by George Woodcock, *The Princess Casamassima* presents a 'distorted' and unreal depiction of the European revolutionary scene. See Taylor Stoehr, 'Words and Deeds in *The Princess Casamassima*', *ELH*, 37.1 (March 1970), pp. 95–135. Quotation from p. 112. See Lionel Trilling, '*The Princess Casamassima*', in *The Liberal Imagination: Essays on Literature and Society* (London: Secker and Warburg:, 1964), pp. 58–92. Quotation from p. 98. See George Woodcock, 'Henry James and the Conspirators', *The Sewanee Review*, 60.2 (April–June, 1952), pp. 219–29. Quotation from p. 226.

37. See Thomas Peyser, '*The Princess Casamassima* and the Theatrical Metropolis', *American Literary Realism*, 42.2 (Winter 2010), pp. 95–113.

38. See Margaret Scanlan, 'Terrorism and the Realistic Novel: Henry James and *The Princess Casamassima*', *Texas Studies in Literature and Language* 34.3, 1992, pp. 389–402, p. 394.

39. As Scanlan argues, the issue was also politically sensitive: like Stevenson, James disliked the Irish and it would have been difficult for him to mould an aesthetically sensitive hero out of what he considered to be 'an inferior and third rate race, whose virtues are of the cheapest and commonest and shallowest order,' and whose 'vices are peculiarly cowardly and ferocious'. Quoted in Scanlan, 'Terrorism and the Realistic Novel, p. 383.

40. As John Kimmey has suggested, the novel plays out Hyacinth's exploration of his conflicted identity on the streets of the British capital, where the city's arbitrary geography magnifies his consciousness of himself as an outsider. See John Kimmey, 'James's London in *The Princess Casamassima*', *Nineteenth-Century Literature*, 41.1 (June 1986), pp. 9–31.

41. Although here, as in many other novels, including Wilkie Collins's 1860 sensation novel, *The Woman in White*, the term 'comrade' might be too strong, as Hyacinth, in volunteering to carry out the assassination, has

surrendered himself to the deadly authority of his superiors. Despite anarchism's rejection of all forms of authority, late Victorian readers enjoyed following stories about supposedly free-thinking terrorists who blindly follow the orders of master-anarchists.

42. See Walter Benjamin, 'The Work of Art in the Age of Mechanical Reproduction', in *Illuminations*, trans. from *Schriften* (Verlag: Frankfurt-am-Main, 1955) by Harry Zohn (London: Fontana, 1992), pp. 211–44.

43. See Mike Fischer, 'The Jamesian Revolution in *The Princess Casamassima*: A Lesson in Bookbinding', *The Henry James Review*, 9.2, Spring 1988, pp. 87–104, p. 92.

Chapter 2

Imperialism and the Late Victorian Dynamite Novel

. . . facts have sometimes beaten fiction, and among such facts have been, and yet possibly may be, Fenian outrages.[1]

In contrast to Robert Louis Stevenson, who complained that the Irish reminded him of toads,[2] some nationalist authors confronted British imperialism by writing fiction that promoted republican separatism and tried to explain the rationale behind the 1881–5 bombing campaign. Some of these dynamite novels even ended with the Fenians achieving political independence and becoming the 'undisputed masters of the whole of Irish soil'.[3] Displaying a global perspective, from which the planting of bombs in England and attacks on British forces in Ireland are compared to the anti-imperial efforts of the Transvaal Boers and Zulus, the pro-Fenian fiction that was written during the 1880s offered its readers a radical political perspective by criticising the concept of empire *per se*. This re-imagining of the dynamite novel as a medium for Irish nationalist discourse repeated the political logic found in the threats that were published in the pages of republican journals like Jeremiah O'Donovan Rossa's *The United Irishman* and Patrick Ford's *The Irish World*. Bombs are rarely defused in these tales nor do they, as in Stevenson's yarn, offer imperialist readers a reassuring sense of closure by conveniently exploding prematurely in the hands of their makers. Instead, they speculated over what could happen if Rossa's and Ford's hopes of experiencing 'the satisfaction of seeing London laid in ashes',[4] and of witnessing the destruction of Britain's 'most cherished public buildings', were realised.[5] By translating such propaganda into popular literary capital, these fictions conjured lurid scenes of urban chaos and all-out warfare against the British in an attempt to shock readers into paying attention to the separatist ideology that motivated the Fenians. In doing so they produced counter-narratives to mainstream fictions like *The Dynamiter* and invested militant republicanism with meaning, appealing to an alternative reading public consisting of diasporic, nationally minded Irish and Irish-American readers who supported the Fenian cause.

Republican Propaganda

When Alfred Nobel patented dynamite in 1867 he intended high explosives to serve as an industrial commodity, not as the weapon of choice for Irish revolutionaries who would use them to wage what they called 'scientific warfare' against the British empire.[6] The Fenian movement also engaged in a bitter propaganda war, believing that the printed word could have as forceful an impact upon the political establishment as the destructive force of a bomb. In 1882 an alarmed British Secret Service agent reported from New York that O'Donovan Rossa was inciting assassination and 'outrages of all kinds, by fire and dynamite' in his newspaper, the *United Irishman*, where his new political arguments seemed to offer Irish militants 'a departure from the original object of the conspiracy, which was ostensibly the establishment of an Irish Republic by open warfare'. Warning that the veteran Fenian was advising republicans to 'strike terror' into England, the spy included a cutting from Rossa's journal along with his own report:

> we go further than all, in as much as we recognize the superior forces with which we have to contend, and are prepared to accept stratagem and enlightened science, to assist our weaker numbers ... We want and must have that little Green Isle, no matter what agent may be employed so long as it promises ultimate success.[7]

The *United Irishman* demanded that all British politicians should perish, or 'meet the fate' of Lord Frederick Cavendish and Thomas Henry Burke, respectively the Chief Secretary and permanent Under Secretary to the Irish administration in Dublin Castle. Both men were stabbed to death by a republican splinter group, the Invincibles, in a bloody daylight attack in Phoenix Park in Dublin in May 1882. Rossa also called for the assassination of the Liberal prime minister, William Ewart Gladstone, along with the entire cabinet, and promised to reduce London 'to ashes' with his organisation's secret cache of dynamite.[8] When the bombing campaign was at its height in 1884, Patrick Ford went further by celebrating the 'simply indescribable' impact that dynamiting had on the British public.[9] *The Times* reacted to such claims by describing how the 'very name and thought' of dynamite short-circuited the Fenian imagination by suggesting 'ideas to the writer which he can hardly find language to express'. This, the newspaper claimed, led excited conspirators to publish incoherent but passionate ideas that were forged in 'the intense central heat of the soul'.[10] What is certain is that, by unleashing what it considered a 'bold, masculine, defiant sentiment, sublime in volume and terrible in intensity', the Fenian press gave expression to an unlimited form of rhetorical violence that was designed to amplify the political shocks caused by the bombing campaign in Britain.[11]

According to John Littlechild, the detective who headed Special Branch efforts against Fenianism during the 1880s, Rossa's dynamiters lacked the recognisably 'patriotic element' that he encountered among the earlier Irish revolutionaries of 1867. 'Terrorism was the object of this later movement,' he recalled, and it was carried out 'in order to compel legislation in a desired direction'.[12] The dynamite attacks were launched from the United States with Rossa's bombers, the Skirmishers, competing with activists belonging to the rival Clan na Gael organisation but both groups became known collectively as the 'Dynamite Party'[13] or 'dynamitards'[14] in the British popular imagination. The opening salvo of their campaign was launched at the start of 1881 when Rossa's group bombed Salford Barracks. The attack was followed by attempts on London's Mansion House in March and further explosions in Liverpool in May and June. There was another attack on the Mansion House in 1882 and in 1883 there were explosions at the offices of *The Times* and on the London underground railway, one of which injured sixty-two commuters at Paddington Station. The Clan na Gael campaign began in 1884 with further attacks on railway stations, the demolition of the Special Branch headquarters at Great Scotland Yard, and an attempt to blow up London Bridge, as well as the capture of John Daly, en route to Westminster with a case of 'perfectly made' grenades. His plan to attack Parliament was realised the following year with the bombing of the House of Commons, which was accompanied by a synchronised explosion at the Tower of London.[15] In October 1884 more bombs were left on the London underground and in December three Fenians died in the attempt on London Bridge. Further explosions occurred in Ireland during the following decade, where a detective was killed while inspecting a bomb left in the grounds of Dublin Castle on Christmas Eve 1892, and another exploded at the city's judicial centre, the Four Courts, in 1893. This 'dynamite war',[16] as the Fenians labelled it, was the first instance of the bombing of symbolic targets and infrastructure on British soil and its explosions both frightened and enthralled the British public whom it subjected to the kind of political violence associated with continental revolutionaries since the blowing up of Tsar Alexander II in St Petersburg in 1881.

Rossa's plan to inflict 'nervous terror'[17] on the British public culminated with a series of coordinated attacks on central London on Friday, 30 May 1884. The day began with two explosions: one bomb went off at the Junior Carlton Club, home to the Intelligence Department of the War Office (this device exploded on a window sill of the building's crowded morning room), and another detonated at the Army and Navy Club at the entrance to St James's Square from Pall Mall. It concluded at 7.30pm with a third, larger explosion inside Great Scotland Yard. The last bomb had been placed in a public urinal directly underneath the archival headquarters of the newly formed Political Investigation Department where the Special Irish Branch, known since as 'the Special Branch', was based and a fourth, unexploded device was found at dawn the next morning at the base of Nelson's Column, in Trafalgar Square, where it had been planted to provide a spectacular *finale* to the day with the destruction of the famous landmark.[18] Across the Atlantic in New York, the *Irish World* noted with delight that the attack stunned the British establishment, which, it claimed, was left gazing at 'the chaotic debris that covered the scene of destruction and discussing with bated breath the meaning of the occurrence'.[19]

The gleeful journal also reported that this 'audacious piece of business' left the city's 'Paralyzed Peelers' unable to respond to the explosions, while terrified horses were seen 'ploughing through' the 'awe-stricken crowds' of onlookers.[20] Aimed at wrecking the intelligence work of the Special Branch, this coordination of explosions and propaganda underlined the Fenians' awareness of the value of the modern media, and suggests that as well as serving as a destructive weapon, dynamite also had significant purchase as a medium in its own right. This fact was not lost on the British editors who tried to contain the political impact of Fenian bombs by describing them as harmless devices. While *The Times* glibly dismissed Rossa's 'Dynamite Club' as a loud but harmless entity 'with a terrible name and object' dedicated to 'expending its energy in talk', the *Illustrated London News* also condemned Fenianism for arousing 'popular excitement' with its explosive 'acts of mischief', while the *Saturday Review* dismissed dynamiting as a combination of cowardice, clumsiness and scoundrelism.[21] But in its description of an aftershock that followed the Scotland Yard bombing, when a false alarm at St James' Theatre led to mass hysteria as ladies fainted and gentlemen 'started to their feet ready to stampede', the *Irish World* indicates how propaganda complemented the planting of bombs: the act, the journal announced, was designed to infect the British 'public mind' with the 'prevailing impression that the whole of London was going to be blown up'.[22] Although he disagreed with dynamiting, the veteran Fenian John

Devoy described its objective in terms similar to Littlechild: 'to strike terror into the Government and the governing class'.[23] If terrorism was an unusual mode of warfare for traditionalist rebels, images of shattered buildings and rubble-strewn streets conveyed a uniquely shocking and particularly modern message of their own, bluntly teaching the British what Patrick Ford termed 'The Lesson of Dynamite'.[24]

As Michael Denning argues, late nineteenth-century popular fiction had a reflexive, even journalistic role.[25] This chapter discusses the relationship between the bombers, the mainstream press and the authors of political fiction during the 1880s and 1890s. This relationship could emerge rather explicitly in the pages of the dynamite novel, as it does in J. D. Maginn's 1889 potboiler, *Fitzgerald the Fenian*,[26] in which a Fenian leader, William Brady, propounds a series of 'modern revolutionary theories' that justify attacking both the British government and the media. His 'London work' includes bombing *The Times*, a 'filthy and most-offensively conducted organ' that has been 'opposed to the demands and wishes of the Irish people', and his list of symbolic political targets includes Westminster, the Home Office, Scotland Yard and Windsor Castle. Even cultural sites like the Crystal Palace and the British Museum are included. Brady's desire to 'shatter' the newspaper suggests Maginn's awareness of the power of the late Victorian media to challenge or promote terrorism. The Fenian's plan to 'push on the war with vigour in the metropolis', to 'terrify John Bull out of his senses' and then 'sack and burn every city and town in England' echoes Rossa's violent rhetoric of destruction. 'I am sanguinary', the almost vampiric Brady declares to his men, announcing 'I will have nothing but blood', as he promises to 'drench' London with English 'gore'. Brady's skill as a villain lies in his ability as a manipulator of the popular urban imagination whose attacks are designed to capture 'the attention of the city'. His admission that that bombing is 'a very fascinating business' also suggests nineteenth-century terrorism's role as a thoroughly meditated form of subversive political spin.[27] Despite its greater length, Maginn's two-volume tale, like the Stevensons' much briefer shilling shocker, reveals that novelists were responding to Fenianism by integrating its political shocks into their writing.

Popular Imperial Literature

Dynamite fiction was by no means restricted to the expression of imperialist discourse. The anti-Irish prejudice expressed in many of these popular tales was criticised by Arthur Conan Doyle whose early short story, 'That Little Square Box', published in *London Society* in 1881, features a bogus dynamite plot. Doyle's narrator, a passenger on a transatlantic steamer, believes he has discovered a Fenian plan to 'make a noise in the newspapers' with the sinking of the ship but the bomber turns out to be a pigeon-fancier and his 'infernal machine' no more than an elaborate bird cage. A decade later Doyle offered a more layered critique of imperialism in his Victorian gothic mystery, 'Lot No. 249', which appeared in *Harper's Magazine* in 1892. Set in Oxford in 1884, the yarn centres on the mysterious activity of a reclusive and socially challenged catholic, Egyptomaniac and 'demon' scholar of oriental languages, Edward Bellingham, who is suspected by his fellow students of involvement in Fenianism. Doyle's hero, Abercrombie Smith, declares that if Bellingham is 'about to blow a place up with dynamite, no pledge will stand in my way of preventing him' but he eventually discovers that Bellingham has been terrorising the university with a re-animated mummy and has not, in fact, been experimenting with high explosives.[28] The haunting of Britain and its metropolitan culture by imperial commodities like Bellingham's monster is a familiar Doylean theme but this story is unusual in that it equates Smith's anti-Irish views with his anti-Egyptian prejudice. This imperial gothic fantasy encodes Irish political violence by discussing it at a remove, translating the Fenian threat into the far more exotic cultural terrorism practised by a fiendish orientalist and his mummy. The story questions to what extent colonialism, with its absorption of the cultures of the colonised, destabilises the perspective of imperial, metropolitan subject position. While the process of imperial assimilation is symbolised by the private museum that Bellingham keeps in his rooms, packed with colonial commodities such as relics, ancient scrolls, weapons, carved deities, a stuffed crocodile and, of course, his murderous mummy, it seems in the end that it is the mummy and not he who is in control. While the nefarious influence of the colonial artefacts comprising his collection of 'filthy Egyptian tricks' is a staple of late Victorian imperial gothic fiction, typical of the commodities and presences that haunted the British imagination in bestsellers like Richard Marsh's 1897 novel, *The Beetle*, these exotic horrors are directly linked in 'Lot No. 249' to the more immediate problem of Irish subversives at large in England.[29]

John Coulson Kernahan's 1897 shocker, *Captain Shannon*, presents a more frantic vision of Fenian violence. Loaded with graphic scenes of mass death and urban destruction, this strangely prescient tale revisited Stevenson's theme of the railway platform explosion but in a far more spectacular fashion. Serialised in the *Windsor Magazine* from July to November 1896, *Captain Shannon* was hurriedly issued in book form just weeks after an unclaimed bomb exploded on the Inner Circle line of the London underground railway in April 1897 (one reviewer of *Captain Shannon* thought that by rekindling memories of the Fenian campaign of the 1880s, the explosion would 'cause people to read the book').[30] The explosion that went off in a first-class carriage at Aldersgate Street Station killed one passenger and injured nine, including a plain clothes detective. The force of the explosion flung wreckage onto the platform and destroyed a passing train, and its force was felt in the neighbouring Farringdon Street and Moorgate Street stations.[31] The blast was initially blamed on faulty gas fittings but this was ruled out by Her Majesty's Chief Inspector of Explosives, Sir Vivian Majendie, who examined the scene and declared that a 'gross outrage' had been perpetrated with dynamite. Majendie's 'very simple' explanation for the catastrophe caused public uproar and fuelled rumours that the Fenians had returned to London to disrupt the approaching celebration of Queen Victoria's Diamond Jubilee.[32]

Like his morally ambivalent amateur sleuth, Max Rissler, Kernahan himself was a self-confessed hack journalist and hard-pressed 'devil of a writer' of racy magazine articles and lurid detective stories.[33] A chaotic and unstructured novel, *Captain Shannon* is littered with abruptly inserted characters, anomalous scenarios and unconvincing plot convolutions, such as Rissler's unexplained escape from a Scotland Yard 'shadow': instead of describing how his hero evades the detective, Kernahan simply states that to have done so would have taken too much time. Irrelevant characters and unnecessary scenes are included 'for several reasons, one of which is that this story would then have been shorter, and perhaps less interesting' than without them (p. 222), but despite this padding the novel never fails to entertain. Clearly, Kernahan was under pressure to supply the market and in his moralising short story, 'A Literary Gent: A Study in Vanity and Dipsomania', he described how his insecure living forced him to produce copy at very short notice which, even if it 'lacked finish ... would certainly be the stronger for being written at white heat'. His 'overwrought' style[34] left little to the imagination, particularly when describing scenes of violence, as when Rissler compares the shock of an explosion to witnessing 'a drink-maddened man pick up a child whom he afterwards dashed head foremost against a wall' (p. 258).

The novel's hectic form and production mirror the economic chaos of capital that Rissler, as a private detective in search of financial gain, participates in. Pursuing the dynamiter in order to win a £20,000 reward and 'please myself', his mercenary approach to detection makes him a morally ambivalent character. Risking, and often wasting, the lives of friends, accomplices and even innocent passers-by in order to succeed, his ruthless pursuit of the dynamiter reflects the unstructured nature of capitalist business practice. In one scene, when Rissler removes evidence from the body of a rival sleuth who has been murdered by the bomber, he dumps his colleague's body in the sea and prevents its discovery by the police (p. 101). The hunt for the bomber is a shambolic free-for-all, with private detectives competing with one another and against the 'vast network' of official police organisation (p. 52) for profit and professional 'kudos' (p. 93). Counter-terrorism appears as a form of enterprise with high stakes, but not just for the entrepreneurs who take part, as a multitude of unfortunate bystanders and hired hands end up dead as a result of Rissler's decisions and mistakes. As an independent freelancer he mirrors Sherlock Holmes, who is also 'his own master',[35] but whereas Doyle's hero eventually shares intelligence with the police, Rissler never does. Driven by an inherently pathological 'self-interest and inclination', he avoids engaging with the law, even if doing so might save lives. After one explosion demolishes the Bank of England, killing scores of innocents, he keeps evidence from the Scotland Yard investigation to prevent official interference in the 'enterprise' on which he has spent so much of his own 'time, thought and money' (pp. 202, 223). Meanwhile, dangerous surveillance work is contracted to several working class helpers, all of whom end up dead. Rissler's amorality continues unabated in the novel's 1906 sequel, *The Dumpling*, in which he drowns an informant during interrogation, causes an innocent man to have his throat slit by communists and keeps potentially life-saving information from a rival investigator whose mutilated corpse is later found in the Thames.[36]

The novel opens with the eponymous Irish terrorist, Captain Shannon,[37] retaliating against the passage of anti-Fenian legislation by destroying a large section of the London underground railway. Rather than planting a straightforwardly destructive device, the bomber constructs an elaborately symbolic one with which Kernahan makes a statement about contemporary literary culture:

> All that was known was that a respectably dressed young man, carrying what appeared to be about a dozen well-worn volumes from Mudie's, or some other circulating library, had entered at Aldgate Station an empty first-class carriage on the Underground Railway. These books were held together by a strap – as is used when sending or taking volumes for exchange to the libraries – and it had occurred to no one to ask to examine them, although the officials at all railway stations had, in view of the recent outrages, been instructed to challenge every passenger carrying a suspicious-looking parcel. The theory which was afterwards put forward was that, what appeared to be a parcel of volumes from a circulating library, was in reality a case, cunningly covered with the backs, bindings, and edges of books, and that this case

contained an infernal machine of the most deadly description. The wretch in charge of it was supposed purposely to have entered an empty carriage, and, after setting fire to the fuse, to have left the train at the next station. (pp. 4–5)

Disguised as a parcel of books, this bomb points once more to the reflexive nature of the dynamite novel, as Kernahan's fantasy of exploding literature provides a rather focused commentary on the relationship between political violence, popular fiction and late Victorian modernity. Circulation is the predominant motif here, as the movement of bombs, literature and subversive individuals are connected by the explosion. The device goes off at Blackfriars Station, killing all of the passengers on an arriving train, destroying a passing engine and wiping out the commuters and railway workers standing on the platform. However, the blast strangely spares a group of W. H. Smith's bookstall boys, whose 'miraculous' survival reflects the contemporary market success of popular literature, which Smith's bookstalls had come to symbolise. Selling cheap novels and newspapers on sites like railway platforms since 1848, the chain embodied the process of expansion that literary culture had undergone since the closing decades of the eighteenth century. The growth of mass literacy and an expanding cultural consciousness had created a process of profound intellectual change that was linked, as Raymond Williams has shown, to the progress of democracy.[38] By having Captain Shannon conceal his bomb inside a set of popular volumes, Kernahan makes the relationship between political violence and literary culture appear very apparent and links mass literacy with the disruptive forces of democracy, revolution and anti-imperialism.

Above ground is a scene of total destruction, with the demolition of New Bridge Street, part of the Embankment, St Paul's station, and De Keyser's Hotel. The damage leaves central London resembling a dismembered corpse, with a collapsed Blackfriars Bridge looking like 'a limb which had been rudely hacked from a body'. As the cleaning-up operation begins, massive casualties are found beneath the rubble:

I have no intention of sickening the reader by giving a realistic description of the awful sights which were witnessed when, after the first paralysing moment of panic was over, the search for the injured, the dying and the dead was commenced. The number of lives lost, including those who perished in Blackfriars station, in the two trains, in the street, and in the surrounding buildings, was enormous. (p. 7)

Zero's railway platform death is a tame affair compared to the carnage and infrastructural damage done to London by Captain Shannon's bomb. The explosion also succeeds in killing its real target, the Irish Chief Secretary, who is among the huge number of casualties but who, like Zero, is vaporised in the explosion and his body never found. While *The Dynamiter* ends with Zero's comforting demise, *Captain Shannon* opens with this 'terrific' (p. 5) and voyeuristically described attack in which the British Empire's 'Number One' in Ireland is erased by a Fenian. The explosion is quickly followed by the release of a manifesto announcing the formation of a broad revolutionary front composed of 'the whole of the secret societies of the world'. The new World Federation for the Advancement of Freedom promises to replace the repeated operational failures of anarchism, nihilism and Fenianism with a new campaign against the 'common enemy' of capitalism and 'English tyranny'. Threatening further 'righteous punishment' against the 'monsters of Monarchy and Imperialism', the Federation vows to 'destroy society, as society now exists' by starting a series of localised national revolts beginning in Ireland. These, the manifesto promises, will lead to the combined collapse of the European monarchies and capitalism, systems that it claims are already 'undermined to the very core' by socialism and anarchy. But the planned series of international revolts with which Captain Shannon promises to make the French Revolution look like 'an accidental outbreak' never happens: like a Hollywood film that has run out of budget long before its completion, Kernahan's novel runs out of imaginative steam and is scaled down before its *finale*, with Rissler pursuing a lone dynamiter (pp. 8–10). The 'terrible' revolutionary power of the 'swarming millions', which is promised but not delivered in this novel, was not unleashed by Kernahan until the publication of *The Dumpling* in 1906, in which Rissler fails to prevent a revolutionary meltdown as tens of thousands of British *sans-culottes* attack the centre of London.[39]

The popular press is quickly targeted for publishing portraits of wanted Fenians and offering rewards for the capture of Captain Shannon. The move presents independent, entrepreneurial investigators like Rissler with a chance to profit from the attack but by forcing the dynamiter underground, it also causes an abrupt slump in the newspaper market as the cessation of the bombing campaign leaves the press appearing 'flat' and 'tame' to readers accustomed to receiving their news 'with apprehension and anxiety'. This 'want of a sensation' is finally satisfied when the editor of the *Daily Record* is stabbed to death in broad daylight in Fleet Street and a Unionist editor is murdered in Dublin for reprinting the Fenian portraits (pp. 21, 23). The popular sheets are revived by the assassinations, producing more copy for a public addicted to what L. Perry Curtis has described as the 'sheer entertainment value'[40] of the late Victorian press. As a review in *The Times* of *Captain Shannon* joked, the 'blowing up of quite humble individuals and the destruction of public buildings' mattered little compared to the 'really serious' murders of newspaper editors.[41] The episode also carries echoes of Edgar Allan Poe's media-focused story of 1842, 'The Mystery of Marie Rogêt', in which news 'sensitive' Parisians are roused to a state of 'intense' curiosity and excitement by speculative reporting on the murder of a young woman. The huge volume of available information on the case is filtered through the popular press, whose lurid suggestions colour its subsequent reception by the reading public. Poe's story of the unsolved murder is as much a reflection on the purpose of the modern media which, he claims, is to 'create a sensation' and not 'further the cause of truth', as it is a narrative of crime.[42] The mystery predates *Captain Shannon* by more than half a century but its portrayal of the popular appetite for shocking news and the canny manipulation and the distortion of facts by the newspaper press is no less intense. Poe's undiscovered murderer kills for private and unexplained reasons but the political logic of Kernahan's terrorist intensifies popular interest in the violence that he directs indiscriminately against the 'whole community', as well as the press and politicians (p. 2).

By means too convoluted to describe here, Rissler finds correspondence from the bomber's sister, and learns that she almost died from a brain haemorrhage after reading reports of the underground bombing in another reflexive scene that suggests how popular fiction transformed the actual shocks of political violence, and their mediation via newspapers, into exciting literary capital. Kernahan's preoccupation with such processes also underlines Ben Singer's discussion of how sensation impacted upon the melodramatic consciousness of late nineteenth- and early twentieth-century publics. Pointing to the intensity of the 'experiential milieu' of 'modernity-as-stimulus', Singer describes how its sensational aspects were exploited by the performed narrative forms of stage melodrama and early cinema. Both of these entertained audiences by reflecting a range of actual, felt phenomena like urbanisation, the ongoing acceleration of everyday life, advertising, the rise of mass communications and transport. Although they were everyday experiences, they were novel and exciting and produced states of emotional excess in the modern subject. Like the popular stage plays and films Singer describes, *Captain Shannon* dwells on this character's agitated (and suitably exaggerated) emotional response to the distressing details of newspaper reports about her brother's murderous activity. While the plays and early films that Singer discusses feature heroes and heroines who fall into danger and must rescue others or be saved themselves, the bomber's sister is almost killed by the more passive but no less dangerous act of reading the news.[43]

After a captured Fenian reveals Captain Shannon's identity he is named as James Mullen and, when his photograph is published by all of the dailies, Rissler is reminded of a man he once met on a train who 'vanished into space' (p. 52). Underlining Benjamin's theory of the *flâneur*'s transformation into the amateur detective,[44] the novel also suggests that the Fenian defies the surveillant authority of this bourgeois urban type. By erasing proof of his existence as well as his movements ('effacing his footmarks', Rissler observes, is the 'key-word to his criminal code' and political designs (p. 167)), this inexplicable mobility also defines the terrorist in *Fitzgerald the Fenian*, where the Irish bomber appears similarly 'strange'. Maginn's dynamiter, who appears and disappears at will 'like the Wandering Jew',[45] denies the Benjaminian notion that existence inevitably means leaving physical traces or clues about oneself that provide the detective with fragments of data that can be reconstituted to produce a revelatory narrative.[46] The detective's power to detect and describe is denied by these fictional Irish bombers whose significance as signifiers of a subverted modernity rests in their ability to, up until a certain point at least, avoid leaving any signs that might betray their personal identities.

Mullen, it turns out, is the man Rissler saw on the train and when he returns to the station he finds him and follows the bomber into the City. But instead of apprehending the dynamiter, the sleuth finds himself 'paralysed' by the sight of his prey priming another bomb that explodes before he can recover his composure:

> the solid ground seemed to stagger and sway beneath me, and, from the neighbourhood of the General Post Office, came a sudden blaze of light, by which I saw a tall chimney crook inwards at the middle, as a leg is bent at the knee, and then snap in two like a sugar-stick. There was a low rumble, and a roar like the discharge of artillery, that was followed by the strangest ripping, rending din, as of the sudden tearing asunder of innumerable sheets of metal. I was conscious of the falling of masonry, of a choking limy dust in my eyes, nostrils and throat, and then a red darkness closed in upon me with a crash, and I remember no more. (p. 195)

Unlike Rissler's second-hand account of the underground attack, this description stresses the strangeness of experiencing an explosion. Material reality is distorted by the bomb, which makes the urban environment suddenly appear brittle and vulnerable. As the device goes off, the scene is illuminated by the flash of the blast, while time slows down and the surrounding buildings bend and fall apart. Its destructive force induces a state of psychic derangement in Rissler, in whom the experience of rapid and violent trauma causes mental overload and collapse: mirroring the stupefying impact of the newspaper reports read by Mullen's sister, the very sight of the bomb shocks his nervous system to the deep and its detonation leaves him in a coma of several weeks' duration. When he emerges, he learns that the bomb has wrecked the General Post Office, devastated Cheapside and, once again, killed countless bystanders.

Tracking Mullen back to the dynamite hulks moored off Canvey Island, he experiences another, equally disturbing shock when he discovers that the dynamiter is an effeminate cross-dresser. As he watches Mullen paring his nails and wearing women's clothes, Rissler realises that the dynamiter does so for sexual thrills as well as for the purpose of disguise: 'I could not help noticing how small, white and beautifully shaped his hands were, and that he had the long tapers of the artists, and pink, carefully trimmed nails'. Just as he was frozen by the sight of the latest bomb, Rissler is also captivated by Mullen's sensuously feminine appearance:

> The bright, prominent eyes, beautiful as a woman's, the delicately clear complexion, the straw-coloured hair, the aquiline nose with the strange upward arching of the nostrils, the curious knitting of the brows over the eyes, the full lips that spoke of voluptuousness, unscrupulous and cruel, the firm, finely-moulded chin – all these there was no mistaking, in spite of his woman's dress. (pp. 228–30)

Having earlier assured his readers that *Captain Shannon* does not feature 'that sickliest of subjects – the New Woman' and describing Mullen's bombing campaign as 'one of the few pieces of mischief that have happened in this world, since the days of Eve, concerning which . . . no woman ever had a hand in', Kernahan's take on the masculine 'boys' own' genre and his determination to tell 'a story without a woman in it' (pp. 172–3) is literalised within this scene. The transvestite bomber is the nearest thing that *Captain Shannon* has to a female character and his sexual otherness has a sequel in another confusion of political and sexual thrills in Kernahan's 1908 novel, *The Red Peril*. Here, another amateur detective, Arthur Maxwell, is captured by anarchists while eavesdropping on their plot to assassinate an MP. Tied to a pipe bomb, he is forced to defuse the device, giving the reader an unusually graphic description of the art of bomb disposal:

> I raised my head and chest so that my face was exactly over it. Then – mouthing, I fear like a madman – I worked my lips and rolled round my tongue to stimulate the flow of saliva, and, stooping, took the fuse between my lips and literally sucked and slobbered till I knew it was extinguished . . . Then, with my face pressed as in ghastly caress against the foul thing that a moment before had threatened my life, I fell forward in a faint. (p. 44)

Having no choice but to fellate the device, Maxwell recovers the following morning feeling objectified, dirty and used:

> Remembering my agonized efforts to free myself on the night before, my thrills, my terrors, but most of all my faint, I felt uncommonly 'cheap'; I felt, if I may borrow a legend which one often sees displayed in shop windows, like an article which has become 'slightly soiled' and is in consequence marked down. (p. 51)

A thinly disguised homoerotic experience, his escape from the pipe bomb provokes embarrassment rather than relief, suggesting the emotional state of a repressed homosexual who is left feeling feminised and 'cheap' after an encounter with another man. It is not until Maxwell has had 'a cold bath, a shave, a change of linen, some breakfast, and a smoke', after which he feels cleansed, rejuvenated and 'like a new man' (pp. 51–2, 54), that he can slip back into his normal heterosexual routine. Even the bomb has a different appearance the next morning: when he looks at it in 'the unsympathetic light of day', it also assumes a normal and unsuspicious appearance – that of 'a bit of once respectable, not to say church-going, but now groggy and dissolute gas-pipe' (p. 50). Returning to his hotel and smiling to himself in his 'soiled' and dishevelled evening dress (p. 52), his memory of the event is coloured by titillation rather than shame. Smug and self-satisfied rather than feeling elated at having survived a murder attempt by anarchists, Maxwell, like Rissler, experiences terrorism as a form of sexual epiphany; that the exclusively masculine sexual elements of these scenes are barely disguised by Kernahan strongly suggests that both novels appealed to readers for reasons that were other than political.

In *Captain Shannon*, Mullen's sexual ambivalence emphasises the strangeness and alterity of terrorism. The aesthete-terrorist's lack of manly qualities (as well as being a sexual deviant he is also 'the greatest artist in crime of the century' (p. 200)) becomes apparent when, screaming 'like a drunken, screeching, hysterical Jezebel' he attacks Rissler and, lighting another fuse, accidentally blows himself up (p. 257). Again, the day is saved and the political threat contained by the terrorist's clumsy self-destruction or, as Kernahan puts it, his arrest by 'Detective Death' (p. 258). But his vision of rampaging political violence is much darker than Stevenson's, whose reining in of the chaotic possibilities of Fenianism limits the political scope of *The Dynamiter*. As well as lingering on catastrophic scenes of mass death and ruin, Kernahan presents a political subversive whose sexual difference makes him doubly degenerate. The chaotic quality of his political fantasy is also amplified by the ruthlessness of its morally ambivalent protagonist who, like any capitalist set on extracting profit from an enterprise, will stop at nothing in pursuit of the bomber. While the threat posed by Kernahan's political 'devil' (p. 195) is also exorcised by a premature explosion, we remain uncomfortably aware at the end of *Captain Shannon* that the madness of capital, embodied by Rissler's uninhibited desire for material gain, has not been brought to heel. Readers consumed this vision of unrestricted political violence with relish: three editions of *Captain Shannon* were published by Ward, Lock in Britain, and the novel stayed in print in the United States under the imprint of the International Association of Newspapers and Authors until 1901. The pleasure they experienced in reading the novel suggests how late Victorian industries of popular culture fed a voyeuristic appetite for political shock.

The Anti-Imperial Dynamite Novel

As well as providing source material for conservative novelists, dynamiting also inspired writers who supported the cause of Irish independence and, while Kernehan and Stevenson regarded Fenianism as a form of political 'perversion',[47] other writers rationalised dynamiting by comparing its relatively limited violence to the unrestricted force used by the British in their imperial wars. Donald MacKay's novel *The Dynamite Ship* and Tom Greer's techno-fantasy, *A Modern Dædalus*, were both published at the height of the dynamite war in 1885. Focusing on the revolutionary possibilities of dynamiting, they fuse Irish nationalism with tropes of science fiction. Both adventures conclude with victory for the Fenians and the establishment of an independent Irish republic, and their treatment of political violence exploits the separatist discourse published on the pages of the Fenian dynamite press. Reversing the ideological thrust of pro-empire shilling shockers like *The Dynamiter*, both novels combine the popularity of this form as a commercial, cultural and political product with the novelty-appeal of their anti-imperial narratives.[48] They also differ from other dynamite novels in their characterisation of Irish bombers as reasonable patriots whose actions are justified by comparison with the greater evils of imperialism. As Daniel Pick has shown, late nineteenth-century Europe was immersed in cultural debates about the nature and function of warfare, discussions that circulated ideas of national identity and destiny-fulfilment, or political 'becoming'.[49] Both Greer's and MacKay's novels offer a fictional treatment of the possibilities of fulfilling Irish republican aspirations by suggesting that the successful application of martial skill and technological prowess could awaken a militant national consciousness and encourage the Irish to perform the necessary and spectacularly violent deeds that would result in the creation of a modern Irish nation state. As in the columns of the *United Irishman* and the *Irish World*, this potential is explored in these novels through the idea of dynamite, its unstoppable power and unmatchable precision.

MacKay's novel was published simultaneously in London and New York where, it seems, there was popular demand for narratives focused on the possible collapse of the British empire. It opens by suggesting that developments in weapons technology could allow force to be applied 'in a new way' by republicans (p. 13). Inspired by US naval experiments on dynamite missiles – high explosive shells fired from lightweight guns that threatened to render ironclads obsolete – the novel plays on contemporary anxieties over new military technologies that appeared to mark the twilight of British naval power. Already conscious of the 'fearful ravages' wrought by the O'Donovan Rossa's Skirmishers, *The Times* speculated on the possibility of a bombardment of England with dynamite shells:

> The prospect of such a change in the condition of warfare is appalling . . . comparatively small gunboats carrying one large gun might approach by night or even by day, near enough to a seaport to throw several dynamite shells into an inhabited city, and with a devastating effect which recent events can suggest . . .[50]

From the Fenian perspective, the weapon promised to place Irish separatists on an equal footing with the British and even bring imperial power to its knees,[51] and in *The Dynamite Ship*, MacKay speculates over what might happen if such technology were to fall into Irish hands. It opens in the near futuristic setting of June 1889, with a group of exiled militants discussing the failure of previous insurrections. The meeting, held in Battery Park in view of the emigrant port at Ellis Island, discusses every available and tested method of revolt, including 'rebellion, moral suasion, parliamentary tactics, protests from the people, murders, fires, explosions'. These, the conspirators agree, have all failed to liberate Ireland while the recent bombing campaign has only irritated the British. The conversation turns to the need to replace the traditional strategy of fighting with 'pike and musket' (p. 13) with more modern weapons and the Fenians come to a decision to try fighting with the pneumatic dynamite gun, a weapon that can 'kill a man at the rate of two hundred thousand miles a minute!' (p. 91). One of the plotters, Heyward, goes on to design a mobile weapons platform for the gun, a petrol-powered vessel, or dynamite ship, with which he proposes to launch an attack against London. The *Atlantic* (its very name suggestive of the new diasporic and global reach of Irish insurgency) is built by a team of non-Irish scientists who 'care no more for the freedom of Ireland than for three straws' but who are dedicated to developing the craft's super technology: 'Give them their invention' Heyward remarks, 'and they are happy' (p. 39). While the ship is prepared in a secret dock in the Carribean, its crew is recruited from exiled Fenians in New York, whose involvement in the project indicates that despite their movement's access to foreign scientists and new technology, it remains dependent on the support and participation of America's urban underclass of Irish migrants.

The ship's dynamite guns are invented by a freelance scientist named Mellerkoff, a character modelled on the Brooklyn-based scientist, Professor Mezzeroff, who was reputed, according to contemporary newspaper reports, to have been a Russian nihilist hired to train 'the Scientific School of the Fenian Brotherhood'. 'With dynamite', he instructed the Irish, 'the ironclads and army of Great Britain could be destroyed, and other immense damage done'. Mezzeroff recommended explosives as 'the best weapon obtainable for freeing Ireland from tyranny, and sweeping every British vessel from the sea', and also advised the Fenians on the use of fast cruisers armed with flamethrowers, the employment of torpedoes against naval targets and the practicalities of shelling British cities.[52] While his advice might have seemed like the stuff of science fiction to the hostile writers who filed reports on his meetings to *The Times*, the Irish Republican Brotherhood in New York did sponsor research on a submersible torpedo-armed craft which it christened the 'Fenian Ram' until the expensive prototype sank in the East River in 1883.[53] The idea provided MacKay with the futuristic motif of sea-borne terror and, as one of the ship's crew explains, its maiden 'scientific expedition' to London is a futuristic endeavour belonging properly 'somewhere in the next century' (p. 129).[54] MacKay's hope seems to have been that if his idea for an attack on London should remain impossible for the time being, then perhaps a future generation of separatists might take inspiration from the novel.

Mellerkoff loves the gun, finding 'beauty' as well as pleasure in the 'perfect and unvarying certainty' of its firepower. Heyward, on the other hand, wonders whether such technology is dehumanising mankind and pauses during its construction to reflect on the morality of using it in the coming conflict:

> 'It is a cruel thing' he, at length, said, laying his hand upon the grim cannon. 'Science is dreadful in its teachings, when it places such a gun as this in the hands of men swayed by the passions of hate or revenge. It seems to me that the world is growing more bitter; that men are becoming less human toward one another.'

'The gun's all right,' ventured Mellerkoff. 'The gun is not to blame.' (pp. 91–2)

Like the phallic pipe bomb in *The Red Peril*, the dynamite gun is another erotically charged machine of destruction. The sentiments of Mellerkoff, who has fallen in love with the weapon and defends it against Heyward's anti-war sentiments, represent the confusion of the human with the inanimate but scientifically perfect material. Unlike the Russian who has become engrossed by the gun's precision and capacity to destroy, Heyward remains uncomfortable with its role in the forthcoming attack. A romantic nationalist, he insists that the weapon should be used transparently lest it should disgrace his cause: 'Used secretly, dynamite, or even gunpowder, is not a legitimate article of warfare. Used openly, and in sight of all men, it is as fair as the sling of David'. Adopting the moral high ground, he justifies the shelling of British cities by arguing that the dynamite gun, if brandished in conventional battle, will 'do its work openly, honestly, and fairly in the sight of all men' (pp. 95–6). According to MacKay, therefore, warfare can be legitimised if it is made visible, and bombing, if carried out in this way, as opposed to its employment in a campaign of urban terrorism, will undermine imperialism by subjecting Britain to greater violence than that wielded by its own armed forces. Heyward plans to achieve this transformation in the moral perception of warfare by turning the power of his 'new machine' (p. 123) against a selection of political targets in London, thereby subjecting the city to violence on the scale of that used by the British against Egyptian and Sudanese insurgents during the 1880s.

Armed with enough dynamite 'to blow the island of Cuba out of water' (p. 110), Heyward launches his campaign by abducting two British royals who are forced to acknowledge the attack as being 'in the way of fair, open and legitimate warfare' (p. 154). The *Atlantic* is then moored at London Bridge on the eve of the 'undying and forever glorious Fourth of July', and an ultimatum is delivered to the British government, which is read to MPs gathered in Westminster by the Speaker of the House:

> 'What I have feared,' he continued, 'has occurred. The growing discontent of the Irish in Ireland . . . raised the question in my mind whether some disinterested person, moved to pity by fancied distress, would not organize an expedition, armed with the most scientific of modern weapons, and seek to gain by force the independence of Ireland.' (p. 171)

The 'dread word' 'dynamite' causes panic in the Commons as the Speaker warns that parliament could be 'blown to fragments at any moment'. He adds that Heyward's group, the Irish League, 'has no connection with the skulking, secret-killing dynamiters that have infested the British kingdom for years' and that they plan to engage in hostilities 'openly and above board, face to face ... like Englishmen, in a fair field, and with no favour' (p. 178). When the deadline passes without an announcement from the British of their intention to withdraw from Ireland, Heyward turns his gun on London and lets dynamite do its 'usual work' (p. 208). While a high-tech pneumatic canon rather than the more mundane reality of abandoned Gladstone bags are the method of delivery, the impact is the same as symbolic targets like Westminster, the Bank of England, London Bridge and the Custom House are shelled from the Thames. The British quickly surrender, granting independence to Ireland, and MacKay's fantasy closes with the establishment of 'the Great Irish Republic' (p. 208). By abandoning the underhand methods of terrorism in favour of another form of visible, and therefore legitimate, warfare, the Irish League defeats the British empire, yet its methods carry the same logic as Rossa's Skirmishing campaign as it is only through inspiring fear that the Irish can achieve their goal of national self determination.

Tom Greer also furthered nationalist politics by other means in his political fantasy, *A Modern Dædalus*,[55] in which Irish revolutionaries conduct aerial bombing against British forces. The subversive potential of flight was also explored by E. Douglas Fawcett in his 1893 shocker, *Hartmann the Anarchist; or, The Doom of the Great City*, in which a German anarchist deploys the 'incalculable force' of a dirigible against the population of London, shattering the metropolis and destroying 'the trophies of centuries'.[56] Greer's dynamiters also employ this method but his novel opens by criticising the morally questionable methods of Skirmishing, yet his condemnation of dynamiting is tempered by the idea that the development of high explosives will bring the struggle for Irish independence to an 'unprecedentedly destructive' (p. 233) level:

> Is it necessary to point out to any candid reader how widely different is the employment of dynamite in open war from its use as the instrument of secret murder and assassination, and of the destruction of public monuments which are a heritage and possession, not of the English people alone, but of mankind? The incidents of this story are purely imaginary; but the ideas and forces with which it deals are real, and may at any moment be brought into active play by the inevitable development of the 'resources of civilisation.' Such development is certain to take place; it is in rapid progress at this moment ... Come it will in some form as little expected, as impossible to control. (v–vi)

Despite his formal criticism of Fenian bombing, Greer defends the ideology behind Skirmishing and addresses the overwhelming imbalance of forces that made terrorism inevitable. Like MacKay's fantasy, Greer's adventure hinges on the levelling possibilities inherent in the invention of new technology and in this case it is the development of a flying machine that opens up a new dimension in anti-imperial warfare. Overnight the novel's hero, Jack O'Halloran, changes from a liberal catholic unionist and aspiring professional with ambitions to become a millionaire into a dogged revolutionary who puts his invention and scientific knowledge to use within the Fenian movement. After graduating from a technical college in Belfast and returning home to Donegal, O'Halloran is at first happy to avoid politics and concentrates on perfecting his flying apparatus for mass production and commercial sale. The machine will allow its user to take off 'with a speed equal to that of the eagle, and far surpassing our swiftest railway trains' (xivxv), but before he gets a chance to market the device O'Halloran finds that he must press it into service in a ruthless campaign against the British.

From the outset, the very appearance of the invention – a pair of canvas wings supported by steel rods, its 'form almost exactly resembling that which the popular mythology attributes to angels' (p. 66) – anticipates its use for Miltonian, revolutionary purposes rather than for furtherance of science and exploration, while O'Halloran's discovery that the Donegal peasantry is resisting a 'Tory millennium' also suggests to the reader that revolution is afoot (p. 8). Widespread political oppression, starvation and mass evictions provoke the peasantry into open rebellion and the inventor learns that the crisis has radicalised his own formerly passive family:

> I returned to find them gloomy, idle, suspicious, filled with a literature of whose very existence I was previously unaware, but of which they were as keen students as I myself was of mathematical and physical science. The whole history of Russian Nihilism, of German Socialism, of the Italian Carbonari, of the French Commune, was at their fingers' ends. (pp. 6–7)

As well as keeping well stocked libraries of up-to-date revolutionary literature, the Donegal peasants have also been working hard to acquire modern weapons and explosives, including long-range rifles with telescopic sights and US-manufactured dynamite bombs (p. 10). In *Fitzgerald the Fenian*, a 'cheap education' (Vol. II, p. 147) also results in radicalisation as Maginn's hero, Dick Fitzgerald, is politicised by his father's library of works promoting an 'anti-English point of view'. These include editions of Milton, Byron and Thomas Moore along with back issues of the Young Ireland journal, *The Nation*, and volumes of romantic nationalist poetry by his father's one-time companion,

Thomas Davis (Vol. I, p. 25), all of which inspire Fitzgerald to write his own best-selling prison memoir, *Meditations of a Prisoner*. Reared on the radical politics contained within these 'old books' (Vol. I, p. 69), the heroic Fenian is both a cultural and political figure whose adventures include thwarting dynamite plots hatched by less refined revolutionaries and struggling with a villainous landlord who demolishes an ancient round tower to make way for a piggery. Maginn also makes clear that the twinned spheres of politics and intellectual culture are an exclusively masculine domain as Fitzgerald's mentally inferior sisters are only interested in observing the local 'beaux and belles' and following 'the mysteries of the fashions' (Vol. I, p. 29).

Jack O'Halloran is unconvinced of the need to fight, disagrees with his family's radicalism and refuses to get involved in the revolution. However his views are changed when, during a test-flight over County Donegal, he has a bird's-eye view of an eviction. The sight of wanton destruction and suffering convinces him that he must act:

> I actually caught sight of the smoke rising from the still smouldering thatch that had been stripped off by the 'crowbar brigade,' and saw the houseless wretches who had lived under it standing like statues of despair upon the roadside among the broken and worthless furniture . . . I gave way to feelings unworthy of a philosopher, and cursed the proprietors of the soil in language borrowed from the vocabulary of my brothers. (pp. 14–15)

From his Olympian perspective O'Halloran rejects his reformist beliefs and is overcome by the 'unscientific' emotion of the militant (p. 14). Giving way to the impulsive and romantic character of his peasant kin, he comes to realise that the supposed objectivity and empirical values he learned as a student of science represent the standardisation of his thought into an imperial mould and have been designed to undermine his sense of Irishness and instil a particularly British professional identity. When the conflicted hero is accused by his brother of being the 'spawn' of an 'accursed Government college' (p. 53), Greer suggests that O'Halloran is the product of two Irelands, and that modern nationalism must learn how to reconcile their seemingly polarised values. Torn between his professional roots in the urban and industrial north-east, where unionist and imperial technocracy reigns, and his emotional origins in the 'other', romantic and Celtic Ireland represented by County Donegal, O'Halloran learns that for the national cause to succeed it must re-educate nationalists like his brother in order to convince them that these cultures should not necessarily be antagonistic towards one another. This explains why Greer's political fantasy spends so much time describing the peasantry's interest in revolutionary literature, high-tech weaponry and the anti-imperial campaign of the Boers in South Africa. With their expanding political perspective, the tenant farmers of Donegal are experiencing a rapid process of political, cultural and technological modernisation that is fuelled by knowledge of science, European radicalism and global anti-imperialism. Fantastic as this story of flying Fenians is, O'Halloran's 'wings' symbolise the contemporary modernisation of Irish nationalism, and the novel's repeated scenes of destruction by means of dynamite, which are always witnessed from above, imply possible realignments of the republican military and political perspective by late Victorian technology.

On another flight O'Halloran witnesses a sniper kill a detested landlord's agent 'with a shot that might have won the Queen's prize at Wimbledon' (p. 29) and when he argues with his brother, Dick, over the morality of political murder he is told that local rebels have been studying Boer guerrilla tactics. When he realises that his son has invented the flying machine, Jack's father orders him to use it to 'ensure the triumph of Old Ireland' by training the rebels to fly. Still objecting to political violence and hoping that he can use the machine to improve relations between the Irish and the British, O'Halloran refuses:

> 'Oh, father,' I answered, 'how can I make the first use of my discovery in causing war and bloodshed? It is not for war, it is for peace! it is not for one people only, it is for all the world! I would rather bury it in the sea than that one life should be sacrificed, much less a bloody war provoked.'
> 'You talk like a silly girl,' said he. (p. 36)

Pacifism is feminised by old O'Halloran, who wants to use the machine to 'exterminate' the enemy (p. 37). Mid-argument, another brother, Dan, returns home covered in mud, and shows Jack the Metford rifle (nicknamed 'my dark Rosaleen') that, he reveals, he used to shoot the agent, boasting: 'they have to reckon with a different sort of weapon now' (p. 40). Jack is then told that an enormous underground revolutionary organisation has been raised across the country, but he is disowned when he again refuses to train the rebels. When his brothers take the flying machine from him, he builds a second model with which he flies to London in the hope of persuading the Conservative government to repeal its coercive legislation. However his faith in British politics is shattered when he learns that an aerial display that he gives over Trafalgar Square causes mass panic and anti-Irish hysteria: 'I heard shouts and screams, not all of wonder and amazement, but of anger and terror as well'. After landing on the cupola of St Paul's Cathedral, O'Halloran stashes his wings and goes for a walk among the frightened Londoners only to learn from the news vendors that his attempt at conciliation has got off to a bad start: '*Globe* or *Echo*, sir! last edition! full description of the flying man!! sixteen people trampled to death in the streets!!! great dynamite plot to blow up St Paul's!!!' Like Kernahan, Greer integrates news consumption into his plot but does so from an exclusively nationalist perspective. O'Halloran counters the press's portrayal of his invention by confronting the editor of the *Echo*, who invites him to write a column describing the apparatus and his philanthropic plans for its use. But when he is taken to Westminster to meet the government, he learns that the Home Secretary is manipulating the panic in order to advance the ongoing coercion in Ireland: 'He did not wonder that the popular instinct, which was always a more reliable guide than the theories of philosophers or the shifty explanations of politicians, connected this incident with the machinations of that party from whose ingenuity the country had suffered so much, ie – dynamiters' (p. 91). He finally acknowledges his mistake after he escapes from a police trap laid by the British politicians:

> I felt a proud and exhilirating (*sic*) sense of freedom as I surveyed the city spread like a huge ant-hill beneath me, and tried to make out the exact position of Whitehall and Downing Street. 'That is where a dozen crawling insects are sitting at this moment,' I soliloquised, 'to determine whether they will allow me to give these powers to men, or even to exercise them myself at their beck and call? . . . I will trust them no further, I laugh at their puny authority . . . I may remember I am an Irishman still.' (pp. 130–1)

Once more, O'Halloran's panoramic point of view puts the Irish situation into perspective and contextualises British imperial policy in terms of political and scientific modernity, as represented by the invulnerability, freedom of movement and unlimited vista that he enjoys whilst in flight. Having made his decision to return home and join the rebels in the struggle against British 'tyranny' (p. 134), he tries to make contact with Irish MPs outside Westminster but is caught in a crowd surge and captured.

Imprisoned in St Stephen's Clock Tower, he learns that revolution has broken out all over Ireland with fighting in every district except Belfast (in contrast to this scenario, George A. Birmingham's 1912 fantasy, *The Red Hand of Ulster*, portrays a unionist rebellion by northern loyalists that cuts Belfast off from nationalist Ireland before being suppressed by the British military).[57] An independent republic is declared in Dublin and the leader of the Irish Parliamentary Party, who escapes from London, is appointed president. Jack is rescued from the British by his brother, Dick, who has taught himself to fly with the original apparatus and the pair return home to finally 'sweep the English into the sea' (p. 181). He builds more flying machines and trains the new Irish national army in how to attack British positions with dynamite (p. 185), bringing Fenian violence into new political and tactical dimensions. His campaign opens with a spectacular aerial attack on Dublin Castle, where the Fenians launch an 'infernal rain' of explosives after the building is floodlit by electric lamps. The light renders the attackers invisible and unstoppable while providing O'Halloran and his men with a 'gloriously' illuminated display of the death and destruction that they unleash on the garrison below:

> I balanced myself above them for a moment, and dropped a bomb, which struck the pavement close to their feet and burst with a loud report, enveloping the entire party in smoke and dust.
>
> It was perhaps well that the immediate effects were thus concealed from our eyes. Shell after shell dropped in quick succession, and in a moment nothing was visible but a dim rolling cloud of dust, momentarily torn asunder by the quick flashes of the explosions . . . As it slowly cleared away, a scene of desolation met our eyes . . . Broken roofs and shattered walls stood up in ghastly nakedness under the glare of the electric light; below heaps of bricks and mortar, plaster and broken glass, and bodies of men in uniform half buried among the ruins. (pp. 201–2)

With this attack and a further series of graphically described engagements, Greer shows how politically reflexive the dynamite novel could be. His fiction suggests what might happen should O'Donovan Rossa's call for a global anti-imperialist revolution be answered by 'heroes who will initiate and keep up without intermission a guerrilla warfare – men who will fly over land and sea like invisible beings – now striking the enemy in Ireland, now in India, now in England itself, as occasion may present'.[58] This fantasy of airborne Fenianism is also alluded to by Maginn, whose dynamiters look forward to 'the day that the Irish may float over the burnt and smoking ruins of the English capital!' (Vol. II, p. 182). By suggesting that the future wars of Irish liberation will not only be fought on land but also in the air (or from the sea, as MacKay predicts), Greer's fantasy hinges on the rapid transformation and modernisation of contemporary Irish political culture, and of Fenian political violence, by the dynamite war of the 1880s. The rapid success of Jack O'Halloran's Fenian 'flying brigade', a highly mobile unit that can 'go anywhere and do anything' (p. 36), also indicates the extent of late nineteenth-century Irish nationalism's awareness of the political potential of its global diaspora. The Fenian movement had exploited the international spread of nationalist and anti-imperial politics since at least the 1860s: the Fenian uprising of 1867 included an abortive invasion of Canada launched from the United States, and was followed by the much-publicised escape of prisoners from the penal colony of Freemantle, Australia, while plans were made to flood Ireland and Britain with corps of professional revolutionaries who had experienced combat during the American Civil War. Indeed, Fenianism was described by its enemies as 'the American Celtic revolutionary movement',[59] and while it failed politically these symbolically loaded events afforded it powerful cultural and ideological purchase among Irish emigrant communities. The 'New Departure' programme of the late 1870s and 1880s also established a broad front of Home Rulers, Fenians and Land Leaguers, uniting separatists, agrarian revolutionaries and even constitutional nationalists against British imperialism in Ireland and the United States.[60] The profound 'alteration' (p. 228) of modern warfare by O'Halloran's highly mobile flying machines reflects the modernisation of militant Irish nationalism, which, by the 1880s, had become aware of its global spread. Like Rossa's political dream of an 'invisible' army of airborne Skirmishers, Greer's fantasy allegorises this shift in Irish nationalist politics.

The surrender of the Castle is followed by the 'brilliant' (p. 212) destruction of a fleet of ironclads blockading Dublin Bay and the final deployment of the flying machines in Ulster, where a British expeditionary force, pinned down by Fenian sharpshooters, is finished off. Jack arrives to find his brother rejoicing: '"Ah! Majuba Hill! . . . Do you know the Boers fought for the independence of Ireland that day? They showed what could be done against the British army by really good shooting, and set Irish men to work to organise the body that has done good service since"' (p. 216). During the Transvaal's war of independence of 1880–1, Boer marksmanship and guerrilla tactics culminated in the British defeat at Majuba Hill in northern Natal but the fact that the British actually won the first Boer War does not diminish the significance of this symbolic victory for Dick, whose main interest is in creating a similarly bloody spectacle in Ireland. Like the escapades of the Fenians in 1867, this 'striking spectacle' of resistance (p. 212) engages with the militant republican consciousness.

Hovering over the countryside around Belfast, which has held out against the rebels, O'Halloran views the carnage from the air, finding 'everything that I had associated with the idea of a pitched battle in the field . . . conspicuous by its absence', as precision arms and aerial bombardment have rendered the deployment of troops into 'continuous lines' useless. His final attack on the British rear lines turns their ammunition and fuel dumps into an 'Inferno', incinerates the helpless soldiers and transforms the battlefield into a 'hellish phantasmagoria' (pp. 228, 237, 249, 235). With its combination of guerrilla warfare, dynamiting and aerial bombardment, Greer's novel concludes with the humbled British asking:

> What disgrace can there be in accepting the inevitable? Why not recognise the fact that the Irish have a weapon against which it is vain to fight – a weapon by which we are placed at as great a disadvantage as were the Zulus, with their assegais and ox-hide shields, when compared to our battalions with Martini-Henry rifles and Gatling guns? (p. 250)

His futuristic war of national liberation combines dynamite – the signal motif of individualised political terror – with the limitless potential of flight, and in doing so points to the novelty with which the Fenian dynamite war struck the late Victorian imagination. Greer's climactic battle points to the transformation of Irish political violence which, having abandoned the earlier tactic of direct confrontation, or reliance on outmoded weapons like gunpowder (which was used with disastrous results during an attempted breakout of Fenian prisoners in Clerkenwell in 1867). Both his and MacKay's novels concentrated on the new possibilities inherent in dynamiting, and the manner in which it involved and interested the nationalist diaspora through the spectacle and media coverage of explosions. Both novels discussed the apparent invisibility or untraceability of the dynamiter, celebrated the harnessing of modern technology in the republican cause and explored the shocking quality of Fenian bombs in their political, conceptual and sensory registers. By fusing every late nineteenth-century strategy of militant anti-imperialism, including Skirmishing, Land League violence and Boer guerrilla tactics, *A Modern Dædalus* offered contemporary readers a subversively structured and imagined political commentary on the unstable moment during which it was published. Going to press in 1885, it appealed to readers who were conscious of the direct and violent challenges being posed to imperial power in Britain and Ireland as well as the challenge being posed to imperialism in more distant colonial territories. With its themes of unstoppable rebellion, the technological superiority of the Irish and the possibility of republican victory, the novel mimics the alarming dynamics of popular imperial crisis novels like George Tomkyns Chesney's 1871 fable, *The Battle of Dorking*, in which a militarily unprepared Britain is vanquished by brilliantly efficient Prussian invaders while, at the same time, subverting their political message. In this novel the British invaders suffer complete destruction at the hands of the Irish as Greer 'writes back' in the sense that has been attributed to later, postcolonial writers,[61] countering the conservative and imperialist response to the dynamite campaign with his own spectacularly violent resistance narrative. From his nationalist perspective the technological and military 'resources of civilisation' (p. v) offered to empower the colonised, offering them the kind of destructive might wrought by British forces against rebellious colonial populations throughout the late Victorian period. O'Halloran reflects on this reversal at the end of the novel:

> when men do make war they ought to be in earnest. Their weapons should be the deadliest they can use; their blows the heaviest they can deal. To say that they must make war, indeed, but that they must not make it too effectively; that to kill a man with a solid bullet is legitimate, but to wound him with an explosive one is atrocious; that to blow your enemy to fragments with gunpowder is civilised warfare, but to employ dynamite for the same purposes is worthy only of savages; is a species of cant born of the idea that war is a magnificent game for kings and nobles, and must be carried out under rules that disguise its essentially revolting nature, and prevent it from being too dangerous or disagreeable to them. (p. 247)

Moving away from allegorical territory and into more clearly polemical ground, Greer suggests here that an Irish victory will improve Britain by leading the English toward the 'discovery' of democratic, socialist and republican alternatives to monarchy and imperialism (p. 251). By refusing to distinguish between conventional warfare and the more unusual methods of terrorism, he legitimises the Fenian strategy of dynamiting and, having drawn the reader toward what he believes is the only possible outcome to the conflict between Britain and Ireland (a resounding British defeat and victory and independence for the Irish), Greer ultimately contradicts the condemnation of Skirmishing with which his novel begins. His opening disclaimer also reveals the political restrictions within which the novel was published as it was only after defining itself as an anti-Fenian text that it could open. Yet the limits of his political imagination are also apparent, as his manipulation of the genre of scientific romance allowed him to sidestep the problematic question of how to portray the reality of dynamiting in a realist mode. Clearly Greer, like MacKay, would have found it difficult to represent Skirmishing as it was advocated by Rossa and Ford in their newspapers, and both novelists were forced to represent political violence as the work of revolutionaries who employed their forces in as highly controlled and disciplined a manner as conventional soldiers engaging in open warfare. In this way, the conceptual force of terrorism, along with its power to frighten, is both exploited and contained in both novels because, in re-imagining dynamiting in this manner, Greer and MacKay restructure the unpredictability of the infernal machine within the imaginative framework of the more conventional and acceptable methods of the dynamite gun and aerial attack. Fantastic as these methods are, they were nonetheless recognisably conventional in the eyes of contemporary readers who found such tactics less offensive than the anonymous bombings that were carried out by the Fenians. But even this attempt at moral and political distancing could not separate the novel from the disagreeably radical objectives of the dynamiters. 'The story is told with judicious spirit', wrote one reviewer in the Irish Catholic periodical, the *Dublin Review*, who cautioned readers that although the story was entertaining, its political message was just as dangerous as that of the Fenians, adding 'we have not much belief in the judiciousness of writing such narratives'.[62] Likewise, the English press wondered at Greer's political motivations and the underlying 'moral' of the novel which, 'although quite contrary to his intention', was nonetheless regarded as politically 'suspect'.[63] Its political content made it appear 'hardly a novel', complained another reviewer, who was convinced that that 'Saxon readers' would be unable to forget 'the unpleasant taste which it is calculated to leave in their mouths'.[64]

The Fenian bombing campaigns of the 1880s altered the popular consciousness of Irish violence. Terrorism transplanted the kind of shocks associated in the Victorian imagination with Ireland, which was England's close colonial other, directly onto the streets of Britain and into the political centre of imperial rule. Lasting 'only a minute', Greer's brief but spectacularly violent and gruesome *finale* counters the imaginative and political limitations of Stevenson's ending, which suggests that terrorism, quite literally, accomplishes 'Zero'. *The Dynamiter* served the ideological needs of the pro-imperial reading public by attempting to contain Fenianism and, in writing it, Stevenson tried to halt Irish nationalism's potential to contaminate the public mind with its idea of independence. However, its popularity did not stem the growing appetite for narratives of political chaos and imperial collapse: the repeated publication of *Captain Shannon* over a decade later indicates the extent of the widespread appeal of the dynamite novel even when Fenianism failed or – just as often – when it refused to reassure its readers of the security of the British metropolis from the threat of Irish separatism. In each of the fictions addressed here, dynamite is treated as highly malleable political stuff: whether underlining conservative anxieties or publicising the cause of Irish independence, these authors exploited popular fascination with the Fenian strategy of shocking the public by 'blowing up ships, buildings, and people with infernal machines'.[65] They all tell us something about the nature of terrorism in the late nineteenth century, when the political content of both conservative and radical texts became blurred beneath the exciting experience of writing and reading about terrorism. Globe-trotting, anti-imperialist novels portrayed Skirmishing in a very different light to Arthur Conan Doyle's sympathetic parodies but all of these tales profited by exploiting the popular fascination with political terror. Their narratives of Irish political violence reveal how the threat of being bombed could induce thrills as well as inflict shock.

Notes

1. *Times* journalist A. F. Walter to Colonel Brackenbury of the Secret Service, 20 June 1882, Crime Branch Special, B File, B29, National Archive, Dublin.
2. Stevenson, letter to Anne Jenkin, (undated) April 1897, *The Letters of Robert Louis Stevenson*, Vol. 5, July 1884–August 1887 (New Haven and London: Yale University Press, 1995), p. 390.
3. Tom Greer, *A Modern Dædalus* (London: Griffith, Farran, Okeden & Welsh, 1885), p. 245
4. 'London Bridge', *The United Irishman*, 10 January 1885, p. 2.
5. 'Dynamiters the Thing to Terrify all England', *The United Irishman*, 7 March 1885, p. 2.
6. By the 1880s it was being manufactured under licence by a number of companies and the Irish bombers often used a variant manufactured by the Atlas Powder Company in Philadelphia. See Henri Le Caron, *Twenty Five Years in the Secret Service*, reprinted from the 10th Heinemann edition, 1893 (Wakefield: EP Publishing, 1974), p. 243.
7. *United Irishman*, untitled cutting, dated 1882, Chief Secretary's Office, Dublin, B 171, National Archive, Dublin.
8. Ibid.
9. 'The Dynamite War: A Well-Planned Engagement and Brilliant Achievements of the Irish Forces', *The Irish World*, Saturday, 14 June 1884, p. 13.
10. 'A Press Organ of the Dynamite Party', *The Times*, 24 March 1884, p. 8.
11. 'An Emergency Fund', *The Irish World*, Saturday, 5 January 1884, p. 4.
12. John Littlechild, *Reminiscences of Chief Inspector Littlechild* (London: The Leadenhall Press, 1894), p. 12.
13. 'A Press Organ of the Dynamite Party', *The Times*, 24 March 1884, p. 8.
14. Anonymous, *Parnellism and Crime, or 'The Bloody Work of the Two Leagues'* (reprinted from *The Times*, London, c. 1887), p. 1.
15. See K. R. M. Short, *The Dynamite War* (Dublin: Gill & Macmillan, 1979), pp. 180–1, 259–60.
16. 'Civilized Warfare', *The Irish World and American Industrial Liberator*, Saturday, 5 January 1884, p. 4.
17. 'Intense Excitement in England', *The United Irishman*, 3 January 1885, p. 1.
18. Established to counter republican activity in April 1883, the Special Branch was an offshoot of the CID, which had been monitoring Irish nationalists since 1867. The same month Parliament passed the Explosives Substances Bill, which updated the Explosives Act 1875, so as to prevent not only the illegal use of any 'explosive substance' but also to proscribe 'any apparatus, machine, implement, or materials used . . . or adapted for causing, or aiding in causing, any explosion'. Outlawing the possession of bombs and bomb components, the bill was a political measure as it made conspiracy to

cause explosions a crime and, the Tory press hoped, would 'discourage the future visits to the United Kingdom of the disciples of O'Donovan Rossa'. See Tony Bunyan, *The History and Practice of the Political Police in Britain* (London: Quartet Books, 1983), p. 104. See 'The Explosive Substances Bill', Editorial, *The Times*, Tuesday, 10 April 1883, p. 10.

19. 'The Dynamite War: A Well-Planned Engagement, and Brilliant Achievements of the Irish Forces', *The Irish World*, 14 June 1884, p. 3.
20. Ibid.
21. 'Irish Agitation in New York', *The Times*, Saturday, 12 April 1884, p. 11; *Illustrated London News*, Vol. lxxxiv, Saturday, 7 June 1884, p. 542; 'Reply by Dynamite', *The Saturday Review*, No. 1429, Vol. 55, 17 March 1883, p. 1.
22. *The Irish World*, 14 June 1884.
23. John Devoy, *Recollections of an Irish Rebel* (Shannon: Irish Universities Press, 1968; originally published New York: Chas D. Young, 1929), p. 212.
24. 'The Lesson of Dynamite', *The Irish World*, 21 February 1885, p. 2.
25. Michael Denning, *Mechanic Accents: Dime Novels and Working-Class Culture in America* (London: Verso, 1998), p. 119.
26. Subsequent citations are from J. D. Maginn, *Fitzgerald the Fenian*, 2 vols (London: Chapman and Hall, 1889).
27. The novel is, in fact, a fusion of two stories. It begins with a melodramatic romance, in which a moderate Fenian falls for the daughter of a landlord, and then adopts the plot convention of the dynamite novel, with a sub-narrative centring on Brady's plot to bomb London. When his plan fails, Brady returns to Ireland and turns his attention to Fitzgerald's father-in-law, but blows himself up before he can demolish the local big house and kill the county's Anglo-Irish elite. Quotations from Maginn, *Fitzgerald the Fenian*,Vol. 2, pp. 21, 259, 182, 222, 224, 227.
28. See Doyle, 'That Little Square Box' and 'Lot No. 249', in *Complete Sherlock Holmes & Other Detective Stories* (Glasgow: HarperCollins, 1994), pp. 1–13, quotations from pp. 4–5, 11; 444–65, quotations from pp. 445, 456.
29. Earlier in the century, colonialism in Ireland was directly criticised in Thomas Carlyle's 1840 pamphlet, 'Chartism', which denounced imperialism as a cursed endeavour and warned that the Irish had become, like the Egyptians would later in the century, part of 'our own wretchedness', bringing their political 'Curses' with them. See Thomas Carlyle, *Chartism* (Boston: Charles C. Little and James Brown, 1840), pp. 50–1.
30. 'Recent Novels', *The Times*, Wednesday, 9 June 1897, p. 11.
31. 'Explosion on the Metropolitan Railway', *The Times*, Tuesday, 27 April 1897, p. 9.
32. 'The Explosion on the Metropolitan Railway', *The Times*, Wednesday, 28 April 1897, p. 12; 'The Explosion at Aldersgate-Street Station', *The Times*, Tuesday, 25 May 1897, p. 15.
33. This we learn in Kernahan's 1906 sequel, *The Dumpling*, where Rissler also confesses to having an 'Irishman's love of fight'. See John Coulson Kernahan, *The Dumpling: A Detective Love Story of a Great Labour Uprising* (London: Cassell & Co., 1906), pp. 14, 207.

34. See John Coulson Kernahan, *A Literary Gent: A Study in Vanity and Dipsomania* (London: Ward, Lock & Co., undated), pp. 23–4, 47.

35. Doyle, *The Valley of Fear*, in *Complete Sherlock Holmes & Other Detective Stories*, p. 1204.

36. *Captain Shannon* presents counter-terrorism as a private pursuit rather than the business of the state, as does Arthur Conan Doyle's 1915 tale of Irish-American industrial violence, *The Valley of Fear*. Doyle's plot centres on the dismantling of a secret society called the Scowrers by an Irish Pinkerton detective (the group is modelled on the Molly Maguires, a militant organisation of Irish miners that was broken up by Pinkerton agents in Pennsylvania in the 1870s). Seeking revenge, the Scowrers contract the detective's assassination out to Professor Moriarty's criminal empire. The Pinkerton Detective Agency succeeds in infiltrating the Scowrers because it is 'a dead earnest business proposition' funded by 'all the millions of the capitalists' and not a mere 'take-it-or-miss-it Government concern', but Moriarty's assassins succeed in eliminating the spy because his criminal counter-corporation is a venture that 'cannot afford to fail' in its deadly line of business. See Doyle, *The Valley of Fear*, pp. 1270, 1261–2.

37. The villain's *nom de plume* suggests the rural unrest that gripped parts of Ireland throughout the nineteenth century, when threatening letters were issued under the signature of 'Captain Moonlight'. Thomas Moore's 1824 novel, *Memoirs of Captain Rock*, describes the 'eternal struggles', or endless dialectic of conflict, within which the Irish peasantry are portrayed as having locked themselves and criticises the 'abuse of Government' by agrarian rebels as a form of political terror. See Thomas Moore, *Memoirs of Captain Rock, the Celebrated Irish Chieftain, With Some Accounts of His Ancestors* (London: Longman, Hurst, Rees, Orme, Brown and Green, 1824), pp. ix, xi. The sobriquet Captain Shannon also echoes agrarian resistance to the automation of rural labour in England during the 1830s, when threatening letters were written under the pseudonym of Captain Swing. See Eric Hobsbawm and George Rudé, *Captain Swing* (London: Phoenix Press, 2001), esp. pp. 239–49.

38. Raymond Williams, *Culture and Society* (Harmondsworth: Penguin, 1971; first published, 1958), pp. 13–19.

39. Kernahan, *The Dumpling*, pp. 10–11.

40. L. Perry Curtis, *Jack the Ripper and the London Press* (New Haven and London: Yale University Press, 2001), p. 56.

41. 'Recent Novels', *The Times*, Wednesday, 9 June 1897, p. 11.

42. See Edgar Allan Poe, 'The Mystery of Marie Rogêt', in *Tales of Mystery and Imagination* (London: Dent, 2000), pp. 448, 450, 455, 460.

43. See Ben Singer, *Melodrama and Modernity: Early Sensational Cinema and Its Contexts* (New York: Columbia University Press, 2001), especially chap. 1, 'Meanings of Modernity' and chap. 2, 'Meanings of Melodrama'.

44. Walter Benjamin, 'The Paris of the Second Empire', in *Charles Baudelaire: A Lyric Poet in the Era of High Capitalism*, trans. Harry Zohn (London: Verso, 1997), p. 69.

45. Maginn, *Fitzgerald the Fenian*, Vol. 2, p. 237.

46. Benjamin, 'Paris – the Capital of the Nineteenth Century', in *Charles Baudelaire*, p. 169

47. Robert Louis Stevenson, 'Confessions of a Unionist: An Unpublished "Talk on Things Current"' (Cambridge, MA: privately printed, 1921), p. 11.

48. For a discussion of the relationship between content, form and politics in popular spy fiction written during the twentieth century, see Michael Denning, *Cover Stories: Narrative and Ideology in the British Spy Thriller* (London and New York: Routledge & Kegan Paul, 1987).

49. See Daniel Pick, *War Machine: The Rationalisation of Slaughter in the Modern Age* (New Haven and London: Yale University Press, 1993), p. 143.

50. 'The Dynamite Gun and Shell', *The Times*, Tuesday, 18 August 1885, p. 13.

51. 'Bring on Your Foreign Navies', *The Irish World*, Saturday, 29 March 1884, p. 3.

52. See 'The Trial of O'Donnell', *The Times*, 31 December 1883, p. 6; 'The Invincibles in Paris', *The Times*, Saturday, 12 April 1884, p. 5; 'Irish Agitators in New York', *The Times*, Saturday, 12 April 1884, p. 11; 'Foreign News: American Dynamiters in Ireland', *The Times*, Friday, 23 September 1887, p. 3.

53. 'The United States', *The Times*, Wednesday, 18 April 1883, p. 7. The Spanish socialist Narcis Monturiol first came up with the idea of using submarines for advancing utopian political purposes. See Matthew Stewart, *Monturiol's Dream: The Submarine Inventor Who Wanted to Save the World* (London: Profile Books, 2003).

54. In 1901 George Griffith wrote a similar but less politicised fantasy about submarine warfare, 'The Raid of the *Le Vengeur*', featuring a French submarine attack on the British fleet that is repulsed by light-beams and torpedoes. See George Griffith, 'The Raid of Le Vengeur', in Alan K. Russell (ed.), *Science Fiction by the Rivals of H. G. Wells* (New Jersey: Castle Books, 1979), pp. 85–97.

55. Greer was an unsuccessful Home Rule candidate for the North Derry constituency in the election of 1892. See Stephen J. Brown, *Ireland in Fiction: A Guide to Irish Novels, Tales, Romances and Folk-Lore* (Dublin: Maunsel, 1916), p. 98.

56. E. Douglas Fawcett, *Hartmann the Anarchist; or, The Doom of the Great City* (London: Edward Arnold, 1893), pp. 12, 66.

57. See George A. Birmingham, *The Red Hand of Ulster* (London: Smith, Elder & Co., 1912).

58. *The Irish World*, December 1875, quoted in K. R. M. Short, *The Dynamite War*, p. 38. The rhetorical appeal of dynamite never wore thin: by 1913 Thomas Clarke's IRB paper, *Irish Freedom*, was still hoping for 'a wonderful force that, working like dynamite, would blow up British rule in this country, leaving no trace here of the might of England, saving the shattered fragments of British institutions and creations and instruments of government'. The first signatory of the Proclamation of the Irish Republic, which was read at the launch of the Easter Rising of 1916, Clarke was executed by firing squad at the end of the rebellion. He served fifteen years in prison for his part in the dynamite campaign. See Louis N. Le Roux, *Tom Clarke and the Irish Freedom Movement* (Dublin: The Talbot Press, 1936), p. 118.

59. Anon, *Incipient Irish Revolution: An Exposé of Fenianism To-Day in the*

United Kingdom and America (London: Eglington & Co., 1889), preface, p. i.

60. See Paul Townend, '"No Imperial Privilege": Justin McCarthy, Home Rule, and Empire', *Éire Ireland: An Interdisciplinary Journal of Irish Studies*, 42: 1 & 2, Spring/Summer, 2007, pp. 201–28.
61. See Bill Ashcroft, Gareth Griffiths and Helen Tiffin, *The Empire Writes Back: Theory and Practice in Post-Colonial Literature* (London and New York: Routledge, 1989).
62. A. H., 'Notices of Books', *Dublin Review*, Vol. 14, No. 1, July 1885, p. 235.
63. 'Belles Lettres', *Westminster Review*, Vol. 124, No. 247, July 1885, p. 289.
64. C. E. Dawkins, 'New Novels', *The Academy*, 4 April 1885, p. 239.
65. 'Dynamite Operations in the United States', *The Times*, Wednesday, 5 July 1882, p. 4.

Chapter 3

Exploiting the Apostles of Destruction: Anarchism, Modernism and the Penny Dreadful

Dynamite is their argument!'
(Richard Henry Savage, *The Anarchist*, Vol. 1, p. 40)

In the 1892 potboiler, *The Anarchist: A Story of To-Day*, Richard Henry Savage distinguished anarchism from Irish nationalism by portraying it as a politically unreadable phenomenon. Focusing on its foreignness, he blamed the 'fleeing scoundrels' of Europe for radicalising American industrial workers, provoking riots and masterminding strikes across the modern industrialised world[1] (Vol. 2, p. 205). He observes that the 'reasonably quiet' Irish, on the other hand, avoid participating in the American class war and they are praised by the novel's hero, the tycoon, philanthropist and militia leader Philip Maitland, who advises his plutocratic colleagues: 'Say what you will of the Irish, they are not anarchistic!' (Vol. 2, p. 229).[2] In contrast to militant Irish republicans, late nineteenth-century anarchists seemed completely pathological in the eyes of contemporary conservatives and, as a result, their perceived heinousness earned them a special place in the right-wing imagination. These 'murderers of the State' (Vol. 2, p. 28) who were dedicated to causing the downfall of existing political and economic systems were, according to Savage's bourgeois logic, the 'mad apostles of Destruction' (Vol. 2, p. 228) whose radical ideas were beyond the comprehension of the rationally minded. Yet as they described themselves as people who 'no longer wish to obey the law',[3] it comes as no surprise that anarchists appeared so shocking to those with more mainstream political sensibilities. Promising to break entirely with every form of authority and even tradition itself ('We have heard of free trade, free religion, free rum, free love', wrote one of its American propagandists, and added: 'Anarchy is free everything'),[4] anarchists became associated with the enduring popular image of the bomb-throwing and knife-wielding terrorist. This popular perception was magnified and proliferated on an international scale as a result of the attacks carried out by European and American anarchists during the 1880s and 1890s, when cafés and theatres were bombed, heads of state assassinated and attempts made on the lives of industrialists and financiers. While these deeds were designed to expose what anarchists regarded as the essentially 'criminal'[5] nature of modern capitalism, they had an unavoidably negative impact on how anarchism was received and understood by the middle classes in Europe and the United States.

Propaganda by Deed

Impressed by the assassination of Tsar Alexander II by nihilists in St Petersburg in 1881, the anarchist Congress of London, held the same year, applauded terrorism, or 'propaganda by deed', as did the subsequent 'Black International' held a few months later in Paris.[6] But it was not until another decade had passed that systematic anarchist terrorism broke out in Europe when, from March 1892 until June 1894, the French capital was shaken by a wave of explosions that killed nine and injured dozens. This bombing campaign was not the work of a structured militant grouping like the Irish Fenians but was instead the work of independent revolutionaries including the alienated writer,Émile Henry, the failed entrepreneur Auguste Vaillant and the militant cabinet-maker Théodule Meunier. These solitary 'propagandists of the deed'[7] were united by a cold if rational analysis of the oppressive nature of capitalism. Inspired by the politically ambivalent figure of the criminal-turned revolutionary, François-Claudius Koeningstein, or Ravachol, a burglar and grave-robber-cum-anarchist, they represented in the popular imagination the 'incarnation of the revolt of the individual'.[8] They even provided the French language with a new verb, *ravacholiser*: 'to blow up'.[9] During his trial in 1891 Ravachol revealed what appeared to be the particularly capitalist motivation for his actions by explaining that he killed 'first of all to satisfy my personal needs, then to come to the aid of the anarchist cause'.[10] This ambivalence has been explained by Jeffory A. Clymer, who suggests that propaganda by the deed provided anarchists with a linguistic and conceptual metaphor of action and belief, both of which they regarded as indistinct phenomena. Clymer's analysis of the continuum between anarchist words and deeds stresses the importance of interpretation and meaning to revolutionaries in this period: pointing to the 'cultural work performed by a terrorist act', he suggests that they struggled first of all to gain discursive control of the event or act of political violence.[11] Resembling the literary struggles that were fought over the meaning of Fenianism in the 1880s, this cultural and political conflict occurred both in popular literature and in more 'highbrow' fiction, as well as in the columns of the popular press and in writings and proclamations issued by the anarchists themselves who used their trials and even the scaffold as platforms for their own contributions to 'the propaganda'.[12]

Ranging from the targeted assassination of heads of state to less discriminate attacks on middle-class diners, anarchist violence was designed to shock the politically enfranchised public and to frighten the national elites of Europe and the United States. When the anarchist labourer Léon-Jules Léauthier stabbed and gravely wounded a Serbian minister in Paris he worked upon the principle that 'I shall not be striking an innocent if I strike the first bourgeois I meet'.[13] Vaillant's spectacularly symbolic attack against the French political establishment consisted of bombing the Chamber of Deputies and yelling 'Long live anarchy!' on his way to the guillotine. He was followed by Henry who had already blown up a police station on the rue des Bon Enfants in reprisal for the quelling of a miners' strike at Carmaux (the device was originally planted in the mining company's offices in the avenue de l'Opéra but it was removed by police and exploded instead in a nearby gendarmerie, killing four officers). Henry avenged Vaillant by bombing the Café Terminus in the Gare St Lazare, so as to 'intrude among that concert of happy tones a voice the bourgeois had already heard but which they thought had died with Ravachol: the voice of dynamite'. One patron died and twenty were injured in the blast and Henry used his trial to justify terrorism by explaining that since the Carmaux miners were collectively punished by their employers, then there would, equally, be 'no innocent victims' in his own single-handed war against the state.[14]

Using his trial to stress the symbolic power of violence carried out by 'a man on his own', Henry described to the jury his reasons for carrying out the attack. By addressing them as 'gentlemen of the bourgeoisie', he indicated his own status as a martyr being tried by people whose class interests would ensure a guilty verdict. At the same time, he was coyly informing the court that he considered them as equally legitimate targets as his victims at the Terminus had been. 'I do not wish to develop on this occasion the whole theory of anarchism,' he explained, 'I merely wish to emphasize its revolutionary aspect, the destructive and negative aspect that brings me here before you'. As an anarchist, Henry felt compelled to blow up restaurants in order to destroy the corrupt 'illusion' of middle-class existence and reasoned that by bombing 'peaceful café guests, who sat listening to music and who, no doubt, were neither judges nor deputies nor bureaucrats', he had carried out a justifiable response to capitalism and its 'violations of freedom'. He even argued that the 'good bourgeois' deserved his share in the reprisals, and that this was why he attacked 'that stupid and pretentious mass of folk who always choose the strongest side – in other words, the daily clientele of Terminus and the other great cafés!' Anxious to shatter the dominant bourgeois reality with bombs, he targeted this conspicuous site of consumption – a place that, according to his militant logic, emblematised the current commercial morality where 'everything is base, everything is equivocal, everything is ugly, where everything is an impediment to the outflow of human passions, to the generous impulses of the heart, to the free flight of thought'. 'That' he declared, was 'why I struck at random and did not choose my victims!' Henry's attack was designed to show the middle-class public that 'henceforward their pleasures would not be untouched' and that it would suffer until it experienced the 'final shock' of a revolutionary millennium. Until then, this 'pitiless war' would continue because his deeds had shown the poor how to act. As he told the court, 'the starving are beginning to know the way to your great cafés and restaurants'.[15]

Henry's speech from the dock was the definitive statement of *fin-de-siècle* terrorism. Its explosive and explicitly violent language underlined his dialectic of unrestricted class warfare according to which café patrons, police, judges and jurors constituted, in the eyes of the anarchists, a single oppressive mass. But its logic was not as spontaneous or impulsive as it appears: his stress on the totality of this new kind of revolutionary politics ('it will end by killing you,' he told the jurors) was carefully structured and intended to cause as much shock and fear as his bombs did.[16] And while unsuspecting bourgeois were indiscriminately targeted in these restaurant attacks, even bigger game was being marked for assassination by more ambitious and unknown terrorists whose actions would terrify the political classes. The stabbing of President Sadi Carnot by Cesare Caserio in June 1894 marked the crescendo of propaganda by deed in France and set the revolutionary tempo for the rest of Europe: the Spanish prime minister, Antonio Canovas, was shot in 1897, Empress Elizabeth of Austria was stabbed to death in 1898, and in 1900 King Umberto of Italy was murdered while attending a country fête. These attacks on heads of state were accompanied by indiscriminate deeds in Spain, where in 1894 twenty died in an explosion in Barcelona's Liceo Theatre and more perished when the city's Corpus Christi procession was bombed in 1896. In the United States, anarchists were blamed for bombing police in Chicago's Haymarket Square in 1886. Alexander Berkman's unsuccessful attempt on the life of the industrialist Henry Clay Frick in 1892 was followed by the assassination of President McKinley, who was shot dead by a Polish anarchist, Leon Czolgosz. Britain, meanwhile, experienced its own anarchist scare with the bombing of the Greenwich Observatory in 1894, a relatively undistinguished event in comparison with these bloody *attentats*, but one that became famous for its literary rather than political consequences, as the premature explosion in which the unfortunately clumsy Martial Bourdin perished inspired Joseph Conrad's classic of modernist fiction, *The Secret Agent*. The same year also saw the discovery of a bomb plot against the London Stock Exchange and the firing of shots at the Speaker's house in Westminster.[17]

In the English translation of his 1894 best-seller,[18] *Le péril anarchiste*, the French journalist Félix Dubois warned his British and American readers that the 'hydra-headed' threat posed by anarchism could not be contained by traditional policing methods because its fanatical adherents were devoted to the 'spirit of individualism' and were not members of a political party.[19] The construction of the anarchist as an unstoppable individualist mirrors the self-definition of his sworn enemy, the capitalist, whose political and economic identity is also based on the concept of unrestricted movement and freedom of action.[20] This chapter begins by discussing how late nineteenth-century anarchism mirrored capitalism by demanding absolute independence from authority and tradition. Moving toward modernism through early twentieth-century popular fictions, including Edgar Wallace's *The Four Just Men* and G. K. Chesterton's *The Man Who Was Thursday*, anarchism is then read as the cultural and political source of an aesthetically productive breakdown of literary order. For example, H. G. Wells's 1897 political fantasy, *The Invisible Man*, reads the anarchist as an individual whose anonymity and relative ability to move at will through England and reflects contemporary concerns over the political identity of the figure of the revolutionary. Like Chesterton's fantasy, it also treats anarchism as an unreadable literary and political code.[21] I conclude by examining how this political chaos became fuel for literary modernism in Joseph Conrad's 1907 novel, *The Secret Agent*, and in his earlier short story, 'The Informer' (1906). The construction of the anarchist as an outsider, or 'alien fanatic' (Savage, Vol I, p. 262), worked on two levels, as his foreignness underlined his political strangeness but the cryptic quality of this identity lay in his or her attempt to completely transform society by overthrowing moral values as well as toppling existing political structures. This even included attacking the very concept of time, so central to the collection of shocking qualities that Conrad termed the anarchist's '*chambardement general*', or 'general blow-up', of the routine of bourgeois experience ('The Informer', pp. 92–3). Such politics made the anarchist a charismatically unreadable subject: like Wells's Invisible Man, whose transparent body symbolises the indecipherability of these radical ideas, this figure existed and performed beyond the ken of bourgeois and capitalist rationality. These enigmatic qualities, along with anarchism's capacity to inflict 'shock and alarm' (Savage, Vol. II, p. 255), made it an appealing fixture in popular literature, eventually attracting the attention of Joseph Conrad's modernist imagination.

Chaos, Capital, Culture

At the end of the nineteenth century the word 'anarchism' had a profoundly pejorative ring and was applied by conservatives to practically every shade of radical opinion.[22] However, the popular American novelist Richard Henry Savage went beyond this construction of socialism with his 1894 potboiler, *The Anarchist*, in which he compared the shocks of anarchist violence to the jarring and chaotic impact of modern industrial capitalism, which he portrays as sharing its revolutionary and anti-hierarchical principles. In this loosely cobbled-together novel, anarchists, the author insists, are not the only wreckers of 'creeds, codes ... (and) countries', and the reader is warned that these institutions are also threatened by the unlimited power of the 'self-made' plutocrat (Vol. 1, pp. 269, 14). Savage warns that American capital and its destructive 'money-riot' will undermine the integrity of the nation state as much as anarchists and their 'class attacks' against the wealthy (Vol. 1, pp. 16, 98). The unregulated 'maelstrom' of corporate finance is shown to mirror the 'red whirlpool' of anarchy (Vol. 1, pp. 57, 6), with Savage describing the 'damnable trade of terrorism' as an essentially commercial endeavour. Unusually for a conservative novelist, he portrays political violence as a symptom of widespread economic disorder and equates the 'shock of anarchy' with the 'nerve-destroying' powers of capital (Vol. 1, pp. 21, 39, 87). Savage even suggests that individuals become unpredictable 'human cannon-balls', transformed by the frantic energy and 'high explosive manner' of life under capitalism. Unlike the monarchical and more aristocratic systems of countries like Britain, where subjects prosper from the cultural and economic stability that have arisen from centuries of wise and benevolent rule, the modern nightmares of capitalism and democracy, he warns, promise to create a situation where 'every malcontent and rioter has his vote' (Vol. II, p. 27).

Savage's critique mirrors Peter Kropotkin's view of 'capital-rule', which found 'no ... unanimity about order, and still less about the "order" which is supposed to reign in our modern societies'. In

Kropotkin's opinion, capitalism had no unifying structure and operated under a false sense of order. Criticising the 'bourgeois age' for its 'frenzied' and unprincipled drift toward economic and political meltdown, he believed that the revolutionary individualism of the anarchist reflected the egoistic tendencies of the competitive capitalist. He even pointed to the usefulness of the economic and infrastructural 'net' that connected each of the different 'organizations for exploitation' to one another as the ideal vehicle for spreading revolutionary propaganda: while this grid reinforced the authority of capital it could, if put to use by revolutionaries and other 'better inspired' individuals, actually facilitate resistance. As a network of competing and decentralised systems, capitalism, with its unparalleled resources, presented the modern subject with the option of acting either 'in accordance with anarchist principles or on an opposite line'.[23] It was precisely because capitalism and its systems were designed to unlock human potential that its political other, anarchism, did not seem unrealistic to revolutionaries like Kropotkin but appeared by the close of the nineteenth century as a possible alternative to the existing political, economic and moral dispensations. With its promise of a new reality built upon capitalism's existing structures, anarchism seemed like a realistic possibility and opportunity to revolutionaries like Kropotkin and it was for the same reasons that it appeared so threatening to conservative writers like Savage and Dubois.

By comparing the 'modern lunatics' of the left with the equally modern 'demon' of plutocracy, Savage breaks down the political constructions that distinguish between capitalism and anarchy. He does so by arguing that the United States has 'no real permanence' because it is a country where 'government does not always govern' (Vol. II, p. 62; Vol. I, pp. 200, 176, 228). Capital is ungrounded, unstable and unanswerable to any centralised authority, sense of tradition or system of moral values, a fact recognised by another character, the corporate lawyer Edgar Alton, who complains that capitalist modernity, with its commercial imperatives is a political and cultural void with 'no beginning or end' (Vol. I, p. 226). Capitalism is portrayed as undermining the traditionalist logic of aristocratic rule by allowing the 'money autocrat' to go ahead and 'make his own crown'. The result is that self-reliant individualism and newly made wealth are as dangerous to the integrity of the state as the actions of any revolutionary (Vol. I, p. 97; II, p. 107). The unrestricted acquisition of wealth by these new rulers threatens to plunge the United States into chaos because it appears capable of dismantling the formerly intangible fabric of the state.

The epitome of the irrationality of revolutionary thought, anarchism is presented in an equally negative light as 'the final development of human brutality and insanity' (Vol. I, p. 260), Savage suggests that its anti-state ethos is grounded in cultural as well as political hatred for the bourgeoisie. The anarchists, who are out to 'undo the triumph of Time', are determined to vandalise culture itself by reducing 'all existing systems, and differences, to a dark plane of nothingness'. According to this logic, their plots are not straightforwardly political as Savage, like James, argues that their ideology opposes the 'slow emergence of arts, science, literature, and a cultured society' (Vol. II, pp. 63, 254–5). By constructing anarchism as a purely negative phenomenon, or 'nameless terror' (Vol. I, p. 86), Savage emphasises its mysteriousness and reinforces the notion that its political demands and proposals for radical change cannot be rationalised. But, for all of his anti-anarchist sentiment, Savage clearly states his belief that class warfare is an inevitable reaction to the 'cold and secretive' operation of capital. Unlike Kropotkin, however, he recommends state violence as a remedy (Vol. II, p. 25). America is threatened because its vulgar and self-invented elite lacks the necessary 'higher patriotism' with which to combat the threat of the international left. Founded upon 'culture, nobler thoughts and a distinctive moral elevation', patriotism becomes the weapon with which the stateless anarchists can be defeated because the class war is, for Savage, primarily a cultural one. America's financial masters are unequipped for this battle because they are 'less aesthetic' (Vol. I, pp. 176, 189) than the ruling classes of Europe (although European governments are criticised for exiling the masses of revolutionaries who destabilise the immigrant communities of the United States). As these villains are mostly highly educated individuals, they are perfectly placed and impeccably trained to infiltrate the upper echelons of American society by serving as professors and tutors to the offspring of the super rich. Thus, the German Jew Carl Stein ingratiates himself into the plutocratic circles surrounding the society beauty Evelyn Hartley by using his 'cultured erudition' to befriend her and unlock the 'secrets of politics' along with her wealth (Vol. I, p. 270). Stein involves a renegade Polish aristocrat, Stanislas Oborski, a 'compound of voluptuary, egoist and barbaric poet' (Vol. I, p. 203), whom he tries to marry off to the heiress in order to access her fortune for revolutionary ends. His plan fails when, after Maitland exposes the plot, Oborski is shot dead while attempting to murder Hartley, and Stein, who escapes after leading a failed industrial revolt in Cleveland, is killed in Europe. The novel closes with Maitland running for Congress, demanding stricter naturalisation laws, the establishment of a passport system and the imposition of government controls on the sale and distribution of high explosives.

Even by the standards of the late Victorian potboiler, *The Anarchist* has a flimsy, rather arbitrary feel as Savage uses the novel to deliver lengthy polemics on the dangers of capitalism and its potential to provoke revolution. Scenes and characters develop in a random, stagey fashion in order to serve the novel's principle function – the airing of the author's views. The plot ultimately suffers from Savage's tendency to forget that he is writing fiction rather than a monograph on the root causes of political violence. Yet this is precisely why *The Anarchist* is valuable as an artefact of late nineteenth-century literary culture; for all of its short fallings as a work of fiction it reveals the formal distortions that the popular novel could endure in its role as a vehicle for (as well as a chronicle of) contemporary political discourse. Despite Savage's obvious exploitation of the literary form of the novel, *The Anarchist* remains an unusual but entertaining example of political journalism masquerading as fiction.[24]

Frank Harris's 1909 novel, *The Bomb*, also deals with the American class conflict but is narrated from the perspective of the revolutionaries and is written in a less didactic style. Set during the events leading up to the 1886 Haymarket Square explosion in Chicago, Harris's 'new telling' (p. 184) of this episode in the history of anarchism counters the official narrative of the tragedy as established at the trial of the eight socialists who were accused of carrying out the attack. The bomb was thrown when police charged a demonstration called to protest against an earlier attack on striking workers demanding an eight-hour day. One officer was killed immediately (six more died from their wounds) and his colleagues proceeded to fire on the crowd and at each other. The exact number of protesters who died in the melee is uncertain (George Woodcock estimates it to have been over twenty)[25] and the tragedy sent shock waves across the United States, Britain and Europe. The Haymarket bomb also symbolised the transference of revolutionary power away from the urban mob and into the hands of the solitary terrorist because, as Jeffory A. Clymer has it, the explosion had a cultural impact: by shifting popular attention away from the collective agency of the crowd, it refocused anxiety by bringing to light the subversive individual's 'more invisible, more powerful, and more dangerous ability to commit specific and deadly acts of mass violence'.[26]

The Haymarket trial ended with the hanging of four socialists and the suicide of a fifth, Louis Lingg, in prison. Harris's fictionalised Lingg is a cultured revolutionary who believes that 'one good book is worth a thousand deeds' (p. 186), while the bomber, Schnaubelt, is also a literary figure who regards writing as 'proper' revolutionary work (p. 49). Unlike Savage's anarchists, who are the enemies of culture, Harris's are literary men who enjoy the 'modern pleasure' of reading and praise mass publishing for offering workers the freedom to achieve self-awareness and the power of expression: 'the greatest pleasure in one's life is reading ... Today the poorest can have dozens of masterpieces' (p. 89). Lingg also compares the aesthetic power of art to the politically symbolic force of terrorism:

> The writer ... tries to find a characteristic word; the painter some scene that will enable him to express himself. I always wanted a characteristic deed ... One should be strong enough to bend and constrain deeds to one's service, and they are more stubborn than words ... (p. 141)

The deed, then, is intended to function as a counter-shock designed to deflect the destructive tendencies of capitalism, which Lingg describes as having a putrescent effect upon workers, transforming 'flowers into manure' (p. 88). His theory of the aesthetic power of the political shock is graphically rendered when Harris describes the aftermath of the explosion:

> The street was one shambles; in the very centre of it a great pit yawned, and round it men lying, or pieces of men, in every direction, and close to me, near the sidewalk as I passed, a leg and foot torn off, and near lay two pieces of bleeding red meat, skewered together with a thigh-bone ... We saw fire-engines with police on them, galloping like madmen in the direction whence we had come. The streets were crowded with people, talking, gesticulating, like actors. Everyone seemed to know of the bomb already, and to be talking about it. I noticed that even here, half a mile away, the pavement was covered with pieces of glass ... (p. 155)

The grisly deed captures the popular imagination with its 'infectional' power (p. 164) while the city's news consumers are equally impressed by Linng's eloquent performance in court. This is, in turn, countered by the gratuitous publication of images of bombs by the mainstream press that gives the explosion a mediated afterlife, prolonging its trauma and symbolic currency. By recycling the horror of the original event, the newspapers repeat its violence for their readers and intensify the political fear reverberating across the city. As Clymer suggests, the constant coverage of the Haymarket trial by actual newspapers heightened tension by amplifying the threat of socialist violence and, via a voyeuristic process of 'ideological invocation', gave readers a sense of personal investment in the conflict of which this deed was a part by transforming them into involved spectators.[27]

Anarchist Modernism: *The Man Who Was Thursday*

The notion that anarchism contains aesthetic as well as political possibilities was also suggested, although from a radically different perspective, by G. K. Chesterton whose surreal 1908 novel of pseudo-anarchism and police-inspired intrigue, *The Man Who Was Thursday: A Nightmare*, fuses conservative politics with a decidedly experimental theme and structure (like Joyce's *Finnegans Wake* its narrative takes a circular, dream form). A far more avant-garde affair than its prefatory poem, 'To Edmund Clerihew Bentley' with its attack on the withering 'Green Carnation' of the aesthetic movement of the 1890s would suggest, Chesterton's tale offers a modernist interpretation of terrorism. The novel integrates the physics of the explosion with a more philosophical 'notion of a bomb' and compares these to the growth of artistic consciousness: 'It expands; it only destroys because it broadens; even so, thought only destroys because it broadens. A man's brain is a bomb . . . A man's brain must expand, if it breaks up the universe' (p. 63). Chesterton develops the destructive-creative dynamic associated with anarchist political thought as a thoroughly aesthetic matter and reads its revolutionary character both as a symptom of political modernity and as a generator of literary modernism. Despite his own dislike for 'chaos' (p. 11), he allows the 'anarchic' poet and committed Paterite, Lucian Gregory, to air this view:

> 'An artist is identical with an anarchist,' he cried. 'You might transpose the words anywhere. An anarchist is an artist. The man who throws a bomb is an artist, because he prefers a great moment to everything. He sees how much more valuable is one burst of blazing light, one peal of perfect thunder, than the mere common bodies of a few shapeless policemen. An artist disregards all governments, abolishes all conventions. The poet delights in disorder only. If it were not so, the most poetical thing in the world would be the underground railway.' (p. 10)

Gregory regards the interface between literature and revolutionary politics as an incendiary phenomenon. His views recall Walter Pater's theory of aestheticism as much as they do any kind of anarchist theory, repeating the master aesthete's stress on the momentary impact of the intense and 'elementary' power of art. For Pater, this aesthetic energy is most pronounced in the inner space of the artistic mind, which he describes as an 'inward world of thought and feeling', a rapidly turning 'whirlpool' or fire with a 'devouring' flame.[28] Gregory's political-aesthetic theory applies Pater's original stress on the intensity of aesthetic experience to the shock caused by the blast force of a bomb, which is more important to the artist-terrorist than the incidental matter of destroyed and 'shapeless' bodies. With this statement Chesterton reveals his belief that shock, chaos and uncertainty are the aesthetically productive constituents of modern experience.

The novel's hero, the amateur detective Gabriel Syme, defends the established order against the values represented by Gregory by stressing that he has little time for pre-Raphaelite posturing and its 'old cant of the lawlessness of art and the art of lawlessness' (p. 8). But this tale of modernity-as-nightmare, in which a 'neurotic' popular imagination is 'tickled' as well as terrified (p. 9) by anarchism, presents it as posing a problem for the literary intelligence as much as it does for the political imagination. Chesterton's construction of anarchism as an 'intellectual crime', or the product of 'knowledge you should never dream about' (p. 17), posed his own conservative catholic imagination with a number of contradictions as its 'visions from the verge' (p. 135) appear to inspire rather than confuse the modern mind. In this way, *The Man Who Was Thursday* suggests that anarchism is an inherently literary phenomenon as much as it is a political one, and that its revolutionary imperatives could provide inspiration for modernist practice. The novel's 'cultured discussion' of revolutionary politics (p. 135) interrogates the anarchist's destructively 'pure' thoughts (p. 57) as a form of modernist conscious-ness, so that, while Syme's swipe at aestheticism and revolutionary poli-tics underlines Chesterton's own political and religious conservatism, the novel also suggests that anarchy offers a suitably artistic position for the writer engaging with the 'attractive unreality' of modern experience to occupy. Thus Syme's infiltration of the anarchist Council of Days (the members of which all turn out to be police agents) introduces him to a 'capsized' and confusing universe (p. 81) where art and chaos meet during his pursuit across the French countryside by what he believes to be a mob of anarchists (who turn out to be conservative vigilantes). Syme takes refuge in a wood along with several fellow police agents where, camouflaged by broken patterns of 'shattered sunlight and shaken shadows', he experiences a living nightmare as the fractured light that illuminates the forest obscures his colleagues in a particularly modern play of brightness and shadow that reminds him of 'the dizzi-ness of a cinematograph'. His disrupted field of vision reveals one man's head 'lit as with a light of Rembrandt, leaving all else obliterated' while another's face is 'cut . . . so squarely in two that it seemed to be wearing one of the black half-masks of their pursuers'. The very nature of per-ception and the objective reality that it registers are brought into ques-tion by this confusion of light and shade that symbolises the contortion of objective material facts by conspiratorial politics. The detective finds himself in a shapeless, almost fluid reality, 'in which men's faces turned black and white by turns, in which their figures first swelled into sun-light and then faded into formless night, this mere chaos of chiaroscuro . . . seemed to Syme a perfect symbol of the world in which he had been

moving for three days' (pp. 124–5). The confusion of the scene is intensified by the disrupted sunlight that reflects the fractured, shifting quality
of an unstable modernist culture, which, Chesterton suggests, produces
an aesthetic condition founded on anarchic principle of revolt and its
result of fragmentation and disorientation. The linear conventions of the
popular romance narrative are taken apart in the forest where Syme's
surreal experience prevents him from distinguishing between his friends
and enemies. More importantly, the episode's destabilisation of perception mirrors the essentially chaotic quality of modern art and culture:

> Everything only a glimpse, the glimpse always unforeseen, and always forgot-
> ten. For Gabriel Syme had found in the heart of that sun-splashed wood what
> many modern painters had found there. He had found the thing which the
> modern people call Impressionism, which is another name for the final scepti-
> cism which can find no floor to the universe. (p. 125)

Syme experiences modernity through the eyes of an impressionist painter
and his field of perception appears as a confusion of visual signals.
Resembling a hybrid of the modern forms of cubism and impressionism, the aesthetic instability of this scene mirrors the political chaos of
anarchy, which Chesterton holds to be just as sceptical of philosophical,
aesthetic and political authority. By proffering its vision of modernity
as a series of unrelated and unstructured points of of sensation, impressionism counters the ability of the romance to represent reality, along
with its generally conservative ideological thrust. As a form of art it has
little if no tolerance for the high idealism associated with the conventions of romance or for finding a unifying narrative or meaning that can
rationalise experience according to bourgeois norms, forms that must,
according to Chesterton, be capable of providing a 'floor to the universe'
(p. 78). But despite his rejection of anarchism as an incomprehensible
belief, Chesterton's use of surrealism highlights the aesthetically productive meeting of literature and subversive politics.[29] His experimental,
non-linear narrative and the novel's labyrinthine plot both centre on
Syme's gradual discovery of the 'horrible meaning' of anarchy (p. 45),
which he unearths by experiencing a fragmented modernity where, as
another police spy tells him, the subjective consciousness is forever tested
by an unpleasant combination of abstraction and cruelty (p. 165).[30]

Like the moments captured by the impressionist painter, whose art
renders uncertain images of what is seen momentarily and indirectly,
the unsettling experience of modernity is amplified in this scene. This
also occurs earlier in the novel in Chesterton's representation of the
'inhuman landscape' of London, where estrangement, abstraction and
cruelty are characteristic experiences of modern urban subjectivity

(p. 49). The 'philosophical entities' of time, space and even being are repeatedly dissolved in Chesterton's metropolis, which appears to Syme as an 'unthinkable polygon'. Anticipating the impressionistic chaos that he experiences in the wood, his more explicitly political experience of the city's urban 'maze' (p. 74) lacks any discernible British characteristics, as Leicester Square becomes the base of European dynamiters and the 'headquarters of hell' (p. 53). Transformed into an 'alien' space, it is symbolic of the new modernist world that lacks political coherence and fails to provide adequate signs of native identity. This process of denationalisation reflects the disharmonious character of modernity because, for Chesterton, true anarchy lies in its uncertainty: as the complexities and contradictions of modern and metropolitan existence radically alter the terms upon which subjective consciousness is experienced, they also shift experiential focus away from the norm of a stable British identity and re-orient the subject in the direction of a disrupted, decentred and profoundly fractured identity. The confusion of the senses and the estrangement of subjectivity that is described in *The Man Who Was Thursday* registers the transformation effected in national culture by anarchism, which so many contemporary writers and readers took to be an inherently foreign and unassimilable belief. It appeared to Chesterton as a symptom of an unsynchronised modernity characterised by the failure of romantic idealism, disorientation, sensory shock and political anxiety.

Edgar Wallace's 1905 thriller, *The Four Just Men*, also addresses the slippage of Britain's 'national' character by questioning the increasingly chaotic quality of modern experience but, rather than focusing on the kind of psychological explored by Chesterton, Wallace exploits contemporary paranoia over immigration. The 1905 Aliens Act, which is fictionalised as the Aliens Political Offences Bill, provokes a cell of assassins known as the Four Just Men into acting against the British political establishment. Their plot against the Home Secretary, Sir Philip Ramon, whom they eventually assassinate within his 'anarchist-proof' office, allows Wallace to discuss these cultural and political concerns within the popular generic formula of the 'locked room' mystery. While the Four are never described as anarchists proper, their anonymity (they are 'four men whom no person had consciously seen' (p. 22)) functions as popular shorthand for the anarchist's politically subversive anti-identity; their only identifying trace is the tellingly Latin script left on their threatening letters and claims of responsibility.[31] Unrestrained by national borders, they kill for justice, executing politicians, generals, industrialists and even decadent poets across the globe. They introduce London to the decidedly continental methods of the 'coward alien and deadly anarchist' (p. 67) by planting a hoax bomb in Westminster, giving twentieth-century England its first taste of 'hidden terror': 'Why, argued London, with suspicious side-long glances, every man we rub elbows with may be one of the Four, and we none the wiser' (pp. 20–1). The presence of the 'Four Foreigners' (p. 24) makes continental anarchism appear not as reassuringly remote as it should in Briton's traditionally 'ungeographical' imagination (p. 22), and the supposedly unbreachable *cordon sanitaire* set up around Downing Street and Whitehall fails to protect the Home Secretary, who is electrocuted by a current transmitted along a telephone line. Wallace's novel discusses the impossibility of sealing domestic political space from 'alien' influences in an age of growing communication technologies and mass media, as the impact of the Four and their campaign is mediated by *The Daily Megaphone*, a newspaper based on Wallace's employer, *The Daily Mail*.[32] The novel also suggests that political modernity is collapsing the formerly clear cultural and political boundaries separating Britain from the continent, undermining even the internal perimeters that seal sensitive political spaces like Whitehall and Downing Street not only from penetration by the anarchist but also from the curious gaze of the assembled crowds who gather to witness the seemingly impossible assassination. This political locked-room mystery, then, offers a study in the impossibility of closing national space both to foreign political influence and to the rising power of the British masses.[33]

H. G. Wells and Anarchism

The theme of anarchism receives one of its most sustained treatments in H. G. Wells's 1897 novel, *The Invisible Man*, which explores the problems posed by the illegibility of terrorism. In this political fantasy, violence results from the failure of an aspiring but unsuccessful bourgeois, Griffin, whose experiments in invisibility have led to isolation rather than fame and professional acceptance. It was not the first story in which Wells explored this theme: two of his earlier stories, 'The Stolen Bacillus' and 'The Diamond Maker', both published in the *Pall Mall Budget* in 1894, also dealt with anarchism.[34] The former yarn is a satire on revolutionary individualism; the titular bacillus, supposedly a cholera culture, is shown to an anarchist who plans to use it to infect London's water supply but the terrorist's true motivation is his competitive desire to outdo his comrades. In his quest to outdo these unprepared 'rascals' and 'blind fools' who use bombs when indiscriminate chemical warfare is possible (p. 4), he mirrors his enemy, the capitalist entrepreneur:

No Anarchist before him had ever approached this conception of his. Ravachol, Vaillant, all those distinguished persons whose fame he had envied dwindled into insignificance beside him. He had only to make sure of the water supply, and break the little tube into a reservoir . . . The world should hear of him at last. (p. 6)

Intent on martyrdom, the anarchist drinks some of the sample and walks off, yelling 'Vive l'Anarchie!', unaware that he has ingested a harmless bacteria rather than a deadly strain of cholera. Such parodies of radicalism were common during the late Victorian and Edwardian periods,[35] and with this story Wells pandered to the popular construction of anarchism as morbid irrationality. But in 'The Diamond Maker' he looked more closely at the relationship between capitalism and anarchism, exploring the politics of the 'transitional age' during which these stories were written. It begins with a chance encounter between a tramp and an investor. The tramp, claiming to have a 'big business in hand', describes his attempt to manufacture synthetic diamonds, but as a non-person who is paradoxically marked by his undistinguished status, his claim amuses the capitalist who wants to know if he has 'anything to tell . . . worth the money' (pp. 48–9). The tramp does, revealing that he had planned to make a fortune by producing the diamonds *en masse* by mixing high explosives, South African clay and a carbon compound inside a strong steel cylinder that he heated until it exploded. Accused by a drunken neighbour of being a 'Structive scoundrel' and 'Nerchist', he flees and his laboratory is raided by the police who, on finding his materials, believe him to have been making pipe bombs.[36] Forced underground and having to make himself socially invisible, the tramp is denied a prosperous life along with the chance of experiencing the upper class prerogative of 'gratification in display' (p. 49).

In the figure of the Invisible Man, we find a political villain whose invisibility mirrors the Diamond Maker's lack of social status. While Griffin's condition has traditionally been read as signalling the early Wells's views on science,[37] it is clear the novel was written in an allegorical mode. Wells presents invisibility as a political 'idea' with revolutionary potential, 'the mystery, the power, the freedom' of which (p. 84) leads inevitably to violence. In carrying out his research into invisibility, Griffin is really exploring the limitations imposed upon will by modern capitalist society, and, in doing so, he reveals that its political potential could rival capitalism's logic of material transformation: 'This was not a method, it was an idea, that might lead to a method by which it would be possible, without changing any other property of matter – except in some instances, colours – to lower the refractive index of a substance, solid or liquid, to that of air . . .' (p. 81). With his experiments the

Invisible Man applies rather Marxian principles to the phenomenon of material devaluation, something that he compares to the transformation of a discernibly precious commodity like 'a valuable stone' into something worthless. By applying this kind of political economy to himself through the allegorical means of his fantastic experiments, he achieves his condition of 'personal invisibility' (p. 81). In politically metaphorical terms he embodies the reduction of the individual's social value which is based, as the wealthy narrator of 'The Diamond Maker' makes clear, on one's *apparent* economic status. Both Griffin and the tramp men are associated with anarchism by Wells because they vanish from the deliberately visual bourgeois public sphere.[38] Threatening nineteenth-century bourgeois culture, invisibility is configured by Wells as the result of capital but, nonetheless, it is a threat that must ultimately be contained. Invisibility was also seen by political writers to have subversive ramifications: in *The Psychology of Revolution*, published in English in 1895, Gustave Le Bon warned that 'invisible powers' and 'invisible forces'[39] were directing revolutionary socialism, while Mikhail Bukunin described the anarchist movement as an 'invisible dictatorship' which, lacking 'insignia, titles, or official rights', was 'all the stranger for having none of the paraphernalia of power'.[40] Along with Le Bon's theory of the subversive potential of the unseen, Bakunin's description of anarchism as 'a force that is invisible, that no one admits'[41] indicates how the concept of invisibility had become political shorthand for this particular brand of revolutionary subversion prior to the publication of *The Invisible Man*.

Whereas 'The Diamond Maker' closes with the tramp entertaining the hope that some day he might be able to enter the world of commerce, the Invisible Man quickly decides to attempt to destroy the system that has ruined him. Critics have tended to view his campaign against the village of Port Burdock as a pathetic and preposterous affair,[42] and, in so doing, have overlooked the fact that with this short novel the early H. G. Wells offered an allegorical critique of the complexities facing British radicalism in the 1890s. The political problems that are raised in *The Invisible Man* are never resolved but by drawing attention to the lone, alien and rampantly revolutionary ego of the terrorist, and to the responsibilities that he imagined were facing British workers as a result of this threat, Wells raised difficult questions about how the proletariat and the middle classes should respond to the two major strands of contemporary revolutionary thought – collective socialism and the ungovernable, individualist tendencies of anarchism. Griffin's anarchic rampage against society culminates with his unsuccessful attempt to control the village of Port Burdock, where he tries to realise his 'brutal dream of a terrorised world' (p. 119) by threatening the locals and then challenging the British state, which he plans to replace with a revolutionary dictatorship.

After arriving at the village of Iping, where he has a suggestively 'explosive' argument with his landlady (p. 18), the Invisible Man is quickly suspected by the villagers of setting up a bomb factory in his rooms. Taken for 'an Anarchist in disguise' (p. 19), these allegorical hints at the Invisible Man's political origins underline the explicitly subversive character who emerges later in the novel to threaten Sussex with a Jacobin 'Reign of Terror' (p. 115). Announcing 'day one of year one of the new epoch – the Epoch of the Invisible Man', Griffin declares a new revolutionary calendar for England and the first day of terror begins with treason: 'Port Burdock is no longer under the Queen', according to Griffin, but has become subject to the alternative sovereignty of 'Invisible Man the First' (p. 123). Wells's use of political metaphor continues when he describes the scene at Dr Kemp's house which, after being wrecked by Griffin, is left resembling the scene of 'a violent riot' (p. 131). For Wells, clearly, the Invisible Man represents the destructive potential of undisciplined revolutionary power.

Griffin's alien or 'out-cast' identity (p. 113) is underlined by the entries found by the locals in his diary, where his scientific notes are kept. Containing notes in Russian, Greek and even cipher, the diaries, with which the novella closes, are unreadable to the locals but they carry more symbolic freight than at first appears. The records of his experiment in invisibility are, like anarchism, unreadable and exotic phenomena that suggest Griffin's closeness to exotic and terroristic forms of European radical thought like nihilism.[43] But despite his metropolitan origins, the Invisible Man has great difficulty moving around urban settings. Before turning on Kemp, he reveals to the scientist that he had to leave London because the very matter of the city undermined his invisibility, with pollution and smog restoring him to a 'greasy glimmer' of residual visibility (p. 106). His adventure begins with some negative encounters with 'sordid commercialism' – a series of scrapes that ends in a failed sequence of arson, robbery and violence (p. 84). Recalling how he was confronted by the spectacle of commodity capitalism in London, he describes lying low in the shopping arcade, Omniums, after first becoming invisible and burning his lodgings. His fugitive presence in a 'big establishment where everything is to be bought' (p. 99) reveals that his campaign has been launched during a period of profound political and cultural change in which the ethos of the politicised individual is being displaced by the rise of mass consumerism. Forced to spend his first night as the Invisible Man in retail premises, he fails to realise that the commercial purpose of the site is eroding the kind of political activity that he now stands for. Competing with capitalism, which also 'trades' on the striking imagery of its publicity strategies, the anarchism that he represents is, as Wells suggests, about to be displaced by the more flexible methods of modern consumer culture. In a later essay, 'The Labour Unrest', published in 1912, Wells warns that this process was eroding the collective loyalty and stability of the working class, a phenomenon that he cites as having begun during the 1870s and peaked by the 1900s; offering workers 'luxury, amusement, aimlessness, and excitement', capital, with its inexhaustible 'parade' of commodities could only disappoint the poor of Britain. Wells regarded its vulgar 'Spectacle of Pleasure' as a blind constructed to distract the population from the onset of 'real and irreparable class war', a crisis that would provoke 'anarchistic' crimes by the poor. Although this essay was composed fifteen years after the publication of *The Invisible Man*, it shares Wells's earlier concerns with the pressures of modern commodity capital, as its ethos of provocatively conspicuous consumption seems designed to goad 'insurgent'[44] revolutionaries in the twentieth century as much as it does the Invisible Man, who is forced to loot the emporium for clothes and to fight with its staff (p. 104).

Rural Sussex proves to be as restrictive a place as London for the Invisible Man as Kemp sets out to mobilise the entire community against him. Wells's model of a conservative pastoral England resembles the treatment accorded to Scotland by John Buchan in his 1913 novel, *The Thirty-Nine Steps*, in which the fugitive Richard Hannay becomes implicated in an anarchist plot to destabilise international relations. Pursued across the seemingly unlimited Scottish countryside, 'a wide green world with glens falling on every side and a far-away blue horizon', both by terrorists and the police, Hannay finds to his horror that even in the illimitable highlands he has nowhere to hide: 'there was not cover in the whole place to hide a rat', he discovers. Starting to 'suffocate' in the deceptively open spaces of the glens, he realises that the 'free mooorlands were prison walls, and the keen hill air was the breath of a dungeon' as Scotland, like rural England in *The Invisible Man*, turns out to be a model of surveillance and containment.[45] Once Griffin commits murder, he meets the same difficulties faced by Hannay and is transformed from being 'a legend, a terror' into a 'tangible antagonist, to be wounded, captured, or overcome' (p. 119). Kemp prevents the Invisible Man's escape by causing a stoppage of goods traffic, and by restricting the flow of commodities in this part of England, he traps the anarchist. As in the commercialised space of Omniums, where Griffin thought he could evade detection by hiding among shop displays, his ability to traverse rural space is also limited by the modalities of commodity culture.

Forced to return to the unwelcoming environment of a country town, Griffin is eventually brought to ground in Port Burdock by a group of navvies who, rushing to save Kemp, capture the Invisible Man and beat him to death. The anarchist's intentions remain illegible to these men as, in death, his political obscurity is embodied by the 'dim outline' of his now partially visible corpse (p. 135). Like Chesterton, who believed that 'not many working men are anarchists' (*The Man Who Was Thursday*, p. 126), Wells regarded British the British working class as stable and politically reliable. Griffin is only contained when he is finally defeated by labourers whose loyalty provides reassuring closure to this political tale. Paradoxically, by defending England from the threat posed by the political alien, who is presented throughout the novel as a grotesque 'stranger' (p. 5), a crowd of urban workers, the very entity that also seems to give rise to political spectres like the anarchist, brings a gruesome end to his campaign of super individuality. Shortly before the publication of *The Invisible Man*, Gustave Le Bon theorised that the collective would always outmatch the individual because modernity undermined the 'conscious activity of individuals' and facilitated the 'unconscious' and therefore dangerous action of crowds.[46] This sociological observation is reversed by Wells, who portrays the unthinking bravery and violence of the collective as the basis of political order (he would in later years suggest replacing the nineteenth century's 'sublimation of individuality' with the more anonymous machinery of the World State).[47] The fragmented modern society that was replacing the traditional and more coherent pattern of English rural life in the 1890s[48] appears disruptive in *The Invisible Man*, but in this tale the superimposition of modern urban political patterns on rural England by the individualistic anarchist is shown to be doomed to failure.

Conrad, Anarchism and *The Secret Agent*

The fictions examined so far exploit the strangeness of anarchism and the shocks of revolutionary violence by showcasing its disruption of political norms, and consider how these impacted upon contemporary literary conventions. Joseph Conrad's 1907 novel, *The Secret Agent*, dwells upon anarchism as a kind of literary intervention that carries a particularly modernist resonance, as its revolutionary demands are portrayed as bearing considerable cultural utility. Like James, Conrad treats anarchism as a phenomenon that grows almost organically out of the London streets. His treatment of the aesthetic value of political chaos links these popular texts with the more highbrow concerns of modernism, which was originally intended to shock readers into questioning established literary values. The connection is explicit, as Conrad experimented with this theme less than a year before the publication of *The Secret Agent* in a melodramatic short story of 1906, 'The Informer', which appeared in *Harper's*. The tale narrates the downfall of an undercover police agent who has infiltrated an anarchist cell and falls in love with an idealistic young woman who allows the terrorist group to use her property as, among other things, a bomb factory. As John Batchelor has shown, Conrad wrote 'saleable' romances like this when he was under financial pressure[49] but as well as satisfying his own commercial needs the story also served as a skillful negotiation of a less apparent theme: the contiguous and mutually profitable exchange between anarchist politics and the aesthetics of modernism. Constructed around a series of interviews between Conrad's framing narrator and the sinister anarchist 'X', who is also a collector of Chinese bronzes and porcelain, 'The Informer' considers the relationship between publicity and political violence while also testing the limits of romance. Renowned as a 'destructive publicist' and the greatest 'insurgent (*révolté*) of modern times' (p. 92), X professes the shocking belief that '(t)here's no amendment to be got out of mankind except by terror and violence' (p. 94). Yet with this figure, Conrad subverts the contemporary 'popular idea' of the anarchist as a lunatic, armed with 'a dagger in one hand and a dynamite bomb in the other'.[50] With X, Conrad suggests that terrorism is in fact the product of more refined, sophisticated and culturally attuned sensibilities than the stereotype admits. An essentially bourgeois character, he appears 'beautiful' to the narrator who is taken by his 'polished' manner and finds him 'in a sense even exquisite', conferring aesthetic value upon X despite his reputation as a 'monster' (p. 94).

'The Informer' also addresses the political illegibility of the anarchist and his beliefs as the narrator fails to rationalise X's 'simply inconceivable' character, to which he cannot relate 'mentally, morally, logically, sentimentally, and even physically' (p. 110). As the 'mysterious unknown Number One of desperate conspiracies suspected and unsuspected, matured or baffled' (pp. 91–2), X's background smacks of Fenianism, but these enigmatic qualities also suggest the modernist qualities of the cultured anarchist. The story's articulation of a dialogue between modernism and revolution is highlighted by the collector's fascination with the terrorist: while his own life is structured upon the more 'suave and delicate discrimination of social and artistic values' (p. 94), X blurs these distinctions by fusing his political beliefs with his highly developed appreciation of beauty. 'The Informer' begins by drawing attention to the interface between aesthetics and violence, suggesting that the anarchist's shocking political values can mirror the literary pursuits of the modernist. Until the publication of this story anarchism was – with the notable exception of *The Princess Casamassima* – the concern of sensational literature that combined lurid thrills with the contemporaneousness of its subject matter. Whereas Conrad pointed to the connection between anarchism and culture, James, as we have seen in Chapter 1, viewed the two as antagonistic formations. The distinction between politics and culture is much less certain in 'The Informer', as Conrad's anarchist is as dedicated to the destruction of political systems as he is to the preservation of the collectables that are their finer material products. The narrator is introduced to X by a fellow collector and thinly disguised caricature of Ford Madox Ford[51] who is engaged in the 'delicate' work of accumulating distinguished acquaintances. This 'true collector of curiosities' keeps a mental record of his 'subjects' that is suggestive of the recently introduced archival policing methods pioneered by Francis Galton and Alphonse Bertillon: 'He observes them, listens to them, penetrates them, measures them, and puts the memory away in the galleries of his mind'. Through his interest in these human 'specimens' (as opposed to the commodities acquired by the narrator and by X) he familiarises himself with people whose 'value' goes unrecognised by 'the vulgar' and whose real worth remains 'unknown' because it cannot be read according to the standards by which society measures 'popular fame' (p. 91). The narrator, who specialises in rare objects rather than interesting individuals, is nonetheless eager to acquire some of X's political knowledge for his own cerebral *wunderkammer*. By discussing the proximity of popular commodity culture, represented by the collector of oriental artefacts, to the intellectual sphere populated by esoteric curiosities like the anarchist, Conrad suggests that terrorism invests itself with considerable cultural purchase. The allure of the anarchist lies in his personal symbolic capital that, for the narrator, is analogous with the collectability of the objects that he acquires, making X appear like a markedly strange product of contemporary political culture. Unlike the objects that he hoards, this 'rare item' (p. 114) cannot be categorised in accordance with normal bourgeois value. X is deemed 'monstrously precious' (p. 93) by virtue of his possession of valuable 'underground' knowledge (p. 96) that cannot be assimilated into the narrator's materialist imaginary. His passion for 'collecting things which are rare, and must remain exquisite even if approaching the monstrous' (p. 93), suggests that the secret knowledge that X effectively sells in the process of disclosure resists being categorised or stored according to bourgeois norms.

X's belief in the 'necessity of the *chambardement general*', or 'the general blow-up', leaves the 'routine acts' of a stable bourgeois life, such as having a family or collecting commodities like bronzes and china pieces, 'quite out of the question' for him (pp. 92–3). This renders him unintelligible to the narrator who cannot read any kind of rational motivation in his desire to disrupt rather than accumulate. The radical possibilities that he represents contradict the narrator's values but what makes the revolutionary appear truly monstrous is his realisation that he shares his cultural and class identity with him: 'He was alive and European; he had the manner of good society, wore a coat and hat like mine, and had pretty near the same taste in cooking. It was too fright-ful to think of' (pp. 93–4). Looking, behaving and even eating like a bourgeois, X's indulgent lifestyle and nefarious political activities are supported by the profit that he makes from the commercial sale of his writings (books that 'were at one time the rage, the fashion – the thing to read with wonder and horror' (p. 95)). Like the subversively named *bombe glacée* ice cream with which he ends his meal, these publications are designed to titillate middle-class consumers inexperienced in the art of revolution. By reading his books they gain a voyeuristic insight into the thrills of 'sheer terror', by which '(a)ll other sensations' are 'swept away' (p. 105). Like Conrad himself, X enjoys the irony of plying his popular readers, whom he considers mere 'amateurs of emotion' (p. 95), with literary shocks that exploit their fascination with political violence.

X describes how the middle class's love for 'mischief . . . even if it is made at its own expense' underlines its misunderstanding of the basic symbolism of political violence. Its own essentially artificial existence, 'being all a matter of vestment and gesture', prevents it from appreciat-ing 'the power and danger of real ache'. X describes how these sensa-tions can only be expressed by 'words that have no sham meaning', without which readers experience a shielded encounter with the world of revolution. This criticism of middle-class values allows Conrad to explain the imaginative power of terrorism in the words of a fictional anarchist whose writings mirror the purpose of 'The Informer', a story that itself is designed to flatter the bourgeoisie's 'silly vanity' with its pseudo-romantic plot. Conrad, like X, plays to the desire of his popular readership to become conversant with chic doctrines and the 'ideas of the day after tomorrow', and X even recognises this weakness in the narrator, whom he warns that collecting satisfies equally shallow desires among those who are incapable of appreciating the genuine 'marvellous-ness' of his artefacts (p. 95). Like the narrator's specialised knowledge of oriental objects and the equally refined field of literary modernism, the real meaning of anarchism is unsuitable for popular consumption and can only be understood by the initiates of a higher, more elite culture.

Whereas Henry James regarded anarchism as threatening the necessary boundary between 'the common and the rare' (p. 115), Conrad's story ends with the collector of acquaintances reassuring the narrator that this 'unique' terrorist and his disturbing tale of the unfortunate police spy is 'worth knowing' (p. 114). With its affirmation of the finer knowledge of those who, like the gently caricatured Ford, are both aesthetically *and* politically aware, this short story discusses anarchism as an intellectual and literary matter that is beyond the cognitive scope of mainstream materialist consciousness. While James advised the rigid separation of literary and political culture into separate spheres that could be policed by guardians of culture like himself, Conrad acknowledged anarchism's potential as a source for modernist production.

When Conrad wrote to his agent, J. B. Pinker, to stress that *The Secret Agent* was not intended for consumption 'on popular lines'[52] he tried to distinguish his signally modernist novel from the shilling shocker genre of terrorist fiction. Unlike these popular works in which anarchism appears as the negative underside of modernity, Conrad explored it as an aesthetically productive phenomenon. The notion that anarchism cannot be processed by rational logic is suggested by the detective, Chief Inspector Heat, who ruminates over the human remains found at the scene of the explosion around which Conrad's plot centres:

> The echo of the words 'Persons unknown' repeating itself in his inner consciousness bothered the Chief Inspector considerably. He would have liked to trace this affair back to its mysterious origin for his own information. He was professionally curious. Before the public he would have liked to vindicate the efficiency of his department by establishing the identity of that man. He was a loyal servant. That, however, appeared impossible. The first term of the problem was unreadable – lacked all suggestion but that of atrocious cruelty. (p. 108)[53]

The death under investigation is that of the brother-in-law of the police informer, embassy spy and *agent provocateur*, Adolf Verloc. The young victim, Stevie, is an innocent in every sense whose gruesome death links the enigma of anarchist politics to the aesthetic concerns of modernism. Echoing John Littlechild, the Scotland Yard detective who distinguished between the 'inventive genius' of the ordinary criminal and the political motivation of the terrorist,[54] Heat's view of anarchism is that it is an 'unreadable' phenomenon that exists outside the norms not just of legality but also outside the very terms according to which crime itself is understood. Unlike the burglar or pickpocket the anarchist has no financial motivation and is therefore impossible to classify. Heat's definition of anarchism as a mystery that defies the economic logic of crime proper conveys more than a hint of modernism's relationship with mass-market literature.

As is well known, the event that that inspired *The Secret Agent* was the explosion of 15 February 1894 that killed the young French anarchist, Martial Bourdin, who was brother-in-law to the pamphleteer and police agent, H. B. Samuels. Bourdin died when, while making his way through Greenwich Park to the Observatory, he tripped over a tree-root and accidentally set off his bomb. The improvised device, consisting of a glass-bottle casing containing an acid time fuse, explosives and iron shrapnel, was also sensitive to shock and the blast blew off Bourdin's hand and tore open his stomach. He succumbed to his injuries in less than an hour and a police search of his clothes found £13 in getaway money, a document providing bomb-making instructions and Bourdin's membership card for the Autonomie Club on the Tottenham Court Road. The explosion focused already heightened anxiety over the presence of foreign anarchists in Britain: *The Times* declared that London was the 'headquarters' of international anarchism thanks to a lax asylum policy that 'disquiets honest men in England'. Perhaps the explosion, the paper speculated, would discourage the 'comfortable belief that . . . Anarchists will do nothing to impair their asylum' as the incident had forced the Home Office to turn its attention to the presence in London of revolutionaries 'who have waged war against society in Paris, in Barcelona, and in other places on the Continent'. The police were, it noted, about to close in on the foreign 'miscreants' who until now had enjoyed immunity 'so long as the actual "operations" had been excluded from British soil'. The British public, *The Times* claimed, was now prepared to abandon its illusions about these 'desperadoes' and accept the reality that it faced a domestic threat posed by the presence on English soil of alien troublemakers like Bourdin.[55]

In *The Secret Agent* Conrad used the Greenwich Park tragedy to depict terrorism as the manipulation of the public imagination by governments and subversives alike, with both sides in the political struggle participating in a political simulation, or 'game' and behaving as if they are, as one of the anarchists puts it, 'identical' entities or products of 'the same basket' (p. 94). The mystery surrounding the explosion, along with the provenance of Bourdin's symbolic target, appealed to Conrad's modernist imagination as he depicts the bomb as a carrier of violent ideas and a 'means of expression' (p. 67) that is designed to shock. Greenwich was chosen as the Prime Meridian during the 1884 International Meridian Conference and the actual explosion seemed to have been planned to undermine the very concept of uniform public time. Bourdin's attempt on the very site that provided late nineteenth-century modernity with a centralised chronological framework (fixed time-keeping facilitated the flow of capital through time and across geographical space)[56] allowed Conrad to explore terrorism as an attack on both bourgeois rationality and the very fabric of capitalist reality.

Conrad's political doubling is most evident in his comparison of the official terrorist and boorish Russian diplomat, Vladimir, with the moral nihilism of the novel's 'perfect anarchist', the Professor (p. 103),[57] in whom we also find something of a perfect modernist. Both characters' reflection of one another's values and concepts is inevitable since it is Vladimir who dreams up the 'idea' of a conceptually flawless and 'purely destructive' demonstration against science (pp. 64, 67) and it is the Professor who provides his scheme with the required explosives. The pair never meet but their intentions neatly collide with brilliant Conradian irony in Stevie's fatal stumble at the Greenwich Observatory. In his coldly rational and politically reactionary lecture to Verloc, Vladimir warns the *agent provocateur* that he wants no less than to blast the British middle classes out of their complacency with the 'startling fact' (p. 61) of an outrage against their most 'sacrosanct' object: science. The 'source of . . . material prosperity' and held by Vladimir to be the popular 'fetish' of the British public (p. 67), it is, like the bomb that kills Stevie, vulnerable to shock, or so he believes. The attack is intended by the diplomat as the first in a series of outrages that will persuade the British to support coercive measures against the anarchists who are enjoying political asylum in England, and he contends that the dreamed-up pseudo-campaign will also rejuvenate an ongoing international anti-anarchist conference in Milan, where the slowness of proceedings is frustrating his government. By causing an explosion in a building representative of the framework within which capitalism works, Valdimir intends to portray anarchists as having gone 'beyond the intention of . . . terrorism' (p. 66) by carrying out as 'an act of destructive ferocity so absurd as to be incomprehensible, inexplicable, almost unthinkable; in fact, mad' (p. 67). As Heat's reaction shows, his plan succeeds.

Requiring 'all the shocking senselessness of gratuitous blasphemy' (p. 67) (he dismisses the possibility of bombing the National Gallery as lacking sufficient seriousness), Vladimir's almost juvenile plot to create 'a jolly good scare' is rich in irony. His desire to capture the popular imagination by engineering a 'psychological moment' (p. 64) by assaulting the principle of unified, coordinated time also has a distinctively modernist quality. The Russian's plan to make a 'clean sweep of the whole social creation' (p. 66), echoes an earlier statement of Conrad's in which the author revealed his own appreciation of literature's capacity to cause shock. In an important letter written to the critic Edward

Garnett ten years prior to the publication of *The Secret Agent*, Conrad explained that the written word has, at once, a creative imperative and a decidedly subversive quality: 'the illumination, the short and vivid flash' of 'words', he wrote, explodes 'like stored powder barrels ... An explosion is the most lasting thing in the universe. It leaves disorder, remembrance, room to move, a clear space'.[58] For Conrad the experience of reading had the potential to transform the imagination with an explosive violence that, despite its momentary existence, leaves permanent impressions on the psyche. Conrad's modernist theory of aesthetic renovation, achieved through the violence of language, is echoed by Vladimir's desire to shock the British public; like the modernist writer intent on revolutionising literature by dint of the sheer energy of his art, the diplomat's planned series of unreadable and excessively violent statements will be distinguished by the intensity of its 'shocking senselessness'. In its very incomprehensibility, the 'absurd ferocity' of an attack on the meridian will, he believe, influence the English public more thoroughly than the explosion of a bomb on a busy street or in a theatre. The symbolic, disruptive power of this deed lies in its very negativity and its worth is measured in terms of its impact as an offence against knowledge and culture, as the explosive concept of 'blowing up ... the first meridian' will prove more outrageous even than throwing a bomb 'into pure mathematics' (pp. 67–8). Of course, Vladimir's model of propaganda by deed presents Verloc with the problem of having to handle such a provocative statement of excess that, as the informer correctly expects, will prove far too clever for its own good.

The novel closes with Vladimir's subversive other, the Professor, walking away from the debacle caused by Vladimir. Moving, 'unsuspected and deadly, like a pest in the street full of men' (p. 269), he is, despite his professed opposition to humanity, a modern man of the crowd, finding the kind of solitude in anonymity that Benjamin described Baudelaire experiencing among the urban masses.[59] In his cameo appearance in 'The Informer', we find him developing new bomb technology (these devices prove his eventual undoing) and experimenting with the high explosives that provide him with 'his faith, his hope, his weapon, and his shield' (p. 103). The Professor bears more than a passing resemblance to the entirely abstract figure outlined by the Russian nihilist, Sergei Necahev, in his 1869 pamphlet, *Catechism of the Revolutionist*, which describes the model terrorist as knowing 'only one science, the science of destruction'.[60] Emphasising the purity of his own, chaotic intentions by distinguishing himself from the rest of Conrad's 'insignificant' anarchists, whom he derides as mere 'revolutionists', the Professor holds himself to be, in contrast to them, a 'true propagandist'

(p. 94). His identity is encoded in the personalised bomb that he carries in order to frustrate Heat's desire to have him arrested. Like Conrad's explosive words, this particularly modernist symbol of creative destruction is designed, as he explains to Comrade Ossipon, to make a 'clean sweep' of his enemies and mark a 'clear start for a new conception of life' (p. 97). However the remarkably integrated system of violence that he has designed for achieving this end is far from complete:

'I walk always with my right hand closed around the indiarubber ball which I have in my trouser pocket. The pressing of this ball actuates a detonator inside the flask I carry in my pocket. It's the principle of the pneumatic instantaneous shutter for a camera lens. The tube leads up – '

With a swift, disclosing gesture he gave Ossipon a glimpse of an indiarubber tube, resembling a slender brown worm, issuing from the armhole of his waistcoat and plunging into the inner breast pocket of his jacket . . . 'The detonator is partly mechanical, partly chemical,' he explained, with casual condescension.

'It is instantaneous, of course?' murmured Ossipon, with a slight shudder.

'Far from it,' confessed the other, with a reluctance which seemed to twist his mouth dolorously. 'A full twenty seconds must elapse from the moment I press the ball till the explosion takes place.'

'Phew!' whistled Ossipon, completely appalled. 'Twenty seconds! Horrors! You mean to say that you could face that? I should go crazy – '

'Wouldn't matter if you did. Of course, it's the weak point of this 'special system, which is only for my own use. The worst is that the manner of exploding is always the weak point with us. I am trying to invent a detonator that would adjust itself to all conditions of action, and even to unexpected changes of conditions. A variable and yet perfectly precise mechanism. A really intelligent detonator.' (pp. 91–2)

Hard-wired into his body, which is penetrated by the phallic rubber tube, and ready to explode at just twenty seconds' notice, this chemical, mechanical and also partly biological device anticipates a key concern of political modernity as the Professor's attempt to invent an artificially intelligent bomb offers a commentary on the protean thrust of revolutionary doctrine. But for Conrad the transformation that the perfect anarchist has undergone represents a gradual shedding of his own humanity. In his effort to create a purely destructive artificial intelligence, the Professor must become partly inorganic by integrating himself into the system that he has invented and fusing his body with the bomb's variable and delicate operation. In order to achieve his ideal of a sentient device he must temporarily overcome its technological limitations by becoming part of this infernal machine. The bomb requires the input and agency of its conscious biological component – the human carrier – who camouflages the device and triggers its detonation and whose role in its mechanism suggests the danger posed by abstract revolutionary doctrines. Carried out 'absolutely alone' (p. 94), the dangerous work of bomb-making, to which the Professor sacrifices so much of his own time, capital and freedom, is a philosophical labour as much as it is a physical one.

The bomb's delayed detonation, which is initiated by a process resembling photography, suggests that bombs, like cameras, generate images of their own. The Professor's description of the device provokes Ossipon into conjuring a hellish vignette when, as he dwells on the horror of knowingly experiencing the hiatus between the moment at which the detonator is triggered and the explosion of the bomb inside the underground Silenus Restaurant, he imagines the instant of destruction. The transformation of the restaurant into 'a dreadful black hole belching horrible fumes, choked with ghastly rubbish of smashed brickwork and mutilated corpses' can be produced by the slow-working mechanism of the Professor's bomb, the delay sufficient to provide any carrier with a 'distinct' and realistic perception of the ruin that the device will inflict on its target. What Ossipon has come to realise here is that, in contrast to the long-winded theoretical discussion of revolution that takes place in Verloc's parlour, the Professor's revolutionary absolutism encapsulates the more frightening, because all the more real, impact of actual political violence. The shock that is produced by an act of pure terrorism (remember here Henry's 'theoretical' [61] anarchism, articulated by means of his indiscriminate attack on the Café Terminus) is magnified by the contradiction between the bomb's delayed detonation and the instantaneous 'principle' of the explosion. This weakness means that this invention does not yet have the universal application that the Professor intends for it and, as he explains, the detonator that so clearly defines him is wholly dependent, in the meantime, on the incorruptibility of his own 'character' (pp. 91, 92).

The perfect detonator requires an individual prepared to accept the final, drawn-out phase of his existence. Incorporating mechanical, chemical, biological and chronological components, the Professor's design for a 'special system' imagines modern subjectivity in a manner consistent with the theories presented by Martin Heidegger in his 1927 study, *Being and Time*. It is deeply ironic that the novel's two real terrorists – the amoral diplomat, Vladimir, and the absolute anarchist, the Professor – are both engaged in addressing time theory, if in different ways. Vladimir's pseudo-plot is designed to cause outrage by damaging the Greenwich Observatory and attacking the concept of an ordered modernity; but the Professor's threat to auto-destruct at twenty seconds' notice is predicated on the consciousness of modern being and time that the Meridian was designed to regulate. Centred on the private horrors and political disturbance caused by the 'day of shocks' made possible by the pair (p. 228), *The Secret Agent* explores the momentary and singularly modern quality of terrorism. Dealing with the relatively short period of time surrounding the explosion, and with the limited number of people affected by it (ultimately Stevie's death does not bother the 'unconscious stream' of Londoners (p. 89)), it presents the event of being, much as Heidegger did later, as a phenomenon that is focused on the instantaneousness of experience. Conrad's own time theory, articulated by Chief Inspector Heat, is suggestive:

> In the close-woven stuff of relations between the conspirator and police there occur unexpected solutions of continuity, sudden holes in space and time. A given anarchist may be watched inch by inch and minute by minute, but a moment always comes when somehow all sight and touch of him are lost for a few hours, during which something (generally an explosion) more or less deplorable does happen. (p. 105)

The terrorist shocks the temporal scheme and its disciplinary, spatial reality on two levels: firstly, by disengaging from it and disappearing, and then by momentarily disrupting it with the destructive force of an explosion. By withdrawing from what the Professor terms 'the game' (p. 94) and thereby becoming nothing, the anarchist, Heat fears, will achieve 'something'. Conrad presents in the Professor a closely focused study of a revolutionary being in time, and one who is conscious of, and even physically attached to, an emblem of what Heidegger termed the approaching ontic 'imminence' of 'Being-Toward-Death'. This condition is manifested in the mechanical, chemical, biological and chronological composition of the Professor's bomb. For Heidegger death is not so much a final state of being as one that, in its potential immediacy, is always present; no state of being highlights his theory of the continual imminence of death more than that of being subjected to political terror; nothing magnifies the existence and 'facticity' of being, or 'Da-sein', quite as acutely as 'the ever-present phenomenon of death itself'.[62] With its built-in pause between detonation and death, the Professor's personal device lacks the instantaneous cruelty and unexpectedness of the bomb that vaporises Stevie on the knoll at Greenwich: the horrific sight of the boy's remains convinces Heat of the impossibility of his not having experienced in that brief moment 'pangs of inconceivable agony', a reflection that causes the policeman's now fearful consciousness to rise 'above the vulgar conception of time' (p. 107). The Professor's specially adapted detonator and its delayed action (more carefully designed than the 'ingenious' but hastily constructed 'combination of time and shock' handed to Verloc (p. 99)) acquaints Ossipon with the possibility of experiencing Stevie's fate because, as he realises in the Silenus restaurant, it will leave enough time, once triggered, to allow its carrier to reflect on the magnitude of its destructiveness. For Heidegger and, it must also be added, for the Professor, this particular passage of time is the surest 'horizon' or confirmation 'of every understanding and interpretation of being' (p. 15), as existence is comprehensible only in relation to its movement. This explains the Professor's desire to perfect an absolutely sensitive device that will prove more reliable than any human carrier, particularly the ineffective delegates of the International Red Committee, whose indecisiveness convinces the bomb-maker that, unlike him, they have 'no character whatever' (p. 93).

The Professor endows his own bomb with an ontic quality, much as Heidegger's theory of modern subjectivity, structured around the 'theroretical 'representation' of a continuous stream of nows', underlines the temporality of being. 'Being', in this sense, constructs itself according to its own 'time calculation', providing a lived, or 'phenomenonal aspect of temporality', giving Heidegger's idea a very Conradian resonance when we consider the Professor's essentially temporal device, not to mention Vladimir's choice of target for the launch of his own bomb-plot. The Professor's preoccupation with perfecting the detonator's 'system' also conforms to Heidegger's model of temporal experience as a 'project of a meaning of being' that 'can be accomplished in the horizon of time'.[63] His description of the workings of the bomb provokes Ossipon into considering the magnitude of the short but torturous and imaginatively prolonged period leading to its detonation. His anxiety over the possibility of an explosion in the Silenus Restaurant reveals how the connection of the philosophical concept of the importance of time to the interpreation of being might reveal the cultural significance of the terrorist's bomb: time, as Da-sein, or as temporal existence, is re-inscribed in Ossipon's imagination by the lapse between the triggering of the device and the moment of its explosion. Rather than causing a break in time, as Heat fears, an explosion magnifies, with symbolic force as well as with sheer violence, the instant of its detonation. The detective comes to realise this when, pondering over Stevie's mangled remains, he contemplates the 'horrible notion that the ages of atrocious pain and mental torture could be contained between two successive winks of an eye' (p. 107). The time bomb, which operates according to its own internal 'time calculation', would appear to validate Heidegger's concept of temporality's bearing upon being, since the time calculated by its mechanism records a temporality that 'blows up' with its detonation. This detonation interrupts the 'everyday' and 'vulgar' understanding of time that Heidegger wanted to see beyond with his time theory, while the Professor's promise to auto-destruct in the event of his arrest mirrors the absolutely existential state of Being-toward-Death described by the philosopher as an ongoing 'being-toward-the-end', rather than as an approach towards some distant, terminal horizon.[64] Like present-day suicide bombers, the Professor does not view his death as an event that will bring an end to his terrible work or beliefs, and the novel's chilling conclusion presents the 'incorruptible' terrorist as a purely ontic figure: 'He had no future. He disdained it. He was a force' (p. 269). *The Secret Agent* closes with this image of the terrorist at large, intent on realising his philosophy of pure violence, which is what he eventually does: as X relates to the collector in 'The Informer', the Professor dies some years after the setting of that story when one of his 'improved' detonators explodes prematurely ('The Informer', p. 103). In death he achieves the most extreme Heideggerian 'possibility of being', or the 'ownmost potentiality' implicit in his politically motivated death-drive.[65]

Existence, according to the Heideggerian model, is dominated by the overarching fact of 'everydayness'. The Professor struggles against normality and advocates 'the destruction of what is' as it is expressed in routine and in 'everyday' media, such as newspapers, which in *The Secret Agent* function both as a kind of calendar and map of events. Indeed, the novel closes with him feeling oppressed by the contemplation of 'mankind as numerous as the sands of the seashore'. The masses, occupying what Ossipon terms the 'damned hole' of eternity, threaten to overwhelm the Professor's sense of his own, individuated being and those of his devices, as the 'sound of exploding bombs' promises to vanish amid the crowds and become 'lost in their immensity of passive grains without an echo' (p. 265). Still struggling to invent the 'perfect detonator' (p. 93), its system, of which he is a constituent part, remains flawed since the impact of its irreversible operation cannot halt the everydayness of modern, urban experience. The 'experience that is objectively present' – the momentary now in the flux of an ongoing present – is the temporal space within which the explosion occurs – combined with the newspaper response, carried by dailies and evening editions, constitutes the modern attempt to capture or negotiate this ever-enduring present through which being and objective reality, according to Heidegger's model, travel, or 'stretches along'.[66] Only the present is real, because time exists within being, and this is why the Professor is so absorbed by a newspaper report on Stevie's death as it relays the temporal, momentary being of the bomb he constructed for Verloc. The bomb can be understood to have performed a being of its own that is constructed via the temporal function of its operation. Conrad negotiates with modernity in many ways in *The Secret Agent* but this is done most strikingly through this treatment of bomb technology. As the Professor's morbid nihilism suggests, waiting for one's death in political struggle has an ontic quality, something that also characterises the anarchists in Richard Henry Savage's potboiler, one of whom declares: 'death in the struggle of humanity is the open gateway of eternal freedom!' (Vol. 1, p. 89). But of all the fictions written on the subject of terrorism, *The Secret Agent* offers the most sustained examination of the particularly modern character of revolutionary political violence. While Savage viewed it as no more than a mindless drive toward self-destruction, Conrad regarded terrorism's shocking qualities as reflecting the forceful impact of modernism upon the literary consciousness.

Conrad's Alien Nation

Like Edgar Wallace's *The Four Just Men*, *The Secret Agent* also discusses immigration's impact upon the collective, political identity of Britain. This issue reached critical mass with the passage of the 1905 Aliens Act (having become a naturalised British citizen in 1886, Conrad, as a Pole, was conscious of his own status as an invited Englishman). This legislation formalised what Conrad termed the 'unreasonable terror' of xenophobia in the short story 'Amy Foster' (1901),[67] the tale of a Carpathian immigrant, Yanko Gooral, who, shipwrecked in England on his way to the United States, bears the 'indelible stamp' (p. 155) of foreignness. This distinction is a distinction shared by Adolf Verloc who, as the son of a Frenchman, never acquires full Englishness despite being a natural-born British subject. While Yanko remains trapped in rural Kent, anarchist immigrants are decidedly urban figures in *The Secret Agent*, and Conrad represents London as an unstable place that is susceptible to their foreign influences. The Assistant Commissioner's walk through the 'dark corners' between the Strand and Charing Cross becomes a 'descent' into an unclean atmosphere of 'gloomy dampness' resembling a 'slimy aquarium', where he is 'enveloped' and 'assimilated'. Emerging looking like one of Soho's 'queer foreign fish'[68] (pp. 150–1), the policeman's experience of urban uncertainty corresponds with Ford Madox Ford's notion of the transformative power of the metropolis appears in his homage of 1905, *The Soul of London*, where he provides bodily and liquid metaphors for cultural deconstruction and re-composition. Ford describes the city as a body that 'slowly digests' newcomers, irrespective of their nationalities or beliefs, 'assimilates' them and transforms them by 'converting them, with the most potent of all juices, into the singular and inevitable product that is the Londoner – that is, in fact, the Modern'.[69] For Conrad and Ford this process occurs as the city's cultural essence, which is imagined by both as fluid material, is soaked up. Once contaminated, the subject is irreversibly cast as a new metropolitan being.

While the Assistant Commissioner feels 'unplaced' (152) in Soho, he finds the experience of de-Anglicisation to be an easy, even pleasurable, one. The loss of his established identity is accompanied by a 'rather pleasant' 'sense of loneliness, of evil freedom'; clearly, Conrad's metaphors of wetness, ooziness and slipperiness in a metropolis lacking stable cultural boundaries is suggestive of London's other role as a site of erotic transformation. Leaving the restaurant, the Assistant Commissioner adapts himself to fit more closely the indistinct urban types that surround him:

> he saw himself in the sheet of glass, and was struck by his foreign appearance. He contemplated his own image with a melancholy and inquisitive gaze, then by sudden inspiration raised the collar of his jacket. This arrangement appeared to him commendable, and he completed it by giving an upward twist to the ends of his black moustache. He was satisfied by the subtle modification of his personal aspect caused by these small changes. 'That'll do very well,' he thought. 'I'll get a little wet, a little splashed –' (pp. 151–2)

So effective is this new identity that he is mistaken for a foreigner by Winnie Verloc when he enters her shop. The watery city reflects the image of the modern subject back onto himself, soaking him, in the process, with its transformative juices and reshaping him as a suitably 'denationalized' (p. 152) individual. According to Conrad's modernist logic, the process of becoming foreign and unfamiliar need not be a negative experience: the almost instantaneous assimilation of the Assistant Commissioner into the otherness of Soho's back streets would have been an impossible feat for him in the colonies where, as a director of counter-insurgency methods, he applied imperial power by tracking down secret societies and breaking them up, a responsibility that was, essentially, an act of detection and definition of the anti-colonial Other. In the fluid and levelling atmosphere of London, however, which is depicted by Conrad as a kind of cultural swamp, any shift in identity appears possible. The Briton and the foreigner meet halfway in its interpenetrative processes of mutual contamination and cross-fertilisation that transform one another's formerly fixed identities. The 'pleasurable feeling' of experiencing this unfixed condition continues as the Assistant Commissioner leaves the restaurant and makes his way to Verloc's pornography shop, which caters for other fantasies of sexual exchange and transmission. The very materiality of the streets along which he walks appears soft and malleable, even vulnerable to a kind of sexual violence as he passes through 'an immensity of greasy slime and damp plaster' that is 'enveloped, oppressed, penetrated, choked and suffocated by the blackness of a wet London night' (p. 152). As with the sexual transmission of bodily fluids, the British capital's juicy atmosphere of cultural exchange and collision carries a risk of infection (Conrad introduces the Gallic Verloc at the beginning of the novel as having returned from the continent 'like the influenza' (p. 47)), while its characteristic wetness penetrates the buildings themselves which, with their decomposing skins of damp plaster, seem ready to break down as readily as the Assistant Commissioner's British identity has done.[70]

This rotting, shifting, liquefied 'world of contradictions' (p. 105) is an apt setting for a modernist tale that also deconstructs the distinction between the organised forces of the state and the subversive agents of anarchy. The 'modern pest'[71] of terrorism infects revolutionaries, police and governments alike, suggesting the chaotic and ill-defined character of capitalist and imperialist modernity. Conrad's politically upside-down world is, like Chesterton's nightmare vision, saturated by a moral nihilism that influences every actor in the conflict except, of course, for the doomed Winnie Verloc and her innocent brother, Stevie. Sham anarchists, double agents, ambitious policemen and diplomatic staff are linked by their suitability for their respective roles in the 'cruel' and morally ambivalent metropolis where, as the Assistant Commissioner's experience reveals, there is no solid ground. Again, Conrad's urban imaginary echoes Ford's description of London which, with its 'lack of unity, of plan', appears as ideally modernist terrain.[72] In his 1920 Author's Note, Conrad describes how the city's 'monstrous' character afforded his imagination with 'room enough . . . to place any story', its bleak 'vistas' seeming filled with literary potential (pp. 40–1). Anarchism also offers the modernist writer an unlimited literary scope because, unlike the neatly packaged popular fictions that end with the containment of anarchism, the fluid political morality of *The Secret Agent*, held together by endless interlocking intrigues, seeps into every corner of twentieth-century politics and culture. Its pervasive secrecy infiltrates and confuses any sense that we might have of the oppositional ideologies of government and revolution, of legitimacy and corruption, as the reader comes to realise that in this 'simple tale', moral anarchy is what characterises the political practice of the state and its agents.

The threat of anarchist terrorism, like Irish dynamiting, fitted into a range of late Victorian sensational phenomena. Its illegibility, coded for popular writers like Savage and Chesterton by its anti-capitalist ideals, is also what made anarchism such an appealing and commercially viable subject for mass-market publishing, while also inspiring Conrad's more experimental modernist fiction. Anarchism crossed the boundary between elite and popular literary culture, its shocking tactics suiting the modernist preoccupation with the fragmentation of experience and of the self, while the continental violence of the early 1890s gave the 'shilling shocker' a very contemporary flavour. As a result the methods of modern political violence coincided with the methods of modern literary culture, reflecting a growing preoccupation with the cultural politics of individual agency. By assuming its place within the popular imagination, anarchism, despite its strangeness, appeared than more than a passing fad or foreign political trend. Although conservative scaremongers warned the public that 'there is no crime, however horrible, which is not gathered under the aegis of Anarchism', it appealed to Conrad as much as it did to the writers of pacier yellow-back novels. Peter Latouche complained in 1894 that '(t)he very fact that certain crimes might especially shock the public, commend them to the Anarchistic mind which delights in shocking and terrifying the bourgeoisie'.[73] The same could have been said of its appeal to the literary imagination.

Notes

1. Richard Henry Savage, *The Anarchist: A Story of To-Day*, 2 vols (Leipzig: Tauchnitz, 1894). Hereafter cited in the text.
2. A similar distinction is made again in G. K. Chesterton's 1908 novel, *The Man Who Was Thursday*, when a new recruit to the 'New Detective Corps' is advised not to equate anarchism with Russian nihilism or Irish dynamiting: 'Do not confuse it ... with those chance outbreaks from Russia or from Ireland, which are really the outbreaks of repressed, if mistaken men.' See G. K. Chesterton, *The Man Who Was Thursday: A Nightmare* (New York: Modern Library, 2001), p. 45.
3. Pierre Kropotkine (also Peter Kropotkin), *The Place of Anarchism in Socialistic Evolution*, translated from the French by Henry Glasse (London: International Publishing Company, 1886), p. 1, pp. 4–5.
4. C. L. James, *Anarchy: A Tract for the Times* (Eau Clair, WI, 1886), p. 30.
5. Émile Henry, 'A Terrorist's Defence', from *Gazette des Tribuneaux*, 27–28 April 1894, trans. George Woodcock, in George Woodcock (ed.), *The Anarchist Reader* (Glasgow: Fontana, 1977), pp. 189–96, p. 190.
6. See Peter Weir, *Anarchy and Culture: The Aesthetic Politics of Modernism* (Amherst: University of Massachusetts Press, 1977), p. 76; and Roderick Kedward, *The Anarchists: The Men Who Shocked an Era* (London: Library of the Twentieth Century, 1971), especially chap. 2, 'Individual Terror'; see George Woodcock, *Anarchism: A History of Libertarian Ideas and Movements* (Harmondsworth: Penguin, 1970), p. 276.
7. Émile Henry, 'A Terrorist's Defence', p. 196.
8. Félix Dubois, *The Anarchist Peril*, trans. Ralph Derechef (London: T.

Fisher Unwin, 1894); originally published as *Le péril anarchiste* (Paris: Flammarion, 1894), p. 238.

9. Peter Marshall, *Demanding the Impossible: A History of Anarchism* (London: Fontana, 1992), p. 438.

10. Quoted in Woodcock, *Anarchism*, pp. 289, 290.

11. See Jeffery A. Clymer, 'Introduction: Terrorism in the American Cultural Imagination'*America's Culture of Terrorism* (Chapel Hill and London: The University of North Carolina Press, 2003). Quotations are from pp. 15–16, 20. Anthony Kubiak has also drawn attention to this aspect of modern terrorism by pointing to the process of 'theatricalization' of political violence. An essentially mimetic phenomenon it is, according to Kubiak, a form of coercion by performance. See Anthony Kubiak, *Stages of Terror: Terrorism, Ideology, and Coercion as Theatre History* (Bloomington and Indianapolis: Indiana University Press, 1991). Quotation from p. 2.

12. Émile Henry, 'Propaganda By Deed', *The Torch*, New Series, No. 4, October 1894, p. 5.

13. Quoted in Woodcock, *Anarchism*, p. 291.

14. Henry, A Terrorist's Defence', p. 193.

15. Henry, quoted in Woodcock, *Anarchist Reader*, pp. 189, 194, 196.

16. Having served as editor of the anarchist journal, *L'Endehors*, Henry was a skilful propagandist. His staff included the famous Parisian aesthete and wit, Félix Fénéon, who was later charged with lending a dress to Henry that he used as a disguise during the rue des Bon Enfants attack, and with keeping detonators for his editor. Fénéon was also suspected of bombing the restaurant of the Hôtel Foyot in April 1894, when the poet Laurent Tailhade – who had famously supported Henry's bombing of the Café Terminus by asking 'Qu'important quelques vagues humanités si le geste est beau?' – lost an eye. Therefore, dynamite was given a 'voice' by a literary man who like the unfortunate Tailhade appreciated the shocking aesthetic and cultural value of propaganda by deed. As he told the court that sentenced him to death: 'I am almost tempted to say, with Souvarine in *Germinal*: "All discussions about the future are criminal, since they hinder pure and simple destruction and slow down the march of the revolution . . .".'. Tailhade had been entertaining his mistress at the restaurant which was popular with staff and senators from the Palais de Luxembourg. See Luc Sante, 'Introduction' to Félix Fénéon, *Novels in Three Lines* (New York: New York Review of Books, 2007, translated from the series 'Nouvelles en trios lignes', *Le Matin*, 1906), pp. xvii, xix, xv. Henry is quoted in George Woodcock, *Anarchism: A History of Libertarian Ideas and Movements* (Harmondsworth: Penguin, 1970), p. 191.

17. While Britain afforded political sanctuary to European anarchists, those who remained at home too often suffered internment, torture and even extra-judicial execution. This was particularly the case in Spain and France. Woodcock describes how in both countries negative 'deeds' like bombing cafés, theatres and religious processions were desperate reactions to extraordinarily harsh official repression. See Woodcock, *Anarchism*, chap. 10, 'Anarchism in France' and chap. 12, 'Anarchism in Spain'.

18. 'Literary Notes', *New York Times*, Wednesday, 4 August 1894, p. 3.

19. Dubois, *The Anarchist Peril*, pp. 53–4.

20. This was recognised by C. L. James, who suggested that 'competition, *if really free*, might do as much good as it does harm.' See James, *Anarchy*, p. 30.
21. The construction of anarchism as an unreadable phenomenon also owes much to what Arthur F. Redding has termed its essentially unreal and 'perplexed' sense of itself. Lacking the theoretical structures associated with scientific socialism, anarchism is 'inextricably and immediately at war with coherence' and, he suggests, ought to be considered 'as 'fantastic,' in its own terms.' As a consequence, it has a primarily emotive quality, thriving on psychic tension and producing violence via the exploitation of sentiment. See Arthur F. Redding, *Raids on Human Consciousness: Writing, Anarchism, and Violence* (Columbia: University of South Carolina Press), pp. 78–9.
22. See Haia Shpayer-Makov, 'Anarchism in British Public Opinion, 1880–1914', *Victorian Studies* 31, Summer 1988, pp. 487–516, especially pp. 491–2.
23. See Peter Kropotkin, 'Anarchist Communism', 'Law and Authority', 'The Spirit of Revolt', 'Anarchism: Its Philosophy and Ideal', in *Anarchism: A Collection of Revolutionary Writings* (Mineola: Dover, 2002), first published as *Kropotkin's Revolutionary Pamphlets* (New York: Vanguard Press, 1927), pp. 44–78, p. 52. Quotations from pp. 199, 36–7, 65, 132, 65, 75.
24. Such was the popularity of *The Anarchist* that it was published by Bernhard Tauchnitz as part of his popular Collection of British and American Authors series which in its lifespan issued 3,500 titles by over bestselling 400 authors. Tauchnitz specialized in publishing, in English, sensational fiction by authors such as Mary Elizabeth Braddon and Ouida. H. G. Wells was also on his list. See Siegfried Mews, 'Sensationalism and Sentimentality: Minor Victorian Prose Writers in Germany', *MLN* 84, no. 5, October 1969, pp. 776–88. See also David Lake, 'The Current Texts of H. G. Wells's Early Science Fiction Novels: Situation Unsatisfactory', in John S. Partington (ed.), *The Wellsian: Selected Essays on H. G. Wells* (Oss: Equilibris, 2005), pp. 167–88.
25. As Clymer has pointed out, in contrast to the exact record of police fatalities 'the actual number of casualties among the protestors, like the bomb thrower's identity, was never determined.' See Clymer, *America's Culture of Terrorism*, chap. 1, 'Imagining Terrorism in America: The 1886 Chicago Haymarket Bombing', quotation from p. 33. See also George Woodcock, *Anarchism*, pp. 436–9.
26. Clymer, *America's Culture of Terrorism*, p. 36.
27. Clymer regards such reports as initiating America's fascination with 'wound culture' or its 'fascination with 'torn, or devastated private bodies and their representation across a wide range of print and visual media.' See Clymer, *America's Culture of Terrorism*, pp. 38, 44.
28. Walter Pater, *The Renaissance: Studies in Art and Poetry* (Oxford: Oxford University Press, 1998), pp. 150–1.
29. *The Man Who Was Thursday* influenced Jorge Luis Borges's complex story about the disruptive but fascinating 'enigma' of Irish political revolt, 'Theme of the Traitor and the Hero'. See Jorge Luis Borges, 'Theme of the

Traitor and the Hero', *Labyrinths* (London: Penguin, 2000), pp. 102–5, pp. 102–3.

30. Here Chesterton is recognising the collapse of what Samuel Beckett later termed conventional literature's 'neatness of identifications'. See Beckett, 'Dante. . . Bruno. Vico.. Joyce', in *Disjecta: Miscellaneous Writings and a Dramatic Fragment* (London: John Calder, 1983), p. 19.

31. David Glover argues that the placeless anarchist functioned within the popular and modernist literature that surrounded the Aliens Act as the key political symbol of 'the evacuation of signifiers of identity'. See David Glover, 'Aliens, Anarchists and Detectives: Legislating the Immigrant Body', *New Formations*, 32, Autumn/Winter 1997, pp. 22–33. Quotation from p. 30.

32. See Glover, 'Aliens, Anarchists and Detectives', p. 31.

33. Of course Wallace was not the first writer to draw this analogy. In Arthur Conan Doyle's 1892 story, 'The Adventure of the Speckled Band', the villain uses an Indian swamp adder, which accesses his victim's sealed bedroom through a ventilator, as a murder weapon. Here the penetration of the locked room serves as a metaphor for imperial recoil with the invasion of metropolitan British space by a colonial entity that is both subject and commodity.

34. Subsequent quotations are from H. G. Wells, 'The Stolen Bacillus' and 'The Diamond-Maker', in *The Complete Short Stories of H. G. Wells* (London: Phoenix Press, 2000).

35. Examples include Robert Louis Stevenson's *The Suicide Club* (1882), Harry Blythe's 'The Accusing Shadow' (1894) and Coulson Kernahan's *Scoundrels and Co* (1908).

36. This process of creation through destruction, whereby commodities are produced by an explosion, reveal that the 'creative' processes of modern capitalism are inherently destructive, exploding 'all that is solid' in order to create a surplus of commodities of ever-increasing value. As Marshall Berman suggests, this indicates the dual role of capital which, while promising growth and transformation, also enacts a storm of 'perpetual' disintegration and renewal. The Diamond Maker reverses this Marxian theory by making something out of nothing by means of the explosion that produces something, a solid diamond, out of mud, if not out of thin air. See Marshall Berman, *All That is Solid Melts Into Air: The Experience of Modernity* (London: Penguin, 1988), p. 15.

37. Bernard Bergonzi, for example, has interpreted *The Invisible Man* in 'strictly mythical' rather than political terms, reading the novel as a discourse on power in which Wells presents Griffin as a 'scientist-magician' and representative of the pre-modern patterns of folk culture that, he felt, had to be exorcised from modern British society. See Bernard Bergonzi, *The Early H. G. Wells: A Study of the Scientific Romances* (Manchester: Manchester University Press, 1961), p. 120.

38. Jürgen Habermas describes how the 'aura' of this sphere was dependent on a 'publicity of representation' as ownership of the political process required that its participants be figures of 'publicness'. See See Jürgen Habermas, *The Structural Transformation of the Public Sphere: An Inquiry into a Category of Bourgeois Society*, trans. Thomas Burger and Frederick

Lawrence from *Strukturwandel der Öffentlicheit*, Hermann Luchterhand Verlag, Dermstadt and Neuwied, 1962 (Cambridge: Polity Press, 1989). Quotations from pp. 7, 10.

39. Gustave Le Bon, *The Psychology of Revolution*, trans. Bernard Mall from *La psychologie des revolutions* (London: T. Fisher Unwin, 1913), pp. 16, 12.

40. See Mikhail Bakunin, letter to Albert Richard, 1 April 1870, translated from the French by Stephen Cox, in Mikhail Bakunin, *Selected Writings* (London: Jonathan Cape, 1973), pp. 180–1.

41. Bakunin, letter to Sergei Nečaev, 2 June 1870, *Selected Writings*, p. 192.

42. See Bergonzi, *The Early H. G. Wells*. See also Frank McConnell, *The Science Fiction of H. G. Wells* (New York and Oxford: Oxford University Press, 1981).

43. The clandestine quality of Griffin's notes recalls the communications used by Russian revolutionaries in Sergei Stepniak's 1889 novel of Russian revolutionaries, *The Career of a Nihilist*, which opens with Andrey Kjukhov, an expert in 'revolutionary literature', decoding secret messages sent by his comrades. The code, written in invisible ink, is rendered visible by chemicals. Its 'endless variety of signs' can only be read by specially trained nihilists whose role as code breakers distinguishes them from the rest of the reading public. This presents Kjukhov with a literary paradox because, as well propagandising, he must shield his movement from popular and police scrutiny. Stepniak's discussion of this complex textual barrier of ciphers (written in invisible ink, the code must be rendered visible and then made sensible by its translation into Russian) reveals the importance of reading, or, more precisely, of not being read by the wrong people, to revolutionaries. See Sergius Stepniak, *The Career of a Nihilist* (1889, reprinted London: Walter Scott, 1901), pp. 13, 7. Like Griffin's cipher, Sepniak's decoding scene mirrors Ezra Pound's notion of the necessary specialisation of modernist writing, outlined in his essay 'The Serious Artist', which was published in Richard Aldington's journal, *The Egoist* in 1913. Pound's insistence that highbrow literature should appear illegible to the popular reader is based upon his notion of modernism as literary 'science' and the result of 'patient experiment'. The complex rules dictating the composition and form of the modernist text create an aura of difficulty that is designed to provide an alternative to the purely market-oriented values of popular literature. See Ezra Pound, 'The Serious Artist', in *Literary Essays of Ezra Pound* (London: Faber, 1954, reprinted 1968), pp. 41–57, pp. 42, 55.

44. H. G. Wells, 'The Labour Unrest' (London: *The Daily Mail*, undated, originally published 13–20 May 1912), pp. 1, 11, 14–18.

45. John Buchan, *The Thirty-Nine Steps* (London: Penguin, 1991), pp. 13, 39, 57, 59.

46. Gustave Le Bon, *The Crowd: A Study of the Popular Mind* (London: T. Fisher Unwin, 1896), pp. v–vi.

47. See Wells's 'anticipatory' outline of the breakdown of nations and the rise of the World State in his part-fiction, part-polemic, *The Shape of Things to Come*, which was published in 1933. Wells declared that 'as much a colonial organism as any branching coral or polyp . . . We are all members

of one body'. See H. G. Wells, *The Shape of Things to Come: The Ultimate Revolution* (London: Penguin, 2005), pp. 443–5.

48. See Peter Bailey, *Popular Culture and Performance in the Victorian City* (Cambridge: Cambridge University Press, 1998), p. 28.

49. John Batchelor, *The Life of Joseph Conrad: A Critical Biography* (Oxford: Blackwell, 1994), p. 151. For an account of Conrad's stressful effort to balance his experimental modernist principles against the demands of the literary market, see chap. 6, 'Towards Verloc, 1904–1907'.

50. G. O. Warren, *Freedom: Rent, Interest, Profit and Taxes, the True Causes of Wage-Slavery* (London: William Reeves, 1894), p. 3.

51. For Ford's relationship with Conrad, see Norman Sherry, *Conrad's Western World* (Cambridge: Cambridge University Press, 1971), especially chap. 20, 'The Informer'. While Ford notoriously exaggerated his own influence on Conrad, Sherry argues that his presence in this story acknowledges his role as the primary source for these political fictions.

52. 30 July 1907. Quoted in Batchelor, *The Life of Joseph Conrad*, p. 163. Conrad also complained to Methuen that flashy American publicity described the novel as 'A Tale of Diplomatic Intrigue and Anarchist Treachery', fearing that it might attract less discriminating readers than *The Secret Agent* was intended for.

53. Subsequent quotations are from *The Secret Agent* (London: Penguin, 1990).

54. John Littlechild, *Reminiscences of Chief Inspector Littlechild* (London: The Leadenhall Press, 1894), p. 12.

55. For a detailed account of the historical background to the composition of *The Secret Agent*, along with a close discussion of Conrad's sources, see Norman Sherry's *Conrad's Western World*, chapters 22–31. See also David Mulry, 'Popular Accounts of the Greenwich Bombing and Conrad's *The Secret Agent*', *Rocky Mountain Review of Language and Literature*, 54.2 (2000), pp. 43–64. Although George Woodcock offered the unlikely theory that the device was not intended for domestic use, he acknowledged the symbolic importance of the Greenwich Observatory, as was recognised by *The Times*, which accused Bourdin of planning an attack on the building. See Woodcock, *Anarchism*, p. 414. See *The Times*, Editorial and 'Bourdin's Antecedents', Saturday, 17 February 1894, p. 5.

56. See Stephen Kern, *The Culture of Time and Space: 1880–1914* (London: Weidenfeld and Nicholson, 1983), p. 33.

57. Their similarities are perhaps inevitable, since, as Alex Houen has suggested, 'effective government is shown (in *The Secret Agent*) to depend on blurring the distinctions between crime and law'. See Alex Houen, *Terrorism and Modern Literature: From Joseph Conrad to Ciaran Carson* (Oxford: Oxford University Press, 2002), p. 50.

58. Conrad to Edward Garnett, Friday, 12 March, 1897, in Karle R. Frederick (ed.), *The Collected Letters of Joseph Conrad*, Vol. 1 (Cambridge: Cambridge University Press, 1983), pp. 331–2.

59. See Walter Benjamin, *Charles Baudelaire*, p. 50.

60. Nechaev wrote that the true revolutionary was a pitiless opponent 'of the State, of class,' and even of 'so-called culture'. See Sergei Nechaev,

Catechism of the Revolutionist, in Walter Laqueur (ed.), *The Terrorism Reader* (London: Wildwood House, 1979), pp. 68–70.

61. Isabel Meredith (pseud. Christina and Olivia Rossetti), *A Girl Among the Anarchists* (first published London: Duckworth & Co, 1903, reprinted Lincoln and London: University of Nebraska Press, 1992), p. 189.

62. Martin Heidegger, *Being and Time: A Translation of* Sein und Zeit, trans. Joan Stambough (originally published Tübingen: Max Niemeyer Verlag, 1953; reprinted Albany: State University of New York Press, 1996), p. 231.

63. Heidegger, *Being and Time*, pp. 376, 216–17.

64. Heidegger, *Being and Time*, pp. 231–2.

65. See 'The Possible Being-a-Whole of Da-sein and Being-toward-Death' in Heidegger, *Being and Time*, pp. 223–45.

66. Heidegger, *Being and Time*, p. 343.

67. Joseph Conrad, 'Amy Foster', in *Typhoon and Other Stories* (London: Penguin, 1990), p. 160.

68. As Joseph McLaughlin has suggested, the Assistant Commissioner's entry into this urban abyss invokes the mythic topography of a descent into hell that was common in nenteenth-century urban writing from William Blake to Jack London. See Joseph McLaughlin, *Writing the Urban Jungle; Reading Empire in London from Doyle to Eliot* (Charlottesville and London: The University Press of Virginia, 2000), p. 150.

69. See Ford Madox Ford, *The Soul of London* (London: Alston Rivers, 1905; reprinted London: Dent, 1995), pp. 12–13.

70. This vision of London as a dirty aquarium overflowing with cultural fluids echoes Arthur Conan Doyle's famous description of London as the great 'cesspool' of empire, with which he opened the first Sherlock Holmes adventure, *A Study in Scarlet*. See Arthur Conan Doyle, *A Study in Scarlet*, in *Complete Sherlock Holmes and Other Detective Stories*, pp. 83–4.

71. Untitled, *The Times*, Saturday, 17 February 1894, p. 5.

72. See Ford, *The Soul of London*, p. 13

73. Peter Latouche, *Anarchy! An Authentic Exposition of the Methods of Anarchists and the Aims of Anarchism* (London: Everett & Co., 1908), p. 143.

Chapter 4

'The Doctrine of Dynamite': Anarchist Literature and Terrorist Violence

Everything is at an end.
Do what you choose.
Everything is Everybody's.
'The Anarchist Doctrine'[1]

Like Fenianism, late nineteenth-century anarchism was an intensively mediated form of radical politics. Despite its association with violence in many of the political novels of the period, printed propaganda was by far the most characteristic form of anarchist activity in late Victorian Britain.[2] Stressing the continuum between anarchist words and deeds, such journals, pamphlets and, sometimes, also fiction written by anarchists and former revolutionaries suggested the revolutionary function of writing. As if responding to Joseph Pierre Proudhon's claim of 1840 that 'equality failed to conquer by the sword only that it might conquer by the pen',[3] anarchist writers challenged the authority and power of the state by celebrating revolutionary action throughout the 1880s and 1890s. Even the renowned pacifist Peter Kropotkin praised the contemporary 'spirit of revolt' that motivated 'actions which compel general attention' and won converts. 'One such act', he wrote, 'may, in a few days, make more propaganda than thousands of pamphlets'. Deeds, Kropotkin maintained, were the one thing that bred daring.[4] This kind of revolutionary violence was dependent on its communication via the printed word as the concept of 'propaganda by the deed' owed much to its advertisement in the anarchist press. A single act might, in Kropotkin's estimation, accomplish more publicity than a large run of pamphlets but, in order to have much of an impact, it still depended upon being written about. The attention that these publications attracted amplified the shock of the deed itself, linking political language to revolutionary violence and showing that while deeds were paramount, the importance of Proudhon's pen had not diminished. Although outrageous actions like Henry's *attentats* against cafés and the bombing of theatres were not replicated in England, some anarchists there called for 'War to the Knife', praised the 'immortal bomb' in print and advised their comrades to 'terrorize the tyrannical administrators of the law'.[5] This chapter will examine how this kind of revolutionary literature fuelled the negative perception of anarchist ideas and practice in Britain. Showing how the rhetoric of terrorism exercised an enduring cultural influence, it will examine how anarchism became synonymous with violence during the late nineteenth and early twentieth centuries.[6] The optimistic but largely theoretical opinions of moderate anarchists was countered and undermined by their militant comrades;[7] although only a minority carried out acts of terrorism during the 1890s, their belief in the primacy of the act of revolt became a staple of the anarchist press. This hardening of attitudes is evident in a number of late nineteenth-century radical journals, such as *The Torch*, *Freedom*, *Anarchy* and *Commonweal*, all of which were influenced by the militant style of the German-language paper, *Freiheit*, and its uncompromising editor, Johann Most. Helen and Olivia Rossetti, former anarchists who eventually distanced themselves from revolutionary politics, also reflected on the relationship between words and deeds in their autobiographical novel of 1903, *A Girl Among the Anarchists*, which describes their experiences of writing, editing and distributing *The Torch* from 1891–7. Their novel describes an erratic but vocal revolutionary movement that depended on the cooperation of foreigners whose extreme views and theoretical approaches ignored what both women came to regard as the necessity of adapting to British political circumstances.

The Haymarket Affair and the Anarchist Press

The reaction of British and American anarchists to the Haymarket tragedy illustrated the developing militancy of anarchism. This became particularly apparent with the transformation of *The Torch*, an initially moderate journal that quickly went on to support the most militant European anarchists and even circulated back-issues of Johann Most's notorious paper *Die Freiheit (Freedom)*, not long after it was launched in 1891. Although published in German, *Freiheit* influenced subsequent anarchist journalism in English, earning notoriety for its author's 'wild talk'[8] and earning him several terms in prison. A committed 'propagandist-of-the-word',[9] Most embodied the connection that bound language to revolutionary action. Banished from Austria in 1871 after being imprisoned for his radical activities, he subsequently became the most sensational writer and public speaker of the left, both in Europe and in the United States. After the suppression of his *Freie Presse* in Germany in 1878 he emigrated to London where the more relaxed political atmosphere facilitated the publication of *Freiheit*, but Most quickly tested the boundaries of British tolerance and in 1881 he was sentenced to sixteen months' imprisonment for publishing the infamous issue of 19 March that celebrated the assassination of Tsar Alexander II as 'Sterling propaganda-by-the-deed!' Declaring 'Let more monarchs be killed!', a column framed in red and headed 'AT LAST', 'Triumph!, Triumph!' announced: 'One of the vilest tyrants corroded through and through by corruption, is no more'. The bomb that killed the Tsar 'fell at the despot's feet, shattered his legs, ripped open his belly, and inflicted many wounds . . . Conveyed to his palace and for an hour and a half in the greatest of suffering, the autocrat meditated on his guilt. Then he died as he deserved to die – like a dog'. *Freiheit* called for more assassinations 'until the last tyrant, the last plutocrat, and the last priest are dead'[10] and recommended further attacks on every head of state 'from St Petersburg to Washington'.[11] The jail term failed to control Most's rhetoric and in 1882 he shocked British imperial sensibilities by loudly applauding the double killing of Frederick Cavendish, the coercionist Lord Lieutenant of Ireland, and his Chief Under Secretary, Thomas Burke, who were stabbed to death in Dublin's Phoenix Park by the republican 'Invincibles'. Back on form, *Freiheit* praised this 'admirable deed' and 'heroically bold act of popular justice' that 'splendidly annihilated the evil representatives of a malignant government'.[12]

After emigrating to the United States Most turned his hand to more practical affairs, writing a comprehensive DIY manual for the 'non-expert' or 'layman' revolutionary, entitled *Science of Revolutionary Warfare*, which was published in German in 1885. With its instructions on causing havoc 'without help from very specialized people', the pamphlet was designed to make terrorist action against a variety of urban targets 'extremely easy . . . and very inexpensive'. As well as advising on a variety of 'jobs', such as dynamiting, arson, stabbing, poisoning and letter-bombing, the pamphlet also discussed the psychological impact of terrorism on its key target, the 'Property-Monster', and the potential of such violence to 'inflict surprise, confusion and panic on the enemy'. Most suggested that small professional teams of revolutionaries could wreak a disproportionate level of havoc without being detected or captured, and warned his readers that the first step towards success as a terrorist was not to assume that 'you may safely write whatever comes into your head, as if you were having a private conversation'. He also criticised 'unnecessary risks' and unsuccessful attacks like 'stabbings that did not penetrate deeply enough, shots that merely grazed' and 'blows that missed altogether'. Instead, he stressed the more practical qualities of the successful terrorist: 'Many simple-minded people talk glibly about revolutionaries not needing to do more that (*sic*) be courageous and risk their lives. This is utter nonsense: the real plan is for others to lose their lives'. Self-sacrifice, while admirable, was counter-productive and contrary to the interests of the anarchist cause because an attack could deal 'a much harder blow . . . when the perpetrator remains unknown'. Most also recommended that it was only when captured and facing a hopelessly long jail term, or worse, that an anarchist should make his views public, which should be done by converting the court into a political 'platform' and defending his actions from the dock by speaking from the 'revolutionary-anarchist point of view'.[13]

Most bluntly advised his readers: 'If you want to carry out a revolutionary act, don't talk to others about it first – go ahead and do it!' His pamphlet advised anarchists that, unlike their comrades in Europe, they had considerable freedom to carry out such actions in the United States, where 'everything' – including dynamite – 'can be had for money'. By encouraging his readers to save up and purchase 'the best weapons you can afford', Most also suggested that the country's capitalist ideology was itself a form of anarchism. He also kept his argument simple and avoided overly technical language, or 'jargon', to give basic but deadly instructions on how to manufacture 'respectable' bombs suited for a number of purposes, ranging from strikes against 'large assemblies of people' containing 'riff-raff of the upper-class variety' to more elaborate attacks. These ranged from controlled 'mini-explosions' designed to kill individuals (these devices could be 'planted under the table at a high society banquet, or . . . thrown through a window') to more destructive bombs that could destroy buildings such as palaces, churches, barracks and courts.[14] As well as adapting capitalism's ideology of economic and organisational freedom for his own revolutionary purposes, Most's discussion of terrorism and its tactics also contains something of the bourgeois ethos of professionalism. His call for 'respectable' deeds, by which he meant attacks that were well planned, adequately funded and successfully executed without loss on the part of the 'operational team', was made against a background of failed attacks, inspired by a laudable but ultimately unsuccessful amateurism that, he felt, had come to characterise anarchist violence.

The Haymarket bomb detonated less than a year after the publication of *Science of Revolutionary Warfare*, by which point its author had considerable influence over Chicago's German-speaking anarchists, some of whom appeared at protests carrying arms under banners bearing the slogan 'Read Most'.[15] The official hysteria that followed the explosion reached a crescendo with the show trial of the 'Haymarket Martyrs', five anarchists – Albert Parsons, August Spies, George Engel, Adolph Fischer and Louis Lingg – who were convicted of writing inflammatory articles and making speeches that inspired the unknown bomber. Four went to the gallows while Lingg cheated the hangman by exploding a detonator inside his mouth in his cell. As George Woodcock has pointed out, the executions amounted to 'judicial murder' as Illinois governor John Altgeld's 1893 enquiry found that none of the accused was involved in the bombing.[16] The explosion itself was a result of a political conflict in which anarchist writers, including Parsons, had directly confronted state and corporate power; as editor of the fortnightly journal *The Alarm*, Parsons had highlighted the state of virtual warfare between striking workers and Chicago's political and industrial elite, and spelled out the terms by which revolutionaries understood the word 'violence':

> According to 'law' there is no violence employed when employers starve the workmen into subjection, but it is 'unlawful and disorderly' for the worker to resist the starvation process known as the lock-out, discharge, etc. To resist these compulsory methods is what the law terms 'violence', and the authorities are called upon by employers to suppress it. The police, guardians of law and order, are set upon the unarmed people to quell the disturbance, the militia being held as a reserve to reinforce them when necessary. Workingmen are thus driven to the choice of quiet submission or cracked heads, broken bones and slaughter. In such cases arms become a necessity.[17]

As the anarchist press reveals, the crisis that culminated with the explosion was one that had a long history of conflict between workers, industrial corporations and the state and the Chicago anarchists were not prepared to passively endure starvation or suffer baton charges lightly. Their own political culture was, as Clymer has pointed out, a 'boisterous' one, in which large picnics, singing clubs and holiday celebrations accompanied other revels such as fetes commemorating the Paris Commune of 1871 and the assassination of Alexander II.[18] These events also featured more serious business, as seen in the same issue of *The Anarchist*, which advertised a workers' sharp shooting competition:

> It is needless to say that nothing is more important to the wage-slave than a knowledge of how to handle the rifle, pistol and bomb. Recent attacks of the authorities upon defenceless working people makes such a knowledge the prime necessity for self-preservation. A pleasant time is expected. Bring your families.[19]

Such calls for defensive action with bombs and guns, made less than a year before the explosion, point to the deepening spiral of class warfare that had taken hold in Chicago and would permanently alienate

American anarchism from mainstream politics: 'Not because you have caused the Haymarket bomb,' Judge Gary told Parsons and the other accused, 'but because you are Anarchists, you are on trial'.[20] After sentencing, Parsons gave a lengthy oration in which he called on his comrades to continue the work that he had begun in the city by continuing to write and publish for his revolutionary cause: 'Though fallen, wounded perhaps unto death, in the battle for liberty, the standard – the press- which my hands bore aloft in the midst of struggle is caught up by other hands'. *The Alarm* soberly noted that this eight-hour 'speech of defiance', during which Parsons followed Most's instructions on transforming the court into a political battleground, failed to win any favour with the judge and sealed his fate at the gallows.[21] The five Chicago anarchists lost their lives because of the threat posed by the combination of subversive violence and the written word in an atmosphere of intense political and economic repression; as Emma Goldman later recalled, the official 'terror' that climaxed with their executions had a profound influence over the next generation of anarchists in the United States,[22] while British anarchist journals reveal how revolutionaries in London also began discussing what they regarded as the need to strike back.

Richard Henry Savage was not the first writer to point out the inherent weaknesses of modern capitalism. Years after the Haymarket executions *The Alarm* suggested that modern capitalist society contained the potential for its own destruction:

> The very grandeur of its factors make them more powerful for destruction if they work the wrong way. A rich and powerful class, with all the earth to revel in, will the sooner burn and wither itself to destruction. A huge mass of humanity, knowing many wants and capabilities, yet deprived of the very means of life and development, and weakened by apathetic helplessness will sink an easy prey to death, disease, ignorance, slavery . . . We may be factors in the great whole, atoms working toward a grand upheaval as really as the symptoms themselves are resolving into elements of their own destruction.[23]

Echoing Most's views on the inherent weakness of capital while also applying the language of empirical, scientific analysis, *The Alarm* suggested that the depersonalising force of corporate wealth and government power could be turned against what were, in fact, the most vulnerable structures of authority. The dehumanising effects of industrial advancement were proving disastrous for workers who had been transformed into a shapeless collective 'mass', but what the capitalist fails to recognise, the journal suggests, is that this seemingly amorphous body is a vibrant collection of anonymous 'atoms' capable of independent action. According to this model, capitalism is itself an inherently anarchic and unregulated process that creates powerful subversive energy capable of destroying it from within if this energy is harnessed in the service of revolutionary change. Ignorant of the uncontrollable individual particles that form its whole, capitalism is deeply vulnerable to the constitutive 'elements of progress' that form it and influence its development.[24] The greater and more ruthlessly accumulative that the effects, or 'factors', of capital appear to be, the more it exposes itself to the uncontrolled actions of these anarchic atoms. As this kind of scientific-revolutionary rhetoric makes clear, anarchists found inspiration in the rational imperatives of science and evolution that seemed to provide a more coherent explanation of modernity than the chaos of industrial capitalism.

In a situation that appeared like open class warfare, the symbolism and destructiveness of high explosives appealed to the anarchist imagination with considerable rhetorical power. For those desperate enough to use it, dynamite offered a solution to their political and economic plight that was at once both practical and strikingly metaphorical, as the very 'thought of the humble bomb' promised to level the conflict between the individual terrorist and the forces of the state. This idea also provided radical writers and propagandists with a powerful emblem of resistance:

> Dynamite has come and our proud chevaliers and dainty dames hold up their hands in pious horror, and exclaim: 'What! Our institutions are at stake, our privileges endangered, our very lives rendered insecure!' . . . But this has been the work of slow evolution? Yes, because the bullet could reach but one individual. The new factor is far more powerful in its effects and in just so for far more rapid will be its work. Governments have no monopoly of it. One small bomb has already shaken the world. Will it be the last?[25]

Again, the logic of capital is used to highlight its weaknesses as the mass production of dynamite undermines the power of governments to monopolise its use or control the distribution of this explosive commodity. Appealing to the popular memory of the first skirmish between American revolutionaries and the British at Lexington, Massachussetts, the claim that the Haymarket explosion had 'shaken the world' echoes Ralph Waldo Emerson's description of the opening salvo of the American Revolution in the 'Concord Hymn' as 'the shot heard 'round the world': despite their status as aliens, the Chicago anarchists aligned themselves within the traditional discourse of American revolutionary politics, comparing the 'despotism' of the 'un-American'[26] forces of state and corporate power to British imperial tyranny and carving a place for themselves within a nativist radical tradition. Less discriminate than bullets or even cannon, the concept of dynamite, along with the notion that it was easy to acquire, made it an ideal propaganda weapon as, after the Haymarket crisis, British and American anarchists began to appreciate how a solitary revolutionary could terrorise the middle classes.

Some British anarchists were advocating dynamite before the Haymarket explosion. The London journal, *The Anarchist*, drew inspiration from attacks on London and St Petersburg carried out by Fenians and Russian nihilists and praised dynamite as 'The Modern Agent of Revolution'. Having appeared to have shifted the balance of power by reducing the 'supremacy of brute force and mere number', the new revolutionary strategy of 'dynamite warfare' that was being practised in the British capital showed the public how exposed 'vast cities' had become to the actions of revolutionaries. No longer protected by their police forces, each of these 'vulnerable points of attack', it argued, were now open to the possibility of 'wholesale destruction':

> At this moment a single wayfarer, with dynamite in his pocket, throws the cities of England in greater terror than would an army of a hundred thousand men landing at Dover . . . A handful of hunted homeless Nihilists are, able to terrorize all of the Russias, forcing its Emperor to live the life of a fugitive, and making his very coronation a problem of chance. Jupiter with his lightnings was scarcely more a master of the ancient world than is the mob with its bomb of dynamite, the avenging Fate of modern monarchies.[27]

On both sides of the Atlantic dynamite had become in the anarchist imagination a symbol of the unlimited agency of the solitary revolutionary. Having transformed cities into a new kind of battlefield, it promised to threaten the entire political system in Britain, according to *The Anarchist*. Just as *The Alarm* celebrated the humble bomb for democratising class warfare, *The Anarchist* viewed the revolutionary armed with high explosives as a new political force who posed a greater threat to British power than any foreign army.[28] The fusion of dynamite and desperation in the figure of the lone, unpredictable bomber or in the image of the bomb-wielding mob also reveals a transformation in the terms by which the urban poor were viewed. Since the 1790s, the image of the revolutionary crowd had been associated with republican revolutionary terror but, now that it might be armed with dynamite, the subversive potential of the mob was increased *ad infinitum*. Instead of throwing themselves in waves *en masse* against lines of troops or police, individuals within the crowd could now throw bombs at them. Thus, the 'triumphs of science and invention' could aid what the journal termed the 'individual war-maker', expanding his or her political power and even subjectivity through 'some agency like the perfected dynamite bomb and electrical battery', which could now reduce the anarchist's formerly omniscient enemies to 'mere targets for destruction'.[29]

The portable and concealable dynamite bomb, it seemed, was promising to make terrorism a fail-proof strategy; 'proclaimed from the house-tops', this 'Doctrine of Dynamite' would frighten every capitalist, from employers to judges, who would 'tremble at an outraged and maddened movement'. Such propaganda signals an abandonment of anarchism's enlightenment-inspired idealism in favour of urban terrorism because, according to *The Anarchist*, 'the science of chemistry', or material facts, was much 'stronger than public opinion, and can readily adapt itself to the open street'.[30] Echoing Most's concept of class warfare, the journal viewed dynamite as a scientific breakthrough and evolutionary leap in the cause of revolution that had particularly urban applications, since, in the city, individual revolutionaries could go underground and disappear from the surveillant gaze of the state: 'They can never know but some individual in a crowd has a bomb ready for use, for they are easily made. No accomplices are necessary, consequently the danger to the police is very great'.[31]

By announcing their belief in the virtue of high explosives, these British anarchists fuelled popular anxiety over the presence of the anarchist on English soil.[32] In a reflexive turn, paranoia over anarchism was lampooned in socialist journals like *Commonweal*, which pointed out that revolutionaries were not the only people prepared to set off explosions. Reporting the attempted assassination of the American financier, Russell Sage, it described how even failed capitalists were reverting to terrorism. Sage was attacked by a man who, on gaining access to his office:

> exploded a dynamite bomb which created wide-spread havoc, killing the intruder and one other man and severely injuring several clerks and visitors. Mr Sage, with the true instinct of his class, escaped serious injury by clutching hold of another person, a clerk, who happened to be in the office, and keeping him between himself and the threatened danger. The identity of the dynamiter who was blown to pieces by the explosion was for some time doubtful and conjectures concerning a conspiracy of anarchist desperadoes to blow up millionaires were ventilated by the press and accepted by the New York police authorities. Latterly, however, the victim of his own desperate deed has been identified as Henry L. Norcross, a Boston broker, whose mind had become unhinged owing to losses in stock speculations. The affair has, of course, created a wide-spread sensation . . .[33]

The shocks of dynamite were so democratic that they offered everyone from the politically disaffected to capitalist malcontents with spectacular opportunities to avenge themselves on the powerful governments and entrepreneurs who were crushing them out of existence. With this report, *Commonweal* highlighted to its readers how the unregulated anarchy of finance capitalism was producing violence within its own ranks. In the decade following the Haymarket tragedy, anarchist and socialist journals explored how the solitary, revolutionary or, indeed, simply disgruntled 'wayfarer' bearing a personal grudge and armed with dynamite might attempt to demolish the state and attack corporate power. The anarchist press tried to convince its readers that both of these entities had become vulnerable to terrorism and it seemed to the *Alarm*, the *Anarchist* and even *Commonweal* that modern capitalism had finally produced not so much its gravediggers, dedicated to 'the inevitably impending dissolution of modern bourgeois property',[34] as Marx and Engels had predicted, as its demolitionists.

Terrorism and *The Torch*

The Torch was the most noted British anarchist newspaper of this period. Published from 1891 until 1897, it was edited for five years by Helen and Olivia Rossetti, daughters of William Michael Rossetti, nieces of the Pre-Raphaelite artist Dante Gabriel Rossetti and the poet Christina Rossetti, and granddaughters of the painter Ford Madox Brown. The Rossetti sisters began publishing the *Torch* when the precociously politi-cised Helen Rossetti was aged only thirteen and Olivia sixteen, printing the first issue in the basement of their Primrose Hill home (the journal went into print in July 1892 after the initial reproduction of handwritten copies by hectograph). It survived until 1897, collapsing less than a year after their abrupt departure from the anarchist scene. Its originally mod-erate tone was transformed as *The Torch* began providing a literary and platform for anarchist militants. The journal's assimilation of extremist views boosted the Rossettis' position within British anarchist circles, with work attributed to the likes of Émile Henry appearing alongside that of moderates such as Kropotkin, who unsuccessfully tried to dis-suade the sisters from associating with the movement's more desperate characters.[35] Their idealistic association with revolutionaries is fictional-ised in Conrad's short story, 'The Informer', in which a wealthy young lady and anarchist 'Patroness' allows her upper middle-class home to become the headquarters of a militant anarchist group. Here literature gets published downstairs while bombs are manufactured in the attic, and her limited practical experience is compensated for by a 'severe' if purely theoretical outlook that she expresses in a series of 'sentimental articles with ferocious conclusions'. Published in the journals *Alarm Bell* and *Firebrand*, her pieces advocate 'the most advanced things . . . advanced . . . beyond all bounds of reason and decency', including calls for the abolition of 'all social ties', by which Conrad's narrator means the institution of marriage, and the dissemination of opinions 'intolerable to my sentiment of womanhood' including the 'licentious doctrine' of free love and, presumably, the circulation of abortion information. The articles reveal that she knows 'little of anything except of words', as the language of revolutionaries, like their deeds, lacks substantial meaning for Conrad. The dogmatic and unfeeling communication of radical ideas by means of deliberately overloaded language fails to express inherent truths, and the void that lies between reality and the imagined, idealised world contained in the naive expression of the young woman's 'abominable sentences'[36] is profound. As with Vladmir's bomb plot in *The Secret Agent*, Conrad treats terrorism in this story as the ultimate version of political 'spin', or as a public relations exercise that employs revolutionary language replete with striking imagery but which, lacking reason, has no meaning or potential to lift consciousness. By drawing attention to this particular anarchist's political and linguistic emptiness, Conrad points to the lapses of reason contained in her deliberately shocking revolutionary theories. These ideas are designed to capture popular attention but remain hopelessly insufficient to express, with any degree of truth, the reality they are intended to transform. Indeed, such is the gulf that separates ideology from reality in the story that the young woman falls in love with an anarchist who turns out to be a police agent and not a revolutionary at all.

In its 'Statement of Principles', *The Torch* describes itself 'as a journal advocating International Revolutionary Socialism' and condemns 'the present division of Society into rich & poor, oppressors & oppressed' for creating 'every evil under which we now labour'. Criticising hierarchically-driven attempts at 'Revolution from above', it instead advocates a widespread programme of political education as 'the only means by which the people can be brought to a true understanding of their wrongs, their duties and their rights'. Its principal purpose, then, was indoctrination and the dissemination of suitably written 'propaganda of every description', including pamphlets, lectures and foreign works translated into English and even work culled from rival anarchist journals.[37] Copying the methods of Christian pamphleteers, distributors left copies in public spaces such as railway carriages, waiting rooms, tramcars and cafés, a practice that, given some of its more shocking content, amounted to a form of literary terrorism. While Olive Garnett admired the young editors for 'inking their fingers in the cause of freedom',[38] she also disapproved of the journal's increasingly violent tone and was convinced that it had fallen under the influence of militant French anarchists at an early stage. Nevertheless, like Kropotkin, she continued to help with its publication and distribution, working with the Rossettis while Olivia wrote pamphlets advocating the use of bombs.[39]

A report on the London anarchists' annual Haymarket commemoration in 1892 gives an indication of the Rossetti sisters' direct, if theoretical, brand of anarchism. It describes how one banner on display at the event read 'To be Free is to dare and do',[40] and records that the crowd were told that 'the present society, unless quickly changed for the better must unavoidably bring its results in the shape of Ravachols'. James Tochatti, editor of the more cautious *Liberty*, addressed the meeting to advocate the use of 'protective force' while at the same time condemning 'Paris dynamite outrages',[41] and Kropotkin also spoke. He warned his British audience that the Haymarket explosion was the first instance of a worldwide revolution 'because the first sign of the rebellion, which is now breaking out everywhere, occurred there'.[42] Kropotkin shared the platform with the French anarchist Louise Michel, who, having survived the defeat of the Paris Commune in 1871, compared the plight of the executed Chicago anarchists to her own experience, asking: 'How, indeed, should one not wish for Anarchism when one has seen Paris red with the blood of the Communards, when one has seen old men homeless and starving lie down on the cold pavement to die?'[43] Michel presented revolt in relation to urban space and alienation,[44] reasoning that, should the city continue as the focus of human abandonment, then further violence was inevitable.[45] Regarding themselves as the armed vanguard of the politicised urban proletariat, the Communards considered the city to be the place where the symbolic 'instruments of monarchist and bourgeois oppression' were most pronounced and could be defeated.[46] This was precisely the space wherein the anonymous bombers glorified in the pages of the London *Alarm* were imagined both by militant anarchists and popular novelists to be roaming. Michel's words reinforced the concept that modern revolution would be a particularly urban phenomenon.[47]

The Communards' revolt was the most sustained anarchist effort against what they termed the 'traditional conceptions of the unified, centralized, despotic State'.[48] Lasting for three months, from March until May, it ended with all-out war between the revolutionaries and the Versailles-based government in which swathes of Paris were destroyed by artillery, public buildings were burned by the Communards and thousands of lives were taken in drastic government reprisals. Michel's concern about urban abandonment and the wreckage of people at the hands of an indifferent capitalism is an enduring trope in anarchist thought, and her theory of the integration of urban space with political violence, which was so heavily influenced by this context, also appeared in the *Alarm*. Statements such as those made by Michel indicate the extent to which British anarchists at the *fin de siècle* were conscious of the distinctly urban purchase of their ideas and actions. Kropotkin, who also viewed the city as the place where revolution would break out 'in the open, on the street', believed that anarchist writers and intellectuals would ultimately be carried by angry and untheoretical 'mobs' to victory. Like Marx, he was sure that capitalism, with its contradictions, was hurtling to its inevitable destruction as industrial modernity had created the conditions that made revolution unavoidable.[49] The totalising and spectacular processes of modernity, from industry, to the World Fair, to the bloody quelling of the Paris Commune and to the sight of the urban poor starving to death, were all evidence of what they perceived as modern capitalism's self-destructive tendencies.

These calls to action were followed to the letter by British revolutionaries like C. C. Davis who, when convicted for breaking a jeweller's shop window, gave his own hard-hitting speech from the dock. He was applauded by the *Torch*, which hoped that the unemployed would follow his example and 'not only break windows but sack the shops and take back some of the food, clothing and other necessaries of life which have been stolen from them by rich idlers'.[50] The same issue that lauded this practical, if relatively symbolic, deed also encouraged Germans to 'polish off the Kaiser'[51] and described Ravachol as the 'signal instance of a man whom our present society has driven to be a murderer and a dynamitard'.[52] Using Ravachol's example, Gustave Mollet also suggested that capitalism created terrorism:

> When such a man rises in his indignation and strikes (maybe blindly) at the cause of such misery, when he gives up everything that tends to his present comfort that he may but hasten the dawn of the day
> 'When man to man the world o'er
> Shall brothers be'
> Is [*sic*] not a criminal, even though, to bring nearer that day he commits deeds which are repulsive to our better nature.
> Such a man was Ravachol.[53]

Terrorism is rationalised by comparing it to the greater evils of capitalism, which is held to be the ultimate source of unhappiness. By defending this most notorious anarchist and explaining his actions, the Rossettis aligned their journal with the most militant strain of the revolutionary movement in Europe. When official patience with foreign anarchists wore thin after the Greenwich Park explosion of February 1892, *The Torch* also rushed to condemn the extradition to France of another bomber and friend of Émile Henry, Jean-Pierre François, who retaliated for Ravachol's execution by blowing up the Café Very in Paris. Fleeing to England soon after Henry's capture,[54] he was arrested in London and deported, *The Torch* complained, for merely 'speaking in a way that had become so common at public meetings'.[55]

The political crime of subversive speech is the central theme of Joseph Conrad's short story, 'An Anarchist', published in *Harper's Monthly Magazine* in 1906. This is in fact a tale of petit-bourgeois revenge in which an escaped South American convict and former Parisian mechanic describes his downfall after succumbing to 'Gloomy ideas – des idées noires' during a drinking bout with a pair of anarchists that ends with him drunkenly roaring 'Vive l'anarchie!' His own bourgeois values are subverted by the revolutionaries who convince him that the world is 'a dismal place' where 'poor wretches had to work and slave to the sole end that a few individuals should ride in carriages and live riotously in palaces'. Persuaded by their ideas he concludes that only one path is possible – 'Demolish the whole sacrée boutique':

> With a howl of rage he leaped suddenly upon the table. Kicking over bottles and glasses he yelled: 'Vive l'anarchie! Death to the capitalists!' He yelled this again and again. All round him broken glass was falling, chairs were swung high in the air, people were taking each other by the throat. The police dashed in. He hit, bit, scratched and struggled, till something crashed upon his head.[56]

As in 'The Informer', Conrad suggests that chaos, violence and personal tragedy are produced by the undisciplined and thoughtless expression of political language. On release from prison the mechanic is fired by his *patron*, denied any chance of re-entering the bourgeois sphere (he had hopes of starting his own business) and becomes a reluctant '*compagnon*' of the anarchists. He quickly learns that his comrades are more criminal than political as his involvement becomes less and less meaningful and he is finally coerced into taking part in a bank robbery during which, for a spectacularly destructive *finale*, 'a bomb would be thrown to wreck the place'. Betrayed by an informer (or possibly by another *agent provocateur?*), he is deported to French Guiana where he takes his revenge under the cover offered by a mass escape. The mechanic avenges himself on two of the gang for ruining his life 'with their phrases' and, armed with a warder's abandoned revolver, he turns on his former friends by realising his dream of becoming a bourgeois. Forcing them to row the boat that they have escaped in, he tells them: 'There are no comrades here. I am your *patron*' (pp. 80–1, 87). He also tells them that they have destroyed the language and political meaning of anarchism by ruining the word 'Comrade' and making it 'accursed', before shooting one and forcing the other to beg for his life:

'Mercy,' he whispered, faintly. 'Mercy for me! – comrade.'

'Ah, comrade,' I said in a, low tone. 'Yes, comrade, or course. Well, then, shout *Vive l'anarchie.'*

He flung up his arms, his face up to the sky and his mouth wide open in a great shout of despair. '*Vive l'anarchie! Vive –*'

He collapsed all in a heap, with a bullet through his head. (p. 89)

The mechanic's deadly embitterment is the result of the depoliticisation of radical language by the gang. His rage is caused by the disconnection of revolutionary words from their original, political sense – a dislocation that, for Conrad, symbolised the death of all hope. Even worse than his betrayal to the police, his imprisonment and deportation to South America, or his enslavement by the criminal gang, the mechanic's sense of the gang's worst outrage – the violence that it carries out against language and its meaning – is what drives him to kill. Permanently barred from re-entering the social class that he aspired to join, the mechanic re-asserts his earlier, pre-anarchist self by temporarily reclaiming his aspirant bourgeois identity, forcing the revolutionaries to work for him by rowing at gunpoint while, at the same time, repudiating the emptiness of their false political rhetoric. Like his ruined life, slogans no longer make any sense but the mechanic's attachment to the social and political purchase of the position of '*patron*', which he might have enjoyed had he not become entangled with the anarchists and their sham revolutionary politics, is equally pointless: when the narrator finds him he is the virtual slave of the corporate cattle baron, Harry Gee, by whom he was rescued when he washed up on his ranch. His short-lived spell as an overseer or manager ends in what he hopes will be an act of restorative violence with the killing of the anarchists but his hopeless position is renewed with his re-enslavement by a company manager. In this story Conrad criticises the idea that subversive words are worthy 'methods of propaganda'. As shown by the speeches made by Henry and his British comrade, C. C. Davis, anarchist language has a performative quality that Conrad viewed as being just as illusory as the narrative of capitalist improvement, since neither revolutions, governments or corporate power are capable of tolerating individual agency and innocence.

Conrad's criticism of the Rossettis' increasingly abstract political vision is underlined by their attempt to rationalise the explosion that killed twenty during a gala performance of Rossini's *William Tell* at Barcelona's Liceo theatre in 1893. *The Torch* described the attack as an act of class revenge:

Doubtless the act was brutal and terrible . . . But when reflecting on the barbarity with which workers are treated, thinking of the people murdered by poverty, shot down if they dare to complain . . . one is filled with hatred of our whole society, and, if one cannot approve of such ferocious vengeance, one excuses it, and feels sympathy for its author, for this unknown man who stands out from the crowd and single-handed against the whole forces of society, poor, persecuted, avenges with one blow his friend shot down, his comrades transported, and his ideal despised and persecuted.[57]

From this perspective, the act of political violence transforms the terrorist from an anonymous member of the collective population into the individuated 'author' of his own deed. By allowing him to assert his agency in the face of the depersonalising 'forces of society' and power of capital, the deed has distinguished the bomber from the mass (represented by the theatre audience), who, according to the Rossettis' logic, stand in for 'the whole'. Bombing the opera is justified by virtue of its having targeted middle-class power at its weakest point: culture. A context is also provided – that of repression in general and the indirect but no less brutal killing off of the poor through poverty – and the bomb, thrown in an equally indiscriminate manner in the theatre, is seen to counter the murderous methods of capitalism which, the anarchists argued, were consciously applied tools of repression. But while capital functions in a cold and impersonal, if no less deliberate manner, the lone terrorist, valorised as a 'soldier who devotes himself entirely to the Cause, and who, for a moment, strikes terror into the hearts of the middle-classes', exercises his revolutionary individuality and personal agency in the powerfully symbolic gesture of resistance-through-destruction. As in Émile Henry's speech from the dock, this article locates and embodies the wrongs of capital in the persons of anonymous bourgeois consumers – those enjoying an evening of culture at the theatre in this instance – who, like Henry's equally random targets in the Café Terminus, are held collectively responsible for the wider evils of capitalism, as their cultural or culinary pleasure is made possible by enormous inequality.[58] Despite the apparently motiveless appearance of such attacks, *The Torch* reasoned that they were responses, albeit brutal ones, to the indiscriminate effects of capital which could only be met by the equally blunt but ostentatiously symbolic tactic of terrorism.

In another article entitled 'Propaganda By Deed', which was attributed to Émile Henry and contained excerpts from his courtroom speech, *The Torch* explained to its readers that these attacks occurred because the 'abstract' institutions of power depended upon 'men of flesh and blood who represent them'. This meant that anarchists were left with no option other than violence:

There is therefore only one way of striking at these institutions; *ie*, to strike the men themselves, and we are happy to vindicate any energetic act of revolt against the Bourgeois society, for we do not lose sight of the fact that the Revolution can only result from the individual acts of rebellion all together.[59]

In order to counter the violent 'reality' of capitalism,[60] anarchists like Henry bombed, shot and stabbed the bourgeoisie, whom they regarded as worthy targets because they embodied the power of the state. As Henry's attacks on cafés illustrated, there was, according to his logic, a very broad degree of middle-class culpability. His theoretical model of resistance, based on the equation of bourgeois 'flesh' with the institutions that it represents, echoes Edmund Burke's earlier model of an organic body politic grounded in the very persons of its political representatives. Henry used his trial to publicise this belief and to publicly defy the power of the disciplinary state, exploding the possibility that his trial and execution might serve as a showcase for the authority of official power and its ability to bring the revolutionary individual under control. As Michel Foucault has explained, the judicial process was designed to symbolically re-inscribe authority but its coercive force was halted by such performative assertions of subversive political identity.[61] Such speeches given from the dock, often followed by yells of defiance at the executioner, and their circulation in journals like *The Torch*, were powerful gestures of resistance in their own right made by anarchists against their re-integration, by means of *la guillotine*, back into the dynamic of state power.

Salvador Franch, the anarchist who carried out the Liceo attack, was quickly arrested and, like Henry, asserted his own political agency on the scaffold:

> Stoical in the last, he asked the executioner to be quick, and, with his last breath, exclaimed 'Vivre [*sic*] l'anarchie!'
> The crowd hooted the priest and the executioner, and the death of Franch has done more for the propaganda of Anarchy than his act itself.[62]

Unlike Conrad, who read such slogans as exclamations of 'imbecility',[63] *The Torch* viewed them as symbolic statements of individualised resistance that were even more politically powerful than the 'author's' original terrorist action. Franch, it argued, intensified the impact of his attack by applying speech, and therefore meaning, to the deed and in doing so transformed his own death into a platform for the anarchist cause. While the dangers of public execution and its potential for creating political martyrs had been acknowledged in Britain with its abandonment in 1868 in favour of a more privatised form of judicial killing (which suddenly made the British imperial 'spectacle' appear much less spectacular), continental anarchists were afforded opportunities to publicise their actions to the bitter end.[64] By publishing these statements, *The Torch* answered Parsons's call for the left-wing press to continue his own political 'work and duty'.[65] Quoting the novelist Maurice Barrès, it claimed that such examples of undiluted revolutionary language affected, even infected, the less radical when, '(o)verwrought by that terrible alcohol called death ... moderates behaved like madmen'. As a result, Barrès claimed, the words '"Vive l'Anarchie" appeared "on many lips"'.[66]

Alexander Cohen, a Dutch anarchist and friend of Henry's, lived in exile in London after his deportation from France in 1893,[67] where he wrote for the Rossettis' journal. Cohen described his comrade as the 'most logical' but also the 'most terrible of all the Anarchists' because the meaning of his deeds could only be absorbed by pausing to understand 'what he himself said':

> no one could explain his acts more eloquently and at the same time more lucidly than he himself did ... The clear, incisive sentences of his speech, now sparkling with wit and now again solemn, but always marked by their formidable logic fell like blows dealt by a sledge hammer on the brains of these poor imbeciles. Poor jurors! Trembling with superstitious fear, their brows clammy with sweat, there they sat, fascinated, hypnotised looking at this disdainful youth, this impassioned destroyer; fear tortured them, the fear of a whole society which must die and which will not go![68]

According to Cohen, the clarity, power and rational precision of Henry's speech served his enemies with an object lesson in the political sublime, simultaneously captivating and terrorising the jury at his trial. In contrast to bourgeois cowardice and vulgarity, his stance even had aesthetic purity: 'As to the middle-classes, the rulers, jurors, and judges who, piteous dwarfs, undertook to sit in judgement on this man, they were crushed by the beauty of his character and by his proud stoicism'.[69] For Cohen, Henry's courtroom speech about the impending doom of capitalist society illustrated the power of anarchist propaganda to capture, enthral and occupy the bourgeois imagination. Even mainstream journalists, he argued, could not resist the persuasive, even hypnotic force of his words, and Cohen repeated the description of Henry given in the conservative *L'Echo de Paris* as 'the most formidable adversary that the existing organisation of capitalist society has raised against itself'.[70] Henry's threats were also understood by politicians like Henry Maret, who considered his speech as the key to appreciating why such 'unimpeachably courageous' but desperate young men 'hurl hap-hazard their engines of destruction': 'If they strike the rich – well, whosoever they may be, they are oppressors. If it strikes the poor, it is still well, for they were resigned and did not revolt ... this sect does not pretend to deal justice, but to make room for it'.[71] These views, Cohen believed, justified

Henry's 'unimpeachable' logic, which would outlive the infamy of his actions; his unscripted courtroom declarations, 'translated into every tongue and read by millions of persons', he believed, would do more 'to propagate the idea of revolt and liberty than a hundred thousand polished speeches'.[72] *The Torch* also celebrated Sadi Carnot's assassination in 1894 for similarly focusing worldwide attention on its cause. It did so, the journal claimed, by highlighting the vulnerability of heads of state, instantaneously sending 'the Bourgeoisie, the world over, into a paroxysm of rage and terror' and teaching them that the 'persecuted, the outcast, had proved themselves the strongest'.[73]

But *The Torch* did not just carry militant opinion columns and speeches from the dock. It also made room for the literary efforts of its contributors, one of which suggested that London had the potential to become a site of anarchist terror:

> Cruel City, London, London,
> Where, duped slaves of devil's creeds,
> Men and women desperate, undone,
> Dream such dreams and do such deeds.
>
> London, London, cruel city,
> By day serpent, by night vampire,
> God in thy great pity, pity,
> Give us light – though it be fire![74]

Like Commune-era Paris, London is imagined here as being ripe for destruction on a millennial scale. Such calls for the annihilation of the British capital were accompanied by poems praising assassination and applauding the men of 'despair and death' who 'steal on and kill' their oppressors to die 'like men', claiming 'An eye for an eye, and a tooth / for a tooth, and a life for a life!'[75] According to this untitled poem, terrorism restores the anarchist's agency and selfhood along with his masculinity. Such contributions to the journal reveal that a violent imagination was not the sole preserve of writers of 'penny dreadfuls', while the expression of revolutionary sentiment in specially penned music-hall songs also indicates the social quality of the London anarchist scene:

> Capitalism's got to go
> (Got to go *go! to go!*)
> The capitalist had better know,
> And so we've come to wake him,
> And if he points to the door,
> (To the door, to the door,)
> And turns him around to sleep and snore,
> Why then we'll have to shake him.

And if he calls his bobby in
(Bobby in, bobby in,)
Or sets his priest to cant of 'sin'
Why then we'll have to fight him,
And if he points his maxim gun,
(Maxim gun, maxim gun)
'Twill be his final bit of fun,
For we will dynamite him.[76]

Celebrating the shocks of political violence (the capitalist, priest and policeman are shaken by dynamite) such songs, much like Rudyard Kipling's pro-empire ballads, were designed to transmit ideology on the level of popular culture. While their rowdy enthusiasm for blowing people up contrasted with the milder ideas of Kropotkin or Errico Malatesta, they do suggest that the Rossettis were nonetheless sticking to the educational focus outlined in their 1892 mission statement. Their publication in *The Torch* points to a distinct revolutionary lifestyle and an associated sense of community, centred on the reading of radical journals and the sharing of the militant ideas that they contained. Written to be performed in chorus in venues like the Autonomie Club on Tottenham Court Road, they reveal how revolutionary ideology could also be spread by Bakhtinian, even folkish means.

The News as Fiction: *A Girl Among the Anarchists*

In their collaborative, confessional novel, *A Girl Among the Anarchists*, Helen and Olivia Rossetti gave an autobiographical account of their experience of publishing the *Torch*. Describing their journey along 'the path of the propagandist' (p. 95), their vivid analysis of the London anarchist movement comes complete with internal conflicts and contradictions. The novel charts the political development and eventual disillusionment of a teenage revolutionary, Isabel Meredith, who comes to appreciate the need to distinguish British identity from the alien values of European revolutionary politics. An ultimately conservative work, its realistic description of British anarchism presents the movement from within, charting the gradual erosion of Meredith's initially unlimited sympathy for her foreign comrades. Capturing the inherently chaotic nature of anarchism, the Rossettis provide character sketches of eccentric personalities, discuss topics like culture, assassination and free love, and finally distinguish between British domestic politics and the inherently 'foreign' circumstances fuelling terrorism in Europe (p. 105). As her insight deepens, Meredith's initially romantic conception of radical politics wanes along with her idealism, and she comes to realise that anarchism is an essentially alien ideology.

A political and social nonconformist from an early age, it seems inevitable that Meredith should fall in with revolutionaries: along with her sister, Caroline, and a brother, Raymond, she is subjected to her father's 'advanced' ideas, which include some eccentric schooling and allowing the children 'full liberty to follow our various bents': 'The idea of providing us with suitable society, of launching us out into the world, of troubling us to see that we conformed to the ordinary conventions of society, never occurred to him'. Their bohemian home in Fitzroy Square is visited by a stream of foreigners and political 'cranks', exposure to whom politicises the 'precocious' children at an early age. The visitors even nickname Meredith 'Charlotte Corday', after Jean-Paul Marat's Girondist assassin, for showing an unusually deep interest in the French Revolution, which she expresses in her 'ambition . . . to die on a scaffold or a barricade, shouting Liberty, Equality, Fraternity' and in her recitals of political poetry. One guest even warns her father that it will not be long before the child 'will be making bombs . . . and blowing us all up' (pp. 1–3, 7–10).

Upon their father's death the children become financially secure enough to pursue their individual interests. Meredith's revolutionary idealism intensifies when a socialist editor publishes her work in his paper but it is only after meeting the famous nihilist, Nekrovitch, a character modelled on the Russian political refugee, Sergius Stepniak, that she converts to anarchism. Drawn by the anarchist's 'right to complete liberty of action' and the conviction that 'morality is relative, and personal and can never be imposed from without', she enters the world of the revolutionary:

> The bold thought and lofty ideal which made of each man a law unto himself, answerable for his own actions only to his own conscience, acting righteously towards others as the result of his feeling of solidarity and not because of any external compulsion, captivated my mind. (p. 18)

Here she encounters an eclectic circle of radicals and 'pseudo-Bohemian' types, including Russian nihilists, liberals, socialists and Fabians, along with plenty of artists. Although Nekrovitch's contacts are mostly insincere 'faddists', Meredith makes contact with anarchists 'of all nationalities' (p. 22), and the Russian soon confides in her that his movement is in desperate need of 'propagandists' possessing both 'brains and money' (p. 33). She accepts his invitation to write for his journal, *The Bomb*, where she finds evidence of the connection between revolutionary politics and the world of art. Upon entering its offices, she finds the premises scattered with objects left by its founder, an artist, whose 'relics' include portraits of anarchist martyrs, an obsolete revolver and bottles filled with chemicals (p. 44). The staff consists of Russians who speak no English, an alcoholic, a painter and some 'fishy and nondescript characters of the Hebraic race' (p. 47), and as Meredith begins her work they discuss the strange death of Augustin Myers, an 'obscure little French anarchist' who has just blown himself up in a London park (p. 39). His brother, Jacob, a former editor of *The Bomb*, is suspected of being an informer and of setting his brother up with a faulty device, as the explosion was followed by several arrests, including those of the paper's publisher, Banter, and its printer, O'Flynn. Meredith's first experience of anarchist politics is modelled on the circumstances surrounding the Greenwich Park explosion and the police-inspired 'Walsall Plot' of 1892, in which five anarchists, including the Italian Jean Battola and the French refugee Victor Cailes, were arrested in possession of chloroform, bomb casings and bomb-making manuals. It becomes clear to Meredith that the state is determined to convict the men on the strength of the only evidence that it has: 'gaseous speeches' made by the pair calling for 'wholesale assassination' and 'war to the death' (p. 72). Their conviction and sentencing to five years' hard labour introduces her to the dreary and unromantic reality of anarchist politics:

> Holloway and Newgate, Slater's Mews and the Middle Temple, barristers and solicitors, judges and juries and detectives; appointments in queer places to meet queer people – all this had passed before me with the rapidity of a landscape viewed from the window of an express train; and now that the chapter had closed, I found that it was but the preface to the real business I had set my shoulder to. (p. 74)

Meredith's transformation by her sudden immersion is followed by her appointment as editor of *The Bomb*, which, rather wisely, she renames *Tocsin*. So begins her career in a type of sensational political journalism that 'would never consent to destroy the effect of a tale by slavish subservience to facts' (p. 86) and, as her reputation as a propagandist grows, so too does the paper's list of contributors. Starting with the entire staff of a French journal who, having escaped to England to avoid trial under the *lois scélérats*, are the 'very reincarnation of Murger's Bohemians' (p. 105), *Tocsin* expands with further 'unannounced invasions':

> Unexpected persons would arrive at the office, of whom nobody perhaps knew anything ... The most rudimentary notions of Anarchist etiquette forbade any of us from inquiring the name, address, or intentions of such intruders. They were allowed to stay on or to disappear as inexplicitly as they

came. They were known, if by any name at all, as Jack or Jim, Giovanni or Jacques, and this was allowed to suffice. (p. 117)

These intrusions leave the journal vulnerable to police infiltration but Meredith develops a natural ability to identify plain-clothes men: 'Every Anarchist learns in time to spot a detective at first sight, and we relied on this instinct as a safeguard against spies' (pp. 117–18). The cranks gathering at the office include 'argumentative people with time on their hands', and even 'downright lunatics' while the foreigners begin to dominate as the movement's 'English element' is overwhelmed and the office 'swamped' by refugees from abroad. Suspecting that the anarchists are the product of more serious political conditions on the Continent, Meredith wonders whether her ideology is suited to address- ing domestic British problems. Meanwhile, the *Tocsin* office, with its 'magnetic' appeal and promise of unquestioned asylum, becomes a miniature version of modern Britain, replicating on a smaller scale the attraction of contemporary London, housing a 'strange medley' of politicised foreigners (pp. 131–2). However this does not prevent Meredith from distinguishing between anarchists and undercover detec- tives, as she quickly learns to spot the policemen who try to spy on the movement because their Englishness makes them stand out. At the same time, despite the air of camaraderie at the paper, she also becomes increasingly aware that *Tocsin* is failing to articulate native radicalism: as the propaganda at *Tocsin* degenerates into a chaotic 'Babel of voices' (p. 117), Meredith comes to realise that, as an ideology, anarchism is a profoundly denationalised phenomenon that is dependent on the input of a loosely affiliated network of unconnected foreigners and 'declasses', (*sic*) a cross-section of whom appear at her office at will (p. 131).

As Meredith's involvement deepens, so does her realisation that the movement is not exclusively composed of idealists and martyrs. She encounters others whom she describes as 'degraded' individuals, similar to Conrad's criminally-minded anarchists, who are motivated by a combination of 'dissatisfaction and covetousness', but Meredith also distinguishes these from the sincere revolutionaries who are committed to the principle of 'personal revolt'. This section of the movement is represented by anarchists like Émile Henry who progress 'from words to deeds' and whose 'totally different viewpoint' cannot be rationalised by the rest of society. Echoing Henry's speech from the dock, Meredith describes how it is impossible for the bourgeois, or 'normal man', to 'understand or judge fanatics. He cannot grasp their motive, their point of view, and is therefore morally incapable of judging them'. Not only do these anarchists explode the interpretative faculties of the average middle-class spectator with their actions, they also deny the 'futile' political-psychological categorisations and definitions established by right-wing specialists: 'men of science', like Nordau, Le Bon and Cesare Lombroso, who try to 'dissect and classify abnormal people and abnormal ideas, to discover that geniuses are mad' and that political rebels are 'born criminals'. Unlike the models of decadent, subversive and criminal behaviour suggested by these writers the 'strangely and intricately' constructed revolutionary consciousness contains 'the most heterogenous qualities'. These defy the linear, descriptive imperatives of conservative psychology, which are exploded by the fusion of 'fanaticism, heroism, criminality, and not unfrequently a spicing of genius' in the personality of a genuine anarchist. Meredith also suggests a connection between political violence and brilliance, stressing the intellectual qualities of the terrorist, whose violence is the 'offspring of ideas' and 'abstract' thought that are beyond the range of bourgeois comprehension. Because it cannot be processed within this imaginary, the 'thrill of horror' that is generated by terrorism appears like the work of genius (pp. 187–8, 190). Yet, despite her swipe at early sociology and criminal psychology, Meredith's equation of the 'ordinary forces of life' with bourgeois experience betrays her growing uneasiness with anarchism.

Henry's deeds are understood by Meredith to be the product of a superior, enlightened and 'pervertedly logical' consciousness:

> He committed them not in moments of passion, but with all the *sang froid* of a man governed by reason. His defence when on trial was a masterpiece of logical deduction and eloquent reasoning . . . when he threw his bomb among the crowd in the Café Terminus, maiming and killing indiscriminately, Émile Henry was performing his duty according to his own lights . . . (pp. 188–9)

A coldly rational man of 'intellect and some culture', Henry put his purely 'theoretical' brand of anarchism into effect by attacking 'society at large' instead of opting for the more personalised strategy of targeted assassination. The result is the death and injury inflicted on society's most 'indifferent members' – the café frequenters who, in his eyes, were culpable of the equally indifferent abuses committed against the poor by capitalism:

> 'Society at large is guilty; society at large must suffer. Society is fairly well represented by the mixed crowd in a café. I will attack this crowd indiscriminately, and kill as many of their number as I can. I will unreluctantly end my days on the scaffold in order to accomplish this very obvious duty . . .' (pp. 189–90)

Troubled by the continuum between anarchist language and revolutionary violence, Meredith finds herself considering the paradox of propaganda by deed: while morally unsettling for her, it remains, so far as she can see, a logical reaction to the circumstances being experienced by the continental revolutionist, whose struggle is entirely different to that being waged in Britain. The values that it represents, therefore, are entirely alien. She accepts his speech from the dock as a 'masterpiece' of logic, recognising it as a statement of reason, as opposed to an outburst of passion, and acknowledges that in inflicting such 'horror' on his victims (p. 188), Henry adopted for his own revolutionary purposes the brutal indifference of the capitalist. His café-bombing, based on the assumption of the collective guilt of his targets, is the result of a keen intellect misguided not by ideology but by the harsh material conditions of political and economic life in late nineteenth-century France. Meredith does not dispute the correctness of Henry's conclusion, in so far as it has reached through the direct experience of class conflict in Europe, but her discussion of his motivations divulges an awareness of the danger of possessing such knowledge: Henry embodies the idea of propaganda by deed, being represented in anarchist propaganda and in the movement's revolutionary mythology as representing the acme of individual agency. But in her view, this type of 'theoretical protest translated into deeds' is the brutal materialisation of reason in an unreasonable, un-British and uniquely latin world of suffering, where drastic acts of 'personal and class revenge' (p. 194) are the normal currency of political revolt. As Meredith comes to realise, the movement in London lacks a British cultural grounding because 'what genuine Anarchists there are here are mostly foreigners' (p. 132).

Contrasting with Henry's impersonal tactics, another method of terror is advocated by 'A-', a frequent visitor to *Tocsin* and 'dynamitard by passion' who, we are told, 'belonged rather to the Ravachol type'. One of the 'ignorant confreres' who lack Henry's analytical finesse, his desire to 'exterminate' the rich is a purely personal matter: 'When my stomach is empty and my boots let in water, the mere sight of a replete and well-clothed man makes me feel like murder' (p. 194). In Meredith's view this type of revolutionary, though equally as indiscriminate as Henry, is a less shocking figure because he is practical, passionate and romantic. When she brings the Italian bomber and bank robber, Giacomo Giannoli, to the National Gallery, the sight of Da Vinci's painting *Madonna delle Roccie* provokes an outburst against culture: 'I should love to burn them all, to raze all these galleries and museums to the ground, and libraries with them. For what are libraries but storehouses of human superstition and error? We must free ourselves from the past, free ourselves utterly from its toils, if the future is to be ours'. Giannoli's 'gospel of destruction' is based on the revolutionary concept of 'entirely individual activity', revealing his desire to destroy culture, especially in its catholic, Renaissance expression which he regards as underpinning oppression.[77] Like Henry James's anarchists, he views art as the decadent product of capital but, whereas James himself was unashamed by culture's dependence on wealth, Giannoli views the National Gallery as a potential target with considerable symbolic value. For Giannoli, respect for the aura of art is no more than a bourgeois 'superstition' and he considers the museum's fetishisation of classical works and, by extension, their authority, as encoding capitalism's ideology. Impressed by Meredith's strength of character and autonomy, he trusts her completely with these views: '"You are a true Anarchist," he said to me one day, "and I would trust you with anything, *even*," and he emphasised the word so as to give greater weight to the compliment, "*even* with *explosives*"' (pp. 210–13). From this moment onward *A Girl Among the Anarchists* documents Meredith's growing distress at her increasingly difficult position within a movement composed of revolutionaries who, like the bank robbers in Conrad's story, 'An Anarchist', are given to using 'long words they barely understood'. The movement's legitimate members, – 'dreamers' and 'incorrigible idealists' like Henry and Giannoli – are outnumbered by its undesirables, or 'heterogeneous elements' (pp. 272–4) and, having once praised anarchism for resisting all known political categorisations, Meredith abandons the movement. She finally quits during a police raid carried out after Giannoli makes a failed attempt on the life of the Spanish prime minister in Barcelona and accepts 'the destined end of the *Tocsin* and of my active revolutionary propaganda'. 'I had changed,' she recalls, asking 'Why not let the dead bury the dead?' But her comrades have not and as she leaves, she hears the Irish printer, M'Dermott, uttering 'bloodthirsty' threats against the police as they make another raid on the newspaper office, promising 'to get rid of them by our insidious means, and then go in for wholesale assassination!' (pp. 298–9).

In his preface to *A Girl Among the Anarchists*, the novelist Morley Roberts expressed his hope that the Rossettis' account of their involvement in the political underground would dispel the popular image of anarchists as 'wild-eyed' fanatics and . . . 'outrage mongers' (Preface, pp. xxi). But Isabel Meredith's experiences, culminating in her decision to abandon her comrades, offer a reinforcement rather than a revision of this view. The anarchist movement is divided, disruptive and incapable of discriminating between political circumstances in Europe and Britain, while the novel's last words on political violence are uttered by an Irish malcontent, whose threats to kill policemen underline the foreignness of anarchists in Britain. Political violence is alien to Isabel Meredith who, as a young woman of bourgeois means, cannot abandon the class to which she feels she ultimately belongs, and her reclamation of her former, bourgeois self sees her walking away from *Tocsin* 'a sadder if a wiser woman' (p. 302). Her final action in the office is revealing: on re-entering the 'normal' world, she no longer finds the police threatening and, despite having expended much time and energy avoiding them thus far, she is able to walk past the detectives, out of the raided premises and back into the political and social mainstream without being stopped or questioned. Her political adventure over, she returns to the security of the bourgeois sphere and, although she leaves the anarchists as a transformed and enlightened woman, her British middle-class identity remains intact and undisturbed.

Anarchism and Literary Politics

Pointing to the decadent movement and its 'revolutionary attitude on purely artistic questions', Félix Dubois maintained that anarchism had a pernicious influence on *fin de siècle* literature.[78] Alexander Cohen also highlighted the subversive connection between art and politics in *The Torch*, where his commentary on Oscar Wilde's trial seemed to validate Max Nordau's model of an 'anthropological family' of degenerates that included anarchist revolutionaries alongside decadent writers, criminals, 'pronounced lunatics' and prostitutes.[79] Cohen read the great literary and sexual scandal of the 1890s as an assault on Wilde's own anti-authoritarianism, which was no secret by the time that he took his own place in the dock in 1895. His decadent views on the pleasures of excess had a decidedly radical edge and blended anarchist politics with aesthetic ideas, with Lord Henry Wotton's discussion of the moral necessity of resisting authority in *The Picture of Dorian Gray* being a case in point: 'Discord is to be forced to be in harmony with others . . . for any man of culture to accept the standard of his age is a form of the grossest immorality'.[80]

Cohen criticised the press for its sensational coverage of Wilde's trial and, in doing so, reversed Nordau's idea of modern degeneracy by applying it to the news media:

> The indecency was in the attitude of the press-jackals, draining hard cash out of this case by means of the artificially increased sale of their prostituted papers, rejoicing themselves in Wilde's pain and distress, and every day giving a detailed account of every wrinkle in his face.
>
> At bottom they had never really forgiven this man his talent, his dramatic and literary success, a success which was due to writings the spirit of which

was quite at variance with the accepted moralities and the base hypocrisies of the Philistines. Hence the savagery of their joy . . . Wilde's sentence was a monstrosity engendered by mere hypocrisy.[81]

Driven by indecent motives and the commercialisation of their trade, those writing for the 'delighted evening-jackal'[82] eagerly punished Wilde for his own celebrity, applying to his radical literary and public persona by means of their printed 'hypocrisies' the kind of disciplinary authority that Émile Henry's earlier trial had failed to impose. Unlike Henry, who would always be an outsider, Wilde was both a revolutionary and a celebrity at the same time whose enemies within the establishment, Cohen believed, were patiently waiting for an opportunity to punish him for his public successes. The radical literary and political beliefs that Cohen believed the trial was really attacking were the product of Wilde's Irish nationalist background, which made his support for revolutionary causes a matter of second nature. His mother, Lady Jane Francesca Wilde, famously wrote nationalist poems and articles in Thomas Davis's Young Ireland paper, the *Nation*, under the pseudonym 'Speranza' and in 1882 her son defended the apparently indefensible by describing the Phoenix Park killings as 'the fruit of seven centuries of injustice'.[83] Wilde was also personally connected with anarchist revolutionaries: in 1892 he paid £100 bail for the anarchist poet, John Evelyn Barlas, who fired shots at the Speaker's residence in Westminster. His response to Barlas's letter of thanks acknowledges the link between the pair's political and literary idealism: 'Whatever I did was merely what you would have done for me or for any friend of yours whom you admired and appreciated. We poets and dreamers are all brothers'. A month later he followed up the favour by sponsoring Barlas's application for a reader's ticket to the Reading Room of the British Museum.[84]

Dubois feared this kind of literary-political 'innovation': by linking aesthetic and revolutionary ideas, the anarchists, he suggested, would attract talented writers to their cause, blurring the boundary between art and politics and creating a new generation of avant-garde subversives capable of producing literary but no less politically inspired work with a broader appeal than straightforwardly polemical writing. Believing that a movement as 'pronounced' as anarchism would never remain confined to the purely political sphere, he warned that its infiltration of the world of art was only a matter of time. Given the existing tendencies of anarchist and decadent writers to promote the 'shadier sides of contemporary society', the convergence of their common literary 'delineations' was inevitable.[85] Cohen also recognised this, and his defence of Oscar Wilde attempted to broaden the anarchist movement by associating him with its aims. He regarded Wilde's prosecution as an anarchist *cause celèbre* that summarised what was wrong with society:

> In Wilde's case . . . there is no question of violence done to anybody. There was neither violation nor even seduction. Subject to a passion, which it is not my place or anybody else's to judge of, Wilde sought to satisfy this passion, with the free consent of the creatures who so vilely turned round and gave evidence against him.
>
> These individuals having all, long since, reached the age of discretion, and having all prostituted themselves before they made Wilde's acquaintance, I fail to see the harm done to society, and consequently the right of society to claim redress, *ie.*, to punish.
>
> And, again, I ask in the name of what principle, whether 'sacred' or not, Wilde was interfered with?[86]

Wilde's case shed light on a number of issues. To begin with he had corrupted no-one but only followed his sexual preference, or 'passion', which, Cohen argued, was the business of none to make judgement upon as he had solicited with consenting men who were sex workers before he had ever encountered them. Cohen's main point, however, lies in his questioning of the real motivation behind Wilde's prosecution and public humiliation by the 'prostitutes' of the press, which suggested to him that the trial was politically motivated. Wilde's persecution for his sexual and political choices also allowed *The Torch* an opportunity to draw attention to his status as an Irishman and to compare its own anti-authoritarianism to the anti-imperial stance of the rebellious Irish when, a fortnight after the publication of Cohen's condemnation of the Wilde trial, it praised subversive Irishness. Its comparison of anarchist belief with Irish republicanism provides an interesting sequel to its sympathetic discussion of the aesthete's underground sexuality:

> Our position is somewhat akin to that of the Irishman, who, when asked his political opinions, said he was 'ag'in the government'. We are forever 'ag'in the government' no matter whether it be Tory or Liberal, Monarchy, Autocracy, or Democracy, convinced that only in the overthrow of government in all its forms and the recognition of individual liberty, is it possible for humanity to lead a pure, free, and natural life.[87]

The connection is made indirectly here, as was Cohen's suggestion that Wilde was subjected to a political show trial, but it is clear that his persecution was interpreted by anarchists as an example of state oppression while they also read his pursuit of personal and sexual liberty as a manifestation of Irish resistance to British imperialism. In Cohen's estimate he was doubly punished, firstly for his homosexuality and then for his literary talent, and in this subsequent article *The Torch* clearly announced its sympathy for Irish nationalism. The relationship between literature and terrorism is highlighted by these instances of solidarity, first with the particular case of Oscar Wilde, the political and sexual 'deviant', and then with the Irish cause in general. An Irishman whose sexual practice equalled subversion in the eyes of the moral establishment, Wilde's doubly rebellious individualism was also read by anarchists as a model for their own anti-authoritarianism as his plight in court seemed to them to mirror their own political struggle. Siding with him, they regarded his martyrdom as equally important for those who wished to live a life that was as 'pure, free and natural' as had been the deaths of Henry, Franch and Ravachol.[88]

Cohen's defence of Wilde explains the simultaneously literary and political character of *fin de siècle* anarchism, as enunciated by Henry's courtroom praise for Zola's fiction and by Ravachol's admission, published in William Morris's Socialist League journal, *Commonweal*, that Eugène Sue 'produced a profound impression upon me'. Ravachol explained this connection between literature and revolution by warning the court that tried him that 'words are not enough', and that only the necessary 'acts of violence' could 'awaken men's minds by giving food for reflection to the self-satisfied, troubling the sleep of the well-filled, and inducing people to study great social questions'.[89] When coupled with deeds, revolutionary language and realistic literature, he suggested, could produce profound social change. *Commonweal*, which by the early 1890s had fallen under the influence of the well-heeled anarchist, David J. Nicoll, and his anarchist circle within the Socialist League, provided another platform for militant views.[90] Nicoll himself proved that radical writing was a form of subversion in its own right when he was tried for incitement to murder along with the paper's publisher, C. W. Mowbray, and sentenced to eighteen months' imprisonment for publishing an editorial that recommended assassination. He also published *An Anarchist Feast at the Opera*, a violently worded pamphlet that was produced in evidence at the Walsall trial in the same issue, even though the accused described it as 'police literature'.[91] The controversial editorial consisted of a speech that Nicoll gave in Hyde Park advising anarchists to 'act ... alone and unaided' against undercover policemen, the 'monster' Secretary of State, Henry Matthews, the High Court judge Sir Henry 'Hangman' Hawkins and the detective inspector William Melville, asking 'Are these men *fit to live?*'[92]

Nicoll's conviction provoked sympathetic poetry from the more moderate anarchist newspaper, *Freedom*, which published the 'Ballad of Scotland Yard':

> There's John Sweeney, he's an Irishman, you see,
> And I call all his comrades to remark,
> Right well he's learnt the lessons of the gallant R.I.C.,
> And practised them in Sundays in the Park,
> For he moved inconspicuously thro' the mob
> In a close-fitting mustard-color'd coat
> With a special duty truncheon in his fob
> And the tablets of his memory for a 'note.'[93]

Again anarchists are found comparing the Irish situation to their own, as dubious counter-insurgency methods ('the lessons of the gallant R.I.C.') are practised by Sweeney's detectives in the domestic arena of London. Despite the charges brought against Nicoll, *Commonweal* continued in the same angry vein and, indignant that someone 'full of love' like Ravachol should have met with the guillotine, it demanded 'vengeance', praised his contribution to 'the propaganda' and expressed hope that it would report in the near future on 'any English Ravachol who will not hesitate to use *all* means, however desperate and unfashionable':

> Our masters have no feeling for us and if we are men, with brains and hands, we must have none for them. It is a war to the knife and up to the hilt. They gain their ends by fraud, exploitation and murder; and we must not blame those who, in order to live and help the Cause, use the same weapons.[94]

Commonweal proved exceptionally unapologetic in promoting this dialectic of endless struggle. Unbothered by the potentially damaging content of 'incendiary'[95] political literature like *An Anarchist Feast at the Opera*, it continued to look forward to the day of all-out revolution, 'when a Government depot of ammunition can be safely and suddenly made to vanish into the hands of those who will use it in self-defence'.[96]

Writing in *The Torch* in June 1893, the politically suspect anarchist H. B. Samuels went even further by proposing suicide as the most autonomous deed possible in the 'living death' of modernity. The modern metropolis, with its 'vast, busy, struggling stream of life hurrying, panting, snatching at every opportunity for personal profit, pleasure or popularity' was a death trap in its own right. So, he reasoned, 'let every reader if he or she cares consider this and give the answer in word or deed to the foul, diabolical, monstrosity, SOCIETY, that produces such inconsistent, incoherent, disconnected beings as we are'.[97] Samuels was the brother-in-law of Martial Bourdin, who killed himself while trying to plant the Greenwich Park bomb, was later accused by Nicoll of being an informer, and is considered the model for Joseph Conrad's *agent provocateur*, Adolf Verloc.[98] His praise for auto-destruction as the ultimate form of political protest is an unusual trope in anarchist writing as it was more commonplace for revolutionaries to blame the system, as did *Freedom: A Journal of Anarchist-Communism*, which warned that modern capitalism, with its 'crushing' competition, was to blame for all of society's ills, even the self-destructing anarchist 'martyrs' and their 'contempt for death'.[99]

The Conservative Response

In his 1904 memoir, *At Scotland Yard*, the retired CID Chief Inspector, John Sweeney, described his dealings with anarchist publications. A native of County Clare and a fluent Irish speaker, Sweeney spent years spying on Irish nationalist groups in London before becoming an expert in the art of 'Anarchist hunting' during the 1890s.[100] Although an immigrant himself, he complained that Britain's lax asylum laws were making England a 'dumping-ground' for Europe's unwanted 'human refuse'[101] and cited the Walsall plot as proof that countless continental anarchist conspiracies were afoot in England. Sweeney pointed to the 'incendiary character' of the anarchists' journals and pamphlets, describing their content as 'astonishing stuff . . . circulated amongst revolutionaries the more thoroughly to poison their minds'.[102] Worse, this literature was also designed to spread political contagion, or 'infect with the Anarchist taint' the minds of those who were 'still comparatively unsmirched'.[103] Like Dubois, Sweeney was also convinced that the ideas communicated by anarchist publications were dangerously infectious. During one raid his men found terrorist paraphernalia that included a box of sulphuric acid, some suspicious-looking powder and a set of notes reading 'Long Live Anarchy' and 'Down with laws and government'.[104] They also found a more sinister text recommending that 'brutal force is indispensable'. This document, which copied almost verbatim Johann Most's handbook, *Science of Revolutionary Warfare*, declared that 'it is absolutely necessary to burn the churches, palaces, convents, soldier-barracks, prefectures, lawyers' and barristers' offices, fortresses, prisons', and 'destroy entirely' the 'business' class: 'we shall contrive also that the blood which will flow in the streets be not ours, *but that of the infamous rich*, who have starved us . . . that is our first and veritable work'. The pamphlet also advised anarchists to attack their enemies with high explosives:

> Well, no more organisations; no more dictators . . . let us occupy ourselves with chemistry, and let us manufacture promptly bombs, dynamite, and other explosive matters much more efficacious than guns and barricades, to bring

the destruction of the actual state of things and above all to spare the precious blood of our comrades.[105]

Owing to the dangerous content of these publications, Sweeney urged that the ownership and publication of anarchist literature should be treated as seriously 'as the possession of explosive materials', called for a muzzling process that would prevent the foreign radicals whom he considered the 'scum of the earth' from promoting their 'poisonous' ideas in Britain, and even recommended an all-out ban on people declaring themselves anarchists.[106] The conservative French writer, Peter Latouche, also acknowledged the link between this type of 'literary activity' and the commission of revolutionary deeds. Citing the spread of subversive ideas via cheap and 'exceedingly popular' anarchist journals and pamphlets, Latouche warned his readers that these publications motivated political crime because 'assassination, which is the outcome of Anarchist views, is practically never the result of conspiracy'. Inexpensively produced and easily circulated, these prints allowed even 'the poorest companions to aid in spreading anarchist principles'.[107] But in contrast to Sweeney, who wanted to introduce a total ban on anarchist expression, Latouche warned that the suppression of this material in France in the wake of the Carnot assassination had alienated radicals even further and intensified the bitterness of their writing. Being 'loud in their promise of murder and every form of crime, and vying with each other in profanity and grossness', the French anarchist presses went on to produce even more violently worded material in the aftermath of the *lois scélérats*. The intensification of political repression made *persona non grata* of writers and editors who, with nothing to lose, went on to express increasingly radical beliefs and ideas. Outlawed by this draconian legislation, moderate French anarchists were driven underground, with the result that their organisations were decentralised even further while the influence of the movement's more 'extreme individualists' simply intensified. As far as Latouche could see, the illegal status of French anarchists encouraged the spread of propaganda that, in its increasingly desperate attempts to capture public attention, had begun to mirror the competitive advertising strategies of the capitalist.[108]

Much as the Rossettis did, Latouche also blamed immigration for transplanting this essentially continental ideology onto British soil, and accused continental coercionists with transforming London into 'the Mecca of all revolutionary exiles' and making the city the European production centre for anarchist propaganda. As proof, he cited the 'perverted' documents, seized during the Walsall arrests, that contained 'explicit' instructions on bomb making, poisoning, burglary, forging and even conducting 'illegal surgical operations', or abortions. But while he regarded them as being 'beyond ordinary comprehension',[109] Latouche stressed the wisdom of the British policy of tolerating political refugees, as he knew that blanket censorship in France had only intensified the anarchists' culture of desperation. Terrorism, he warned, thrived under coercion and, by tolerating the 'undesirable alien' and his publications, the British government was limiting the circulation of potentially more dangerous literature:

> Were these journals allowed to be freely printed and openly circulated, as in England, they must necessarily be shorn of their appallingly criminal character ... although the Continental method may reduce the number issued to a minimum, one of these murderous sheets may reach the hands of a lunatic and inspire him to a foul deed at which nations stand aghast. Far better permit a print shorn of incitement to murder to reach a circulation of sixty thousand, than to limit the circulation of to even six copies by a system which leaves the writers free to inspire the foulest deeds even in the smallest area.[110]

Complete censorship could leave the state vulnerable to the subversive power of the 'unbridled license' of a single article but, Latouche observed, the more sensible 'English method' allowed for the watered-down expression of anarchist opinion, limiting its potential to cause lasting harm. Repressive legislation might reduce the number of subversive journals in circulation but it also left their editors and contributors with no option but to attack the state in a more direct fashion and, as a result, the publication of only one of these 'insidious' pamphlets[111] could have disastrous consequences. The examples cited by Latouche included the 'Anarchist's Guide', a 'complete hand-book for the practical militant anarchist' that provided information on manufacturing home-made bombs like the 'incendiary cigarette' and the booby-trapped tall hat. Another pamphlet, 'Police Spies', offered advice on how to avoid surveillance, and others described terrorism as the new 'front', or 'battlefield of the people ... where deeds of reprisal can be accomplished'. Disregarding his own dire warning about circulating dangerous anarchist ideas, Latouche even published the most notorious document found on the Walsall anarchists, *An Anarchist Feast at the Opera*, which gave practical instructions on theatre-bombing. Claiming to be motivated by hatred for the middle class, its anonymous author describes the 'apotheosis' of a burning theatre and provides, in gloating details, instructions on how to bring about this 'delightful spectacle'. After severing gas-pipes and hiding a time bomb behind the stage, the anarchist could return to watch the rest of the first act and then leave to see the inferno from a safe distance to enjoy 'seeing on a fine evening this splendid building all in flames in the middle of a brilliant feast'. The collapsing ceiling, the reader is told, will have 'the effect of grapeshot on the jolly spectators':

> After all, what do we care for the failings of humanity, even with regard to the women and children of that race of robbers and real criminals? Do not their young become wolves likewise? Are their females less eager for prey than the males? Therefore it is pious work to crown worthily those revels which the bandits throw as a defiance at our misery and sufferings. Would not a single one amongst us feel his heart beat with an immense joy in hearing the shriveling (*sic*) of the grease of the rich, and the howlings of that mass of flesh swarming in the midst of that immense vessel all in a blaze? In fact, what delight in our town to see even at a distance such a red conflagration! A thousand times more beautiful to our eyes than the dazzling of the purest diamond! To hear howlings, the cries of pain and the rage of the wolves, their females and young ones in the midst of the furnace – a thousand times more pleasant and more vibrating to our ears than the songs of half-a-dozen prostitutes above an orchestra. (pp. 129–30)

The crescendo of violence described in *An Anarchist Feast at the Opera* reveals how anarchists like Nicoll, who also insisted on publishing it in *Commonweal* (and, if the document is a forgery, their enemies in the police who planted it), manipulated political fear. Comparing dying women and children to wolves, its disturbing imaginative register reaches much farther than Émile Henry's dispassionate rhetoric with remarkably depraved flourish. While Henry's speech appealed to anarchist reason while simultaneously shocking bourgeois sensibilities, this document, in contrast, expresses joy at the enactment of atrocity. While the practical advice that it offers is very basic (no information is provided on how to access the theatre's gas pipes, or on how to build a time bomb, for that matter), the pamphlet's meaning is contained in the intensity of its description of violence, and, in particular, on the glee with which it describes the indiscriminate killing of women and children. Lacking the logical rationale of even the most militant articles that appeared in anarchist newspapers, the pamphlet would seem to be, most likely, a forgery designed to incriminate as it shares little, stylistically, with the statements of actual terrorists like Henry who justified his war against the 'bourgeois' in chillingly plain language. Driven by violent exaggeration rather than by any political intention, the document's real purpose was to shock and frighten readers and, perhaps, also jurors in a court who would have listened as it was read aloud as evidence during the Walsall trial.

Terrorism and Advertising

Police forgers were not the only writers who recognised anarchism's shock-value. In December 1894, two budding entrepreneurs, Charles Henry Dent and Frank Cannock, used anarchist publicity tactics in an attempt to win a competition that had been designed to publicise the popular periodical, *Answers*. Posting twenty-four hoax bombs to government offices and MPs in London, as well as to the mayors of Liverpool, Manchester, Bradford, Leeds, Exeter, Bristol and Gloucester, their unsuccessful attempt to win the competition's £250 prize money became known as the Tamworth Bomb Scare. The dodge involved sending a copy of the journal along with a detonator fitted to a firing mechanism that exploded when each of the parcels was opened. Dent and Cannock hoped that when the smoke cleared and the recipients found a note telling them 'page 452 explains the joke', they would appreciate the humour of their gesture and back their campaign. On this page, in which the advertisement had been printed, a note was left asking: 'Does this win, say yes, please'. When the pair were brought to trial, it was noted that the fake bombs were modelled on one of the Walsall plotters' devices, and the defence's explanation that they had hoped to 'create a sensation' and advertise the newspaper under-lined Sweeney's point that anarchism was a contagious phenomenon. Adapting the voice of dynamite to entrepreneurial ends by repackag-ing it as a business gimmick, the Tamworth Bomb Scare showed how political violence could also be employed as a marketing tactic because, although it was a purely commercial endeavour, the plot used the sub-versive strategy of generating a 'sudden shock'[112] in order to create publicity. In doing so, it validated conservative fears that, if allowed to go unchecked, anarchism could infect mainstream culture. Indeed, this instance of the hoax bomb-as-advertising concept is perhaps the first example of the manipulation of terrorism for commercial ends. With their transplantation from the world of radical politics into the sphere of competitive capitalist individualism, subversive words and deeds assumed a new role as stimulants for late Victorian consumption. While the Rossettis concluded their novel by arguing that anarchism was an unsuitable model for British politics, the *Answers* scam underlined how its ideology of unrestricted individualism might appeal to the capital-ist imagination. As Félix Dubois noted, '(t)he spirit of innovation is an essential characteristic of the anarchist'.[113]

These examples of anarchist writing underline how propaganda by word and deed impacted upon the public consciousness during late Victorian period and into the Edwardian years. The spectacular political tactic of terrorism occurred alongside a wider panoply of modern excitements but, as Sweeney pointed out, it captured the popular imagination by providing the public with 'the greatest sensation' possible.[114] The closely related practices of terrorism and subversive writing also appeared as a branding strategy, as illustrated by the example of the Tamworth Bomb Scare. Although conservatives like Latouche warned their readers that 'there is no crime, however horrible, which is not gathered under the aegis of Anarchism', its capacity to cause political and moral outrage had an enduring appeal: 'The very fact that certain crimes might especially shock the public, commend them to the Anarchistic mind which delights in shocking and terrifying the bourgeoisie'.[115] Despite disputes over the authenticity of pamphlets like *An Anarchist Feast at the Opera*, anarchist journals are replete with equally militant if not quite so graphic accounts of, and recommendations for, the use of political violence. In attempting to upset middle-class sensibilities, the language of anarchist terrorism became political-aesthetic matter in what Latouche termed its 'murderous sheets'.[116] Denials of the links between anarchist thought and violent political action were undermined by an anarchist literary culture that did not discriminate between the writings of terrorists and pacifists, which were often published side by side.[117] *Fin de siècle* anarchist literature was characterised as much by its expression of political violence as it was by philosophical rhetoric, as propaganda-by-word was an essential aspect of political violence. While moderates tried to counter the negative impressions conveyed by this literary propaganda, their claims that anarchy was 'synonymous with liberty . . .'[118] and that 'the negation of law' was merely the 'expression of equal liberty'[119] were not met warmly by a bourgeois public frightened by the words and deeds of revolutionaries like Henry and Ravachol: the Walsall defendants' claims that detectives planted evidence including bombs and the pamphlet *An Anarchist Feast at the Opera* found little sympathy among jurors representative of a class that was regularly threatened by underground newspapers. Regardless of the extent of their veracity, these publications reflected anarchism's deliberate celebration of its political marginality, its rejection of authority and illegality. The political beliefs of moderates were bound to the actions of Ravachol and Henry, and anarchism was defined not as a purely ideological formation but as a violently subversive pandemic threatening to erupt in England and transform British streets into an urban battlefront. As one of the Haymarket martyrs was attributed with telling his comrades in the British journal, *Freedom*: 'Anybody can make and use bombs; they cost only from ten to fifteen cents a piece. These are facts and I can't help that'.[120]

Notes

1. Quoted in Félix Dubois, *The Anarchist Peril*, trans. Ralph Derechef (London: T. Fisher Unwin, 1894); originally published as *Le péril anarchiste* (Paris: Flammarion 1894), p. 177.
2. See Haia Shpayer-Makov, 'Anarchism in British Public Opinion, 1880–1914', *Victorian Studies* 31.4, Summer 1988, pp. 487–516.
3. Pierre Joseph Proudhon, *What is Property?*, translated from *Qu'est-ce que la propriété?* by Donald R. Kelley and Bonnie G. Smith (Cambridge: Cambridge University Press, 1994), p. 34.
4. Peter Kropotkin, 'The Spirit of Revolt', in *Anarchism: A Collection of Revolutionary Writings* (Mineola: Dover, 2002), p. 40.
5. 'War to the Knife', *The Anarchist*, London, No. 19, September 1896, p. 1.
6. For a contemporary critique of anarchism's association with violence, disorder and confusion in the popular political language of this period, see Errico Malatesta, 'Anarchy Defined', from *Anarchy* (1907), reprinted in George Woodcock (ed.), *The Anarchist Reader* (Glasgow: Fontana, 1977), pp. 62–4.
7. James Joll, *The Anarchists* (London: Methuen, 1969), p. 326.
8. 'Notes on the News', *The Commonweal*, Vol. 5, No. 160, 2 February 1889, p. 33.
9. Frederic Trautmann, *The Voice of Terror: A Biography of Johann Most* (Westport, CT & London: Greenwood Press, 1980), p. xxi.
10. Quoted in Trautmann, *The Voice of Terror*, pp. 50, 52, 44.
11. Quoted in Hermia Oliver, *The International Anarchist Movement in England* (London: Croom Helm, 1983), p. 18.
12. *Die Freiheit*, 13 May, 1882, quoted in Trautmann, *The Voice of Terror*, p. 70.
13. Johann Most, *Science of Revolutionary Warfare* (translated from *Revolutionäre Kriegwissenschaft* [1885]; reprinted Eldorado: Desert Publications, 1978), pp. 11, 30, 50, 47–8, 57–8, 62.
14. Most, *Science of Revolutionary Warfare*, pp. 60, 54, 30, 13–15, 22, 29.
15. Trautmann, *The Voice of Terror*, p. 130. The political chaos gripping Chicago in May 1886 occurred in the context of a decade of relentless and virtually unimpeded state and corporate violence against striking workers and campaigners for labour reform. See Philip S. Foner, 'Editor's Introduction', *The Autobiographies of the Haymarket Martyrs* (New York: Monad Press, 1977).
16. George Woodcock, *Anarchism: A History of Libertarian Ideas and Movements* (Harmondsworth: Penguin, 1970), p. 438. Quoting State Attorney Grinnell's summation speech, Foner also describes how the men were openly tried for their beliefs: 'Law is on trial. Anarchy is on trial. These men have been selected, picked out by the grand jury and indicted because they were leaders. They are no more guilty than the thousands who follow them. Gentlemen of the jury; convict these men, make examples of them, hang them and you save our institutions, our society.' See Foner, *The Autobiographies of the Haymarket Martyrs*, p. 8.
17. 'The Police', *The Alarm*, Chicago, Vol. 2, No. 1, 22 August 1885.

18. Jeffory A. Clymer, *America's Culture of Terrorism* (Chapel Hill and London: The University of North Carolina Press, 2003), pp. 34–5.
19. 'The Military Organization', *The Alarm*, Chicago, Vol. 2, No. 1, 22 August 1885.
20. Quoted in Peter Marshall, *Demanding the Impossible: A History of Anarchism* (London: Fontana, 1992), p. 397.
21. Melville E. Stone, editor of the *Daily News*, visited Parsons shortly before his execution and unsuccessfully pleaded with him to retract the oration. See 'Men Die But Principles Live', *The Alarm*, Vol. 1, No.14, Saturday, 16 June 1888.
22. See Emma Goldman, *Living My Life* (Dover: New York, 1970, originally published by Knopf, 1931), Vol. 1, p. 8.
23. 'Rebellion as a Sacred Duty as Well as a Right – Our Duty as Revolutionists', *The Alarm*, Chicago and New York, Vol. 1, No. 15, 23 June 1888.
24. Ibid.
25. 'The Resources of Civilisation', *The Alarm*, Chicago and New York, Vol. 1, No. 16, 30 June 1888.
26. 'Autobiography of Albert R. Parsons', in Foner, *The Autobiographies of the Haymarket Martyrs*, pp. 56, 36.
27. Unsigned, 'Dynamite: The Modern Agent of Revolution', *The Anarchist*, London, No. 1, March 1885, p. 4.
28. Contemporary paranoia over the possibility of an attack on Britain by rival European powers fuelled the popular literary genre of the invasion narrative and is perhaps most famously captured in George Tomkyns Chesney's anti-Prussian fantasy of 1871, *The Battle of Dorking*.
29. 'Dynamite: The Modern Agent of Revolution', *The Anarchist*, ibid.
30. 'The Doctrine of Dynamite', *The Anarchist*, London, No. 17, 1 July 1886, p. 1.
31. 'Beware', The Anarchist, London, No. 17, 1 July 1886, p. 3.
32. Clymer discusses the reaction of the American anarchist press to the Haymarket tragedy. See Clymer, *America's Culture of Terrorism*, chap. 1, 'Imagining Terrorism in America: The 1886 Chicago Haymarket Bombing'.
33. 'Dynamite Versus Dollars', *The Commonweal*, Vol. 7, No. 296, 9 January 1892, p. 5.
34. Marx Karl and Friedrich Engels, *The Communist Manifesto*, Preface to the Russian Edition of 1882 (Harmondsworth: Penguin, 1967), p. 56.
35. See Olive Garnett, *Tea and Anarchy! The Bloomsbury Diary of Olive Garnett, 1890–1893*, ed. Barry C. Johnson (London: Bartlett's Press, 1989), p. 155.
36. Conrad, 'The Informer', in *The Lagoon and Other Stories* (Oxford and New York: Oxford University Press, 1997), pp. 100–1, 104.
37. 'Statement of Principles', *The Torch*, Vol. 2, No. 2, February 1892, p. 1.
38. Ibid. p. 5.
39. Garnett, *Tea and Anarchy!*, p. 209.
40. 'Chicago Anarchist Commemoration', *The Torch*, Vol. 2, No. 11, 15 November 1892, p. 5.
41. *The Torch*, ibid. p. 6.

42. *The Torch*, ibid. p. 8.
43. *The Torch*, ibid. p. 7.
44. Responding to the resurgence of radicalism that erupted in the Paris street battles of May 1968, the American anarchist, Murray Bookchin, reiterated Michel's stress on the revolutionary potential of a new urban type: the rioter. According to Bookchin:

    crowd actions involve the rediscovery of the streets and the effort to liberate them. Ultimately, it is in the streets that power must be dissolved: for the streets, where daily life is endured, suffered and eroded, and where power is confronted and fought, must be turned into the domain where daily life is enjoyed, created and nourished.

    For Bookchin the Commune was 'a festival of the streets,' enacted by the tradesmen and itinerant intellectuals forming the 'social debris' of their era. Like Michel, he viewed the city as inorganic and criticized urbanisation for inhibiting the growth of 'rounded' consciousness. See Murray Bookchin, 'Post Scarcity Anarchism' and 'Forms of Freedom', in *Post Scarcity Anarchism* (Edinburgh and Oakland: AK Press, 2004), pp. 15, 90, 105.
45. Michel was deported to a penal settlement after the suppression of the Commune where she is described in William Henry Savage's *The Anarchist* as 'musing on the shores of a South Sea island, dreaming of Paris, once more flooded with flaming petroleum!' See Savage, *The Anarchist*, Vol. I, p. 93.
46. This according to the British-based Revolutionary Commune Group, a collective of survivors of the cataclysm, in their 1874 statement, 'To Supporters of the Commune', reprinted in Eugene Schulkind (ed.), *The Paris Commune of 1871: The View from the Left* (London: Jonathan Cape, 1972), pp. 235–6. Quotation is from p. 236.
47. See Kropotkin, 'The Spirit of Revolt', p. 42.
48. Arthur Arnould, from *Histoire Populaire et Parliament de la Commune de Paris* (1878), in Schulkind (ed.), *The Paris Commune of 1871*, pp. 242–3, quotation from p. 242.
49. Unlike Marx they were also convinced that revolution was always immediate. See Karl Marx, Postface to the Second Edition (1873), *Capital*, Vol. 1 (London: Penguin, 1990).
50. 'A Debate: What We Want For Britain', *The Torch*, Vol. 3, No. 3, 15 March 1893, pp. 7–8.
51. Helen Rossetti, 'Notes On News', *The Torch*, Vol. 3, No. 3, 15 March 1893, p. 7.
52. '1892, A Retrospect', *The Torch*, Vol. 3, No. 1, 15 January 1893, p. 2.
53. Mollet, Gustave, 'Ravachol', *The Torch*, Vol. 3, No. 8, August 1893, p. 4.
54. 'Notes on News', *The Torch*, Vol. 3, No. 1, 15 January 1893, pp. 10–11.
55. 'Notes on News: Report on the Extradition of Francois, Accused of Complicity in the Café Very Explosion of April 25, 1892', *The Torch*, Vol. 3, No. 1, 15 January 1892, pp. 10–11.
56. Joseph Conrad, 'An Anarchist' (1906), in *The Lagoon and Other Stories* (Oxford and New York: Oxford University Press, 1997), pp. 78–9. Thereafter cited in the text.

57. 'Spain', *The Torch*, Vol. 7, New Series, 18 December 1894, pp. 5–6.

58. The entire bourgeoisie was held by anarchists to be 'pestilential marauders' who used 'force and violence on all sides.' See 'The Dangerous Classes', *Freedom: A Revolutionary Communist-Anarchist Monthly* (Chicago), 1 June 1891, Vol. 1, No. 8.

59. Émile Henry, 'Propaganda By Deed', *The Torch*, New Series, No. 4, October 1894, p. 5.

60. Ibid.

61. See Michel Foucault, *Discipline and Punish*, trans. Alan Sheridan from *Surveiller et punir: Naissance de la prison* (Éditions Gallimard, 1975) (London: Penguin, 1991).

62. 'Spain', *The Torch*, Vol. 7, New Series, 18 December 1894, pp. 5–6. Quotation from p. 6.

63. Conrad, 'An Anarchist', p. 70.

64. The last public executions to take place in Britain were those of three Fenians, William Allen, Michael Larkin and Michael O'Brien who became known as 'The Manchester Martyrs'. The trio undermined the imperial spectacle by staging their own powerful counter-performance, their last words on the scaffold being 'God save Ireland'. See Paul Rose and Patrick Quinlivan, *The Fenians in England, 1865–1872: A Sense of Insecurity* (London: Calder, 1982).

65. 'Men Die But Principles Live', *The Alarm*, Vol. 1, No.14, Saturday, 16 June 1888.

66. Quoted from *Journal*, 22 May 1894, *The Torch*, October 1894, p. 26.

67. Luc Sante, 'Introduction' to Félix Fénéon, *Novels in Three Lines* (New York: New York Review of Books, 2007, translated from the series 'Nouvelles en trios lignes', *Le Matin*, 1906), pp. xvi–xvii.

68. Alexander Cohen, 'Émile Henry', *The Torch*, Vol. 11, No. 2, 18 July 1895, pp. 24–6.

69. Ibid.

70. Henry Bauer, in *L'Echo de Paris*, quoted in Cohen, 'Émile Henry', p. 26.

71. From *The Radical*, 6 February 1895, quoted in Cohen, 'Émile Henry', pp. 24–5.

72. Cohen, 'Émile Henry'.

73. Benjamin Preig, '1894: A Retrospect', *The Torch*, No. 8, New Series, 18 January 1895, p. 5.

74. Unsigned, *The Torch*, New Series, No. 4, October 1894, p. 12.

75. F. Adams, untitled, *The Torch*, Vol. 3, No. 7, July 1893, p. 4.

76. 'Verses by L. S. B', *The Torch*, No. 8, New Series, 18 January 1894.

77. Giannoli's desire to destroy art is similar to the Futurists' proposed assault on 'museums, libraries and academies': 'let them come, the gay incendiaries with the charred fingers! . . . Set fire to the library shelves! Turn aside the canals to flood the museums! . . . Oh, the joy of seeing the glorious old canvasses bobbing adrift on those waters, discoloured and shredded! Take up your pickaxes, your axes and hammers, and wreck, wreck the venerable cities, pitilessly!' See 'The Founding and Manifesto of Futurism' in F. T. Marinetti, *Let's Murder the Moonshine: Selected Writings*, trans. R. W. Flint and Arthur A. Coppotelli (Los Angeles: Sun & Moon Press, 1991).

78. Dubois, *The Anarchist Peril*, p. 124.

79. See Max Nordau, *Degeneration* (London: Heinemann, 1895), Introduction, vii.

80. Oscar Wilde, *The Picture of Dorian Gray* (London: Penguin, 2000), p. 77.

81. Alexander Cohen, untitled, *The Torch*, Vol. 2, No. 1, 18 June 1895, p. 6.

82. Ibid.

83. Quoted in Declan Kiberd, *Inventing Ireland: The Literature of the Modern Nation* (London: Vintage, 1995), p. 46. Wilde's most obvious and sustained engagement with political violence was, of course, his first, melodramatic play of 1880, *Vera, or the Nihilists*.

84. Wilde to John Barlas, 19 January and 4 February, 1892, *The Complete Letters of Oscar Wilde*, ed. Merlin Holland and Rupert Hart-Davis (New York: Henry Holt, 2000), pp. 511, 512.

85. Dubois cited the example of Octave Mirbeau, whose eulogy for the terrorist Ravachol appeared in the literary periodical *Entreaties*, which also published the chemical formula for dynamite. See Dubois, *The Anarchist Peril*, pp. 124, 126–7.

86. Cohen, untitled, *The Torch*, Vol. 2, No. 1, 18 June 1895, pp. 5–6.

87. 'News At Home and Abroad', *The Torch*, Vol. 2, No. 2, July 1895, p. 17.

88. Cohen was not the only anarchist to appreciate the connection between Wilde's political and sexual identities. Emma Goldman also defended Wilde in her autobiography, explaining that she had no difficulty with 'sexual variation' (p. 269). Goldman had a very broad view of anarchism, which she viewed as a movement of 'intellectuals' (p. 436) that linked 'the world of labor, art and letters'. See Goldman, *Living My Life* (New York: Dover Publications, 1970), 2 vols, Vol. 1, pp. 269, 436, 482.

89. 'Ravachol: His Autobiography', *The Commonweal: The Official Journal of the Socialist League*, Vol. 7, No. 312, 7 May 1892.

90. See E. P. Thompson, *William Morris: Romantic to Revolutionary* (London: Merlin Press, 1976, reprinted 1996), pp. 566–71.

91. 'The Speeches of Our Comrades', *The Commonweal*, Vol. 7, No. 309, 9 April 1892.

92. 'The Walsall Anarchists. Condemned To Penal Servitude', *The Commonweal*, Vol. 7, No. 309, 9 April 1892.

93. 'S. O.', 'A Ballad of Scotland Yard', *Freedom: A Journal of Anarchist Communism*, Vol. 6, No. 68, p. 53.

94. 'Ravachol', *Freedom: A Journal of Anarchist Communism*, Vol. 7, No. 322, 16 July 1892.

95. 'An Incendiary Pamphlet', *Freedom: A Journal of Anarchist Communism*, Vol. 7, No. 309, 9 April 1892.

96. 'Revolution and Physical Force', *The Commonweal*, Vol. 7, No. 325, 6 August 1892.

97. H. B. Samuels, 'Life or Death: Suicide and Insanity', *The Torch*, Vol. 3, No. 6, 15 June 1893, pp. 1–3.

98. See David Mulry, 'Popular Accounts of the Greenwich Bombing and Conrad's *The Secret Agent*', *Rocky Mountain Review of Language and Literature*, 54.2 (2000), pp. 43–64.

99. *The Echo*, 6 February 1895, reprinted in *Freedom*, March 1894, p. 11.

100. John Sweeney, *At Scotland Yard: Being the Experiences During Twenty-*

Seven Years of Service by John Sweeney, Late Detective Inspector, Criminal Investigation Department, New Scotland Yard (London: Grant Richards, 1904), p. 36.

101. Ibid. pp. 70, 203.
102. Ibid. p. 212.
103. Ibid. pp. 204–5.
104. Ibid. p. 242.
105. Ibid. pp. 213–14.
106. Ibid. pp. 271, 295–6, 223–4.
107. Peter Latouche, *Anarchy! An Authentic Exposition of the Methods of Anarchists and the Aims of Anarchism* (London: Everett & Co., 1908), pp. 77, 281, 66, 137–8.
108. Ibid. p. 69
109. Ibid. pp. 22, 26, 126, 11–12, 25, 29.
110. Ibid. pp. 36–8.
111. Ibid. p. 69.
112. Sweeney, *At Scotland Yard*, pp. 160, 164, 165.
113. Dubois, *The Anarchist Peril*, p. 211.
114. Sweeney, *At Scotland Yard*, p. 166.
115. Latouche, *Anarchy!*, p. 143.
116. Latouche, *Anarchy!*, p. 38.
117. One anarchist songbook that featured William Morris's socialist anthem 'All for the Cause' also included ditties by lesser-known bards with titles like 'We'll Turn Things Upside Down!' and 'People Who Wouldn't Be Missed', which lists possible targets for the aspiring revolutionary, including 'patriotic gentlemen', 'emigration-mongers', policemen, jerry-builders, evangelists, 'sweating middlemen', rent-collectors, landlords, employers and businessmen of any class. See *Songs for Socialists* (Aberdeen: James Leatham, 1890), pp. 16–17.
118. Henry Seymour, *Anarchy: Theory and Practice* (London: Henry Seymour, 1888), p. 4.
119. Ibid. p. 8.
120. George Engel, 'Autobiography of George Engel', *Freedom: A Revolutionary Communist-Anarchist Monthly*, Chicago, Vol. 1, No. 8, 1 June 1891.

Chapter 5

Shock Modernism: *Blast* and the Radical Politics of Vorticism

No man, unless he has had a great deal of it, likes government . . .[1]

As Vanessa R. Schwartz has suggested, overt sensationalising and spectacularising provided the means by which experience was commodified in late nineteenth-century popular culture.[2] As we have seen with the dynamite novel, Fenian and anarchist politics were marketed as popular literary spectacles, with revolutionary violence being presented to readers in the guise of popular forms such as detective fiction, imperial quest adventures and science fantasy. While Joseph Conrad's *The Secret Agent* bridged the void separating the various types of dynamite novel of the 1880s and 1890s from literary modernism, Wyndham Lewis's Vorticist movement adopted political violence as the basis of its avant-garde modernist practice. Vorticism brought literary shock to a new aesthetic level in its journal, *Blast*, in which the individualist politics of anarchism were fused with an 'exploding'[3] oppositional ideology of art. Vorticism's deliberately agitational style, which Lewis engineered with the help of Ezra Pound to appear as a subversive literary and artistic 'fashion', was intended to shock the sensibilities of the bourgeois public that it was aimed at; paradoxically, Lewis hoped that the influential circles targeted in *Blast* would ultimately become its sponsors.[4] With its stress on the importance of the individual, the journal shared its anarchic leanings with Richard Aldington's more mainstream modernist journal, *The Egoist*, which stressed the need to examine the workings of the individual 'nervous system', as opposed to the collective imperatives being advocated by Fabian socialism.[5] By attempting to upstage Aldington's journal, *Blast* set out to test the nerves of its readers rather than encourage them to introspectively examine their consciously modern selves. While Aldington promoted Joyce's stream of consciousness technique by serialising *A Portrait of the Artist as a Young Man*, Lewis and Pound proposed a more direct method of securing their readers' attentions by attacking the mainstream of literary, artistic and even political thought. In doing so, Vorticism aped the political practices of anarchism and exploited what Walter Benjamin would later identify as the 'traumatophile' consciousness of the modern subject.[6]

Oversized and characterised by its 'violent' typography,[7] *Blast* flamboyantly voiced the Vorticists' literary discord and dissent and, in doing so, appeared, as Lewis deliberately intended, as a journal designed for the 'militant' modernist.[8] Its striking poetics, particularly as expressed through its manifestos, have been overlooked owing to a critical tendency to regard Lewis's writing in this period as secondary to his painting or as an unimportant forerunner to his later novels and political books. Yet the journal's articulation of an oppositional modernism reveals his lifelong obsession with individualism and his antagonism toward political and artistic authority. Both of these elements of Lewis's writing surfaced within the journal, in which militant posturing and the commercialisation of art went hand in hand.[9] *Blast*'s political stance was paradoxical, allowing it to function, as Lewis described in its promotional catalogue, both as 'a vehicle for the propagation of . . . ideas' and as a promotional 'picture gallery' for Vorticist painters.[10] Its first issue, published in June 1914, was designed to serve as an extended aesthetic shock and although its sequel, the 'War Number', was less overtly radical (Paul Peppis argues that it underwrote British imperialism and supported the general war effort),[11] the journal remained preoccupied with exploring the conflict between the revolutionary individual and the impersonal forces of political authority, offering a critical assessment of its construction of a collective pro-war consciousness. Both issues of *Blast* were designed to undermine the ordinariness of what Lewis described in his essay of 1910, 'Our Wild Body', as the 'barren formula' of ordinary civil life, which, he believed, required being shaken up by the shock of some 'good honest fighting'.[12] When considered together, both numbers of *Blast* presented a much more consistently radical and subversive view of individualism than appeared in contemporary modernist journals like *The Egoist*, and in doing so, they aligned Vorticist modernism more closely to anarchism than any other avant-garde circle had ever done.

Anarchism, Advertising and the British Avant-Garde

Vorticism's political and aesthetic radicalism was influenced by both the style and ideological content of anarchism. Lewis's favourite political philosopher,[13] the nineteenth-century anarchist Joseph Pierre

Proudhon, described bourgeois culture as an unproductive 'catastrophe' and warned writers that instead of seeking literary recognition they should 'precipitate the catastrophe', adding that 'the most deserving of us is the one who plays his part'. Asking, famously, 'What is property?' and answering, 'It is theft', Proudhon expressed disgust for capitalist modernity, or 'everything that exists'. Dismissing bourgeois society as 'tyranny' and proposing revolutionary ideas and 'projects for its destruction', his opposition to privilege, status and authority appeared boundless to his readers.[14] Proudhon's distaste at capitalist and bourgeois modernity underlines Lewis's, and subsequently, Vorticism's, peculiar estrangement from mass-market commodity culture and contextualises the rather elitist but simultaneously anarchic tone of his lifelong hatred of democracy. As made clear in Lewis's key Vorticist story, 'The Crowd Master', which appeared in the second issue of *Blast*, the journal provided a platform for the expression of a decidedly revolutionary kind of modernist individualism.

The group's signal motif of the Vortex, represented throughout the journal by the image of an inwardly spiralling cone, is an ontic symbol of the energy and momentum of an unstoppable modernist present. The Vortex also had political associations, as Vorticist literature and painting expressed for the group the 'free movement' of select individuals and their art as the circulation of modernist 'particles'[15] in a permanent present, liberated from the external considerations of past and future (this, even, despite Ezra Pound's reputation as a *passéist* and literary 'time-trotter').[16] But despite Lewis and Pound's rejection of their rivals in the Italian avant-garde movement, Futurism, and of its stress on style and technology and the fetishisation of machines, the notion of a ceaseless and chaotic Vorticist present, free from anticipation of what might come and from the romanticisation of what had been, was, like Marinetti's Italian movement, heavily dependent on the marketing power of its novelty and potential to shock. The manifestos, or 'rigid propagandas', that expressed this movement's abstract literary and artistic theories were published in the hope that they would be picked up by unusually receptive individuals. According to this logic, the revolutionary message of Vorticism was directed at an aesthetically conscious elect, but while Lewis stated his opposition to the crassness of base or 'commercialised' art, he also exploited the journal's 'telling design' to advertise his Vortex. The hyperbolic messages contained in the pages of *Blast*, along with the striking imagery of the Vorticists' advertising posters, were intended to communicate to readers and potential sponsors the 'essentials' of Vorticist art in a consciously modern and revolutionary way that would allow Lewis's very select circle to compete with rival art collectives like the Omega Workshops. Therefore, despite Lewis's claims as to the importance of its elitist origins (he claimed that Vorticism was an expression of a handful of the very best artists in England),[17] *Blast*'s aesthetic jolts fitted within the marketing strategies already being employed by the popular culture industries.

Walter L. Adamson describes the cultural battles that erupted between the end of the nineteenth century and the outbreak of the First World War, when modernists reacted against the cheapening of cultural markets by establishing avant-garde movements such as Futurism and Expressionism. These groups addressed the ongoing fragmentation, commodification and democratisation of cultural products and cultural discourse by attempting to locate their own forms of high art at the centre of cultural life. Writing manifestos was a central tactic of these decentred, even anarchic groupings which did not engage in purely aesthetic forms of avant-gardism but instead opted to think through, and act upon, a number of alternatives for their art that were based upon loosely coalesced fronts bearing 'alliance-oriented strategies'. As Adamson suggests, these modernisms cooperated, competed and conflicted with one another as their journals and pamphlets took advantage – as the Vorticists also did – of the aestheticisation of capitalism being made so evident by the techniques of early twentieth-century advertising. Their appropriation of the marketing strategies of commodity culture mirrored the competitiveness of nation states and that of emerging but increasingly powerful corporate entities. In this way an aesthetic of active confrontation became the primary operative doctrine of the pre-war avant-gardes, while their techniques of provocation and performance developed into heavily mediated phenomena. As a result of this consciously strategic activity, the presentation of shocking and outrageously composed manifestos became the 'signature avant-garde practice' of the pre-war years across Europe. Clearly, then, avant-gardism had an ambivalent consciousness of its own means and ideology of dissemination, reflected in its tendency to produce literary splinter-groups. As the critic and poet Harold Monro complained of Imagism in *The Egoist*, its deliberate policy of estrangement from the literary mainstream provided a focus for individual cranks and equally 'detached groups of the wrong people'. Yet the Imagists, like the Vorticists, were acutely aware of the need to participate in the commodity culture that they claimed to despise because they knew that doing so was the only way to guarantee the circulation of work that was, after all, produced for the literary market place. As Adamson has shown, European avant-gardists got around this problem by devising strategies for self-promotion, central to which was their offering of competing brands of 'activist' or 'political' modernism for popular consumption.[18]

During the immediately pre-war era, Vorticism was the most aesthetically radical and politically conscious form of British modernism but it was also a commercially oriented endeavour and marketed its politicised aesthetic by exploiting the symbolic capital of terrorism. The critical tendency to associate the movement's politics with extreme right-wing thought is exemplified in the work of Paul Peppis and Frederic Jameson, both of whom have highlighted what they perceive as Lewis's 'proto-fascist' tendencies[19] in readings that are influenced by his later undeniably pro-Nazi views, voiced in the 1931 panegyric, *Hitler*.[20] However, prior to the rise of German National Socialism, Lewis modelled his subversive writing on anarchist theory and practice and its combative qualities support Perry Anderson's theory of the 'imaginative proximity' of European modernism and political violence. The modernists' determined efforts against what they regarded as the pre-war decline of culture mirrored the old régimes' fears of political disintegration, but avant-gardes embraced the meltdown of traditional political structures as a possible basis for new literary and artistic praxis. At the beginning of the twentieth century, when democracy was incomplete and subject to the temporality of markets, its fractured and protean existence was threatened from within by the unpredictable force of labour, which had never been fully co-opted into the bourgeois democratic system. This political confusion and cultural instability spawned the 'insurgent' art movements that emerged across Europe, appropriating the language and imagery of political subversion while also displaying more elite characteristics. This meant that modernism's schizophrenic qualities emerged from a split aesthetic and political consciousness as writers and artists exhibited fashionable revolutionary *chic* alongside their conservative social beliefs. As Anderson suggests, modernism contained these contradictions because it was formed at the intersection of 'a semi-aristocratic ruling order, a semi-industrialized capitalist economy, and a semi-emergent, or semi-insurgent, labor movement'.[21] Anderson's theory of modernist culture reflecting the shifting and unstable surface of the early twentieth century explains the political ambivalence of figures like Lewis and Pound, who developed an anarchic aesthetic while simultaneously viewing their work as the product of a new 'hierarchy' and reflecting the values of an authoritative 'aristocracy of the arts'.[22] Despite the European avant-garde's dislike for the dominant bourgeois ethos, its expression in declarations like Baptiste Von Helmholtz's 'contempt for the citizen'[23] reveals the profoundly reactionary ethos that would later attract some writers to European fascism and Nazism.

Influenced by Georges Sorel's pessimistic conception of the historical role of violence,[24] Lewis's lifelong fixation with the interface between art and conflict is summarised by his belief that the artist is 'always holding the mirror up to politics'.[25] The strategy of repeatedly denying and then acknowledging the link between politics and art characterises his 1937 memoir, *Blasting and Bombardiering*, a text that captures the fractious and contradictory qualities of Vorticist modernism. As Raymond Williams has pointed out, the use of such self-positioning tactics meant that the politics of the avant-garde could, from the outset, have gone either way.[26] Likewise, Renato Poggioli has stressed the ideological and sociological functions of avant-gardism and its 'formulas of logic'. As Poggioli has argued, the political content of avant-garde ideology is contained in its theories, programmes and manifestos and its 'hardening' into positions, rendering it:

> a sociological phenomenon because of the social or antisocial character of the cultural and artistic manifestations that it sustains and expresses. This is why 'the image and the term' were so central to anarchistic and avant-garde revolt, as both were always associated with 'the ambience of the political left.[27]

Given that ideology is the product of social reality, as Peter Bürger has suggested, the politicisation of art is inevitable, as aesthetic production is both deeply involved in and highly critical of bourgeois existence. Stressing the historical relationship between art and bourgeois subjectivity, Bürger argues that modernist avant-garde consciousness developed out of and responded to nineteenth-century aestheticism, and that it broke with bourgeois norms by refusing to assume a singular, definitive style. As a result, imposing defamiliarisation by deliberately 'shocking the recipient' became the key practice and principle of these highly specialised aesthetic vanguards. Traditionally perceived as a 'distinctive sphere of experience', avant-gardism exploits the tension between institutional and political content of art, while its tendency toward self-criticism highlights its duality by drawing attention to its simultaneously contradictory and subversive character.[28]

Anderson has also recognised this 'antithetical' quality of different modernisms, describing Symbolism, Expressionism, Cubism, Futurism and Constructivism as politically 'ambidextrous' affairs.[29] Lewis's later abandonment of his anti-bourgeois and anarchic self-image, which he replaced with pro-fascist leanings in 1931, embodies this contradiction. According to Andreas Huyssen, mid nineteenth- to early twentieth-century modernity was characterised by the volatile engagement between high art and mass culture, in which modernists practised conscious strategies of exclusion; this allowed avant-gardes to counter the threat of becoming engulfed by mass culture by detaching themselves from the practices of daily life while, simultaneously, destabilising the boundaries between high and low culture from within.[30] Vorticism's engagement with the language and imagery of terrorism, which, until the emergence of literary modernism, had traditionally been the stuff of popular fiction, addresses the high-low dialectic of modern art and literature. By exploring the disorientation of mass culture and producing imagistic shocks and experimental textual methods, Vorticism (not to mention Lewis's persistent self-promotion as a subversive figure) is marked by its attempt to commodify terrorism as a form of aesthetic practice. In their quest for notoriety, Lewis and his colleagues constructed an aggressive, modernist version of the explosive advertising strategy that was first developed by Charles Henry Dent and Frank Cannock with the Tamworth bomb scare of 1894.

Alex Houen has shown how the Vorticists' estrangement from mainstream art and politics mirrored French Syndicalism's separation of itself from spheres of production, principally by means of strikes, as well as other methods like sabotage, attacks on shops and the disruption of transport and communications. As Houen suggests, the performativity of the strike can be used to interrogate the theoretical autonomy of the avant-garde as the act of withdrawal, to the Syndicalist, is by no means an admission of the failure of radical agency: 'the (anti-)activity of the strike is asserted to be the most potent means of interfering with state power'. In France, anarchism metamorphosed into Syndicalism following the introduction of the *lois scélérats* after the assassination of President Carnot in 1894. Combined with the political exhaustion of terrorism, this legislation drove many French anarchists into the more conventional, if no less radical, Syndicalist movement.[31] Pointing to Sorel's construction of a 'language of strikes', Houen draws attention to the provocation of revolutionary instinct by the most powerful form of action – the strike that involves language itself. Lewis read Sorel when living in Paris from 1903 until 1908 and, as Houen suggests, he found in his political writing inspiration for new modes of 'literary combat' that would materialise a few years later as Vorticism. As Houen suggests, the belligerent type of modernism that Lewis articulated in *Blast* in 1914–15 exploited the shocking otherness of terrorist violence by presenting its 'disjunctive textuality as a form of violence in itself'. This process translated the metaphoric gesture of revolt into a subversive *avant-gardisme* that had an 'increasingly terroristic' appearance.[32] There can be no doubt that Lewis invented Vorticism with a backward glance at recent political history: his invention of anarchic modernism played

on contemporary anxieties about political violence and recycled revolutionary discourse as the basis of his new literary and artistic aesthetic. As
Ezra Pound put it to readers of *The Egoist*, Vorticism was a combative
'movement of individuals, for individuals' and one that stood for 'the
protection of individuality'. As a result, it was prepared for conflict with
its rivals as it saw itself engaged in a permanent dialectic of struggle,
where art was 'always crashing and opposing and breaking' with contemporary literary and political authority.[33]

Blast 1

Vorticism briefly shocked the literary scene with the publication of two
numbers of its 'revolutionary review',[34] *Blast*, in June 1914 and July
1915. The 'revolutionary spirits'[35] whose writing, painting and sculpture represented the movement styled as the 'Great English Vortex',
gathered around Lewis, who, in turn, borrowed the group's aggressive
modernist identity from his notoriously combative mentor, Pound. The
Vorticists promoted a particularly British form of advanced modernism
that stressed the need for a violent and intensively experienced aesthetic
of 'pleasure in forces'.[36] Basing itself upon the assumption that 'writing
as an art is very susceptible to shock',[37] literary Vorticism was influenced
by the political and cultural impact of the Fenian dynamiters, the anarchists and the Suffragettes, whose radical doctrines were transformed
into modernist capital in the pages of *Blast*.[38] Preoccupied with rebellious art, Vorticism competed with other forms like Expressionism,
Post-impressionism, Cubism and, especially, early Futurism, which also
combined artistic novelty with the possibilities of revolutionary social
change. With its suggestively explosive title, *Blast* titillated its readers
by appearing to blow up the accepted norms of bourgeois politics and
culture.

The journal's avant-garde manifestos showcased Vorticism's shocking
poetics by expressing its desire to construct uncompromising aesthetic
positions. *Blast* presented the Vorticist as an anarchic, aesthetically
conscious individual distinct from F. T. Marinetti's idealised Futurist
subject. Lewis criticised his Italian rival's desire to saturate mass culture
with an ironic primitivism expressed through worship of technology and
the 'Automobile-God'. Unlike Futurism, which praised the collective
imperatives of industrial modernity, Vorticism stressed the agency of
the individual artist in what it perceived to be a negative and backward
bourgeois democratic age (Marinetti's 'worship of 'the people', Lewis
warned, would 'destroy initiative' rather than liberate consciousness

or inspire new art).[39] As Andrej Gasiorek argues, Vorticist art and literature sought to observe and synthesise the tensions that character-ised modern experience rather than submit to them,[40] and its aesthetic anarchy countered Futurism's association with corporate and state power. Lewis later attacked Marinetti for pandering to government by allowing himself to be officially recognised as a 'precursor of fascismo' (Fascism, he later complained, was 'merely Futurism in practice').[41] Vorticism, with its dissociation from centralised authority and advo-cacy of individual subversive aesthetic action, was, then, projected as a British alternative to Futurism. As an expression of literary anarchism, *Blast* provided an avant-garde commentary on the mediated and textual power of terrorism. Of course, Vorticism combined its subversive sense of the responsibilities of the aesthetically-conscious individual with more reactionary and typically modernist fears of the increasing politi-cal influence of the masses. Contemporary anxieties over the integrity of individual agency and the conscious personality of the modern subject underline Vorticism's modernist stress on the aesthetically conscious individual and, while *Blast* reflects Lewis's interest in the 'emotional' appeal of anarchism,[42] the journal also expressed more elitist anxieties over the progress of democracy.

Blast was designed to both shock the aesthetic sensibilities of its readers and to create art out of 'political activity', and Lewis used the journal to publicise a modernist aesthetic that would reflect the influence of radical propaganda over the British avant-garde. He would later look back on this period as one of failure, but at the time he was adamant that his confrontational journal represented the only worthwhile art being pro-duced in England.[43] The very establishment of Vorticism in 1914 was an attempt to unsettle Roger Fry's Omega Workshops (its short-lived headquarters, the Rebel Art Centre in Great Ormond Street, was opened after Lewis split from Fry in October 1913 during a dispute over work submitted for an Ideal Home commission) and, while the decision to establish a rival movement was doubtlessly motivated by Lewis's noto-riously combative ego, *Blast* also marked the beginning of a sustained personal engagement with the sphere of 'art-politics' as a novelist, critic, pamphleteer and painter.[44] Branding the new group was paramount since the Omega Workshops claimed, quite literally, to represent the last word in contemporary art, so Lewis copied Fry's idea that art should be agitational enough to provide the public with an 'electric shock'.[45] The motif of the explosion, rather than that of the still centre of the Vortex, was the movement's original signifier but this less violent emblem was adopted, along with the group title of 'Vorticism', at Pound's suggestion during the closing stages of the production of *Blast*.[46] Its radical literary style was also expressed through bold, experimental typography that, along with its abstract and contradictory content, Vorticism used to alienate readers with more mainstream tastes.

In *Blasting and Bombardiering*, Lewis claimed that Pound defined this 'unassimilable' group's oppositional identity by giving its activity the appearance of '*Bewegung*', or agitation. This, along with the journal's deliberately 'technical militancy' and content (Lewis later described the manifestos as containing obscure but nonetheless 'political contraband'), was intended to provide Vorticism with a radical edge over its competitors.[47] Describing the belligerent American poet as a violent figure, 'born revolutionary' and 'Trotsky of the written word', who encouraged the expression of any 'fractious disposition', and regarded poetry as having the disruptive potential of an 'infernal machine', Lewis remembered Vorticism in his memoir as a thoroughly political avant-garde grouping. Pound publicised his role as the 'destructive' director and manipulator of Vorticism's literary 'force'[48] in modernist circles months before the publication of *Blast*, when he outlined a combination of extreme aesthetic positioning laced with anti-democratic doctrine in his essay, 'The New Sculpture', which appeared in *The Egoist* in February 1914. Describing the gulf between modern sculptors and the 'half-educated simpering general' of the masses, Pound argued that artists, who were 'born to rule', should attack traditional aesthetic values with a combination of 'craft and violence'. The 'wild' and highly original sculpture of Henri Gaudier and Jacob Epstein, he announced, by engaging with '"strife" in the arts' was creating work of 'new beauty' which, he suggested, reflected the condition of 'general combat' that existed between the advanced artist and the rest of society.[49] His model of a modern art that was violently at odds with establishment culture (this would soon include Imagism after its abandonment by Pound the following summer) informed Vorticism's self-construction and basic ideology. A worthy poem, painting or sculpture contained the destructive force of a primed bomb, he suggested, along with the creative potential to recast art and culture with its energy and momentum. Pound's reputation for aggression and his status as a 'rebel' poet was, of course, designed to sell his own, personalised brand of 'extreme-orient' modernism. His association with Vorticism was, according to Lewis, an explosive one and his 'dynamite role' consisted of publicising Vorticism[50] and praising, in Pound's own words, its 'war' on mediocrity.[51] Lewis's recollections of his involvement are littered with metaphors of conflict, explosiveness and shock, and Pound's responsibility as Vorticism's chief 'propagandist' or 'Manager'[52] reveals how Vorticism's anarchic identity rested upon its corporate structure. Its claims to competitive individualism, organised around Pound's administrative role, reflected the group's sense of its art as a branded commodity, suggesting that the aesthetic power of its explosive modernism could also be translated into the economic value of commodity exchange.

Henri Gaudier added his own combative touch to the first issue of *Blast*, which closed with the sculptor's art manifesto, entitled 'Vortex'. Prior to moving to London he had, Pound claimed, taken part in revolutionary activity in Paris in 1910, when he kept an art notebook entitled *Le Chaos*, in which he penned 'his first "Vortex"'. According to this account, Gaudier was involved in an attempt to rescue a condemned anarchist, took part in anti-police riots and even broke out of prison (according to Pound, this was why he emigrated to London in 1911).[53] Gaudier was killed in combat at the battle of Neueville St Vaast just before the publication of the second number of *Blast* in 1915, but not before he described his obsession with fighting Germans, the 'great fun' he found in close-quarter combat and, if we are to take Pound's word for it, the enjoyment he experienced at throwing 'magnificent little bombs' at the enemy.[54] While Pound's claims about Gaudier's involvement in bohemian anarchism are difficult to verify, his belligerent personality and his fascination with the relationship between art and violence are obvious. These aspects of his work and character were realised in his sculpture of a pair of knuckle-dusters, a piece that drew on and even mythologised popular images of urban violence. Gaudier's tough, anarchic streak came into its own amid the chaos of the battlefront where, ironically, he found himself in uniform, giving his life for the very state from which, according to Pound, he fled to London as a political fugitive.

Blast 1 closes with Gaudier's manifesto, in which the sculptor attempts to contextualise Vorticism by explaining its function within the present. For Gaudier its role was to perpetuate art as a kind of life-force: 'VORTEX IS ENERGY! And it gave SOLID EXCREMENTS in the quattro é cinquo cento, Liquid until the seventeenth century, gases whistle till now. THIS is the history of form value in the West until the FALL OF IMPRESSIONISM' (*Blast* 1, p. 156). The threshold that marks the end of vapid art and the emergence of a renewed originality is the close of the nineteenth century with its insistence upon the realism of impressionistic images. According to Gaudier's model of art history, the pure energy of the Vortex is realisable only by modernists who recognise the historical and formal connection between art and conflict. This is manifested in the particularly urban dialectic that Gaudier claims that he and other 'moderns' (he lists Epstein, Brancusi, Archipenko, Dunikowski and Modigliani) now find themselves immersed in. Spending their energy 'through the incessant struggle in the complex city' (p. 156), their experience, or vortex, is one of an endless conflict that registers the new 'form value' of art-as-violence. Gaudier's historicisation of this process gives Vorticism the appearance of synthesis and substance, distancing his movement from what he regarded as the relatively meaningless modernist 'spin' of other avant-gardes. By contextualising Vorticism as a historically grounded phenomenon, he sought to distinguish it from Futurism's celebration of the rootlessness of modern experience. Along with Pound's violently combative approach to culture,[55] Gaudier's sculpted knuckle-dusters and the confession of his enjoyment of warfare suggest that, ultimately, Vorticist modernism was all about having a fight.[56]

Gaudier's manifesto goes on to describe how, as the structural 'elements' of civilisation, these conflicts must be mastered by Vorticists who, through the assertion of their Nietzschean 'will and consciousness', characterise a new moment:

> We have been influenced by what we liked most, each according to his own individuality, we have crystallised the sphere into the cube, we have made a combination of all the possible shaped masses – concentrating them to express our abstract thoughts of conscious superiority. (p. 156)

Gaudier constitutes the 'Vortex' as an aesthetic-political manifestation of transformative individual agency that is activated by desire on the part of the artist to achieve and sustain a fundamental shift in the appreciation of art-objects. Aesthetic empowerment is the operative motif here: in sculpture, an immaterial and inert sphere, or lump, can be agitated or 'crystallised' into a meaningful shape by the artist, who, recasting it as a cube, transforms it into a work of art. This fundamental change in the object's structure and shape suggests that it has been formed by some civilising intelligence. What Gaudier discusses here is the need for the artist to enliven commodity culture by manipulating 'all the possible shaped masses', or available but dormant material, into something more beautiful and alive than conventional, inorganic commodities. His call for an art of vitality is also suggestive of the literary Vorticist's desire, expressed by Lewis in his story 'The Crowd Master', to recast the non-entity that is the democratic crowd into a more active and self-aware formation capable of recognising its own reality and able to interpret the 'conscious superiority' of avant-garde expression. In contrast to its main rival in the visual and plastic arts, the Omega Workshops, which essentially functioned as a marketing collective, Vorticism articulated a more theoretical awareness of the artist's responsibility and suggested that writers, sculptors and painters should explore the possibilities that lay beyond the facilitation of consumption by opposing the devitalising forces of capital.

Despite its contemporary reputation as a variant of Futurism, Aldington recognised in Vorticism a 'new' and suitably British form of modernism. Nonetheless, *Blast*'s manifestos were influenced by Marinetti's enthusiasm for violence, revolution and riot, expressed in writings like 'The Founding and Manifesto of Futurism', which, published in *Le Figaro* in 1909, lauded the 'aggressive action' of 'the punch and the slap'.[57] Struck by *Blast*'s 'tumultuous' arrival on the literary and artistic scene, Aldington was interested in the curiosity that it provoked among the 'ordinary' readers that other modernist journals tended to avoid.[58] In arousing their interest, *Blast* appeared to achieve its goal of influencing its target 'bourgeois' public but Lewis later claimed that his group misinterpreted this popular appetite for artistic shocks. With hindsight, Lewis claimed that the demand for novelty and political notoriety was more conventional than he at first realised: 'I mistook the agitation in the audience for the sign of an awakening in the emotions of artistic sensibility. And then I assumed too that artists always formed militant groups. I supposed they had to do this, seeing how 'bourgeois' all Publics were – or all Publics of which I had any experience'. Lewis's recollection of the events surrounding the publication of *Blast* appeared over two decades later in his memoir, *Blasting and Bombardiering*, and his version of the formation of the group ignores Gaudier's significant contribution to Vorticist theory. By reducing its revolutionary position on art and literature to the status of an advertising gimmick, or 'fashionable stunt',[59] he tried to control the subsequent interpretation of his movement by depoliticising it. Yet, as Paul Edwards has shown, the Lewis who emerged from the First World War was a traumatised writer who was deeply embittered by his experience and dismissive of pre-war politics. This transformation in Lewis's personality explains the shift that marked his political beliefs and literary output during the 1920s. Of a more reactionary character, the post-war Lewis reacted against his younger, more idealistic self and against the left-wing position that he adopted in artistic and literary debates in 1914, before he had any direct experience of the chaos, trauma and psychic alienation that are part of the experience of front-line combat.[60]

Lewis's claim that the Liberal prime minister, Herbert Asquith, 'smelled' revolutionary politics in *Blast* and regarded its manifestos and typographical novelties as coded revolutionary propaganda acknowledges the reaction of contemporary readers to its 'impenetrable' avant-gardism and to its preoccupation with aesthetic revolt. Vorticism, like anarchism, appeared unreadable to the mainstream imagination, and by conjuring images of twentieth-century 'sanscullotism',[61] the journal attempted to fill the imaginary void left by the demise of British anarchism in the pre-war period. Its construction of a 'new art' for a 'new age' was deliberately political[62] but its moment was, of course, cut short by the outbreak of war and although a second issue, subtitled the 'War Number', was published in July 1915, the promised third instalment never materialised. The opening manifesto announcing the 'Great Revolutionary Vortex' proclaimed the journal's dedication to the ontic 'Reality of the Present' as opposed to the 'sentimental' future and 'sacripant Past'.[63] As suggested by the journal's title, Vorticism was configured as a literary and artistic explosion that distinguished itself from other art movements by emphasising the intensity of its vision:

> We do not want to change the appearance of the world, because we are not Naturalists, Impressionists or Futurists (the latest form of Impressionism), and do not depend on the appearance of the world for our art. WE ONLY WANT THE WORLD TO LIVE, and to feel its crude energy flowing through us. (*Blast* 1, p. 7)

Unlike these other movements, which aimed at transforming exterior appearances, the Vorticists' objective was to record and communicate experience. Accepting the 'crude' energy of the present as their medium necessitated the acknowledgement that, as in the past, 'great artists . . . are always revolutionary' (p. 7). In making this statement the Vorticists distinguished themselves from Futurism and its 'identification with the crowd' (*Blast* 2, p. 42), along with its worship of commodities and technology.[64] In contrast, Vorticism promised to interiorise the existential thrill of the moment by treating modernism as a mediated, experiential phenomenon and providing a platform for 'vivid and violent ideas that could reach the public in no other way'. Claiming to have no alternative than to use these aggressive means, Vorticist avant-gardism promised to reproduce the sensational impact of political violence by offering itself as a form of textual shock. This, Lewis hoped, would give his movement a popular, voyeuristic appeal that would register equally with the egotistical consumer of high art:

> Blast will be popular, essentially. It will not appeal to any particular class, but to the fundamental and popular instincts in every class and description of people, TO THE INDIVIDUAL. The moment a man feels or realises himself as an artist he ceases to belong to any milieu or time. Blast is created for this timeless, fundamental artist that exists in everybody.
>   The Man in the Street and the Gentleman are equally ignored.
>   Popular art does not mean the art of the people, as it is supposed to. It means the art of individuals. (p. 7)

The inherent contradiction of this statement adds to the deliberate impenetrability of Vorticism, which, on being advertised as a 'popular' expression of British avant-gardism, suddenly retreats from the manifesto's democratic implications and attempts to transform the modern subject from a constituent of the crowd into a figure resembling the 'timeless' artist. On realising the meaning of the Vorticist aesthetic, this new artist-subject will withdraw from the collective sphere of 'the people' and enter the more specialised and creative realm of individualised art. Echoing the theories of reactionary sociologists like Le Bon, whose anxiety over the 'atavistic' tendencies of the modern crowd[65] mirrored Max Nordau's distrust of the inherently 'degenerate' democratic masses, Vorticism proposed a universal nature – the art-instinct – that is found only in the aesthetically conscious individual who, upon becoming aware of his position, rejects any involvement with the social. Disdain for the 'milieu' and its championing of an art for the individual gave Vorticism a simultaneously anarchic and aristocratic character since its art, while promoting impulsive revolt, has 'nothing to do with "the People"'. Lewis's oppositional, contradictory aesthetic is also expressed in his 'blast' against the entire spectrum of British workers, targeting the 'SPECIALIST' and 'PROFESSIONAL' alongside the 'GOOD WORKINGMAN' and even the reader of the piece 'who will hang over this Manifesto with SILLY CANINES exposed' (*Blast* 1, p. 17). The journal's goal – involving the demolition of existing standards and forcing 'the rich of the community' to 'shed their education skin' – is to eradicate social conditioning and the dominant patterns of artistic taste by destroying 'politeness, standardization and academic, that is civilized, vision' (p. 7). This aim is playfully seditious:

> We will convert the King if possible.
> A VORTICIST KING! WHY NOT?
> DO YOU THINK LLOYD GEORGE HAS THE VORTEX IN HIM? (*Blast* 1, p. 8)

In a similar vein the journal also rejects leftist constructions of working-class identity by pointing to the impossibility of any form of agency modeled on Marxist belief in the power of the collective. In another contradictory turnaround both the wealthy and the poor are attacked:

> The 'Poor' are detestable animals! They are only picturesque and amusing for the sentimentalist or the romantic! The 'Rich' are bores without a single exception, *en tant que les riches*!
> We want those simple and great people found everywhere. (p. 8)

Sentiment and romance have no place in Lewis's revolt against the system and against sense. This opening manifesto presents Vorticism's

'art of Individuals' (p. 8) as a form of refusal characterised by its rejection of the categories of left and right, and by its suggestion that art need
not be comprehensible. Its anti-logic proposes the artist as a completely
autonomous figure detached from socialist orthodoxy, which he finds
to be as restrictive and unbending as capitalism. Having rejected the
binary opposites of revolution and reaction, *Blast* proposes an over-
haul of British politics and art. These 'Blasts' are aimed at a variety of
individuals and national institutions identified in 'MANIFESTO – 1',
including less serious attacks against the 'SINS AND INFECTIONS' of
the British climate and the 'VICTORIAN VAMPIRE' that is London
smog. In a more radical tone, blasts are aimed at the cultural and
political 'MACHINERY' of England, including iconographic phenomena, from the 'DOMESTICATED POLICEMAN' to the 'LONDON
COLISEUM' and the 'SOCIALIST PLAYWRIGHT'. Yet, any seriousness that this statement might contain is undermined by further blasts
against popular culture in the form of 'DALY'S MUSICAL COMEDY'
and the 'GAIETY CHORUS GIRL', while high art is also blasted with
an attack on the Slade academic, Henry Tonks. All of these institutions
are blamed for creating Britain's 'flabby' environment, which will be
attacked with a series of 'necessary BLIZZARDS' against establishment
culture (France is also indiscriminately blasted for its prettiness, sentimentality and sensationalism) (*Blast* 1, pp. 11–14).

However Lewis's most important and intelligible blasts are aimed
at the cultural legacy of the nineteenth century, which he regarded as
'one of the most hideous periods ever recorded'.[66] The tirade against
Victorianism begins by blasting 'years 1837 to 1900' for creating the
'abysmal, inexcusable middle class' along with the aristocracy and proletariat. By offering such a sweeping 'blast' attacking the entire social
spectrum, from the aristocracy to the working class, the manifesto
undermines whatever attempt the reader might make to rationalise its
political content, while also achieving a large degree of self-isolation, as
Vorticism continues to define itself via its refusal of rationalism. This
manifesto reflects Lewis's estrangement from the mainstream of British
culture, his belief in the inherent chaos of modernity, and his recognition of the collapse of Enlightenment ideals in the face of bourgeois
democracy and capitalism.[67] His blast against the 'pasty shadow' cast
by Joseph Edgar Boehm's sculpture and his call for readers to 'WRING
THE NECK' of similar work (*Blast* 1, p. 20), was a protest against both
the 'triumph' of capital in the nineteenth century and against the seemingly 'indestructible' institutions that, he believed, produced the 'zero-
mind' of Victorian philistinism that was embodied in Boehm's 'bourgeois
statuary'.[68] Boehm enjoyed official patronage, having modelled Queen

Victoria for the official Jubilee medal of 1887 and produced busts of other royals, along with those of the artists Whistler, Millais and Holl and of the statesmen Gladstone, Shaftesbury, Lord John Russell (whose statue stands in Westminster) and Rosebery. Boehm's work also included busts of Thackeray, Carlyle and Ruskin and the Victorian imperial martyr, George Gordon, while he also designed the 1889 Wellington Monument in Hyde Park Corner.[69] Given that the Clan-na-Gael campaign was directed in the main against public monuments and buildings, such as London Bridge, the House of Commons and Nelson's Column (Irish Republican dynamiters were also blamed for hatching an 1887 'Jubilee Plot' against Queen Victoria herself) this outburst against the most prominent court sculptor of the late nineteenth century reads as a form of radical aesthetic violence directed against symbols of a 'lazy' (*Blast* 1, p. 14) official culture and the plastic representations of its figures of political authority. However, by targeting the official art of the previous century, Lewis chose not to engage directly with contemporary imperial power.

The closest that *Blast* comes to challenging contemporary power is when it singles out the 'SIMIAN' art establishment for its 'STYLISM', extolling readers to 'CURSE WITH EXPLETIVE OF WHIRLWIND THE BRITANNIC AESTHETE' who represents the cultural elite, or 'CREAM OF THE SNOBBISH EARTH' (*Blast* 1, p. 15) (Pater and the 'Wildeites' are also criticised for being unmanly 'eunuchs and stylists'). Again, Vorticism's deliberate sense of contradiction becomes apparent as Lewis targets established art theories for carrying out exactly the kind of cultural activity that Vorticism is all about: stylisation (in Lewis's case, the stylisation of politics) as commodity art. But as Douglas Mao has pointed out, the radical prescriptions for a new art that were articulated by both the Vorticists and their rivals in the Omega group paradoxically had their origins in the spectacular nature of commodity culture. This problem emerges in modernist ideology precisely because, like Henry James's conflicted fictional anarchist, Hyacinth Robinson, both factions were conscious that 'a broadly based capitalist system had helped to shape the very forms that constituted art as they knew it'. As Mao suggests, modernist 'mandarinism', for all of its radical posturing and anti-bourgeois rhetoric, delighted in and collaborated with 'the ways of the market and mass culture'.[70] When considered against Vorticism's reception in 1914, these anarchic blasts indicate how fashionably marketable subversion had become. Although Lewis later denied it, there is a clear link between the Vortex and political violence, and his journal owed its notoriety to its exploitation of this connection and its fusion of modernism with the destructive rhetoric of revolution.

The tone of the manifesto changes by blessing Britain for its isolated national identity and its uniqueness as an 'industrial island machine' (p. 23). France is also blessed for having vitality, embodied in its 'MASTERLY PORNOGRAPHY', and 'COMBATIVENESS', and in the 'BALLADS OF ITS PREHISTORIC APACHE'. This idealisation of France's criminal and political underground is followed by praise for its unstable political culture, symbolised by the 'GREAT FLOOD OF LIFE pouring out of the wound of 1797' and the 'bitterer stream from 1870' (p. 27). Revolution and violent political upheaval symbolise the release of political energy and momentum that Vorticism claims to embody: by aligning his movement with republican violence, Lewis suggests that, like the actualisation of revolutionary ideology into violent action, the Vortex transforms abstract modernist theory into aesthetic force. That this aspect of French political culture horrified the British during the nineteenth century underlines Lewis's strategy of shocking the contemporary reader into abandoning the residual Victorian sensibilities that were still lingering in 1914 and accepting the fact of the present (this is expressed in his praise for the up-and-coming Irish modernist James Joyce and the popular thriller-writer Marie Belloc Lowndes, a blessing that suggests the movement of literary culture away from the 'blank of genteel fatuity' represented by Boehm's sculpture).[71] Both in its blasts and blessings 'Manifesto – I' reveals Lewis's tendency to punctuate his very technical modernism with intensely political matter.

Criticising England as the 'anti-artistic' and 'unphilosophic' source of the 'idée fixe of Class', 'Manifesto – II' blames the 'incapable', 'stagnant' and inbred British aristocracy for resisting cultural progress. Simultaneously, however, it also praises its production of a uniquely 'compressed' culture that, containing the potential to periodically explode, is credited with the sporadic creation of superior art. This reserve of potential energy is 'the reason why a movement towards art and imagination could burst up here . . . with more force than anywhere else'. Therefore British culture is underlined by the 'discord' that motivates Vorticism's primitive 'Art-instinct' and its blunt, or 'savage', sensibility contrasts with the artificially refined, or '"advanced"', perfected, democratic' qualities of Futurism. Because the Futurist's 'limited imagination' is as synthetic as the technology that he worships, it is unfit for the rough 'desert' of modernity. The incoherence of modern experience, with its 'chaos of imperfection', is embraced by the more organic Vorticist while the Futurist happily submits to technology instead of trying to master it (*Blast* 1, pp. 32–3). Marinnetti's followers are unprepared for the authentic violence of modern chaos where Futurist fetishes such as 'automobilism' (*Blast* 1, p. 8) are of little use because the revolutionary present involves an intimate kind of conflict more suited to a modernist who is capable of utilising Gaudier's brass knuckles. A more delicate type of avant-garde practice, Futurism, with its stylish focus on techno-aesthetics, is protected from this reality by its implication within the industrial and corporate culture that it celebrates.

The Explosive Modernist Present

Stressing its recognition of cultural tradition, Pound described Vorticism as neither 'Pastism' or 'Futurism': 'We do not desire to cut ourselves off from great art of any period, we only demand a recognition of contemporary great art'.[72] Vorticism's insistence on its contemporaneousness (Aldington enthused that it recognised 'its own time')[73] meant that, unlike Futurism, it represented 'art that '*is*' and not art that is '*going*' somewhere'.[74] Rather than praising technology and its links with power, Vorticism claimed to subordinate machinery and promised to remove 'narrow and pedantic Realism at one stroke'. Lewis shared the Cubists' scepticism over realism's ability to represent experience through rectilinear imagery and suggested the model of an uncontained poetics of the explosion. According to this alternative, the destructive brevity of the explosion's blast-wave mirrors the anarchic, omni-directional tendencies of capitalist modernity. Lewis located this energy within the uncontrolled eruption and technological growth of industry: 'the Will that determined, face to face with its needs the direction of the modern world, has reared up steel trees where the green ones were lacking; has exploded in useful growths, and found wider intricacies than those of nature' (*Blast* 1, p. 38). The ontic present of this phenomenon is what Futurism ignores, while the themes of eruption and agency underline the revolutionary aesthetic force with which Vorticism claims to master technology. Lewis's post-romantic imagination acknowledges the spread of inorganic industrial technology but refuses to allow this aspect of modernity to dictate Vorticism's movement from the present toward the future. Defusing the apparently unlimited possibilities of technology by subjecting it to the controlling gaze of the artist, Vorticism resists capitalism (which Lewis describes here as an uncontrolled jungle) along with its power to enthrall, allowing himself to make sense of its material density and intellectual 'complication'. Its 'dramatic tropic growths' are part of the spectacular phenomenon that 'distinguishes externally our time' but which fails to influence Vorticist consciousness. Declaring themselves 'the great enemies of Romance' (of which Futurism is considered to be an unoriginal, updated expression), the Vorticists propose an alternative of a technologically conscious realism that is grounded in a sense of individual agency and defined by its essentially violent character, which Lewis compared to 'Chaos invading Concept and bursting it like nitrogen'. In contrast to Marinnetti's simplistic worship of hardware ('Futuristic gush over machines, aeroplanes, etc.' (*Blast* 1, p. 41)) which reproduces the disengaged awe of Romanticism, Vorticism is critically conscious of capitalism and its construction of a technologically-focused modernity. Modernity is viewed as explosively volatile and art that engages with its 'volcanic'[75] nature reveals a 'new consciousness towards the possibilities of expression in present life' (pp. 38, 41). The novelty of Vorticism is based on the suggestion that the experience of reality is coloured by the relentless spread of industry, infrastructure and mass consumption (heavy machinery, steam-power and factories are cited as tangible evidence of this) and that this, as yet, has been ignored by artists. The Vorticist recognises the influence of the 'crude' and 'insidious' power of capital and resists its technological and corporate chaos 'forcibly and directly' through the pure, oppositional force of his uniquely combative modernism.

The subversive tone of the manifestos continues in some unrestrained if unimpressive verse by Ezra Pound. In 'Salutation the Third' Pound attacks his enemies, the 'gagged' and 'slut-bellied' literary reviewers for objecting to 'newness' in art. Lumping them with the 'fungus' and 'gangrene' of society, he compares them to Jews who were, according to his cultural outlook, somehow connected to the press's 'detesters of beauty':

> I have seen many who go about with supplications,
>   Afraid to say how they hate you.
> HERE is the taste of my BOOT,
>   CARESS it, lick off the BLACKING. (p. 46)

Lacking the analytical thrust of Lewis's manifestos, Pound's angry and incoherent *Blast* poetry is no less shocking. Its deliberate bluntness and offensiveness, and its deeply personalised tone, register a shift away from the generalised and more abstract tone of the journal's opening statements by giving vent to the poet's unrestricted and highly individualised expression. 'Monumentum, Aere, Etc.' also attacks the literary establishment for slighting Pound by accusing him of strutting 'in the robes of my assumption':

> In a few years No one will remember the 'buffo,'
> No one will remember the trival (*sic*) parts of me,
> The comic details will not be present,
> As for you, you will lie in the earth,
> And it is doubtful if even your manure will be rich enough

To keep grass
Over your grave. (p. 46)

Pound did not like having his expertise on literary and aesthetic matters
questioned and the bitterness of these poems is explained by a confrontation that he had with Aldington who, under the pseudonym 'Auceps',
challenged Pound in a letter to his own journal, *The Egoist*. Three
months before the appearance of *Blast*, Aldington announced that he
had had enough of the poet's pretentious 'blaguing' and 'offensive
incompetence', not to mention his impossible claims to literary expertise.
Aldington complained that Pound's reckless self-promotion was based
upon scraps of knowledge and that his cultural pronouncements were
usually uninformed. Pound, of course, took the bait, as did his touchy
friend and protégé, Gaudier, and Aldington succeeded in working the
pair into a defensive frenzy (his dismissal of Lewis's paintings of 'geo-
metric sardine-tins' indicated that he was aware of the formation of
an alternative avant-garde).[76] Gaudier stepped up to defend his friends
by attacking Auceps's personality which, he declared, 'I despise', and
praised Vorticism for its intense expression of feeling. Pound, genuinely
stung by Aldington's dig at his knowledge of European and Far Eastern
culture, replied that his critic's intellect was based on fragments borrowed from Pater and the *Encyclopedia Brittanica*.[77]

The seriousness with which Pound and Gaudier took this criticism
indicates the extent to which Vorticism's claims to intensity cultural
superiority mattered to both writers. Pound, of course, found enemies
everywhere and *Blast* became a useful platform for attacking them, but
his violently worded protests against the sterility of the British literary
scene conclude with a vision of contentment. In 'Come My Cantilations'
he suggests the need for a Yeatsian escape from city life (as well as from
publishing obligations), achieved via moving to a 'fresh' but synthetic
utopia. In this space, 'free of pavements' and other manifestations of
urban and material reality, the poet might sing and rollick with the
'graceful speakers' and 'ready of wit' of the modernist elite:

Let come the gay of manner, the insolent and the exulting.
We speak of burnished lakes,
And of dry air, as clear as metal. (*Blast* 1, p. 46)

While Lewis promised not to indulge utopian fantasy, Pound's image
of a Vorticist idyll blends naturalism with the 'bareness' and 'hardness'
(*Blast* 1, p. 41) of the Vortex and his image of a rather still, lifeless
and metallic pastoral contrasts with the throbbing, organic vision of
William Butler Yeats's 'The Lake Isle of Innisfree' (1890). In contrast

to this image of the collective fulfillment of those who are prepared to accompany Pound on his journey toward the Vorticist paradise, another poem, 'Frateres Minares', makes it clear that unconstructive critics like Aldington could writhe in their erotic frustration:

> With minds still hovering above their testicles
> Certain poets here and in France
> Still sigh over established and natural fact
> Long since nicely discussed by Ovid.
> They howl. They complain in delicate and exhausted metres
> That the twitching of three abdominal nerves
> Is incapable of producing a lasting Nirvana. (*Blast* 1, p. 48)

Both poems are linked as together they make it clear that, unlike their enemies, the Vorticists could create a particularly modernist state of delirium by testing their readers' willingness to tolerate literary shocks (Pound's poetry guaranteed further notoriety for *Blast*, and Lewis, in a deliberate and self-conscious attempt at generating controversy, tried to facilitate this by censoring the poem by having Jessie Dismoor and Helen Sanders ink out its opening and closing lines).[78] At a time when Pound was still experimenting with Imagism, a form in which 'the 'image' is the furthest possible remove from rhetoric', *Blast*'s deliberately offensive and even outrageous style echoed his stress on the poet's need to register 'every emotion and every phase of emotion' and to express this through 'toneless phrase' and rhythm.[79] For Pound, Vorticism was the logical extension of Imagism because it presented the reader with 'an intellectual and emotional complex in an instant of time'. Less willing than Lewis to disown the 'Paterites' and the poetic legacy of the late nineteenth century, he viewed Vorticist art as drawing on 'primary media' that were essentially poetic, and regarded the image as Vorticism's principal 'pigment' (*Blast* 1, p. 154). Gianni Vattimo's theory of modern estrangement is apparent here: with its insistence on poetic oscillation, imagistic shock and the textual practices of the mass media, Vorticism, with its contradictions, underlined what Vattimo terms the precarious structure of modern experience.[80] Producing literature within a capitalist culture that they considered to be defined by its instability, lack of depth and impermanence, Lewis and Pound both suggested that aesthetic condition of twentieth-century modernity was characterised by society's capacity to absorb shock.

The manifestos that Pound contributed to *Blast*, like those of Lewis and Gaudier, offer a more considered analysis of the Vorticist position. His theory of the vortex describes it as a 'point of maximum energy' and 'greatest efficiency':

You may think of man as that toward which perception moves. You may think of him as the TOY of circumstance, as the plastic substance RECEIVING impressions.

OR you may think of him as DIRECTING a certain fluid force against circumstance, as CONCEIVING instead of merely observing and reflecting.

Pound's vortex is an active, sensorial process occurring within the passage of time. Directing its energy against its given moment and producing worthwhile art, its fluid force is subtler than the inert material circumstances that surround the artist-subject. This essential energy is the striking, imagistic content of Vorticism, leading the writer or painter to rely on the 'primary pigment of his art, nothing else'. Echoing the sentiment expressed by Gaudier in his defensive letter to *The Egoist*, Pound describes art as an experiential affair in which emotion is generated by abstract form confronting the 'vivid consciousness' of the artist. The value of this new avant-gardism, he argued, lies in the impact of its forms, which are manifested in 'the picture that means a hundred poems, the music that means a hundred pictures'. Form is Vorticist content, as the movement's literature, painting and sculpture represents 'the most highly energized statement, the statement that has not yet SPENT itself ... but which is the most capable of expressing'. Pound branded Vorticism by claiming that it represented the uncontained expression, limitless force and overwhelming impact of art and constructed its ideology around his earlier theories of Imagism. He presented this doctrine again in his 1916 book on Gaudier, in which he defended both movements' tendencies toward abstraction and held that serious art was that 'which would need a hundred works of any other kind of art to explain it' and described Vorticism as the 'core' of a spiralling abstraction.[81] This construction of the Vortex as a focus of aesthetic energy updates Walter Pater's theory of art-as-force, in which art is seen to suspend material reality 'like some trick of magic' and bombard the observer with the fluid 'passage and dissolution of impressions, images, sensations'. Despite their rejection of all things Victorian, the Vorticists shared Pater's recognition that modern experience was one in which sensations are manifested as an ongoing chain of dispersal and renewal, or as the 'continual vanishing away, that strange, perpetual, weaving and unweaving of ourselves' that, as a result of which, the art-object and artist-subject defy rational analysis. His theory predates Pound's notion that art dislocates the beholder from the materiality, or 'daily irritation' of the 'superficial world',[82] as does his ontic theory that the experience of art is 'the end'. For Pater, art occurs where 'the greatest number of vital forces unite in their purest energy', so that its 'hard, gem-like flame' is permanently lit as to maintain the ecstasy of its experience.[83] Regardless of their intense dislike for Victorian culture, the Vorticists' own theories of intensity and renewal drew heavily on Walter Pater's prescriptive advice for the aesthete.

For Pound, the destructive but simultaneously productive creation of art takes place in a void where anything is possible:

> All experience rushes into this vortex. All the energized past, all the past that is living and worthy to live. All MOMENTUM, which is the past bearing upon us, RACE, RACE-MEMORY, instinct charging the PLACID, NON-ENERGIZED future . . . All the past that is vital, all the past that is capable of living into the future, is pigment in the vortex, NOW.

In Pound's version of the vortex it is the centrifugal power of history, which he terms 'RACE-MEMORY' (explaining his association of avant-garde modernism with anti-semitism), that has built up to form the revolutionary moment out of which *Blast* has emerged. However the Vortex is not a value-free phenomenon as its opposite is 'Hedonism', which he defines as a 'place', or condition, that exists 'without force, deprived of past and future', operating as the 'vortex of a stil (*sic*) spool or cone'.[84] Pound's Vortex corresponds with contemporary constructions of modernism as a series of force fields representing the conflicting energy of rival avant-gardes.[85] W. B. Yeats's theory of opposing vortices, or 'gyres', proposed that the forces of Concord and Discord form two spheres whose meeting constitutes 'one gyre within the other always'. Yeats's symbolism of the 'double cone', which he also defined as a vortex, is driven by the conflict that occurs at the meeting of the gyres, one 'Primary', the other 'Antithetical', updating William Blake's theory of the inner contraries. For Yeats, all experience reflects the permanent state of conflict that exists between the conditions of 'Spectre and Emanation', whereby the 'antithetical tincture is emotional and aesthetic whereas the primary tincture is reasonable and moral'. Operating in a double movement, the gyres move, one against the other, in a series of circlings that fuse subjective unity with its more chaotic 'turbulent instinct' to create, for the Irish modernist, the field of discord that creates identity.[86] Like Yeats, the Vorticists drew on the chaos of contemporary political conflict to suggest that modernity was inherently disruptive yet argued, at the same time, that this was an aesthetically productive condition.

Both Pound's vortex and the turbulence of Yeats's gyre suggest the joint aesthetic-political application of chaos. For Lewis, these force fields impact upon the individual because modern urban life imposes conformity to its 'fraternal moulds'. Although the modern subject should undergo infinite experiences or 'means of life' as part of a universe of 'elements' that he can control, possibility is not unlimited but restricted by the 'disease' of impersonality. This limits the degree of freedom enjoyed by the modern ego that can 'walk around' but is ultimately contained by its entanglement with the social: 'Life is really no more secure, or his egotism less acute, but the frontier's (*sic*) interpenetrate, individual demarcations are confused and interests dispersed'. Even the physicality of the subject is reduced by the experience of restriction and limitation as 'THE ACTUAL HUMAN BODY BECOMES OF LESS IMPORTANCE EVERY DAY' and 'EXISTS, much less'. The real becomes literally intangible within the framework of capitalist modernity but aesthetic consciousness, which protects the physical autonomy of the artist, can reverse this process:

> The human form still runs, like a wave, through the texture or body of existence, and therefore, of art.
> But just as the old form of egotism is no longer fit for such conditions as now prevail, so the isolated human figure of most ancient art is an anachronism. (*Blast* 1, p. 141)

At odds with the modern impetus to conform, the estranged modernist resists the process of dehumanisation that Lewis, like Marx before him, regarded as the 'chief diagnostic' of his age (p. 141). The artistic and literary chaos promoted by *Blast* contains the necessary conditions for individual creation, but we are warned that the full potential of this kind of modernism has yet to be realised as further 'fields of discord' have gone unexploited (p. 142). What makes the vortex so subversive is its availability to the individual artist who, while at large within modern society, can also intensify and exploit its dislocations by turning them against the artificially developed desires of the consuming masses in order to create his own field of chaos. This was read into the textual structure of the journal by a reviewer who interpreted Lewis's alarming spelling and grammar as an assertion of the Vorticists' 'gospel' of individualism.[87]

Blast's shocking aesthetic, with its emphasis on the primary power of artistic and literary forces, was designed to excite a popular consciousness that Lewis believed had been numbed by capitalism. Its aesthetic energy is founded on the promise of violent social and artistic change, as outlined in his essay 'Futurism, Magic and Life', which describes murder as the ultimate creation of sensation: 'Killing somebody must be the greatest pleasure in existence: either like killing yourself without being interfered with by the instinct of self-preservation – or exterminating the instinct of self-preservation itself!' (p. 133). Murder and suicide are the ultimate, nihilistic expressions of autonomy, and all the better if accompanied by some unpredictable, imagistic and incendiary event: 'Surprise is the brilliant and prodigious fire-fly, that lives only twenty minutes: the excitement of seeing him burn through his existence like a wax-vesta makes you marvel at the slow-living world'. As the essay reveals, Vorticism moves away from Pater's stress on leisurely experience by proposing a more frantic modernism where the 'most perishable colours' are also the 'most brilliant' (p. 134). Like Otto Kreisler, the sinister painter, rapist and emblem of 'endless violence', who is the real subject of Lewis's 1918 novel, *Tarr*, the Vorticist is connected to the elemental force of art by his potential to inflict shocks. The blunt energy of Kreisler's particularly modern 'spirit' is unleashed during a duel with his Polish nemesis, Soltyk, whom he kills, and the Pole's death unleashes in him a feeling of something 'fresh loud and new' that heralds an abrupt end to the painter's bohemian existence in Paris. The experience sets Kreisler on a brief but existential journey through the 'novel conditions' of this new mode of experience, which ends with him taking his own life.[88] In this sense, *Tarr* is *the* novel of Vorticism as it claims that violence is the key that will unlock the modernist consciousness, and in it Lewis suggests that the extent to which the painter or writer is aware of this fact is a measure of his greatness or mediocrity. Both in *Tarr* and in *Blast*, Lewis argued that a spectacular end is brilliant and memorable, and in the image of the dying flame he presents a finite but impressive aspect of the Vortex alongside the violent pleasures of auto-destruction. This self-annihilating logic adds to the force of Vorticist avant-gardism, which, in its extremism, burns an imprint onto culture rather than offering a Futurist commentary on the substance of its material or technological surfaces. The first number of *Blast* also included *Enemy of the Stars*, a dramatic piece by Wyndham Lewis in which Vorticism's clear-cut and specifically British aesthetic is emphasised by the protagonist's preoccupation with the energising 'violences of all things', and in the necessary, revitalising destruction of what is. The story ends with the impulsively 'swift anarchist effort' of murder and suicide (p. 74), representing the metaphorical force required to develop this new consciousness, as opposed to Futurism and its belief in capitalist progress.[89]

The *War Number*

Appearing in July 1915, the second and final issue of *Blast* was a more cautious affair. The subversive tone of the first number was overwhelmed by the war and surrounded, as Lewis editorialised, 'by a multitude of other Blasts of all sizes and descriptions'. However he also promised that the journal would 'brave the waves of blood' and continue its radical mission once hostilities ended (*Blast* 2, p. 5). The conflict fuelled the Vorticists' demands for political and aesthetic change and it encouraged their contradictory impulses: Lewis exploited the war, hoping that it would unite Britain and France against the atavistic culture of 'Official Germany', where an atavistic culture driven by 'old Poetry' and Romance were failing to sustain a 'former condition of life, no longer existing' in the rest of Europe. He also acknowledged the progressive and 'unofficial' side of German society, where, he claimed, a lively avant-gardism was being championed by the 'detached individuals' of the Expressionist movement. Regarding the conflict as a fresh start for Europe, he argued that by exposing the anti-modern tendencies of both sides, it would validate the demands for cultural renovation made in the first issue of *Blast* (*Blast* 2, p. 6).

However there is a clear tension between the imperatives of British patriotism and avant-garde propaganda in the War Number. Describing the Vorticists as incidental propagandists, Lewis's criticism of democracy in 'War Notes' gives an early airing to the totalitarian views expressed later in *Hitler*. In his comparison of combat to the ferocity of everyday life, he suggests that in the protective 'fortress' of modern civilisation the modern subject dreams of indulging his desire to wreck chaos. Conflict facilitates this need of modern man who has never outgrown his primitive, naturally violent condition, a state that he can easily revert to, even when surrounded by the clinical, structured and 'scientific' violence of the city:

> The thinkers and Lords of the Earth, then, have fortified themselves in a structure of law. The greatest praise the really wise Lord can bestow on the man in the street is that he is 'actual,' 'of his time,' 'up to date.' Men must be penned and herded into 'Their Time', and prevented from dreaming, the prerogative of the Lord of the Earth. They must also be prevented from drifting back in the direction of their Jungle. And the best way to do this is to allow them to have a little contemporary Jungle of their own. Such a little up-to-date and iron jungle is the great modern city. Its vulgarity is the sort of torture and flagellation that becomes the austere creator. (*Blast* 2, p. 9)

Despite its unreal quality, the urban environment can facilitate man's dual condition of inherent violence and creativity, making it the ideal incubator for Vorticist art. The synthetic, 'scientific ferocity' of urban modernity clashes with man's naturally violent and aesthetically productive character, preventing a drift toward the primal modes of existence and the kind of 'natural' justice praised by Proudhon, who described 'the essence of revolutions' as the destruction of 'modern principles'.[90]

In the War Number these principles underline the mass destruction at the front, and *Blast* criticises the new dystopia of mechanised warfare by measuring its impact on individual consciousness, style and art. With its imposition of the 'impersonal', emblematised by the 'characterless', 'drab and colourless' appearance of the military, (something that Marinetti, with his enthusiasm for mass production would have favoured), Lewis warned that the war's 'universal campaign' would undermine subjective 'quality and uniqueness', replace poetry with the 'abstract hymn' of jingoism and end as a series of indiscriminate 'ant-fights' (*Blast* 2, pp. 25–6). As an alternative, he suggested dissociation from the mass by declaring that: 'One man living in a cave alone can be a universal poet. In fact solitude is art's atmosphere, and its heaven is the Individual's. The abstract artist is the most individual, just as genius is the only sanity' (p. 72). In calling on artists to detach themselves from society and from its synthetically violent extension, modern warfare, Lewis suggested that the solitary experience of reverie, so central to Pater's theory of aesthetics,[91] could be used to counter the dominant structures that unsophisticated popular forms represent and support. By retreating inwardly toward the ego, the British or even German avant-gardist, he suggested, could resist bourgeois culture and find liberation from the tyranny of the everyday.[92]

This idea is manifested in Gaudier's posthumous, paradoxical manifesto, 'Vortex Gaudier-Brzeska', which maintains that the War appears inconsequential in comparison to the power contained within the artist's consciousness:

> WITH ALL THE DESTRUCTION that works around us NOTHING IS CHANGED, EVEN SUPERFICIALLY. <u>LIFE IS THE SAME STRENGTH,</u> THE MOVING AGENT THAT PERMITS THE SMALL INDIVIDUAL TO ASSERT HIMSELF. (*Blast* 2, p. 33)

But Gaudier also entertained the notion that, instead of disenfranchising the individual, the experience of combat could enable 'THE <u>VORTEX</u> OF WILL, OF DECISION' (*Blast* 2, p. 33). His death on the front-line underlined his thesis and provided Vorticism with a martyr, that focal point of sympathy, memory and romanticised re-imagination required by every revolutionary group. His demise earned the journal sufficient patriotic capital to compete with the mainstream Georgian poets, whose popular and more legible poetry countered the cultural elitism of *Blast*'s avant-garde individualism. Pound summed up this oppositionality in the War Number's closing manifesto, 'Chronicles', by arguing that the journal 'dared to show modernity its face in an honest glass' by refusing to ignore the 'actual discords' that existed beneath the surface of European bourgeois society until their eruption in 'open conflict' between the two evils of 'teutonic atavism and unsatisfactory Democracy' (*Blast* 2, pp. 85–6). Although he exaggerated Vorticism's political influence ('Chronicles' claims that *Blast* coloured international affairs), Pound did diagnose the ideological schisms that racked pre-War Europe – contradictions that had been discussed in the previous issue. Pound's and Lewis's hatred for the failure of British democracy were intensified by the War, an event which, in the Vorticists' estimation, magnified *Blast*'s radical aesthetic position along with its anarchic political purchase.

The Great War and Vorticist Individualism: 'The Crowd Master'

Lewis gave vent to his anarchist belief in the fictional fragment, 'The Crowd Master', which can be read as an essay on Vorticism's radical aesthetic of detachment. Lewis regarded literature as the medium most capable of criticising collective consciousness because the writer, a necessarily private figure, is 'nearer to the individualist side than to the crowd side of his readers than are most artists'. This makes reading as an act of private interpretation that is influenced by the master-voice of the writer, whose individual discourse contradicts the corporate political expression unleashed in Britain by the outbreak of war. Initially intended as part of a longer piece, the story was revised and republished in *Blasting and Bombardiering*. The 1915 version opens with a scene of potential revolt as ominously black 'war-crowds' gathering in London are viewed with suspicion by the police who treat them as a political threat:

> THE CROWD
> Men drift in thrilling masses past the Admiralty, cold night tide. Their throng creeps round corners, breaks faintly here and there up against a railing barring from possible sights. Local ebullience and thickening: some madman disturbing their depths with baffling and recondite noise.
> THE POLICE with distinct icy contempt herd London. They shift it in lumps here and there, touching and shaping with heavy delicate professional fingers. Their attitude is as though these universal crowds wanted some new vague suffrage. (p. 94)

The scene is qualified by an air of polarisation and uncertainty as the cold, inert, amorphous and almost lifeless mass of the war crowd is manipulated in the skilled hands of policemen who easily direct its movement around the politically sensitive space of the Admiralty offices (a site bombed by Clan na Gael Dynamiters in 1884), without paying any attention to the collective's real and potentially threatening meaning. The police do not need to interpret the crowd because, by virtue of its collective structure, its intentions, like those of previous movements demanding political reform, are 'vague', indistinct and therefore un-revolutionary. The crowd functions as an uncomfortable reminder of the democratic gains won by British liberalism since the 1850s, but as well as providing the signal motif of this political tradition, it has a dangerous counter-side. Lewis suggests in this story that the structurally flawed democratic state is always vulnerable to any solitary individual with the wit and will to counter police action and then direct the urban crowd toward a more subversive position. Blenner, an invalided ex-sol-dier, is exposed to the conformity and counter-individualistic 'continuity of the Crowd-spirit' that has emerged since the first announcements of the prospect of war. Travelling to London in the hope of enlisting, he finds himself absorbed in a milieu of mass excitement and war-fever: 'Great national events are always preparing, the Crowd is in its habitual childish sleep. It rises to meet the crash half awake and struggling, with voluptuous and violent movements'. Everyone Blenner meets in this unpredictable, fermenting mass is transformed by events, each becoming 'a new person' in the 'temporary Death and Resurrection of the Crowd', but he is satisfied with its impersonal process of generalisation: 'Blenner was not too critical a man to penetrate their disguises or ferret out their Ego. He was glad to see so little of it for once'. He finds sanctuary in the depersonalisation and collective identity of the war-crowd, where the 'Delightful masquerade of everyone' makes its lack of individual-ity appealing: 'The certainty of feeling alike with everyone else was a great relief for over-paradoxical nerves'. But amidst the amorphousness of the expectant and excitable crowds he meets an unusual man, the 'Crowd-proof' individual and leader, or 'professional Crowd-officer', Brown Bryan Multum, an American sociologist whose interpretation of modern man is very similar to Gustave Le Bon's crowd theories. His profession as a scientific observer of modern men makes him the 'only' figure of agency, or 'conscious atom of the Crowd', and this suggests his potential role as a director of modern thought: 'A special privilege with him: to be of the Crowd and individually conscious. He was the King of the Future' (pp. 97–8). Blenner remembers buying one of Multum's books from 'The Bomb', an anarchist bookshop and publishing house on Charing Cross Road.[93] Sharing its name with the title of one of the fictional anarchist newspapers around which the novel *A Girl Among the Anarchists* centres, not to mention the metaphorical significance that it carries within the journal, *Blast*, this 'altruistic Book-Bazaar' serves an

equally subversive function in Lewis's modernist story by providing for
the needs of politicised and estranged avant-garde types like Blenner. He
recalls his first encounter with Multum's revolutionary theories:

> On leaving His Majesty's forces, after a concussion, and become definitely,
> to his family's distress, a crank and very liberal, he began reading sociologi-
> cal books and wandering about London. On passing the Bomb shop he was
> attracted by a poster advertising a new book:

THE CROWD MASTER

By BROWN BRYAN MULTUM

> THE CROWD MASTER, What might that mean? His bright astonished eyes
> fixed on the words, drinking up a certain strength from them.

> An opposition of and welding of the two heaviest words that stand for the
> multitude on the one hand, the Ego on the other.

> That should be something! (p. 99)

The modernist promise of Multum's paradoxical text, which appears
suited to Blenner's own contradictory mind, suggests to him the possibility of possessing a dichotomous consciousness with a much deeper
meaning than 'Master of the Crowd in the sense of a possessive domi-
nation by an individual' (p. 100): what the book promises is not a key
to straightforward political leadership but the fusion of the power of
the masses with the supreme political awareness of the self. Multum's
theories are similar to Max Stirner's elite anarchism which, based on the
notion that the ego functions both as a weapon and as a source of dialectical skill, emphasises an exclusive form of individualism. Regarding
man as a mercenary and amoral being, Stirner equated freedom with
the exercise of arbitrary will in defiance of all authority. Associating the
state with the erosion of individual agency, he regarded the egoist as
'more than "ordinary men"' and therefore as the 'most modern among
the "moderns"'. Like Multum's individualism, Stirner's model of egoism
is based upon the renunciation of collective identity and responsibility
toward the state: his concept of selfhood, or 'ownness', rejects exterior
sources of authority and operates as an ideology of 'Only I, and nothing
but I'.[94] Similarly, Multum fuses the apparently polar binaries of free
will and authority by influencing the as-yet undirected mass with his
superior consciousness and achieves power by sustaining an inherently
modernist awareness of his present. Having purchased the sociologist's
explosive text from the radical bookstore, Blenner finds in its pages
an ideal construction of subversive individualism that forms the basis

of Lewis's own literary aesthetic and political belief in the tyranny of 'Everyman'.[95]

Multum's natural anti-authoritarianism is given theoretical and scientific purchase by his professional status as a sociologist, updating the 'primordial' conditioning discussed in Lewis's essay, 'The God of Sport and Blood'. His unique detachment from the crowd at a moment of mass action and political participation in a national war effort is the measure of Multum as a true avant-gardist. Lewis stressed the autonomy and potential force of the individually focused writer who contrasts with 'mass-artists' like Shakespeare and Dickens, who wrote plays and novels aimed at a popular market that dictated that the ultimate value of a work is economic. For Lewis, engagement with the mass literary market reduces the artist to a commodity-producing 'instrument' and 'property'[96] of the crowd. The autonomous writer or painter contradicts the imperatives of the commercial circulation of art by refusing to become 'the servant of organized man'. Lewis held that freedom is a paradoxical phenomenon existing only 'in the heart of the anonymous crowd'.[97] What Multum's text promises is the possibility of achieving this freedom through total immersion in the mass while, simultaneously, remaining absolutely psychologically distinct from it. This aura of detachment also characterises the protagonist of the 1937 version of 'The Crowd Master', which reveals how Lewis's anarchic belief was intensified by his participation in the Great War. Lewis prefaced this updated version of the story by blaming the Liberals for allowing the conflict to erupt in the first place (he complained that 'it is always a liberal government that makes war',[98] rather than Tories, who are renowned for their war-mongering). This version replaces Blenner, the ex-serviceman, with Cantleman, 'a rough Bohemian' who learns about the declaration of hostilities in Scotland from the 'crashing' headlines of the London press. The atmosphere of imminent catastrophe and conflict is described in much finer detail here, as the ominous possibilities inherent in the assassination of the Austro-Hungarian archduke, Franz Ferdinand, are considered alongside the infinitely chaotic possibilities of the breakdown of central European power: 'Macbeth's witches had gathered at Sarajevo, to preside at a diabolical brew beside which the plots of Shakespeare were storms-in-teacups. Scotland was free of all such presences at the moment, Morpeth living in a golden age'.[99] The allusion to Shakespeare's nightmare play of absolute moral and political collapse, *Macbeth*, is given in hindsight and at a considerable chronological remove of over two decades: Lewis used this re-imagining of the outbreak of war to explore his idea that the conflict had nullified culture and 'stopped Art dead'.[100] In his 1950 memoir, *Rude Assignment*, he also described how, in the popular mind, the war formed a cultural barrier, or 'partition', that abruptly ended the progressive, even innocent avant-gardism of the pre-war years by transforming the period into a cultural 'past' and violently bringing the hopeful, ontic present of Vorticism to a premature end. *Blast* was intended to give voice to the lively, anarchic modernist dissent of this moment but, for Lewis, the outbreak of hostilities put everything on hold, even modernist culture.[101]

Under the headline advertising the Morpeth Olympiad and its 'RECORD CROWD', Cantleman finds the announcement of war expressed in sensational and 'crude violet' newspaper type, the text striking him as the perfect 'distillation' of the political trauma experienced during recent 'suffragetic years of minor violence!' Although relatively low in intensity, the radical activity of the Suffragettes has conditioned the population for a wider and more destructive conflict and, having experienced the shock of feminist radicalism, the country, it seems, is about to undergo further domestic political chaos thanks to the war. The outbreak is announced to a public who, like Cantleman, are already conditioned for fighting by the impact of this earlier militancy:

> Celebrated for minor violence, too, was *he*, a rough bohemian – he savoured violence for its own sake, as a coarse joke, or the crepitation of a Chinese cracker. He was not a man of blood. – He did not understand – he was very stupid. He was a suffragette.
> Eager for news, he went into a shop and got all the popular London papers. *Mails* and *Expresses*, the loudest shouters of the lot. How they hollered 'War' to a thrilled universe! He found all his horizons, by the medium of this yellow journalism, turned into a sinister sulphur. He was as pleased as Punch.[102]

Already desensitised by terrorism and now having his opinions dictated by the popular press and coming under the influence of these newspapers' view of what is possible, Cantleman interprets the war according to the information made available through the print media. Its professionally engineered stories appeal to his 'coarse' toughness, but not being a 'man of blood', his shallow bohemianism is closer to the artificial, synthetic modernism of the Futurist, who is vulnerable to the loud 'shouters' of the daily papers. Arriving after the publicity-conscious subversion of the Suffragettes, to whose militant campaign for the extension of the franchise to women Lewis compares the war, the 'thrilling' breakdown of European politics is rationalised through its comparison with less violent but equally shocking domestic political disturbances.

Lewis expressed his own anxiety over militant feminism in his facetious appeal 'To Suffragettes', in which he offered a 'WORD OF ADVICE':

IN DESTRUCTION, AS IN OTHER THINGS,
stick to what you understand.
WE MAKE YOU A PRESENT OF OUR VOTES.
ONLY LEAVE WORKS OF ART ALONE.
YOU MIGHT DESTROY A GOOD PICTURE BY
ACCIDENT
THEN! –
MAIS SOYEZ BONNES FILLES!
NOUS VOUS AIMONS!
WE ADMIRE YOUR ENERGY. YOU AND ARTISTS ARE
THE ONLY THINGS (YOU DON'T MIND BEING CALLED
THINGS?) LEFT IN ENGLAND WITH A LITTLE LIFE IN
THEM.

IF YOU DESTROY A GREAT WORK OF ART you are
destroying a greater soul than if you annihilated a whole district
of London.

LEAVE ART ALONE, BRAVE COMRADES! (pp. 151–2)

The Suffragettes had added art to their list of targets when they slashed paintings in the Manchester Art Gallery in April 1913 (in the same month Olive Hockin, who was an artist herself, was tried for burning down a croquet pavilion in Roehampton, vandalising an orchid house, cutting telegraph wires and setting fire to a post box)[103] and a year later, in a joint strike against the male dominated spheres of art and literature, Sargent's painting of Henry James was slashed in the Royal Academy.[104] Such attacks on high culture underlined to the Vorticists how the shock-value of terrorism had aesthetic purchase while, in serving blows against the literary and art establishments, they also invested Suffragettism with notoriety and the kind of political credibility that Vorticism lacked. While addressing the Suffragettes as their 'comrades' and acknowledging the radicalism of their actions, the reality of feminist knives tearing establishment canvas challenged the Vorticists, whose theoretically radical agenda appeared wanting in comparison to the directness and radicalism of such action. An imaginary figure representing Lewis's modernist and masculine ideal, Cantleman is his paradoxical answer to the practical challenges that suffragettism posed to establishment art.

The newspapers, as the nation's 'grand messengers of death', announce the war for which Cantleman has unconsciously been prepared by his exposure to the subversive tactics of radical feminism. The new world war and its pervasive 'system' of chaos herald a new atmosphere of 'conventional horror', as political fear is magnified beyond anything that the population of Britain has previously experienced. But, at the same time, Cantleman notices that the masses have been seized by a pleasurable anticipation of the oncoming violence and the novelty of their collective vulnerability:

> Everything was going to be delightfully *different*. There was the closing of the Stock Exchange. What would happen as regards the Banks? Would there be a shortage of small change? No sixpence for a shoe-black, or penny to buy a paper! A host of fascinating contretemps presented themselves to the readers of the newspapers . . . Food supplies had better be laid in at once. And what of course of invasion? What a change an invasion would be! Back to William the Conqueror! The exciting novelties foreshadowed pleased everybody, such a delicious earthquake made children of the party.[105]

This rather exciting 'carnival of fear'[106] reverses *Blast*'s complaint against the Suffragettes and their cultural-political strikes by facing up to the prospect of a possible national meltdown. The financial disaster of a closed stock exchange and the more immediate problems of food shortage excite Cantleman's radical imagination, while the promise of anarchy encourages his subversively bohemian character. This scenario of uncontrolled terror and the saturation of British life by fear and chaos updates older representations of political terror, giving it modernist form by adding the exciting possibilities of the spy-thriller (a genre initiated during the early twentieth century by popular authors such as Rudyard Kipling, Erskine Childers, William Le Queux and John Buchan). Travelling by train to England to enlist, Cantleman reflects on the possibility that his train might be sabotaged, and his anxiety and delight at the possibility of being blown up contrasts with Blenner's eventless train journey to London in the original version of the story:

> When he woke he was evidently upon a bridge. Newcastle-on-Tyne, he found it was. There were sentries on the bridge. It might be blown up otherwise – we were speeding towards all bridges with infernal machines ready for use. Stacks of rifles on the railway platform. More 'mobilization scenes' to delight the *Mail* or *Mirror*.[107]

The omnipresence of the press in this story indicates Lewis's discomfort with the fact that the immediately pre-war period was an intensely mediated moment during which the slightest political scare could be magnified by newspapers serving the political agenda of the state. In the midst of these manipulated 'scenes' Cantleman's excited imagination implicates everyone in the oncoming disaster by involving the collective 'we' in the planting of bombs at railway bridges, while the press's enthusiasm for mobilisation is equalled by its 'delight' at the possibility of sabotage and death. It takes a return of his subversive self to introduce some perspective to these imaginings and to counter the wider atmosphere of paranoia, as Cantleman reflects on the hysteria taking hold of the country. The unfolding of events shocks the British public with an engineered violence that is seen to operate with the invasive force of a sexual attack:

> The 'great historical event' is always hatching; the Crowd in its habitual sleep. Then the appointed hand releases the clutch, the 'great event' is set in motion: the crowd rises to meet the crash half awake and struggling, with voluptuous spasms. It is the Rape of the Crowd. Every acquaintance Cantleman met was a new person. The only possibility of renewal for the individual is into this temporary Death and Resurrection of the Crowd, it appears. The war was like a great new fashion. Cantleman conformed. He became a man of fashion.[108]

Just as the victim of rape is transformed by the violence of rape (manifested here as physical invasion) and by the traumatic disruption of selfhood by the sexual attacker, the psyche of each individual in the war crowd is shocked into a new existential condition by the force of the stage-managed event of war. Lewis's fictional reflection on the conflict offers a modernist theory of shock in which the autonomous and detached individual observes, with gradually lessening autonomy, the domestic hysteria and chaos that prefaces the killing and mass destruction on the front. Like Multum's ego, Cantleman's self or ego is resistant to the manipulated desires of the amorphous crowd, but only to a certain point, resisting its incorporation into a collective movement in the service of official power until a final moment of sensory overload when he is overwhelmed by the persuasive force of authority. Lewis returned to this theme in *Rude Assignment* by arguing that the paradoxical role of government is to, at once, foster and then manage this condition of 'primitive chaos' among the population while, at the same time, shielding the state from the subversive energy of the crowd.[109] As he explains in *Blasting and Bombardiering*, 'The Crowd Master' stressed the agency of the individual capable of recognising this very modern political contradiction:

> what was meant by 'Crowd-master' was that I was master of myself. Not of anybody else – that I have never wanted to be. I was master *in* the crowd, not master *of* the crowd. I moved freely and with satisfaction up and down its bloodstream, in strict, even arrogant, insulation from its demonic impulses.
> This I regarded as, in some sort, a triumph of mind over matter. It was a triumph of the individualist principle. I believed a great deal in the individual. And I still prefer him to his collective counterpart, though recognizing his shortcomings.[110]

Comfortably at large within the throng, Cantleman, like Lewis, goes to war at the end of this confessional story hoping to acquire experiences that will be tailored to his needs as an individual. But in his earlier model, Blenner, and in Multum's ego-inspiring writing, Lewis expressed a more resistant self who functions according to a subversive logic that Benjamin would later describe as 'the metaphysics of the *provocateur*'. This figure of proactive and subversive agency influenced the literature of the unstable bourgeois period, when precariously existing *flâneurs* like Blenner and Cantleman lived in an 'obscure' state of revolt, waiting for the arrival of the moment when they could act and 'feel with those who were shaking the foundations of this society'.[111] This model fits with the reality of nineteenth-century Paris, which Benjamin describes in *Charles Baudelaire*, but its role as a source of modern agency has some resonance for British modernist culture which, Lewis argued, had it not been for the outbreak of the Great War, might have evolved along a different, more anarchic path. Lewis's version of the *flâneur* is of a detached and lonely revolutionary whose agency is limited by circumstances and, ultimately, goes unrealised. Having lost his potential to perform within this moment, he becomes adrift in the war crowd and finds himself at the mercy of the state.

The End of Individualism

Blast petered out after the publication of this second issue. A third was planned but this 'American Number', with which Lewis and Pound hoped to appeal to modernist circles in New York, never materialised.[112] After the war he infamously experimented with far right politics, favouring 'fascism rather than communism',[113] but these earlier writings reveal that, during the pre-war years, his modernism was a decidedly anarchic affair. Lewis thought of himself at this time as a fanatic who 'preferred something more metallic and resistant than the pneumatic surface of the cuticle', such as 'a helmet to a head of hair', or a 'scarab to a jelly-fish'. His preference for the hardness of metallic surfaces incorporates Vorticism's aesthetic principle of an ontic identity invested in the materiality of its present moment. This was embodied in the abstract style and radical immediacy of a modernist movement that assumed a revolutionary position on the function of art, literature and politics within the world in which and by which it was produced. In doing so Vorticism came into conflict with the 'collective Sensation' of the crowd and its 'demonic' impulses, which Lewis also regarded as being as indeterminate as a shapeless polyp, the formlessness of which could only hinder the production of serious art. The equally 'soul-less' and impersonal 'machine' of politics and capital – the system of 'money-government' that drained society of its vitality and transformed the masses into 'half-dead people', like the crowds with which Cantleman contends, in a lifeless state of 'personal extinction' or 'no-living'[114] – was as fraudulent to Lewis as nineteenth-century bourgeois democracy was to the source of his political inspiration, Proudhon. The catastrophic world war between the international factions of modern capital neither settled nor achieved anything, as far as Lewis was concerned, other than imposing a psychological and cultural barrier between pre-war modernism and the culture that followed the armistice of 1918.

In a 1926 review of Beaverbrook's *Politicians and the Press*, Lewis noted that politics is arranged around two extremes: on the one hand, the politically engaged individual who is willing to intervene in a national crisis and, on the other, the more sluggish democratic principle represented by Parliament. He summarised his opinion on individualism by stating that 'Everyman has been proved to be as great a tyrant as the Individual, only slower, less effective and less responsible'.[115] Lewis's condemnation of Futurism can be understood in this light, as its close relationship with the state undermined what he considered the necessary spontaneity, originality and independence of modernist art. Futurism, he fumed while preparing *Blast*, was merely the 'sensational procreation' of Dada and Surrealism.[116] In a review published in *The Egoist*, Frank Denver noted the 'unfortunate' coincidence between both movements' more general aims and, hoping to draw attention away from their 'arriviste' qualities, stressed their differences by describing the Vorticists as 'individually engaging' and audacious artists.[117] While both brands of *avant-gardisme* celebrated modernity as a 'world of ceaseless shocks',[118] Futurism was undoubtedly implicated in the corporate structures of twentieth-century capitalism. Vorticism, in contrast, remained aloof and alienated both from the state and from organised entrepreneurial capital. According to Gianni Vattimo, the difficulties experienced in interpreting modern art are a reflection of the subject's defamiliarisation with the world, and its 'insistence on disorientation' produces an aesthetic experience modelled on the condition of estrangement; instead of recomposing the subject, 'aesthetic experience is directed towards keeping the disorientation alive'.[119] The Vorticists' construction of modernity as a series of 'jangling' and confusing experiences culminating in a condition of sensory 'complication'[120] that is, nevertheless, aesthetically productive, offers a more subversively politicised expressions of estrangement than those offered by Futurism. However it is inarguable that *Blast*'s manifesto modernism owes much stylistically to Marinetti's praise for violence, revolution and riot, voiced in 'The Founding and Manifesto of Futurism', which first appeared in *Le Figaro* in 1909.[121]

Futurism's notorious praise for the 'aggressive action' of 'the punch and the slap', its celebration of struggle as the only source of beauty[122] and its suggestion that poetry should serve as a 'violent attack' on tradition certainly influenced Lewis, but Vorticist modernism did not plagiarise the ideologies of Futurism's early manifestoes. The Vorticists cultivated a British adaptation of Marinetti's shock tactics but in doing so maintained a cautious distance from the centres of artistic and political power, as their characteristic unease with capitalism and its structures is nowhere to be found in the Futurists' demands for progress at any cost.

Futurism, with its love of corporate capitalism and its machine culture, was rounded on by Lewis as the 'disgorging spray of a vortex with no drive behind it, DISPERSAL' (*Blast* 1, p. 153). By paying attention to the cultural surface of modernity, the Futurist aesthetic is superficial, concentrating on technology rather than spirit. Having immersed its art in popular technology fetishes, Futurism offers an arriviste ideology that appealed to a public already indoctrinated in a complex of industrial and commercial ideas that it mimics. With its deliberately unsynchronised style, Futurism appeared uncoordinated and incapable of sustaining lasting change in the world of art. Like the German Expressionist Rudolf Leonhard, who regarded Marinetti's techno-fetishism and its 'hollow inflated verses' as a 'shapeless' celebration of 'din for din's sake',[123] the Vorticists regarded Futurism as unoriginal and self-indulgent, and complained that it bore no relevance to the radically individualist needs of the serious avant-gardist. Regarding their Italian rivals as promoting an 'accelerated form of impressionism', *Blast* condemned Futurism as a combination of the 'CORPSES' of dead art movements and unsophisticated 'POPULAR BELIEFS' (*Blast* 1, p. 154). (In the second number of *Blast* Lewis sarcastically described Futurism's 'merit' as its similarity to Strauss's Waltzes and rag-time dancing, or 'the best modern Popular Art' (*Blast* 2, pp. 41–2).) In contrast to Futurism's cheap lifelessness, *Blast*'s radical and elitist message denies any hope of the Vorticists developing a popular following. Marinetti experienced the limits of popular patience with his worship of machine culture when, after giving a series of readings in Britain in 1912 and 1913, he was heckled shortly before the publication of *Blast* when his troupe of Futurist 'noisicians' was challenged during a rowdy performance of their musical 'principles' at the Coliseum, during which 'weird funnel-shaped instruments' were played to cries of 'No More!' from the auditorium.[124]

Lewis's fusion of aesthetics and politics did not end with the outbreak of the First World War. He tried to resurrect the work done by the 'revolutionary spirits' of the Vorticist group and its short-lived sequel,

X-Group,[125] by outlining his ideas on political and artistic individualism in *The Art of Being Ruled* in 1926, and much later, in 1950, he declared that the state remained 'below the Individual' and that government and violence were 'commutative terms'.[126] *Blast* voiced subversive individualism much more loudly than other modernist publications and, as the first incarnation of 'The Crowd Master' indicates, the war exacerbated Lewis's Vorticist sense of libertarian individualism. Even his temporary but notorious pro-fascist leanings were characterised by scepticism over large-scale political organisation, emerging as they did out of his dislike for Bolshevism's 'top-dog look' and his belief that all revolutionary artists were ultimately 'anarchists' and not slaves to leftist party doctrine.[127] Vorticism's literary and artistic shocks were overwhelmed by the popular war that the story describes but this did not rule out the possibility of subversive individual autonomy. Lewis's experience of the conflict, both as a gunner and then as a war artist, intensified his sceptical aesthetic consciousness and influenced him to re-attempt the Vorticist project when he returned to the art-scene with the 'bang' designed to '"blast" a way . . . through the bourgeois barrage' that was the unsuccessful X Group. Its failure persuaded him to abandon collective projects,[128] but he continued to regard the conflict between the active, aesthetically aware individual prepared to intervene in crises and the slower kind of political action that he felt was represented by parliamentary democracy as *the* key determinant of modern art and politics.[129] In *Blasting and Bombardiering* and in the political essays collected in *The Art of Being Ruled* (which Lewis described as a 'Leftwing' book, written to 'save people from being . . . "ruled" off the face of the earth'),[130] he advocated anarchism and insisted upon the potential of a subversive radical consciousness which, he maintained, could resist the totalising imperatives of the state and of establishment art, forces that he viewed as threatening modernist culture.[131] His theory that a fusion of individuality and revolutionary politics could provoke more intensely felt and therefore genuine forms and expressions of art seemed overblown, even in his own hindsight. But in its very brevity, *Blast*, with its aura of unpredictability, spontaneity and incompleteness, remained true to its impulsive and anarchic influences.

Notes

1. Wyndham Lewis, *Rude Assignment* (London: Hutchinson & Co., 1950), p. 59.
2. Vanessa R. Schwartz, *Spectacular Realities: Early Mass Culture in Fin-de-*

Siècle France (Berkeley and Los Angeles: University of California Press, 1998), p. 11.

3. Wyndham Lewis, 'A Review of Contemporary Art', *Blast* 2, June 1915, p. 38.

4. See Wyndham Lewis, *Blasting and Bombardiering* (London: Eyre and Spottiswoode, 1937), p. 35. *Blast* was, of course, not the first modernist journal to attack the bourgeois 'state of mind', which was described as the target of bohemian contempt in *The Egoist*. See Baptiste Von Helmholtz, 'The Bourgeois', *The Egoist: An Individualist Review*, Vol. 1, No. 3, 2 February 1914, p. 53.

5. See 'Men, Machines and Progress', *The Egoist*, Vol. 1, No. 3, 2 February 1914, p. 42; and Allen Upward, 'The Plain Person', *The Egoist*, Vol. 1, No. 3, 2 February 1914, p. 47.

6. Walter Benjamin, 'Some Motifs in Baudelaire', in *Charles Baudelaire: A Lyric Poet in the Era of High Capitalism*, trans. Harry Zohn (London: Verso, 1997), p. 117.

7. Lewis, *Rude Assignment*, pp. 125, 196–7.

8. Wyndham Lewis, Miscellaneous Art Notes for *Blast* no. 2, 1915, Cornell University Library Rare and Manuscript Collections, Carl Kroch Library, # 4612, Box 22, Folder 12.5.

9. In his seminal study, *The Literary Vorticism of Ezra Pound and Wyndham Lewis: Towards the Condition of Painting* (Baltimore: Johns Hopkins University Press, 1985), Reed Way Dasenbrock writes off the literary merit of *Blast*, neglecting in particular its manifestos and polemical outbursts. Regarding it only as an art journal, Dasenbrock cites Lewis's 1918 novel, *Tarr*, as the first example of Vorticist writing and suggests that the movement's aesthetic tendencies did not have a literary manifestation until the publication of Lewis's later novels and of Pound's poetic cycle of 1925–67, *The Cantos*. Likewise, Paul Edwards's more recent and exhaustive analysis, *Wyndham Lewis: Painter and Writer* (New Haven: Yale University Press, 2000), stresses Lewis's influence as a writer, painter and champion of 'alternative modernism' but argues that his literary potential was not realised at least until the early 1920s.

10. Paige Reynolds argues that *Blast* exploited the shocks of the advertising industry rather than those of revolutionary politics: 'By appropriating the aesthetics of advertising, *Blast* capitalized on this discourse, which insisted that advertising was a shocking, invasive, distinctly modern, and visceral – rather than simply intellectual – cultural form'. However Lewis's notion that the journal would serve artists prepared to adopt and imitate radical political postures suggests that Vorticism was also influenced by contemporary revolutionary discourse. See Paige Reynolds, 'Chaos Invading Concept: *Blast* as a Native Theory of Promotional Culture', *Twentieth Century Literature* 46.2 (Summer, 2000), pp. 238–68, p. 246. See Wyndham Lewis, 'Note for Catalogue', Catalogue for the Vorticist Exhibition, Doré Galleries, 10 June 1915.

11. See Paul Peppis, *Literature, Politics, and the English Avant-Garde: Nation and Empire, 1901–1918* (Cambridge: Cambridge University Press, 2000), especially chap. 4, 'Surrounded by a Multitude of other Blasts: Vorticism and the Great War'.

12. Wyndham Lewis, 'Our Wild Body', *The New Age*, Vol. VII, No. 1, 5 May 1910, pp. 8–10, quotations pp. 8, 10.
13. Lewis, *Blasting and Bombardiering*, p. 152.
14. Joseph Pierre Proudhon, *What is Property?*, translated from *Qu'est-ce que la propriété?* by Donald R. Kelley and Bonnie G. Smith (Cambridge: Cambridge University Press, 1994), pp. 60, 13.
15. Lewis, *Blasting and Bombardiering*, p. 307.
16. See Wyndham Lewis, 'A Man in Love with the Past', in *Time and Western Man* (Santa Rosa: Black Sparrow Press), pp. 67–72, quotation taken from p. 69.
17. Wyndham Lewis, letter to Ezra Pound, July 1915, Cornell, Box 63, Folder 1.
18. See Walter L. Adamson, *Embattled Avant-Gardes: Modernism's Resistance to Commodity Culture in Europe* (Berkeley, Los Angeles, London: University of California Press, 2007), pp. 4, 10–11, 18, 23. While Adamson does not discuss Vorticism, his analysis of the early avant-garde's ambivalent relationship with popular commodity culture and the threat that it posed to the 'sacred' realm of modernist art illustrates how in the pre-war period in Germany, Italy and Russia 'political' modernisms were troubled by the marketing strategies that they adopted. See also Harold Monro, 'The Imagists Discussed', *The Egoist*, Vol. 51 , No. 2, May 1915, p. 78.
19. See Peppis, *Literature, Politics and the English Avant-Garde*, p. 1; and Frederic Jameson, *Fables of Aggression: Wyndham Lewis, the Modernist as Futurist* (Berkeley: University of California Press, 1979), p. 15.
20. Here Lewis praised German National Socialism for its 'passion' and 'impressive conviction', described Hitler as a 'Man of Peace', and dismissed Nazi anti-Semitism as a 'preliminary snag'. See Wyndham Lewis, *Hitler* (London: Chatto & Windus, 1931), pp. 4, 11.
21. Perry Anderson, 'Modernity and Revolution', in Cary Nelson and Lawrence Grossberge (eds), *Marxism and the Interpretation of Culture* (London: Macmillan, 1988), pp. 323, 325–6.
22. Ezra Pound, 'The New Sculpture', *The Egoist*, Vol. 1, No. 4, 16 February 1914, p. 68.
23. Baptiste Von Helmholtz (mis-cited in the original as Bastien Von Helmholtz), 'The Bourgeois', *The Egoist*, Vol. 1, No. 3, 2 February 1914, p. 53.
24. Lewis, like Sorel, indicated the point at which anarchist ideology can meet with far-right thinking. In his notorious 1931 polemic, *Hitler*, he described industrial modernity as a dialectic of 'endless' conflict that produced violence with an inherent 'amusement value'. While these opinions were formed by his observations of Germany, they fit within his imaginary of modern chaos as Lewis's later fascist preoccupation with struggle-for-its-own-sake was inherited from Vorticism (this continuity is reflected by the admiration of trades unionists, anarchists and fascists for the troubling analysis offered by his political role model, Sorel). See Georges Sorel, *Reflections on Violence*, translated from *Réflections Sur la Violence*, ed. Jeremy Jennings, trans. T. E. Hulme (Cambridge: Cambridge Univerity Press, 1999), p. 8; and Lewis, *Hitler*, pp. 35, 74.

25. Lewis, *Blasting and Bombardiering*, p. 6.
26. See Raymond Williams, *The Politics of Modernism: Against the New Conformists* (London: Verso, 1996), pp. 38–51, p. 62.
27. See Renato Poggioli, *The Theory of the Avant-Garde*, translated from the Italian by Gerald Fitzgerald (Cambridge, MA: Harvard University Press, 1968), pp. 3–4, 9, 12.
28. See Peter Bürger, *Theory of the Avant-Garde*, translated from the German by Michael Shaw (Manchester: Manchester University Press, 1984), pp. 8–10, 18, 23.
29. See Perry Anderson, 'Modernity and Revolution', pp. 317–33, 323, 325.
30. See Andreas Huyssen, *After the Great Divide: Modernism, Mass Culture, Postmodernism* (Bloomington and Indianapolis: Indiana University Press, 1986).
31. Sorel, *Reflections on Violence*, footnote p. 152.
32. See Alex Houen, *Terrorism and Modern Literature, From Joseph Conrad to Ciaran Carson* (Oxford: Oxford University Press, 2002), pp. 102–3, 120–1.
33. Ezra Pound, 'Edward Wadsworth, Vorticist', *The Egoist*, Vol. 1, No. 16, Saturday, 16 August 1914, pp. 306–7.
34. See 'The Great Revolutionary Vortex', *Blast: Review of the Great English Vortex*, No. 1, 20 June 1914, p. 7. Subsequently cited in the text.
35. Wyndham Lewis, 'Biographical details for publishing purposes' (publicity released for *The Art of Being Ruled*), 1926, Cornell, Box 3, Folder 12.
36. Ezra Pound, 'The New Sculpture'.
37. Lewis, *Blasting and Bombardiering*, p. 260.
38. Not only did anarchism feature in the anxieties of the immediate pre-war period, so too did radical feminism. For a detailed discussion of the influence of the Suffragette movement on *Blast*, see Alex Houen, *Terrorism and Modern Literature*, chap. 2, 'Wyndham Lewis: Literary 'Strikes' and Allegorical Assaults', pp. 93–142.
39. *Blast* 2, pp. 41–2.
40. See Andrej Gasiorek, *Wyndham Lewis and Modernism* (Tavistock: Northcote House, 2004), pp. 21–2.
41. Lewis, *Time and Western Man*, p. 213.
42. See Wyndham Lewis, *The Art of Being Ruled* (Santa Rosa: Black Sparrow Press, 1989), p. 307. For a near-contemporary discussion of the dangers associated with conformism, see Gustave Le Bon, *The Crowd: A Study of the Popular Mind*, translated from *La Psycologie des Foules* (1895) (London: T. Fisher Unwin, 1896).
43. See Lewis, letters to Alick Schepeler, c. May 1914; and to John Quinn, 24 January 1917; to Ezra Pound, July 1915, Cornell, Box 62, Folder 89, Box 63, Folders 1 and 33.
44. Lewis, *Rude Assignment*, p. 10.
45. Roger Fry, quoted in Judith Collins, *The Omega Workshops* (Chicago: University of Chicago Press, 1984), p. 1.
46. The term 'Vorticism' was coined to describe Lewis's group in opposition to Cubism, Futurism, Expressionism and Imagism. See Dasenbrock, *The Literary Vorticism of Ezra Pound and Wyndham Lewis*, p. 14.
47. Lewis, *Blasting and Bombardiering*, p. 255.

48. Ibid. p. 285.
49. Pound, 'The New Sculpture', p. 68. For Pound the inexplicable force of 'new' art was beyond rational explanation: 'Art is to be admired rather than explained. The jargon of these sculptures is beyond me. I do not know precisely why I admire a green granite, female, apparently pregnant monster with one eye going around a square corner.'
50. Lewis, 'Ezra Pound', draft ms (April 1948), pp. 6–8, 12, Cornell, Box 8, Folder 18.
51. Ezra Pound, 'Wyndham Lewis', *The Egoist*, Vol. 1, No. 12, 15 June 1914, p. 233.
52. Lewis, *Blasting and Bombardiering*, p. 290.
53. Ezra Pound, *Gaudier-Brzeska: A Memoir* (London: John Lane, 1916), pp. 42, 47, 49.
54. Ibid. pp. 82, 78, 67.
55. Lewis recalled how in one of his 'old Ezra-letters' he was advised that 'the one way to deal with an Englishman' was to 'kick him in the teeth'. See Lewis, 'Ezra Pound', pp. 2–3.
56. Long after Vorticism ended, Pound continued to spread his combative approach to letters: Lewis recalled visiting the poet in Paris in 1921 when he found him sparring with Ernest Hemingway, delivering a 'hectic assault' until the aspiring novelist floored him with a blow to the solar plexus. See Lewis, 'Ezra Pound', pp. 6–7.
57. See F. T. Marinetti, 'The Founding and Manifesto of Futurism', in *Let's Murder the Moonshine: Selected Writings*, trans. R. W. Flint and Arthur A. Coppotelli (Los Angeles: Sun & Moon Press, 1991), p. 49.
58. Richard Aldington, 'Wyndham Lewis', *The Egoist*, Vol. 1, No. 12, 15 June 1914, p. 273.
59. Lewis, *Blasting and Bombardiering*, pp. 35, 55.
60. For an account of how this the war transformed Lewis's painting and writing, see Edwards, *Wyndham Lewis*, especially chap. 6, 'The Ideal Giant: Art and the Assaults of Egotism and Life, 1915–1917', and chap. 7, 'War, the *Rappel à l'ordre* and the Continuance of Modernism: Painting, 1917–1923'.
61. Lewis, *Blasting and Bombardiering*, pp. 55, 57.
62. Ibid. pp. 255–6.
63. Subsequent quotations are from '*Blast: Review of the Great English Vortex*', No. 1, 20 June 1914.
64. The Vorticists, who viewed Futurism as mindless 'DISPERSAL' (*Blast* 1, p. 153), were not the only avant-garde that regarded Marinetti as suspect. The German Expressionist Rudolf Leonhard described Futurism as 'shapeless' spin bearing the hallmark 'of advertising slogans', holding that its unfocused 'din' and 'verbal diarrhoea' belonged more properly to the entertainment industries than to the realm of individualised art. See Rudolf Leonhard, 'Marinetti in Berlin 1913', in Paul Raabe (ed.), *The Era of German Expressionism*, trans. J. M. Ritchie (Woodstock, NY: Overlook Press, 1985), pp. 115–18. Quotations from p. 116.
65. Le Bon, *The Crowd*, p. 66.
66. Lewis, letter to Augustus John, summer 1915, Cornell, Box 63, Folder 3.
67. For a discussion of Lewis's concern with the failure of Enlightenment

rationality in the face of a 'perverted' modernity, see David A. Wragg's essay, 'Aggression, Aesthetics, Modernity: Wyndham Lewis and the Fate of Art' in Peters Corbett (ed.), *Wyndham Lewis and the Art of Modern War* (Cambridge: Cambridge University Press, 1998), pp. 181–210.

68. See Lewis, *Blasting and Bombardiering*, pp. 20, 42, 43; and *Rude Assignment*, p. 14.

69. See Maurice Harland Grant, *A Dictionary of British Sculptors, from the XXIIIth Century to the XXth Century* (London: Rockliff, 1958), p. 39.

70. See Douglas Mao, *Solid Objects: Modernism and the Test of Production* (Princeton: Princeton University Press, 1998), pp. 126, 142.

71. Lewis, *Blasting and Bombardiering*, p. 52.

72. Ezra Pound, 'Wyndham Lewis', *The Egoist*, Vol. 1, No. 12, 15 June 1914, p. 234.

73. Aldington, 'Wyndham Lewis', p. 273.

74. Ezra Pound, 'Edward Wadsworth, Vorticist', *The Egoist*, Vol. 1, No. 16, 15 August 1914, p. 306.

75. Ibid. pp. 38–40.

76. Auceps, 'The New Sculpture' (To the Editor), *The Egoist*, Vol. 1, No. 7, 1 April 1914, p. 138.

77. Henri Gaudier-Brzeska, 'On the New Sculpture'; and Ezra Pound, 'The Caressability of the Greeks', *The Egoist*, Vol. 1, No. 6, 16 March 1914, pp. 118–19.

78. See Paul O'Keeffe, *Some Sort of Genius: A Life of Wyndham Lewis* (London: Pimlico, 2000), p. 156.

79. Ezra Pound, *Gaudier-Brzeska*, p. 97.

80. Gianni Vattimo, *The Transparent Society*, trans. David Webb from *La società transparente* (London: Polity Press, 1992), p. 57.

81. Ibid. p. 56.

82. Ezra Pound, 'Exhibition at the Goupil Gallery', *The Egoist*, Vol. 1, No. 6, 16 March 1914, p. 109.

83. Walter Pater, *The Renaissance: Studies in Art and Poetry* (Oxford: Oxford University Press, 1998), pp. 151–2.

84. 'Vortex. Pound.'. *Blast* 1, p. 153.

85. See Anderson, 'Modernity and Revolution', p. 324.

86. William Butler Yeats, 'The Great Wheel', *A Vision* (London: Macmillan, 1978), pp. 68, 70, 72, 94, 105.

87. '"Blast." The Vorticists' Manifesto', *The Times*, 1 July 1914, p. 8.

88. Wyndham Lewis, *Tarr* (London: Penguin, 1982), pp. 281, 284.

89. Lewis's rather extreme fiction was accompanied by contributions from more conventional modernists like Rebecca West, whose short story 'Indissoluble Matrimony' was published in *Blast* 1. The journal also carried the opening section of Ford Madox Hueffer's classic *The Saddest Story*, which was given the more optimistic title, *The Good Soldier*, in 1915. Clearly, Vorticism was not all about making a completely clean sweep of the literary scene, but sought to position itself and function alongside more mainstream (and more comprehensible) modernist writing.

90. Proudhon, *What is Property?*, p. 20.

91. According to Pater, art-impressions impact upon the individual in

isolation, 'each mind keeping as a solitary prisoner its own dream of a world.' See Pater, *The Renaissance*, p. 151.

92. See Jonathan Crary's discussion of reverie-as-resistance in *Suspensions of Perception: Attention, Spectacle, and Modern Culture* (Cambridge, MA: MIT Press, 1999), especially pp. 45–6.

93. See Reg Groves, *The Balham Group: How British Trotskyism Began* (London: Pluto, 1974), p. 45.

94. See Max Stirner, *The Ego and its Own* (Cambridge: Cambridge University Press, 1995), pp. 120, 89, 148.

95. See Wyndham Lewis, 'Britons Shall Never be Bees', *Calendar of Modern Letters*, January 1926, pp. 360–2, quotation from p. 360, Cornell University Library Rare and Manuscript Collections, Carl Kroch Library, # 4612, Box 4, Folder 10

96. Wyndham Lewis, 'The Artist as Crowd', *Twentieth Century*, pp. 12–15 (undated – 1956?), quotation from p. 14, Cornell, Box 44, Folder 5.

97. Lewis, *The Art of Being Ruled*, p. 307.

98. Lewis, *Blasting and Bombardiering*, p. 67.

99. Ibid. p. 69.

100. Lewis to Kate Lechmere (n.d. – summer 1915), Cornell University Library Rare and Manuscript Collections, Carl Kroch Library, # 4612, Box 63, Folder 2.

101. See Lewis, *Rude Assignment*, pp. 137–8, 196–7.

102. Lewis, *Blasting and Bombardiering*, p. 70.

103. 'Suffragist Conspiracy: Lenient Sentence On An Artist', *The Times*, Saturday, 5 April 1913, p. 4.

104. See Houen, *Terrorism and Modern Literature*, p. 128.

105. Lewis, *Blasting and Bombardiering*, pp. 71–2.

106. Ibid. p. 72.

107. Ibid. p. 74.

108. Ibid. p. 81.

109. Lewis, *Rude Assignment*, p. 64.

110. Lewis, *Blasting and Bombardiering*, pp. 89–90.

111. Benjamin, *Charles Baudelaire*, pp. 14, 20.

112. Lewis to Ezra Pound, 29 April 1916, Cornell, Box 63, Folder 22.

113. Lewis, *The Art of Being Ruled*, p. 27.

114. Lewis regarded Gaudier's personal and artistic vitality as an important counter to this condition. See Lewis, *Blasting and Bombardiering*, pp. 110, 89, 115.

115. Lewis, 'Britons Shall Never Be Bees', p. 360.

116. Wyndham Lewis, Galley Notes for *Blast* No. 2, Cornell University Library Rare and Manuscript Collections, Carl Kroch Library, # 4612, Box 4, Folder 1, p. 4.

117. See Frank Denver, 'The London Group, *The Egoist*, No. 4, Vol. 11, 1 April 1915, pp. 60–1.

118. For example, Marinetti praised Mussolini as a walking bomb, or 'a package full of good gunpowder'. See F. T. Marinetti, 'Multiplied Man and the Reign of the Machine', in F. T. Marinetti, *Let's Murder the Moonshine: Selected Writings*, trans. R. W. Flint and Arthur A. Coppotelli (Los Angeles: Sun & Moon Press, 1991), p. 99.

119. Vattimo, *The Transparent Society*, p. 51.
120. *Blast* 1, p. 33.
121. Marinetti, 'The Founding and Manifesto of Futurism', in *Let's Murder the Moonshine*, p. 49.
122. See Marinetti, 'Portrait of Mussolini', in *Let's Murder the Moonshine*, p. 166.
123. Rudolf Leonhard, 'Marinetti in Berlin 1913', in Paul Raabe (ed.), *The Era of German Expressionism*, trans. J. M. Ritchie (Woodstock, NY: Overlook Press, 1985), pp. 115–18. Quotation taken from p. 116.
124. 'Art and Practice of Noise: Hostile Reception of Signor Marinetti', *The Times*, 16 June 1914, p. 5.
125. Wyndham Lewis, 'Biographical details for publicity purposes – Art of Being Ruled', 'The Art Racket' (undated fragment), Cornell University Library Rare and Manuscript Collections, Carl Kroch Library, # 4612, Box 3, Folder 17.
126. Lewis, *Rude Assignment*, pp. 62, 65.
127. Ibid. p. 268.
128. Ibid. p. 211.
129. Lewis, 'Britons Shall Never Be Bees', p. 361.
130. Ibid. p. 303.
131. Lewis believed that if this power went unchallenged, future readers would find 'the period of *Blast*, of *Ulysses*, of *The Waste Land*' to have been a strange and incomparable renaissance for modernism after the moment that European culture failed and 'the day was lost, for art, at Sarajevo'. See *Blasting and Bombardiering*, pp. 256, 261.

Conclusion: Literature and 'the resources of civilization'

In his sensational dynamite novel of 1886, *For Maimie's Sake: A Tale of Love and Dynamite*, Grant Allen addressed the influence that political violence exercised over the late Victorian popular imagination by drawing attention to the fascinating quality of its shocks. Part melodrama, part political yarn and part romance, as well as a satire on British imperialism, the novel initially centres on the efforts of an ambitious scientist, Sydney Chevenix, to invent a noiseless high explosive which he plans to donate to the British government for use as a stealth weapon against anti-colonial insurgencies in Africa. This occurs against the background of Chevenix's pursuit of the titular and amoral heroine, Maimie Llewellyn, the daughter of an anarchist, artist and 'madman' whom he eventually marries. Like Isabel Meredith in *A Girl Among the Anarchists*, Maimie has experienced a 'shocking', even 'heathenish' upbringing at the hands of her bohemian father (pp. 9–10). The novel opens with criticism of British coercion in Ireland but this is as far as Allen, himself the son of an Irishman, pursues the Irish question, which he conflates with anarchism, like many other authors of dynamite fiction. Early on in the novel, Chevenix marvels at the possible application of his silent weapon against the 'uncivilized enemies' and 'unsophisticated savages' that Britain is encountering in Africa (p. 22), but his Polish assistant, Stanislas Benyowski, has other ideas. A member of a secret expatriate revolutionary cell and a man 'redolent of . . . blood-and-thunderous continental Nihilism' (p. 24), he intends to smuggle the silent mixture into Russia and use it to wipe out the Tsarist elite. In an aside to Chevenix, he suggests that there might be alternative use for their 'new stuff':

> 'And its use in politics,' Stanislas Benyowski muttered doggedly. 'You're fighting a lot of enemies of the human kind – emperors and bureaucrats and such-like vermin – and you stick a little of the new explosive under the chief criminal's bed, and it goes off pop in the middle of the night, noiselessly,

silently, unheard, unnoticed, and nobody ever even so much as suspects the miscreant's dead, till some flunky or other goes in in the morning and finds the creature's remains lying in little fragments scattered all about promiscuously over the bed and carpet – here a leg, and there an arm, and yonder a rib or two! Ha! Ha! That would be just magnificent, wouldn't it? That would, indeed, be developing the resources of civilization!' (p. 23)

Here, we are presented in unusually graphic detail with the fatal consequences of political violence and although it is associated with affairs in Russia, Allen is not just discussing the democratisation of class warfare by the introduction of high explosives to radical political protest. His novel is clearly, even if at a remove, treating the consequences of imperialism in Ireland, where overwhelming British power, like Tsarist authority in Russia, is now being met with dynamite bombs. Having silently blown his victim to pieces hours before the discovery of the deed, the now-untraceable murderer leaves only the mangled remains of his enemy as evidence of his action. After his disappearance, the deed is not even noticed until long after the fact of its accomplishment, when the dismembered corpse is stumbled upon by accident. This, Benyowski claims, will become the apogee and high-water mark of modern terrorism – an explosion that goes off unheard, unwitnessed and unacknowledged until some time after the bomber has escaped. But, as Allen suggests later in the novel, it is precisely because it is silent and unnoticeable that that this 'perfectly noiseless' bomb (p. 23) promises to rob terrorism of its charismatic lustre. While it might render the assassin completely untraceable, Chevenix's 'anacoustic' explosive (p. 129) threatens to undermine an important aspect of the bomb's function – its potential to frighten and even thrill its target audience, for whom an explosion without a bang would be both unspectacular and a great disappointment. As Maimie tells Chevenix when she is given a demonstration of the silent compound, terrorism captures the popular imagination because of its ability to shock. In contrast to the 'showiness' of ordinary high explosives, a noiseless bomb, she complains, would be rather sterile and unexciting. As it functions 'without noise, without flash, without smoke, without sign of any sort' (p. 122), its detonation promises to be a very dull affair as it 'goes off too smooth and fast and sudden . . . without any bang, or smash, or flare, or fizzmagig' (p. 130). Despite its destructive power, the material will have 'dissipated itself in the air inaudibly and invisibly' (p. 121) and disappointed eager spectators like Maimie. Its silence could also undermine the impact of the political message that high explosives were used to convey, thereby hindering the very purpose for which Benyowski intends to put it to use: despite his promise that this new invention will 'revolutionize . . . the practice of Nihilism' (p. 121), its novelty goes too far because, in its reversal of the shock-principle of the explosion, a silent detonation contradicts the conceptual basis upon which terrorism depends. As Maimie tells her husband, bombs have such a powerful appeal because 'with . . . ordinary gunpowder, there's a bang and a flash, you see, that excites attention, and gets the murder identified at once' (p. 131). But with its noiseless explosion, she fears, the silent explosive will remove the spectacular element from political violence by erasing what Stevenson's villain, Zero, terms the colour and poetry of his chosen medium of dynamite.[1]

Each of the texts studied in this monograph have, in one way or another, addressed the issue of the appeal of political violence and, from Stevenson to the Vorticists, we have found a continuum that stretches across the divide between 'highbrow' and 'lowbrow' literature, pointing to the existence of what Nicholas Daly has described as the 'popular modernist culture' that fused both types of literary expression and satisfied the tastes and expectations of readers who demanded shocks in both of these literary registers.[2] Combining romantic melodrama, science and political intrigue, Allen's dynamite novel reveals to us how the kind of thrills that were described by Edmund Burke in his *Philosophical Enquiry* in 1756, and were then given political meaning almost four decades later in his *Reflections on the Revolution in France*, lingered long into the late nineteenth century, when they were magnified and transformed by writers who chose terrorism as their subject matter. Mass-produced on an industrial scale and delivered to readers on the pages of popular fiction, where they reached a wider readership than Burke had ever done in his own day, they transgressed Victorian class boundaries so that, by the 1880s, the shock of terror, with its updated 'heightening' effects,[3] presented a new species of literary thrill that indulged the popular fascination with political violence.

The Language of Political Fear

The Fenian dynamite campaign with which this volume opens announced a new age in violent political protest to the British public, and, as we have seen, its distinctly urban shocks generated a new kind of literature. No longer the stuff of three-decker novels, political unrest and revolutionary violence were showcased in a distinct literary form – the dynamite novel which, in itself, constituted a unique sub-genre of the shilling shocker – that had more immediacy than its much longer and far less frantic predecessors. Its violent content mirrored the shocking impact of the politics that it described, marking the sudden shift in popular literary taste to which it appealed by exploiting new reading practices, on the one hand, while exploring the conceptual understanding of revolutionary violence on the other. Since the 1840s, political fiction, like any other genre, had a distinctly drawn-out quality as bestselling Chartist tales like Elizabeth Gaskell's *Mary Barton* and George Eliot's *Felix Holt, Radical*, which were followed by Anthony Trollope's yarn about Irish agrarian resistance to landlordism, *The Landleaguers*, and George Gissing's *Demos*, all treated revolution in convoluted plots that focused on the moral consequences of political violence.[4] The transformation in political protest that was heralded by the employment of high explosives by the Fenian movement during the 1880s, along with the coincident rise of mass-produced popular fiction, changed this aspect of the political novel, as instant shocks became the order of the day, a demand that was satisfied by the availability of this new, cheap fiction. The almost simultaneous appearance of both commodities, one with industrial and political applications (dynamite), the other serving the literary and political needs of both authors and readers (the now easily-accessible yellowback novel), marked a significant change in the literary, political and cultural landscape of Britain.

The Russian nihilist and novelist, Sergius Stepniak, found this transformation to be unsettling, and, in an article published in the *Contemporary Review* in 1884, tried to rationalise dynamiting by presenting it to British readers as an impersonal, even theoretical strategy that lacked the reactive character of 'defence or vengeance'.[5] Thus Stepniak attempted to justify that dynamite attacks that occurred in Russia during this period, including the assassination of Tsar Alexander II in St Petersburg in 1881, as actions that were legitimate by virtue of their comparability with conventional military strategy. But as the Irish Fenian Jeremiah O'Donovan Rossa pointed out, such actions were radical both in cultural and political terms as they caused a tremendous shift in the conceptualisation of political violence (indeed, Rossa's Skirmishers struck before the Russians when they bombed Salford Barracks with fatal results in 1881, over a year before the Tsar was blown up). While Sarah Cole has suggested that anarchism was, above all, the ideology most closely associated with dynamite,[6] it was, to begin with, the Fenians' weapon of choice. The spectre of Irish separatism haunted the British imperial and literary imagination to such an extent that authors from Stevenson to Conrad tried to deflect attention from it by associating its violence with the external, imagined and very uncertain threat posed by anarchism. Recast as an anarchist, the Fenian, who was the original subversive presence both in literary and political spheres and who threatened to avenge Ireland by making Britain 'a smouldering ruin of ashes',[7] exercised a lasting cultural influence. O'Donovan Rossa, like Stevenson's fictional villain, Zero, knew that his cause depended as much upon the sensory shock-effects of dynamite explosions as much as it did upon the radical political content of his republican beliefs. The rhetorical stance of 'Number One' and his fictional counterpart, Zero, explains why more conventionally-minded Fenians like John Devoy considered dynamiting a step that went too far and criticised it as strategic folly, branding William Mackey Lomasney, who died planting a bomb at London Bridge, as 'a fanatic of the deepest dye'.[8] What Devoy did not comprehend was the extent to which political violence had become transformed by late Victorian modernity into a more immediate form of discourse that fought with a variety of competing phenomena for its place in the newspapers and journals of the day. The Russian anarchist Peter Kropotkin understood this process and informed his readers of it in 1880, when he argued that the moment of crisis had arrived for revolutionaries. Recognising that modern industrial capitalism, despite its promise to liberate humanity, was rapidly self-destructing and even degenerating to the point of 'putrefaction',[9] Kropotkin urged that new methods of protest had to be adapted to suit the times, so as to exploit the fast-moving capitalist networks and their media. It was in this atmosphere that Irish dynamiting and the anarchists' politics of the deed provided the late Victorian imagination with a modernised, up-to-date and fully politicised model of the Burkean sublime. Thus, late nineteenth-century political potboilers continued to pursue the terms of Burke's political imaginary, with villains such as Richard Henry Savage's anarchist, Professor Carl Stein, exalting 'in the excitement of the loosening of an avalanche of destruction' and promising to unleash a revolutionary storm, 'loosed in all its fury', that will destroy 'the shaken European autonomies before the first day of the twentieth century' (*The Anarchist*, Vol. I, p. 103).

As outlined in Chapters 1 and 2, the popular dynamite novels of the 1880s and 1890s repackaged the news as exciting fiction, with writers opting to either condemn or support the Irish Fenians. Anarchism, on the other hand, tended to receive overwhelmingly critical treatment, and *The Dynamiter* and *Captain Shannon* were not the only novels to feature ineffective and auto-destructive terrorists. Even when written about by former revolutionaries like the Rossetti sisters, anarchism was subjected to critical inspection from within. But whereas Isabel Meredith narrates the tale of a movement destined to go nowhere, the conservative writer Elizabeth Waterhouse gave her anarchists a chance to set up their utopia in her futuristic political fantasy and cautionary tale of 1887, *The Island of Anarchy*. Waterhouse predicted what would happen if anarchists were given the means of establishing an authority-free utopia, and the reader is treated to the spectacle of its inevitable and brutal collapse as it is transformed from a liberal political dream into a nightmare of uncontrolled savagery. Waterhouse depicts a late twentieth-century Britain, sickened by 'every shade of Nihilism and Dynamitism introduced from the East and West' (p. 18), in which the government decides to round up all of the country's anarchists, whom she describes as 'Law-Deniers' (p. 18) and 'enemies of . . . duty, industry and religion' (p. 23). The prisoners are branded with a circle burned on one hand, and then deported, but instead of being sent to a penal colony, they are taken to a recently formed volcanic island in the South Pacific. Allowed to run it for themselves provided that they will never return to England, they are left to their own devices but the banished anarchists are followed by wealthy sympathisers – 'men and women of a far higher type, mistaken, yet nobly in the wrong' – who volunteer to accompany them. These well-heeled exiles include feminists, radical Christians, artists and writers, and particularly poets, who allow themselves to be branded, having 'stretched out the hand that held the pen . . . for the circle in which they gloried as a sign of their fellowship with the oppressed' (p. 25). Admitting that Britain is a decadent and 'over-ripe civilization', Waterhouse contends that it is only by the expulsion of such characters that the country can recover from decline. She also distinguishes between politically motivated revolutionaries and criminals, noting that, as the deportations continue, the anarchists find their island becoming flooded with 'thousands of the disaffected and idle'. Utopia quickly disintegrates as madness takes hold in the government-free paradise. After annihilating the native societies that they encounter in the surrounding territories in a ruthless search for resources, the inhabitants of the island finally turn upon each other. Surrounded by criminals, the political types prove to be no match for the 'the lowest and most violent class' (p. 25), who descend upon the effete intellectuals, then the artists and women, all of whom fall victim to the natural survival skills of less politicised law-breakers. The crisis ends, suitably enough, with an explosion, as a volcanic eruption kills everyone on the island before it sinks into the sea.

Intended as a warning to sympathisers, including avant-garde literary types, feminists and the wealthy patrons of advanced political causes, Waterhouse's unusual tale suggests that, contrary to the claims of the anarchists themselves, a government-free utopia will never inhibit the natural instincts of the poor to steal, kill and rape. Revolutionaries, she suggests, cannot eradicate the inequalities that are inevitable in any society as governmental structures provide the only reins on such tendencies. Conquering and slaughtering their neighbours before finally killing each other off, Waterhouse's anarchists and criminals also practise a dangerously unstructured imperialism as the savagery that takes hold on their island only occurs after they run out of neighbours to kill. Once their murderous tendencies can no longer be directed outwards, they take hold within the island in an intensifying spiral of political, criminal and sexual violence. The savagery that is contained by modern society, she suggests, must be channelled by the state, or else the human species, if left to its own devices, will self-destruct. Lacking the restraints that are imposed on human nature by the state, the short-lived anarchist utopia inevitably disintegrates into chaos, before sinking into the sea, because no society, unless governed from above, as Waterhouse argues, can withstand its violent internal forces.

Subversive Identities

Some writers contended that these forces were harnessed by revolutionaries. Coulson Kernahan, the highly strung author of hurriedly-written novels like *Captain Shannon*, sometime friend of Oscar Wilde and editor of *The Picture of Dorian Gray* for Ward Lock,[10] suggested in several of his hyperbolic fictions that the terrorist was both driven and characterised by a sense of his own rootlessness. In *Captain Shannon*, as in his other political thrillers, *Scoundrels and Company* (1899), *The Dumpling* (1906) and *The Red Peril* (1908), Kernahan's villains are assigned what Steven Arata, in his study of Wilde, has termed the Irish author's 'liberating mobility of identity'. In *Captain Shannon*, a transvestite Fenian bomber, James Mullan, experiences through his pursuit of an unrealisable political goal a condition that mirrors Wilde's own desire to realise the 'impossible ideal'[11] of an unfixed identity. Like Wilde, who openly supported the Fenian cause, Kernahan's Fenian is a doubly threatening presence, being at once a politically subversive figure and a transgressor of sexual norms whose unpredictability and cross-dressing antics carry more than a hint of Wildean resistance to late Victorian political and sexual respectability. Yet readers were also thrilled by the lawlessness of Kernahan's heroes who, like Stevenson's freelance detectives in *The Dynamiter*, are defined by their inability and even refusal to cooperate with the forces of law and order. Not only does Kernahan's amateur sleuth, Max Rissler, lack official authority, but he also works as hard at avoiding tangles with the law as he does at apprehending the bomber. Completely at odds with the police and, by extension, the state, he is as pathologically driven as the killer he hunts and has no qualms about accumulating a huge collateral body count of uninvolved bystanders as a result of his refusal to share intelligence with the police. Rissler's ruthless success mirrors what Gustave Le Bon described as society's toleration of immorality. By accepting the unacceptable, the state had allowed 'the criminal to "expand" his individuality', which is exactly the process that we find at work in this dynamite novel and its staging of unofficial detection. For Le Bon, such problems were reproduced in 'the "temple" of art', where moral exhaustion had set in and transformed literature, painting and music into a cultural 'asylum' housing the thoughts and ideas of the criminally degenerate and insane.[12] Driven by a Europe-wide collective of egomaniacs, decadents and aesthetes, all art forms, and especially literature, were now, according to the sociologist, giving sanctuary to maniacs and malcontents behind the protective screen of avant-gardism, where 'the refuse of civilized peoples' could be found gathering cultural influence and political momentum.[13] The theme of unanchored identities that, as Arata has suggested, pervades decadent *fin de siècle* novels like *The Picture of Dorian Gray* also influenced the now almost forgotten genre of dynamite fiction. These political fictions fused the enigma of unreadable revolutionary politics with concern over the mysteriousness of the unanchored identities of revolutionaries; Savage, for example, repeatedly turns to the formlessness of anarchism, labelling the anarchist as 'a man without a country', his belief as the 'Cause Without a Name' and his ideology as the 'unspoken code whose sequence is the doom of modern society. "Revolution – Destruction – Annihilation"'[14] (Vol. I, pp. 169, 63, 86). This problem of the fluidity of modern subversive identity also underlines the political crisis that emerges in H. G. Wells's science fantasy of 1897, *The Invisible Man*, which is discussed in Chapter 3. In this novella the transparent villain is received as 'an unusually strange sort of stranger' upon his arrival in rural West Sussex. A figure from London who is 'wrapped-up mystery', the Invisible Man finds himself conforming to this stereotype and coming into conflict with authority by attempting to impose his own 'brutal dream of a terrorised world' upon the mystified villagers.[15] The interpretative and conceptual difficulties associated with defining the essentially indefinable nature of anarchism proved a lucrative source of inspiration for popular authors and the difficulty was resolved in some cases in the distinction that was made between crime and political violence. As Edgar Wallace suggested in *The Four Just Men*, terrorists are fascinating precisely because they operate 'outside the ordinary run of criminals' (p. 55).

Officialdom was also responsible for blurring the distinction between political reality and imperial fantasy, as happened in 1887 when the CID and the Home Office jointly invented, sponsored and supervised the elaborate 'Jubilee Plot' that involved the *agent provocateur*, Frank Millen, in an imaginary Fenian scheme to bomb the thanksgiving service in Westminster. The shady venture ended up on the pages of *The Times*, where it was publicised as yet another example of Irish nationalist villainy. Carried away by this propaganda coup, the paper went on to publish an equally unfounded but no less sensational story when it accused the Irish nationalist leader, Charles Stewart Parnell, of involvement in the Phoenix Park killings, and was successfully sued for libel by the Home Rule leader in 1890. In his study of the bogus plot, Christy Campbell points to the counter-insurgency role played by the late Victorian press, revealing how non-events such as this phantom plot point to the political utility of contemporary cultural fantasies.[16] The unpredictability of modern experience, heightened by cooked-up government plots and the actual 'scientific warfare' being conducted by the Fenians themselves, heightened popular, journalistic and, as Campbell has shown, even official tendencies to imagine the most sensational and potentially violent scenarios possible. As the Stevensons stressed in *The Dynamiter*, the shocking and destructive potential of disrupting British imperial modernity was first realised by the Fenians, who were among the first terrorists to take advantage of drifting metropolis and its labyrinthine geography, revealing to late Victorian consumers of the news and readers of fiction just how modern the destruction of symbolic targets like Westminster or the Tower of London could be. As David Harvey suggests, we inhabit an extended period of modernity within which modernist and post-modern sensibilities have combined to the extent that 'it is almost impossible to tell where the modernist impulse begins or ends'.[17] Therefore, by narrating modernity as a thoroughly chaotic experience, these popular novels reflect not just contemporary but also more recent sensibilities and concerns. Rather than considering terrorism as straightforwardly 'criminal Irishness' from a bluntly imperial perspective,[18] many of the dynamite novels of the 1880 and 1890s examine Fenianism and also anarchism as particularly modern phenomena, and as key elements of the modern imperial and capitalist culture that produced them.

Modernism

Vorticism is the modernist movement whose aesthetic position most closely resembles the political message of anarchism because what was termed by contemporaries as its 'incendiary' character[19] appealed directly to the Vorticist literary imagination. Vorticism illustrates the manner in which anarchism played a key role in the formation of modernist aesthetics, a process that is described by David Kadlec as being characterised by its literary 'appeals to immediacy'.[20] With its improvisational tendencies, Vorticism stressed the concept of spontaneity, promoted ideas of impulsive action and demanded the rejection of aesthetic discipline, much as anarchism opposed the political authority of the state. The threshold text that marks the transition from popular to modernist territory is Henry James's *The Princess Casamassima*, in which the literary ante is increased by an author who was conscious that his work has fed on the public demand for political shocks. While James was keen to distance his work from potboilers and their dependence on the simplicities of 'incident and movement', he did feel that contemporary politics could inspire superior realist fiction.[21] As Gustave Le Bon argued, such refinement could also have a political application because, as he stressed, the final aesthetic judgement of any work of literature was its capacity to convey feelings that were both 'morally beautiful' and aesthetically ideal.[22]

James's novel exploits the political *and* aesthetic condition of the terrorised metropolis and, as he claimed in its preface, it was during his exploration of London that he experienced a sensory 'assault' upon his literary consciousness; his reaction to this bombardment culminated in the writing of his anarchist tale. But as he pointed out later in his preface – and, it should be added, even though he claimed that the novel was initially 'the ripe round fruit of perambulation' – it was, essentially, the spectacle of revolutionary politics that inspired his metropolitan imagination on this occasion. Although James never admitted it, we can consider Irish republicanism to be among the highly 'illustrative' species of urban 'flora' that he encountered, if not directly upon the streets, then in the urban imaginary of London, when he began writing the novel in 1885 (Preface, p. 33). As James insisted, his tale was the product of these streets while its protagonist, Hyacinth Robinson, was an individual who 'sprang up out of the London pavement', along with his conflicted desires (p. 34). His native environment, or 'natural and immediate London' (p. 35), is where the 'human mixture' is to be found in the midst of the city's 'abyss of ambiguities'. This condition of urban hybridity, which James refers to as the 'entangled state' of the metropolis (p. 37), sustained the fascination and bewilderment that inspired the novel and led him to claim a place for it within the same league as the work of Dickens, Thackeray, Meredith, Balzac, Eliot and Austen. The appeal of uncertainty also lies behind Hyacinth's political indecision, which is itself a result of the 'strange experience' (p. 43) of the late Victorian metropolis. This state of confusion leads to the bookbinder's eventual involvement in the anarchists' rather authoritarian revolutionary conspiracy, and it is significant that James chose a producer of literary commodities as the vehicle for his exploration of this phenomenon. The subversive quality of Hyacinth's 'dingy' trade became the stuff of a later literary atrocity in *Captain Shannon*, in which, as we have seen, bombs are concealed inside books. Another branch of publishing, although of an entirely different kind of book, provides cover for Joseph Conrad's *agent provocateur*, Adolph Verloc, who circulates cheap French pornography from his shop in Soho. In James's novel, it is the fault of the protagonist to have 'opinions on "public questions"' – something that is beyond his permitted sphere of social consciousness (p. 44). This mistake draws him, with inevitably fatal consequences, towards anarchism, but what made Hyacinth's story work for James, as Zero's did for Stevenson, is the tantalising proximity, or 'suggested nearness' of terrorism to the everyday and familiar (p. 47). These fictions predate Walter Benjamin's theory of the strangeness of urban modernity, wherein '(t)he harder a man is to find, the more suspicious he becomes' but reveal that the late nineteenth- and early twentieth-century literary consciousness examined the strangeness and inherent mysteriousness of urban experience.[23]

With Vorticism, we encounter the intensification of this literary register. Wyndham Lewis retrospectively claimed that *Blast* was dedicated to 'the cause of 'rebel' or of 'abstract art and revolutionary letters'[24] and to the 'exploitation of discords',[25] a view that was supported by Richard Aldington in 1914, who described it as 'the most amazing, energized, stimulating production I have ever seen'.[26] Reviewers of Lewis's 1926 book, *The Art of Being Ruled*, also suggested that the impact of the journal's revolutionary avant-gardism might have outweighed its brevity when they described the 'hydrochloric' paradoxes of his later political writing as resembling 'chaos caught in a vice'. These contemporary readers did not dismiss avant-gardism, with its rejection of linear models of explanation, as having no place in political discussion but viewed it as a vital response to their own 'contradictory' age.[27] *Blast* reinterpreted the impact of the shock of revolutionary violence on the constitution of the modern subject by offering a modernist 'blueprint' for what Lewis regarded as an 'exclusively political' twentieth century.[28] Both in outline and in detail, Vorticism was an expression of Lewis's aesthetically modelled anarchism, which called for 'decentralized' expression and was organised around a loosely associational 'Art forum, or living Centre', the Rebel Art Centre, that could provide writers and painters with focus by offering free exhibits and stimulate intellectual debate through lectures and discussions.[29] Writing retrospectively, however, Lewis accepted that the difficulties imposed on art by the First World

War also amounted to a barrier to memory that brought an end to the Vorticist project by creating a cultural 'partition' that 'blocked off the past literally as if a huge wall had been set up there'.[30] Vorticism disintegrated in the face of this political and cultural obstacle and its imposition of 'uniformity of thinking' on British society.[31] In *Tarr* we find a reaction against this centralisation of consciousness, but formulated as a much more problematic response than those that are offered in the pages of *Blast*, as the novel is ultimately concerned with deeply personalised forms of violence. Like Henry James, who believed that 'as the picture is reality, so the novel is history', and that fiction 'must speak . . . with the tone of the historian',[32] Lewis also argued for the recognition of the novel's dual status status both as art and as 'history-in-the-making'. Literature, he believed, was 'saturated with politics',[33] and while Lewis ultimately rejected the aesthetic conditioning that James championed in his novel of 1886, both *Tarr* and *The Princess Casamassima*, along with the novels, stories and journals considered here, point to the centrality of political conflict to the modern literary consciousness.

Notes

1. According to Allen's logic, the late Victorian imagination would not be satisfied by violence if it lacked the thrills provided by conventional explosions because the immediately audible and visual shock of detonation was a necessary part of the sensory and political package that constituted revolutionary violence. And Allen knew the value of shock: his sensational novel features a beautiful heroine who is irresistible to both sexes; she accidentally shoots Chevenix who, for her sake, must fake his own death so as to allow her to marry his rival, Adrian Pym, and does so by switching identities with Benyowski, whose corpse is burned beyond all recognition in an accidental hospital fire. In an act of preposterous chivalry, Chevenix goes underground so as to prevent her from facing prison and eventually drowns himself in order to keep the lovers above suspicion. As Peter Morton has shown, demand for Allen's fiction peaked in the late 1880s when he turned out several novels a year. All of these had outlandish plots, and *For Maimie's Sake* was no exception to this best-selling rule. See Peter Morton, *The Busiest Man in England: Grant Allen and the Writing Trade, 1875–1900* (Houndmills: Palgrave, 2005).
2. Nicholas Daly, *Modernism, Romance and the Fin de Siècle: Popular Fiction and British Culture, 1880–1914* (Cambridge: Cambridge University Press, 1999), p. 149.
3. Edmund Burke, *A Philosophical Enquiry into the Sublime and Beautiful* (London: Penguin, 2004), p. 103.
4. The slowness of these plots was, perhaps, related to the decline of indigenous radicalism: the progress of the Industrial Revolution and the seemingly

unstoppable rise of modern capital dealt severe blows to radical working-class consciousness across Europe with the defeat of the revolutions of 1848, when Gaskell's novel was first published; the economic boom that lasted from the 1850s until the early 1870s did not favour the radical left, as prosperity supported the economic and political strength of conservatives, and it was not until the late 1880s that mass protests by British socialists started to gain any momentum. The suppression of demonstrators in Trafalgar Square in November 1887, known as 'Bloody Sunday', came to symbolise the establishment's opposition to the resurgence of organised labour. Nevertheless, labour survived the politically lean decades of the mid nineteenth century and continued to haunt the prosperous middle classes. For an account of the progress of capital and the development of the middle classes during this period, see K. Theodore Hoppen, *The Mid-Victorian Generation, 1846–1886* (Oxford: The Clarendon Press, 1998).

5. Stepniak was describing the assassination of Alexander II in St Petersburg in March 1881. See Sergius Stepniak, (Sergei Kravchinski), 'Terrorism in Russia and Terrorism in Europe', *The Contemporary Review*, Vol. xlv, March 1884, pp. 325–41, p. 337.
6. See Sarah Cole, 'Dynamite Violence and Literary Culture', *Modernism/modernity*, Vol. 16, no. 2, April 2009, pp. 301–28. While Cole's essay points to the melodramatic structure of late nineteenth-century dynamite novels, it overlooks the cultural significance and literary impact of the Fenian scare fiction that abounded during this period.
7. Chief Secretary's Office, Dublin, dated 1882, B 171, National Archive, Dublin.
8. John Devoy, *Recollections of an Irish Rebel* (Shannon: Irish Universities Press, 1968; originally published New York: Chas D. Young, 1929).
9. Peter Kropotkin, 'An Appeal to the Young', in *Anarchism: A Collection of Revolutionary Writings* (Mineola: Dover, 2002), pp. 261–82, p. 277.
10. Richard Ellman, *Oscar Wilde* (New York: Knopf, 1988), p. 322.
11. See Stephen Arata, *Fictions of Loss in the Victorian Fin de Siècle* (Cambridge: Cambridge University Press, 1996), p. 61.
12. Gustave Le Bon, *The Crowd: A Study of the Popular Mind*, trans. from *Le psychologie des foules* (London: T. Fisher Unwin, [1895] 1896), p. 326.
13. Ibid. p. 337.
14. So pervasive is the need for anarchists to function as non-beings in this novel that their International, held in Switzerland, becomes known as the 'Congress without words'. See Richard Henry Savage, *The Anarchist: A Story of To-Day* (Leipzig: Bernhard Tauchnitz, 1894), 2 vols, Vol. 1, p. 93.
15. H. G. Wells, *The Invisible Man*, originally published 1897 (London: Penguin, 2005), pp. 15, 121, 22, 127.
16. See Christy Campbell, *Fenian Fire: The British Government Plot to Assassinate Queen Victoria* (London: HarperCollins, 2002).
17. See David Harvey, *The Condition of Postmodernity: An Enquiry into the Origins of Social Change* (Cambridge, MA and Oxford: Blackwell, 1990), p. 339.
18. See Catherine Wynne, *The Colonial Conan Doyle* (Westport, CT: The Greenwood Press, 2002), p. 22.
19. John Sweeney, *At Scotland Yard: Being the Experiences During Twenty-*

Seven Years of Service by John Sweeney, Late Detective Inspector, Criminal Investigation Department, New Scotland Yard (London: Grant Richards, 1904), p. 205.

20. David Kadlec, *Mosaic Modernism: Anarchism, Pragmatism, Culture* (Baltimore and London: Johns Hopkins University Press, 2000), p. 15.

21. In his 1885 essay, 'The Art of Fiction', James complained that bad novels were full of 'virtuous and aspiring characters, placed in prominent positions' and depended on the resolution offered by 'a "happy ending"' and the 'distribution of prizes, pensions, husbands, wives, babies, millions, appended paragraphs, and cheerful remarks'. The potboiler was, for James, much too predictable and 'full of incident and movement, so that we shall wish to jump ahead, to see who was the mysterious stranger, and if the stolen will was ever found, and shall not be distracted from this pleasure by any tiresome analysis or "description"'. See Henry James, 'The Art of Fiction', *The House of Fiction: Essays on the Novel* (London: Rupert Hart-Davis, 1957), pp. 23–45, p. 27.

22. Le Bon, *The Crowd*, p. 336.

23. Walter Benjamin, *Charles Baudelaire: A Lyric Poet in the Era of High Capitalism*, trans. Harry Zohn (London: Verso, 1997), p. 48.

24. Wyndham Lewis, *Blasting and Bombardiering* (London: Eyre and Spottiswoode, 1937), p. 51.

25. *Blast* 1, p. 142.

26. Richard Aldington, 'Wyndham Lewis', *The Egoist*, Vol. 1, No. 12, 15 June 1914, p. 273.

27. Charles A. Beard, cutting from the *Herald Tribune* and Henry McBride, cutting from the *New York Sun*, collected in Notices of *The Art of Being Ruled* (n. d., 1926?), Cornell University Library Rare and Manuscript Collections, Carl Kroch Library, # 4612, Box 3, Folder 11.

28. Wyndham Lewis, *Rude Assignment* (London: Hutchinson & Co., 1950), pp. 125, 69.

29. 'The Art Racket' (undated fragment), Cornell University Library Rare and Manuscript Collections, Carl Kroch Library, # 4612, Box 3, Folder 12.

30. Lewis, *Rude Assignment*, pp. 137–8.

31. Lewis, *The Writer and the Absolute* (London: Methuen, 1952), p. 38

32. James, 'The Art of Fiction', p. 25.

33. Lewis, *The Writer and the Absolute*, p. 19.

Bibliography of Cited Works

Literary Works

Allen, Grant, *For Maimie's Sake: A Tale of Love and Dynamite* (New York: International Book Company, n.d.; originally published London: Chatto & Windus, 1886).

Amis, Martin, *The Second Plane* (London: Jonathan Cape, 2008).

Beckett, Samuel, 'Dante . . . Bruno. Vico.. Joyce', in *Disjecta: Miscellaneous Writings and a Dramatic Fragment* (London: John Calder, 1983).

Birmingham, George A., *The Red Hand of Ulster* (London: Smith, Elder & Co., 1912).

Blythe, Harry, 'The Accusing Shadow', in Michael Cox (ed.), *Victorian Detective Stories* (Oxford: Oxford University Press, 1993), pp. 303–41; originally published in *The Halfpenny Marvel*, No. 48 (3 October 1894).

Borges, Jorge Luis, 'Theme of the Traitor and the Hero', in *Labyrinths* (London: Penguin, 2000).

Buchan, John, *The Thirty-Nine Steps* (London: Penguin, 1991).

Chesney, George Tomkyns, *The Battle of Dorking*, in George Tomkyns Chesney and Saki, *The Battle of Dorking and When William Came* (Oxford: Oxford University Press, 1997).

Chesterton, G. K., *The Man Who Was Thursday: A Nightmare* (New York: Modern Library, 2001).

Conrad, Joseph, *Under Western Eyes* (London: Penguin, 1989).

—, 'Amy Foster', in *Typhoon and Other Stories* (London: Penguin, 1990).

—, *The Secret Agent* (London: Penguin, 1990).

—, 'An Anarchist' and 'The Informer', from *The Lagoon and Other Stories* (Oxford and New York: Oxford University Press, 1997).

Corelli, Marie, *The Sorrows of Satan* (Oxford: Oxford University Press, 1998).

DeLillo, Don, *Falling Man* (London: Picador, 2007).

Doyle, Arthur Conan, *A Study in Scarlet*, 'Lot No. 249', 'The Adventure of the Speckled Band', 'The Sign of the Four', *The Valley of Fear*, from *Complete Sherlock Holmes & Other Detective Stories* (Glasgow: HarperCollins, 1994).

Fawcett, E. Douglas, *Hartmann the Anarchist; or, The Doom of the Great City* (London: Edward Arnold, 1893).

Fénéon, Félix, *Novels in Three Lines* (New York: New York Review of Books, 2007, translated from the series 'Nouvelles en trios lignes', *Le Matin*, 1906).

Ford, Ford Madox, *The Soul of London* (London: Alston Rivers, 1905; reprinted London: Dent, 1995).

Greer, Tom, *A Modern Dædalus* (London: Griffith, Farran, Okeden & Welsh, 1885).

Griffith, George, 'The Raid of Le Vengeur', in Alan K. Russell (ed.), *Science Fiction by the Rivals of H. G. Wells* (New Jersey: Castle Books, 1979).

Haggard, H. Rider, *She* (London: Penguin, 2001).

James, Henry, *The House of Fiction: Essays on the Novel by Henry James* (London: Rupert Hart-Davis, 1957).

—, *The Princess Casamassima* (London: Penguin, 1987; originally published Macmillan & Co, 1886).

Kernahan, John Coulson, *The Dumpling: A Detective Love Story of a Great Labour Uprising* (London: Cassell, 1906).

—, *Scoundrels and Co.* (London: Ward, Lock & Co., 1908).

—, *The Red Peril* (London: Hurst & Brackett, 1908).

—, *A Literary Gent: A Study in Vanity and Dipsomania* (London: Ward, Lock & Co., n.d.).

Lewis, Matthew, *The Monk* (Oxford: Oxford University Press, 1998).

Lewis, Wyndham, 'Our Wild Body', *The New Age*, Vol. VII, No. 1, 5 May 1910, pp. 8–10.

—, 'A Review of Contemporary Art', *Blast* 2, June 1915, p. 38.

—, *Blasting and Bombardiering* (London: Eyre and Spottiswoode, 1937).

—, *Rude Assignment: A Narrative of My Career Up-to-Date* (London: Hutchinson & Co., 1950).

—, *The Writer and the Absolute* (London: Methuen, 1952).

—, *Tarr* (London: Penguin, 1982).

—, *The Art of Being Ruled* (Santa Rosa: Black Sparrow Press, 1989).

—, *Time and Western Man* (Santa Rosa: Black Sparrow Press, 1993).

Maginn, J. D., *Fitzgerald the Fenian*, 2 vols (London: Chapman and Hall, 1889).

Marinetti, F. T., *Let's Murder the Moonshine: Selected Writings*, trans. R. W. Flint and Arthur A. Coppotelli (Los Angeles: Sun & Moon Press, 1991).

Marsh, Richard, *The Beetle* (Peterborough, Ontario: Broadview, 2004; originally published London: Skeffington and Son, 1897).

Maturin, Charles, *Melmoth the Wanderer* (Oxford: Oxford University Press, 1989).

McEwan, Ian, *Saturday* (London: Vintage, 2006).

Meredith Isabel (pseud. Christina and Olivia Rossetti), *A Girl Among the Anarchists* (Lincoln and London: University of Nebraska Press, 1992; originally published London: Duckworth & Co., 1903).

Messud, Claire, *The Emperor's Children* (London: Picador, 2007).

Moore, Thomas, *Memoirs of Captain Rock, the Celebrated Irish Chieftain, With Some Accounts of His Ancestors* (London: Longman, Hurst, Rees, Orme, Brown and Green, 1824).

Poe, Edgar Allan, 'The Man of the Crowd' and 'The Mystery of Marie Rogêt', in *Tales of Mystery and Imagination* (London: Dent, 2000).

Pound, Ezra, *Gaudier-Brzeska: A Memoir* (London: John Lane, 1916).

Radcliffe, Ann, *The Mysteries of Udolpho* (Oxford: Oxford University Press, 1998).

Savage, Richard Henry, *The Anarchist: A Story of To-Day* (Leipzig: Bernhard Tauchnitz, 1894).

Shelley, Mary, *Frankenstein*, collected in *Making Humans* (Boston and New York: Houghton Mifflin, 2003).

Stepniak, Sergius (Sergei Kravchinski), *The Career of a Nihilist* (London: Walter Scott, 1901).

Stevenson, Robert Louis, *Dr Jekyll and Mr Hyde and Other Stories* (London: Penguin, 1979).

—, *The Body Snatcher and Other Stories* (London: Phoenix, 1999).

—, *A Child's Garden of Verses* (Hertfordshire: Wordsworth, 2000).

—, *New Arabian Nights* (London: T. Nelson, n.d.).

—, with Fanny Vandegrift Stevenson, *The Dynamiter*, originally published as *More New Arabian Nights: The Dynamiter* (London: Longmans & Co., 1885; reprinted Thrupp: Alan Sutton Publishing, 1997).

Thynne, Robert, *John Townley: A Tale for the Times* (London: Henry T. Drane, 1901).

Wallace, Edgar, *The Four Just Men* (Oxford: Oxford University Press, 1995).

Wells, H. G., 'The Stolen Bacillus' and 'The Diamond-Maker', from *The Complete Short Stories of H. G. Wells* (London: Phoenix Press, 2000).

—, *The Invisible Man* (London: Penguin, 2005).

—, *The Shape of Things to Come: The Ultimate Revolution* (London: Penguin, 2005).

Whiteing, Richard, *No. 5 John Street* (London: Grant Richards, 1899).

Wilde, Oscar, *The Picture of Dorian Gray* (London: Penguin, 2000).

—, *Vera, or the Nihilists*, from *The Complete Works of Oscar Wilde* (London: HarperCollins, 2003).

Yeats, William Butler, *A Vision* (London: Macmillan, 1978).

Editions of Collected Letters

Conrad, Joseph, *The Collected Letters of Joseph Conrad*, Vol. 1, ed. Karle R. Frederick (Cambridge: Cambridge University Press, 1983).

Stevenson, Robert Louis, *The Letters of Robert Louis Stevenson*, Vol. 5, July 1884–August 1887 (New Haven and London: Yale University Press, 1995).

Wilde, Oscar *The Complete Letters of Oscar Wilde*, ed. Merlin Holland and Rupert Hart-Davis (New York: Henry Holt, 2000).

Critical Works

Adamson, Walter L., *Embattled Avant-Gardes: Modernism's Resistance to Commodity Culture in Europe* (Berkeley, Los Angeles and London: University of California Press, 2007).

Anderson, Perry, 'Modernity and Revolution', in *Marxism and the Interpretation of Culture*, ed. Cary Nelson and Lawrence Grossberge (London: Macmillan, 1988), pp. 317–33.

Arata, Stephen, *Fictions of Loss in the Victorian Fin de Siècle* (Cambridge: Cambridge University Press, 1996).

Ashcroft, Bill, Gareth Griffiths, and Helen Tiffin, *The Empire Writes Back: Theory and Practice in Post-Colonial Literature* (London and New York: Routledge, 1989).

Benjamin, Walter, *Illuminations*, trans. Harry Zohn (London: Fontana, 1992); originally published as *Schriften* (Verlag: Frankfurt-am-Main, 1955).

—, *Charles Baudelaire: A Lyric Poet in the Era of High Capitalism*, trans. Harry Zohn (London: Verso, 1997).

Bergonzi, Bernard, *The Early H. G. Wells: A Study of the Scientific Romances* (Manchester: Manchester University Press, 1961).

Berman, Marshall, *All That is Solid Melts Into Air: The Experience of Modernity* (Harmondsworth: Penguin, [1982] 1988).

Brown, Stephen J., *Ireland in Fiction: A Guide to Irish Novels, Tales, Romances and Folk-Lore* (Dublin: Maunsel, 1916).

Bürger, Peter, *Theory of the Avant-Garde*, trans. Michael Shaw (Manchester: Manchester University Press, 1984).

Burke, Edmund, *A Philosophical Enquiry into the Origins of Our Ideas of the Sublime and Beautiful* (Oxford: Oxford University Press, 1998).

Carey, John, *The Intellectuals and the Masses: Pride and Prejudice Among the Literary Intelligentsia, 1880–1939* (London: Faber and Faber, 1992).

Clymer, Jeffory A., *America's Culture of Terrorism* (Chapel Hill and London: The University of North Carolina Press, 2003).

Cole, Sarah, 'Dynamite Violence and Literary Culture', *Modernism/modernity*, Vol. 16, no. 2, April 2009, pp. 301–28.

Collins, Judith, *The Omega Workshops* (Chicago: University of Chicago Press, 1984).

Corbett, Peters (ed.), *Wyndham Lewis and the Art of Modern War* (Cambridge: Cambridge University Press, 1998).

Crary, Jonathan, *Techniques of the Observer: On Vision and Modernity in the Nineteenth Century* (London and Cambridge, MA: MIT Press, 1990).

—, *Suspensions of Perception: Attention, Spectacle, and Modern Culture* (Cambridge, MA: MIT Press, 1999).

Daly, Nicholas, *Modernism, Romance and the Fin de Siècle: Popular Fiction and British Culture, 1880–1914* (Cambridge: Cambridge University Press, 1999).

—, *Literature, Technology, and Modernity, 1860–2000* (Cambridge: Cambridge University Press, 2004).

Dasenbrock, Reed Way, *The Literary Vorticism of Ezra Pound and Wyndham Lewis: Towards the Condition of Painting* (Baltimore: Johns Hopkins University Press, 1985).

Debord, Guy, *The Society of the Spectacle*, trans. Donald Nicholson-Smith (New York: Zone Books, 1999); originally published as *La société du spectacle* (Paris: Buchet-Castel, 1967).

Denning, Michael, *Cover Stories: Narrative and Ideology in the British Spy Thriller* (London: Routledge & Kegan Paul, 1987).

—, *Mechanic Accents: Dime Novels and Working-Class Culture in America* (London: Verso, 1998).

Edwards, Paul, *Wyndham Lewis: Painter and Writer* (New Haven: Yale University Press, 2000).

Fischer, Mike, 'The Jamesian Revolution in *The Princess Casamassima*: A

Lesson in Bookbinding', *The Henry James Review*, 9.2, Spring 1988, pp. 87–104.

Foucault, Michel, *Discipline and Punish*, trans. Alan Sheridan (London: Penguin, 1991); originally published as *Surveiller et punir: Naisance de la prison* (Éditions Gallimard, 1975).

Gasiorek, Andrej, *Wyndham Lewis and Modernism* (Tavistock: Northcote House, 2004).

Glover, David, 'Aliens, Anarchists and Detectives: Legislating the Immigrant Body', *New Formations*, 32, Autumn/Winter 1997, pp. 22–33.

Grant, Maurice Harland, *A Dictionary of British Sculptors, from the XXIIIth Century to the XXth Century* (London: Rockliff, 1958).

Gunning, Tom, 'Lynx-Eyed Detectives and Shadow Bandits: Visuality and Eclipse in French Detective Stories and Films Before WWI', *Yale French Studies*, No. 108, *Crime Frictions* (2005).

Harvey, David, *The Condition of Postmodernity: An Enquiry into the Origins of Social Change* (Cambridge, MA and Oxford: Blackwell, 1990).

Heidegger, Martin, *Being and Time: A Translation of Sein und Zeit*, trans. Joan Stambough (originally published Tübingen: Max Niemeyer Verlag, 1953; reprinted Albany: State University of New York Press, 1996).

Hollywood, Paul, *The Voice of Dynamite: Anarchism, Popular Fiction and the Late Political Novels of Joseph Conrad*, PhD thesis, University of Kent at Canterbury, 1994.

Houen, Alex, *Terrorism and Modern Literature: From Joseph Conrad to Ciaran Carson* (Oxford: Oxford University Press, 2002).

Huyssen, Andreas, *After the Great Divide: Modernism, Mass Culture, Postmodernism* (Bloomington and Indianapolis: Indiana University Press, 1986).

James, Henry, *The House of Fiction: Essays on the Novel by Henry James* (London: Rupert Hart-Davis, 1957).

Jameson, Frederic, *Fables of Aggression: Wyndham Lewis, the Modernist as Futurist* (Berkeley: University of California Press, 1979).

—, *The Political Unconscious: Narrative Theory as a Socially Symbolic Act* (London: Routledge, 1996).

Jenkins, Joyce L., 'Art Against Equality', *Philosophy and Literature* 22.1 (1998), pp. 108–18.

Kadlec, David, *Mosaic Modernism: Anarchism, Pragmatism, Culture* (Baltimore and London: Johns Hopkins University Press, 2000).

Kiberd, Declan, *Inventing Ireland: The Literature of the Modern Nation* (London: Vintage, 1995).

Kimmey, John, 'James's London in *The Princess Casamassima*', *Nineteenth-Century Literature*, 41.1 (June 1986), pp. 9–31.

Kubiak, Anthony, *Stages of Terror: Terrorism, Ideology, and Coercion as Theatre History* (Bloomington and Indianapolis: Indiana University Press, 1991).

Lake, David, 'The Current Texts of H. G. Wells's Early Science Fiction Novels: Situation Unsatisfactory', in John S. Partington (ed.), *The Wellsian: Selected Essays on H. G. Wells* (Oss: Equilibris, 2005), pp. 167–88.

Leonhard, Rudolf, 'Marinetti in Berlin 1913', in Paul Raabe (ed.), *The Era of*

German Expressionism, trans. J. M. Ritchie (Woodstock, NY: Overlook Press, 1985), pp. 115–18.

McConnell, Frank, *The Science Fiction of H. G. Wells* (New York and Oxford: Oxford University Press, 1981).

McLaughlin, Joseph, *Writing the Urban Jungle: Reading Empire in London from Doyle to Eliot* (Charlottesville and London: The University Press of Virginia, 2000).

Mao, Douglas, *Solid Objects: Modernism and the Test of Production* (Princeton: Princeton University Press, 1998).

Meissner, Collin, '*The Princess Casamassima*: "a dirty intellectual fog"', *The Henry James Review* 19.1 (1998), pp. 53–71.

Melchiori, Barbara Arnett, *Terrorism in the Late Victorian Novel* (London: Croom Helm, 1985).

Mews, Siegfried, 'Sensationalism and Sentimentality: Minor Victorian Prose Writers in Germany', *MLN* 84.5, October 1969, pp. 776–88.

Morton, Peter, *The Busiest Man in England: Grant Allen and the Writing Trade, 1875–1900* (Houndmills: Palgrave, 2005).

Mulry, David, 'Popular Accounts of the Greenwich Bombing and Conrad's *The Secret Agent*', *Rocky Mountain Review of Language and Literature*, 54.2 (2000), pp. 43–64.

Ó Donghaile, Deaglán, 'Conrad, the Stevensons and the Imagination of Urban Chaos', in Stephen Arata, Laurence Davies and Linda Dryden (eds), *Conrad and Stevenson: Writers of Transition* (Lubbock: Texas Tech University Press, 2009), pp. 159–74.

Parsons, Deborah L., *Streetwalking the Metropolis: Women, Gender and Modernity* (Oxford: Oxford University Press, 2000).

Pater, Walter, *The Renaissance: Studies in Art and Poetry* (Oxford: Oxford University Press, 1998).

Peppis, Paul, *Literature, Politics, and the English Avant-Garde: Nation and Empire, 1901–1918* (Cambridge: Cambridge University Press, 2000).

Peyser, Thomas, '*The Princess Casamassima* and the Theatrical Metropolis', *American Literary Realism*, 42. 2 (Winter 2010), pp. 95–113.

Poggioli, Renato, *The Theory of the Avant-Garde*, trans. from the Italian by Gerald Fitzgerald (Cambridge, MA: Harvard University Press, 1968).

Redding, Arthur F., *Raids on Human Consciousness: Writing, Anarchism, and Violence* (Columbia: University of South Carolina Press, 1998).

Reynolds, Paige, 'Chaos Invading Concept: *Blast* as a Native Theory of Promotional Culture', *Twentieth Century Literature* 46.2 (Summer 2000), pp. 238–68.

Said, Edward, *Orientalism* (London: Penguin, 1995).

Scanlan, Margaret, 'Terrorism and the Realistic Novel: Henry James and *The Princess Casamassima*', *Texas Studies in Literature and Language* 34.3, 1992, pp. 389–402.

Sherry, Norman, *Conrad's Western World* (Cambridge: Cambridge University Press, 1971).

Singer, Ben, *Melodrama and Modernity: Early Sensational Cinema and Its Contexts* (New York: Columbia University Press, 2001).

Seltzer, Mark, *Henry James and the Art of Power* (Ithaca and London: Cornell University Press, 1984).

Stivers, David, 'Narrative Mediation in *The Princess Casamassima*', *The Henry James Review* 28 (2007), pp. 159–73.

Stoehr, Taylor, 'Words and Deeds in *The Princess Casamassima*', *ELH*, 37.1 (March 1970), pp. 95–135.

Thomas, Ronald R., *Detective Fiction and the Rise of Forensic Science* (Cambridge: Cambridge University Press, 1999).

—, 'Revaluating Identity in the 1890s: The Rise of the New Imperialism and the Eyes of the New Detective', in Nikki Lee Manos and Meri-Jane Rochelson (eds), *Transforming Genres: New Approaches to British Fiction of the 1890s* (Basingstoke: Macmillan, 1994), pp. 193–214.

Todorov, Tzvetvan, 'The Typology of Detective Fiction', from *The Poetics of Prose*, trans. Richard Howard from the *La Poétique de la Prose* (Oxford: Basil Blackwell, 1977), pp. 42–52.

Trilling, Lionel, '*The Princess Casamassima*', in *The Liberal Imagination: Essays on Literature and Society* (London: Secker and Warburg, 1964).

Vattimo, Gianni, *The Transparent* Society, trans. David Webb from *La società transparente* (London: Polity Press, 1992).

Virilio, Paul, *Ground Zero*, trans. Chris Turner (London: Verso, 2002); originally published as *Ce qui arrive* (Paris: Éditions Galilée, 2002).

Walkowitz, Judith R., *City of Dreadful Delight: Narratives of Sexual Danger in Late-Victorian London* (London: Virago, 1992).

Weir, Peter, *Anarchy and Culture: The Aesthetic Politics of Modernism* (Amherst: University of Massachusetts Press, 1997).

Williams, Raymond, *Culture and Society* (Harmondsworth: Penguin, 1971).

—, *The Politics of Modernism: Against the New Conformists* (London: Verso, 1996).

Wolfreys, Julian, *Writing London, Vol. 3: Inventions of the City* (Houndsmills: Palgrave Macmillan, 2007).

Woodcock, George, 'Henry James and the Conspirators', *The Sewanee Review*, 60.2 (April-June 1952), pp. 219–29.

Wynne, Catherine, *The Colonial Conan Doyle* (Westport, CT: The Greenwood Press, 2002).

Historical Works

Bailey, Peter, *Popular Culture and Performance in the Victorian City* (Cambridge: Cambridge University Press, 1998).

Bookchin, Murray, *Post Scarcity Anarchism* (Edinburgh and Oakland: AK Press, 2004).

Bunyan, Tony, *The History and Practice of the Political Police in Britain* (London: Quartet Books, 1983).

Campbell, Christy, *Fenian Fire: The British Government Plot to Assassinate Queen Victoria* (London: HarperCollins, 2002).

Curtis, L. Perry, *Jack the Ripper and the London Press* (New Haven and London: Yale University Press, 2001).

Groves, Reg, *The Balham Group: How British Trotskyism Began* (London: Pluto, 1974).

Habermas, Jürgen, *The Structural Transformation of the Public Sphere: An*

Inquiry into a Category of Bourgeois Society, trans. Thomas Burger and Frederick Lawrence (Cambridge: Polity Press, 1989); originally published as *Strukturwandel der Öffentlicheit* (Dermstadt and Neuwied: Hermann Luchterhand Verlag, 1962).

Hobsbawm, Eric, *The Age of Capital, 1848–1875* (London: Abacus, 2001).

—, with George Rudé, *Captain Swing* (London: Phoenix, 2001).

Hoppen, K. Theodore, *The Mid-Victorian Generation, 1846–1886* (Oxford: Clarendon Press, 1998).

Joll, James, *The Anarchists* (London: Methuen, 1969).

Joyce, Patrick, *The Rule of Freedom: Liberalism and the Modern City* (London: Verso, 2003).

Kedward, Roderick, *The Anarchists: The Men Who Shocked an Era* (London: Library of the Twentieth Century, 1971).

Kern, Stephen, *The Culture of Time and Space: 1880–1914* (London: Weidenfeld and Nicholson, 1983).

Le Roux, Louis N., *Tom Clarke and the Irish Freedom Movement* (Dublin: The Talbot Press, 1936).

Marcus, Sharon, *Apartment Stories: City and Home in Nineteenth-Century Paris and London* (Berkeley: University of California Press, 1999).

Marshall, Peter, *Demanding the Impossible: A History of Anarchism* (London: Fontana, 1992).

Oliver, Hermia, *The International Anarchist Movement in Late Victorian London* (London: Croom Helm, 1983).

Pick, Daniel, *War Machine: The Rationalisation of Slaughter in the Modern Age* (New Haven and London: Yale University Press, 1993).

Rose, Paul, and Patrick Quinlivan, *The Fenians in England, 1865–1872: A Sense of Insecurity* (London: Calder, 1982).

Schwartz, Vanessa R., *Spectacular Realities: Early Mass Culture in Fin-de-Siècle France* (Berkeley and Los Angeles: University of California Press, 1998).

Schivelbusch, Wolfgang, *The Railway Journey: The Industrialization of Time and Space in the Nineteenth Century* (Berkeley and Los Angeles: University of California Press, 1986); originally published as *Geschicte der Eisenbahnreise* (Munich: trans. Carl Hanser Verlag, 1977).

Short, K. R. M., *The Dynamite War: Irish-American Bombers in Late-Victorian Britain* (Dublin: Gill and Macmillan, 1979).

Shpayer-Makov, Haia, 'Anarchism in British Public Opinion, 1880–1914', *Victorian Studies* 31, Summer 1988, pp. 487–516.

Stewart, Matthew, *Monturiol's Dream: The Submarine Inventor Who Wanted to Save the World* (London: Profile Books, 2003).

Townend, Paul '"No Imperial Privilege": Justin McCarthy, Home Rule, and Empire', *Éire Ireland*, pp. 201–28.

Whelehan, Niall, 'Skirmishing, *The Irish World*, and Empire, 1876–86', *Éire-Ireland: An Interdisciplinary Journal of Irish Studies*, 42.1 & 2, Spring/Summer 2007, pp. 180–200.

Woodcock, George, *Anarchism: A History of Libertarian Ideas and Movements* (Harmondsworth: Penguin, 1970).

Woodcock, George (ed.), *The Anarchist Reader* (Glasgow: Fontana, 1977).

Biographical Works

Batchelor, John, *The Life of Joseph Conrad: A Critical Biography* (Oxford: Blackwell, 1994).

Ellman, Richard, *Oscar Wilde* (New York: Knopf, 1988).

McLynn, Frank, *Robert Louis Stevenson: A Biography* (London: Hutchinson, 1993).

O'Keeffe, Paul, *Some Sort of Genius: A Life of Wyndham Lewis* (London: Pimlico, 2000).

Thompson, E. P., *William Morris: Romantic to Revolutionary* (London: Merlin Press, 1976, reprinted 1996).

Trautmann, Frederic, *The Voice of Terror: A Biography of Johann Most* (Westport, CT and London: Greenwood Press, 1980).

Contemporary Memoirs, Political Writing and Sociological Works

Anon., *Incipient Irish Revolution: An Exposé of Fenianism To-Day in the United Kingdom and America* (London: Eglington & Co., 1889).

Anon., *Parnellism and Crime* (London: George Edward Wright, 1887).

Arnould, Arthur, from *Histoire Populaire et Parliament de la Commune de Paris* (1878), in Eugene Schulkind (ed.), *The Paris Commune of 1871: The View from the Left* (London: Jonathan Cape, 1972), pp. 242–3.

Bakunin, Mikhail, *Selected Writings*; translations from the French by Steven Cox, translations from the Russian by Olive Stevens (London: Jonathan Cape, 1973).

Carlyle, Thomas, *The French Revolution: A History* (New York: Modern Library, 2002).

—, *Chartism* (Boston: Charles C. Little and James Brown, 1840).

Devoy, John, *Recollections of an Irish Rebel* (Shannon: Irish Universities Press, 1968; originally published New York: Chas D. Young, 1929).

Dubois, Félix, *The Anarchist Peril*, trans. Ralph Derechef (London: T. Fisher Unwin, 1894); originally published as *Le péril anarchiste* (Paris: Flammarion, 1894).

Ellis, Havelock, *The Criminal* (London: Walter Scott, 1890).

Engels, Friedrich, 'The Programme of the Blanquist Commune Refugees' (1874), in Eugene Schulkind (ed.), *The Paris Commune of 1871: The View from the Left* (London: Jonathan Cape, 1972), pp. 237–8.

—, with Karl Marx, *The Communist Manifesto* (Harmondsworth: Penguin, 1967).

Foner, Philip S. (ed.), *The Autobiographies of the Haymarket Martyrs* (New York: Monad Press, 1977).

Galton, Francis, *Finger Prints* (London: Macmillan & Co., 1892).

Garnett, Olive, *Tea and Anarchy! The Bloomsbury Diary of Olive Garnett, 1890–1893* (London: Bartlett's Press, 1989).

Goldman, Emma, *Anarchism and Other Essays* (New York: Dover Publications, 1969).

—, *Living My Life*, 2 vols (New York: Dover, 1970; originally published New York: Knopf, 1931).

Henry, Émile, 'A Terrorist's Defence', from *Gazette des Tribuneaux*, 27–8 April 1894, trans. George Woodcock, in George Woodcock (ed.), *The Anarchist Reader* (Glasgow: Fontana, 1977), pp. 189–96.

James, C. L., *Anarchy: A Tract for the Times* (Eau Clair, WI, 1886).

Kropotkin, Peter, *Anarchism: A Collection of Revolutionary Writings* (Mineola: Dover, 2002), first published as *Kropotkin's Revolutionary Pamphlets* (New York: Vanguard Press, 1927).

—, as Pierre Kropotkine, *The Place of Anarchism in Socialistic Evolution*, trans. from the French by Henry Glasse (London: International Publishing Company, 1886).

Latouche, Peter, *Anarchy! An Authentic Exposition of the Methods of Anarchists and the Aims of Anarchism* (London: Everett & Co., 1908).

Le Bon, Gustave, *The Psychology of Revolution*, trans. Bernard Mall from *La psychologie des revolutions* (London: T. Fisher Unwin, [1895] 1913).

—, *The Crowd: A Study of the Popular Mind*, trans. from *Le psychologie des foules* (London: T. Fisher Unwin, [1895] 1896).

Le Caron, Henri, *Twenty Five Years in the Secret Service* (Wakefield: EP Publishing, 1974; reprinted from the 10th Heinemann Edition, 1893).

Lewis, Wyndham, *Hitler* (London: Chatto & Windus, 1931).

Littlechild, John, *Reminiscences of Chief Inspector Littlechild* (London: The Leadenhall Press, 1894), p. 12.

Malatesta, Errico, 'Anarchy Defined', from *Anarchy* (1907), reprinted in George Woodcock (ed.), *The Anarchist Reader* (Glasgow: Fontana, 1977), pp. 62–4.

Marx, Karl, *Capital*, Vol. 1 (London: Penguin, 1990).

Most, Johann, *Science of Revolutionary Warfare* (Eldorado: Desert Publications, 1978; originally printed as *Revolutionäre Kriegwissenschaft* [1885).

Nechaev, Sergei, 'Catechism of the Revolutionist', in Walter Laqueur (ed.), *The Terrorism Reader* (London: Wildwood House, 1979), pp. 68–70.

Nordau, Max, *Degeneration* (London: Heinemann, 1895).

Proudhon, Pierre Joseph, *What is Property?*, trans. from *Qu'est-ce que la propriété?* by Donald R. Kelley and Bonnie G. Smith (Cambridge: Cambridge University Press, 1994).

Réclus, Élisée, 'An Anarchist on Anarchy', *Contemporary Review*, Vol. xlv (January–June 1884), May 1884, p. 638.

—, *Evolution and Revolution* (London: International Publishing, 1886).

Revolutionary Commune Group, 'To Supporters of the Commune', reprinted in Eugene Schulkind (ed.), *The Paris Commune of 1871: The View from the Left* (London: Jonathan Cape, 1972), pp. 235–6.

Rossa, Diarmuid (Jeremiah) O'Donovan, *Rossa's Recollections, 1838–1898* (Shannon: Irish University Press, 1972; originally published New York: Mariner's Harbor, 1898).

Seymour, Henry, *Anarchy: Theory and Practice* (London: Henry Seymour, 1888).

Sorel, Georges, *Reflections on Violence*, trans. T. E. Hulme from *Réflections Sur la Violence* (Cambridge: Cambridge University Press, 1999).

Stepniak, Sergius (Sergei Kravchinski), 'Terrorism in Russia and Terrorism in Europe', *The Contemporary Review*, Vol. xlv, March, 1884, pp. 325–41.

Stevenson, Robert Louis, 'Confessions of a Unionist: An Unpublished "Talk on Things Current"' (Cambridge, MA: privately printed, 1921).

Stirner, Max, *The Ego and its Own* (Cambridge: Cambridge University Press, 1995).

Sweeney, John, *At Scotland Yard: Being the Experiences During Twenty-Seven Years of Service by John Sweeney, Late Detective Inspector, Criminal Investigation Department, New Scotland Yard* (London: Grant Richards, 1904).

Various, *Songs for Socialists* (Aberdeen: James Leatham, 1890).

Warren, G. O., *Freedom: Rent, Interest, Profit and Taxes, the True Causes of Wage-Slavery* (London: William Reeves, 1894).

Wells, H. G., 'The Labour Unrest' (London: *The Daily Mail*, undated [1912?], originally published 13–20 May 1912).

Contemporary Newspaper and Journal Articles

The Illustrated London News
'Dynamite Outrages in Westminster', *The Illustrated London News*, Vol. lxxxiv, Saturday, 7 June 1884, p. 542.

The Saturday Review
'Reply by Dynamite', *The Saturday Review*, 1429.55, 17 March 1883, p. 1.

The Times
'A Press Organ of the Dynamite Party', *The Times*, 24 March 1884, p. 8.
'Bourdin's Antecedents', *The Times*, Saturday, 17 February 1894, p. 5.
'Dynamite Operations in the United States', *The Times*, Wednesday, 5 July 1882, p. 4.
'Editorial', *The Times*, Saturday, 17 February 1894, p. 5.
'Explosion on the Metropolitan Railway', *The Times*, Tuesday, 27 April 1897, p. 9.
'Foreign News: American Dynamiters in Ireland', *The Times*, Friday, 23 September 1887, p. 3.
'Irish Agitation in New York', *The Times*, Saturday, 12 April 1884, p. 11.
'Suffragist Conspiracy: Lenient Sentence On An Artist', *The Times*, Saturday, 5 April 1913, p. 4.
'The Dynamite Gun and Shell', *The Times*, Tuesday, 18 August 1885, p. 13.
'The Explosion at Aldersgate-Street Station', *The Times*, Tuesday, 25 May 1897, p. 15.
'The Explosion on the Metropolitan Railway', *The Times*, Wednesday, 28 April 1897, p. 12.
'The Explosive Substances Bill', *The Times*, Tuesday, 10 April 1883, p. 10.
'The Dynamite Party, Past and Present', *The Times*, Saturday, 24 April 1886, p. 8.
'The Invincibles in Paris', *The Times*, Saturday, 12 April 1884, p. 5.
'The Trial of O'Donnell', *The Times*, 31 December 1883, p. 6.

Strand Magazine
'Crimes and Criminals. No. 1. – Dynamite and Dynamiters', *The Strand Magazine*, Vol. VII, January-June 1894, pp. 119–32.

The Irish World and American Industrial Liberator
'A Grand Hunt All Round England for Dynamite', *The Irish World and American Industrial Liberator*, Saturday, 29 March 1884, p. 1.
'A Merciless War Must be Waged against the Pirate Empire', *The Irish World and American Industrial Liberator*, January 26th, 1884, p. 3.
'An Emergency Fund', *The Irish World and American Industrial Liberator*, Saturday, 5 January 1884, p. 4.
'Bring on Your Foreign Navies', *The Irish World and American Industrial Liberator*, Saturday, 29 March 1884, p. 3.
'Civilized Warfare', *The Irish World and American Industrial Liberator*, Saturday, 5 January 1884, p. 4.
'England's Fright', *The Irish World and American Industrial Liberator*, 26 January 1884, p. 5.
'Set a Thief to Catch a Thief', *The Irish World and American Industrial Liberator*, 12 January 1884, p. 4.
'The Dynamite War: A Well-Planned Engagement, and Brilliant Achievements of the Irish Forces', *The Irish World and American Industrial Liberator*, 14 June 1884, p. 3.

The United Irishman
'Dynamiters the Thing to Terrify all England', *The United Irishman*, 7 March 1885, p. 2.
'Intense Excitement in England', *The United Irishman*, 3 January 1885, p. 1.
'London Bridge', *The United Irishman*, 10 January 1885, p. 2.

The Torch
'A Debate: What We Want For Britain', *The Torch*, Vol. 3, No. 3, 15 March 1893, pp. 7–8.
'Chicago Anarchist Commemoration', *The Torch*, Vol. 2, No. 11, 15 November 1892, p. 5.
'News At Home and Abroad', *The Torch*, Vol. 2, No. 2, July 1895, p. 17.
'Notes on News', *The Torch*, Vol. 3, No. 1, 15 January 1893, pp. 10–11.
'Notes on News: Report on the Extradition of Francois, Accused of Complicity in the Café Very Explosion of April 25, 1892', *The Torch*, Vol. 3, No. 1, 15 January 1892, pp. 10–11.
'Spain', *The Torch*, Vol. 7, New Series, 18 December 1894, pp. 5–6.
'Statement of Principles', *The Torch*, Vol. 2, No. 2, February 1892, p. 1.
'1892, A Retrospect', *The Torch*, Vol. III, No. 1, 15 January 1893, p. 2.
Adams, F., untitled poem, *The Torch*, Vol. 3, No. 7, July 1893, p. 4.
Cohen, Alexander, 'Émile Henry', *The Torch*, Vol. 11, No. 2, 18 July 1895, pp. 24–6.
—, untitled, *The Torch*, Vol. 2, No. 1, 18 June 1895, p. 6.
Henry, Émile, 'Propaganda By Deed', *The Torch*, New Series, No. 4, October 1894, p. 5.
L. S. B., 'Verses by L.S.B', *The Torch*, No. 8, New Series, 18 January 1894.

Mollet, Gustave, 'Ravachol', *The Torch*, Vol. 3, No. 8, August 1893, p. 4.

Preig, Benjamin, '1894: A Retrospect', *The Torch*, No. 8, New Series, 18 January 1895, p. 5.

Rossetti, Helen, 'Notes On News', *The Torch*, Vol. 3, No. 3, 15 March 1893, p. 7.

Samuels, H. B., 'Life or Death: Suicide and Insanity', *The Torch*, Vol. 3, No. 6, 15 June 1893, pp. 1–3.

Unsigned and untitled poem, *The Torch*, New Series, No. 4, October 1894, p. 12.

The Alarm (Chicago)

'Men Die But Principles Live', *The Alarm*, Vol. 1, No. 14, Saturday, 16 June 1888.

'Rebellion as a Sacred Duty as Well as a Right — Our Duty as Revolutionists', *The Alarm*, Chicago and New York, Vol. 1, No. 15, 23 June 1888.

'The Military Organization', *The Alarm*, Chicago, Vol. 2, No. 1, 22 August 1885.

'The Police', *The Alarm*, Chicago, Vol. 2, No. 1, 22 August 1885.

'The Resources of Civilisation', *The Alarm*, Chicago and New York, Vol. 1, No. 16, 30 June 1888.

The Anarchist (London)

'Beware', *The Anarchist*, London, No. 17, 1 July 1886 p. 3.

'Dynamite: The Modern Agent of Revolution', *The Anarchist*, London, No. 1, March 1885, p. 4.

'The Doctrine of Dynamite', *The Anarchist*, London, No. 17, 1 July 1886, p. 1.

'War to the Knife', *The Anarchist* (London), No. 19, September 1896, p. 1.

The Commonweal

'Dynamite Versus Dollars', *The Commonweal*, Vol. 7, No. 296, 9 January 1892, p. 5.

'Notes on the News', *The Commonweal*, Vol. 5, No. 160, 2 February 1889, p. 33.

'Ravachol: His Autobiography', *The Commonweal: The Official Journal of the Socialist League*, Vol. 7, No. 312, 7 May 1892.

'Revolution and Physical Force', *The Commonweal*, Vol. 7, No. 325, 6 August 1892.

'The Speeches of Our Comrades', *The Commonweal*, Vol. 7, No. 309, 9 April 1892.

'The Walsall Anarchists. Condemned To Penal Servitude', *The Commonweal*, Vol. 7, No. 309, 9 April 1892.

Freedom: A Revolutionary Communist-Anarchist Monthly (Chicago)

George Engel, 'Autobiography of George Engel', *Freedom: A Revolutionary Communist-Anarchist Monthly*, Chicago, Vol. 1, No. 8, 1 June 1891.

'The Dangerous Classes', *Freedom: A Revolutionary Communist-Anarchist Monthly* (Chicago), Vol. 1, No. 8, 1 June 1891.

Freedom: A Journal of Anarchist Communism (London)
'An Incendiary Pamphlet', *Freedom: A Journal of Anarchist Communism*, Vol. 7, No. 309, 9 April 1892.
'Ravachol', *Freedom: A Journal of Anarchist Communism*, Vol. 7, No. 322, 16 July 1892.
'S. O.', 'A Ballad of Scotland Yard', *Freedom: A Journal of Anarchist Communism*, Vol. 6, No. 68, July 1892, p. 53.

Literary Journals

Blast
Blast: Review of the Great English Vortex, 20 June 1914.
Blast: The War Number, 20 July 1915.

The Egoist
Aldington, Richard, as 'Auceps', 'The New Sculpture' (To the Editor), *The Egoist*, No. 7, Vol. 1, 1 April 1914, p. 138.
—, 'Wyndham Lewis', *The Egoist*, Vol. 1, No. 12, 15 June 1914, p. 273.
Anonymous, 'Men, Machines and Progress', *The Egoist*, Vol. 1, No. 3, 2 February 1914, p. 42.
Denver, Frank, 'The London Group, *The Egoist*, No. 4, Vol. 11, 1 April 1915, pp. 60–1.
Gaudier-Brzeska, Henri, 'On the New Sculpture' *The Egoist*, Vol. 1, No. 6, 16 March 1914, p. 118.
Monro, Harold, 'The Imagists Discussed', *The Egoist*, Vol. 5, No. 2, 1 May 1915, p. 78.
Pound, Ezra, 'The New Sculpture', *The Egoist*, Vol. 1, No. 4, 16 February 1914, p. 68.
—, 'Exhibition at the Goupil Gallery', *The Egoist*, Vol. 1, No. 6, 16 March 1914, p. 109.
—, 'The Caressability of the Greeks', *The Egoist*, Vol. 1, No. 6, 16 March 1914, pp. 118–19.
—, 'Wyndham Lewis', *The Egoist*, Vol. 1, No. 12, 15 June 1914, pp. 233–4.
—, 'Edward Wadsworth, Vorticist', *The Egoist*, Vol. 1, No. 16, 16 August 1914, pp. 306–7.
Upward, Allen, 'The Plain Person', *The Egoist*, Vol. 1, No. 3, 2 February 1914, p. 47.
Von Helmholtz, Baptiste, 'The Bourgeois', *The Egoist: An Individualist Review*, Vol. 1, No. 3, 2 February 1914, p. 53.

Contemporary Reviews

A. H., 'Notices of Books', *Dublin Review*, Vol. 14, No. 1, July 1885, p. 235.
Anon., 'Belles Lettres', *Westminster Review*, Vol. 124, No. 247, July 1885, p. 289.
Anon., 'Literary Notes', *New York Times*, Wednesday, 4 August, 1894, p. 3.
Anon., 'Recent Novels', *The Times*, Wednesday, 9 June 1897, p. 11.

Anon., 'Art and Practice of Noise: Hostile Reception of Signor Marinetti', *The Times*, 16 June 1914, p. 5.

Anon., '"*Blast*." The Vorticists' Manifesto', *The Times*, 1 July 1914, p. 8.

Dawkins, C. E., 'New Novels', *The Academy*, 4 April 1885, p. 239.

Archival materials

National Archive, Dublin

United Irishman, untitled cutting, dated 1882, Chief Secretary's Office, Dublin, B 171, National Archive, Dublin.

Walter, A. F., to Colonel Brackenbury of the Secret Service, 20 June 1882, Crime Branch Special, B File, B29, National Archive, Dublin.

Cornell University Library Rare and Manuscript Collections, Carl Kroch Library # 4612

Beard, Charles A., cutting from the *Herald Tribune*, and Henry McBride, cutting from the *New York Sun*, collected in Notices of *The Art of Being Ruled* (n. d., 1926?), Box 3, Folder 11.

Lewis, Wyndham, 'Biographical details for publishing purposes' (publicity released for *The Art of Being Ruled*), 1926, Cornell, Box 3, Folder 12.

—, 'Biographical details for publicity purposes — Art of Being Ruled', 'The Art Racket' (undated fragment), Box 3, Folder 17.

—, 'Britons Shall Never be Bees', *Calendar of Modern Letters*, January 1926, pp. 360–2, quotation from p. 360, Box 4, Folder 10.

—, 'Ezra Pound', draft ms (April 1948), Box 8, Folder 18.

—, Galley Notes for *Blast* No. 2, Box 4, Folder 1, p. 4.

—, Miscellaneous Art Notes for *Blast* No. 2, 1915, Box 22, Folder 12.5.

—, 'The Artist as Crowd', *Twentieth Century*, pp. 12–15 (undated — 1956?), quotation from p. 14, Box 44, Folder 5.

—, 'The Art Racket' (undated fragment), Box 3, Folder 12.

Letters

Lewis, Wyndham, letter to Augustus John, summer 1915, Box 63, Folder 3.

—, letter to Ezra Pound, July 1915, Box 63, Folder 1.

—, letter to Ezra Pound, 29 April 1916, Box 63, Folder 22.

—, letters to Alick Schepeler, c. May 1914; to John Quinn, 24 January 1917; and to Ezra Pound, July 1915, Box 62, Folder 89; Box 63, Folders 1 and 33.

—, letter to Kate Lechmere, summer 1915, Box 63, Folder 2.

Index